# ALSO BY JOHN BIERMAN

Napoleon III and His Carnival Empire
(1988)

Odyssey
(1984)

Righteous Gentile:
The Story of Raoul Wallenberg,
Missing Hero of the Holocaust
(1981)

# DARK SAFARI

# DARK SAFARI

## The LIFE BEHIND
## the LEGEND of
## HENRY MORTON STANLEY

*BY JOHN BIERMAN*

*ALFRED A. KNOPF*    *NEW YORK*

*1 9* 🐾 *9 0*

Copyright © 1990 by John Bierman

Maps copyright © 1990 by David Lindroth

All rights reserved under International and Pan-American Copyright
Conventions. Published in the United States by Alfred A. Knopf, Inc., New York,
and simultaneously in Canada by Random House of Canada
Limited, Toronto. Distributed by Random House, Inc., New York.

Grateful acknowledgment is made to the following for permission to reprint
previously unpublished material:

*National Museum of American Art:* Excerpts from
the Alice Barney manuscript, from the Barney Papers, National Museum
of American Art, Smithsonian Institution.
Gift of William E. Huntington. Reprinted by permission.

*Public Archives of Nova Scotia:* Excerpts from the Captain W. G. Stairs diaries,
from the Public Archives of Nova Scotia, Halifax, N.S. Reprinted by permission.

Library of Congress Cataloging-in-Publication Data

Bierman, John.

Dark safari: the life behind the legend of Henry Morton Stanley/
by John Bierman.—1st ed.

p.   cm.

Includes bibliographical references.

ISBN 0-394-58342-6

1. Stanley, Henry M. (Henry Morton), 1841–1904.   2. Explorers—
Africa, Sub-Saharan—Biography.   3. Explorers—Great Britain—
Biography.   4. Africa, Sub-Saharan—Discovery and exploration.

I. Title.

DT351.S6B53   1990

967'.023'092—dc20                                        90-31089

[B]                                                           CIP

Manufactured in the United States of America

First Edition

BOMC offers recordings and compact discs, cassettes
and records. For information and catalog write to
BOMR, Camp Hill, PA 17012.

For Hilary, who shares
my fascination for Africa,
and for Jonathan,
whom I hope soon
to introduce to that
continent's special magic

Africa will always be the Africa of the Victorian atlas, the blank unexplored continent the shape of the human heart.

*G R A H A M   G R E E N E*

# PART ONE

# THE SELF-INVENTED MAN

The inner existence, the *me,* what does anybody know of? Nay, you may well ask, what do I know? But, granted that I know little of my real self, still, I am the best evidence for myself.

*HENRY M. STANLEY*

# Chapter One

*A*BANDONMENT, rejection, betrayal. These were the themes that haunted the inner life of the swaggering, assertive little man known to the world as Henry Morton Stanley. Evasion, suppression, falsification. These were the defenses he threw up to protect a deeply wounded personality which never recovered from the savaging it received in childhood. Everyone, to a certain extent, wears a mask behind which he hides from the world. For Stanley, a mere mask was insufficient protection; he fabricated for himself a suit of armor, which it has taken almost a century to penetrate.

Even in late middle age, full of honors and feted worldwide as the greatest explorer of his day, which he undoubtedly was, "Bula Matari"—the Smasher of Rocks, as his awed Africans called him—continued to concoct pathetic lies and weave Mittyesque fantasies, as much to win self-esteem as to gain the esteem of others. In bequeathing these mendacities to posterity in his autobiography, he provided "the best evidence for myself" in a way he obviously did not intend.

To be sure, there were grounds enough in the bleak circumstances of his birth and childhood for the suspicion and paranoia that marked Stanley as a man. As he observed in the autobiography: "Those to whom in my trustful age I ventured to consign the secret hopes and interests of my heart, invariably betrayed me."

And yet much of the hostility he sensed all around him in later life was of his own making, the product of his self-defensive brusqueness, boastfulness, and growling lack of social grace. A man more self-aware than Stanley might have been less bemused, if no less wounded, by the realization that "I make enemies every day of my life." By his own account, at the age of forty-four he had "not found one man—and I have travelled over 400,000 miles of this globe—who did not venture to say something unkind the minute I turned my back to him."

Nor had he found a woman who would remain faithful during his long absences. Three broken engagements, compounding what appears to have been a decided sexual ambivalence, had left him unintentionally forbidding and self-defeatingly awkward in the presence of females whom he found attractive. "He hardly looked at me and sat down uncouthly," recalled one woman of great charm and intelligence who met Stanley at the height of his fame and was, by her own account, "keenly interested" in making his acquaintance. "I talked for all I was worth and tried every kind of topic; he hardly responded." Only later did this woman, the Anglo-German writer and artist Marie von Bunsen, learn from mutual friends that Stanley had, in fact, been anxious to know her better because he felt she was "the only woman with the qualities to become his wife."

Together with his hunger for fame, and thereby self-esteem, Stanley's inability to trust men or feel at ease with women was surely a major factor behind his driving need to escape from civilization and return time after time to Africa, where—despite dangers and privations almost beyond imagination in this day of the bush pilot, the outboard engine, the all-terrain automobile, and sophisticated tropical medicine—he could at last feel safe from the torments and frustrations of society and at one with his surroundings. "Oh, I want to be free," he cried out on his deathbed in London, "to go into the woods—to be free!" In those words, perhaps, we find the key to this complex, widely admired, little loved, and deeply misunderstood man whose deeds transformed the face of a continent.


STANLEY'S mother was Betsy Parry, a strapping nineteen-year-old housemaid from rural North Wales. She was, as the Victorians used to say, "no better than she should be," for she was unmarried when she conceived and bore Stanley and would go on to bear three more illegitimate children by various fathers.

A village drunk named John Rowlands claimed paternity of Betsy Parry's firstborn, but there are grounds to doubt he was the father. Persistent legend in the little Welsh market town of Denbigh has it that Rowlands let his name be entered as the father in return for a consideration from Betsy's real seducer, a prominent and respectably married local lawyer named Vaughan Horne. Another version of Stanley's origins—implied by Stanley himself, though not necessarily true, either—is that an unknown third lover got Betsy with child while she was working in London and that she returned from there to Denbigh to give birth in her widowed father's cottage.

Whatever the truth of the matter, neither Betsy nor any of his possible fathers ever showed the slightest interest in, let alone affection for, the child who was born on January 28, 1841, and registered in the records of St. Hilary's Church, Denbigh, as "John Rowlands,

Bastard." It was no light matter in God-fearing, Victorian North Wales to be so designated, and throughout his life Stanley would think of his origins as "base" and "dishonorable."

Even more damaging to his self-esteem, his mother did not display so much as a passing concern for him. She had scarcely recovered from the effort of bringing her bastard into the world before she abandoned him to the care of her father and returned to London and whatever it was that she did there for a living. "One of the first things I remember," Stanley would relate toward the end of his life, "is to have been gravely told that I had come from London in a band-box and to have been told that all babies came from the same place."

It is not clear how the child was cared for after being left with his grandfather Moses Parry, a once-substantial yeoman farmer now in greatly reduced circumstances. In later years Stanley would recall there having been a nurse, but if there was one she seems unlikely to have been more than an occasional baby-sitter. Essentially, it was an all-male household, the old man sharing a cottage in the precincts of the ruined Denbigh Castle with his two unmarried sons.

Stanley would recall his grandfather as "a stout old gentleman, clad in corduroy breeches, dark stockings and long Melton coat, with a clean-shaven face, rather round, and lit up by humorous grey eyes." From that description one may assume that while the old man lived Stanley received at least a minimum of care and affection. But Moses Parry died suddenly at the age of eighty-four, his death being preceded by an incident which Stanley describes in his autobiography without apparently realizing its psychological significance. It seems that the child was carrying a pitcher of water into the house when he dropped and broke it. Old Moses, on his way out to work in a field, "lifted his forefinger menacingly and said 'Very well, Shonin my lad, when I return thou shalt have a sound whipping.'"

It is not difficult to imagine the dread in which the child spent the next few hours. Although Stanley does not say so, it would have been perfectly natural under such circumstances for a five-year-old to wish either himself or his grandfather dead—and equally natural for him to feel a rush of relief on learning that a fatal seizure suffered by the old man that same afternoon had, indeed, saved him from the threatened punishment. We understand enough about child psychology now to know that the boy's relief would be coupled with the gnawing belief that he had caused his grandfather's death merely by wishing it.

Retribution for that imagined crime followed swiftly. With the old man out of the way, his two sons seized the opportunity to rid themselves of the burden of the child. They farmed him out to an elderly couple named Price, to whom they paid half a crown (fifty cents) a week for his keep. This arrangement did not last long. Within a few months the Prices, "dismayed at my increasing appetite," asked for more money. When the two uncles, by now both married, refused either to pay more or to take the child back, the Prices decided on a drastic remedy. Under the pretense of taking him to visit an aunt in a village some miles distant, their son Dick took the child in hand. As Stanley was to recall in later life,

> The way seemed interminable and tedious, but he did his best to relieve my fatigue with false cajolings and treacherous endearments. At last Dick set me down from his shoulders before an immense stone building and, passing through tall iron gates, he pulled at a bell which I could hear clanging noisily in the distant interior. A sombre-faced stranger appeared at the door who, despite my remonstrances, seized me by the hand and drew me within, while Dick tried to soothe my fears with glib promises that he was only going to bring Aunt Mary to me. The door closed on him and, with the echoing sound, I experienced for the first time the awful feeling of utter desolateness.

The place to which young John had been "so treacherously taken" was the St. Asaph Union Workhouse, five miles north of Denbigh. It sounds grim enough and no doubt was, but Stanley's later recollections of the place as "a house of slow death" to the aged and "a house of torture" to the young, may owe more to Dickens than to memory.

"It took me some time to learn the unimportance of tears in a workhouse," wrote Stanley the autobiographer, and the striking phrase has the ring of veracity. Still, it is a fact that after he had achieved fame, the man who had been John Rowlands returned to St. Asaph's to bask in the approval of the board of governors, praise the education he had received there, and urge a new generation of inmates to work hard at their lessons.

There were seventy children at St. Asaph's—forty boys and thirty girls—in addition to the adult and aged destitute. The boys were under the tutelage of a former miner named James Francis, who had lost his left hand in a colliery accident some years before, and whom Stanley depicts as "soured by misfortune, brutal of temper and callous of heart." Others who were at the workhouse at the same time describe Francis more kindly, though he may well have been mentally unstable. He was committed to the Denbigh Lunatic Asylum in 1866, ten years after Stanley left the workhouse, and died in the asylum three years later.

Stanley's description of life under the glowering eye of James Francis is one of unrelieved terror. "Tyranny of the grossest kind lashed and scowled at us every waking hour," he would recall. "Day after day, little wretches would be flung down on the stone floor in writhing heaps or stood with blinking eyes and humped backs to receive the shock of the ebony ruler, or were sent pirouetting across the floor from a ruffianly kick. . . ."

More than mere punitive brutality is suggested by a story which Stanley tells of the death of a boy named Willie Roberts. Willie was "the king of the school for beauty and amiability," he wrote, and "some of us believed that he belonged to a very superior class to our own. His coal-black hair curled in profusion over a delicately moulded face of milky whiteness. His eyes were soft and limpid, and he walked with a carriage which tempted imitation."

Learning of Willie's death, under circumstances which are not elaborated, Stanley and some other boys sneaked into the mortuary, "prompted by a fearful curiosity to know what death was like." They found "the body was livid and showed scores of dark weals," and, Stanley added, "after what we had seen it would have been difficult for anyone to have removed from our minds the impression that Francis was responsible."

Given those circumstances and Stanley's account of young Willie's unusual good looks, a modern reader might well conclude that the boy fell victim to an extreme form of homosexual sadism, a phenomenon over which even the most grimly realistic Victorian writers drew a veil of "decency." The modern reader might also assume that the other boys at St. Asaph's, Stanley included, were exposed to less lethal manifestations of the same perversion. That may well have been the case. Nevertheless, there is compelling evidence to suggest that Willie Roberts and his death were both figments of Stanley's imagination. For the meticulously kept workhouse records fail to disclose the death of any boy of that name, or anything approximating it, at St. Asaph's during the relevant period. And while cause of death could, of course, have been falsified, the simple fact of it could not have been withheld or deleted from the record without trace. All other deaths at St. Asaph's were faithfully entered, and there is no visible evidence of the record's having been tampered with. So we are bound to conclude that there was no Willie Roberts and that, therefore, the episode was pure invention.

While going out of his way to put this dark fantasy into his

autobiography, Stanley—like any good Victorian author—refrains
from making overt reference to the rampant sexuality that clearly
was a feature of workhouse life. A report to the Board of Education
by commissioners who visited St. Asaph's in 1847, shortly after Stanley was admitted, confirms such behavior. The commissioners lamented that little girls admitted to the workhouse came into contact
with prostitutes and quickly "learnt the tricks of the trade." Adult
male inmates "took part in every possible vice," and the children
slept two to a bed, older with younger, "so that from the very start
. . . [they] were beginning to practice and understand things they
should not." For good measure, the *Denbighshire Free Press* reported about this time that the Master of the Workhouse regularly
came in drunk and took "indecent liberties" with the female staff.

Francis may, of course, have been party to such goings-on, but,
whatever his misdeeds, he does at least seem to have had some vocation for teaching and clearly gave Stanley a sound enough basic
education. Up to the time the boy was admitted to St. Asaph's he had
known only his native Welsh, and although Francis spoke only "very
broken English," as the 1847 school inspectors reported, "by cate-
chizing carefully and requiring his pupils always to converse in
English, he has brought them to understand more of what they hear
and read than would be expected in so elementary a school. . . ."

There is also evidence that, far from being the inveterate rebel, as
depicted by Stanley, young Rowlands was a teacher's pet. A strong
enough hint of this is to be found in the autobiography, where,
apparently unaware of the inconsistency, Stanley tells us that in
1856, when Francis went away for a few days to visit friends, he
"appointed me his deputy over the school." A workhouse
contemporary—a "respectable mechanic" named Thomas Mumford
—confirmed this in later years, when he told an interviewer that
"Francis had a very high opinion of young Rowlands and used to put
him in charge of the schoolboys during his absence.

"The boy was quite equal to the task of maintaining discipline,"
Mumford recalled. "He would allow no one to question his authority. Rather than suffer anyone to take liberties with him, he would
give the boys a good thrashing all round, and this he used to do so
effectually that no boy was found to question his authority."

If not for Stanley's own description of how he put down a playground rebellion, Mumford's account of Stanley as the schoolmaster's officiously bullying surrogate might need to be viewed with
some caution. It was given at a time (March 1889) when controversy
raged about Stanley's head over brutalities committed during his last

expedition to Africa. In Stanley's account of the playground revolt, he had to establish his authority by tackling the ringleader, a boy "who had often proved himself my superior in strength." Having subdued his adversary, Stanley recalled, his authority was undisputed, and he added the reflection: "Often since have I learned how necessary is the application of force for the establishment of order."

Another "respectable inhabitant" of the village of St. Asaph—a Mrs. Jones, who kept a little cake shop there during Stanley's workhouse years—gave a description not only of Stanley as teacher's pet, but also of Francis as a kindly man rather than the ogre depicted by Stanley. She told an interviewer that "Whenever he received a shilling or two from friends to spend for the benefit of the workhouse boys, [Francis] used to visit her shop and generally bring Rowlands with him to help to carry the cakes home. . . . He was very fond of the boy, and thought much of him. Again and again he said to Mrs. Jones 'You mark me, this boy will be a great man some day.' "

The informant Mumford also gave some account of young Rowlands' educational attainments, though this may well have been colored by hindsight. The boy, said Mumford, was

> particularly fond of geography and arithmetic, and never seemed so happy as when, pointer in hand, he was able to ramble at his own sweet will over the face of the map. He seemed to his fellow pupils to have the latitude and longitude of each place at his fingers' ends. He was also a good penman and on this account was often selected by the porter to enter the names of visitors in a book kept for the purpose and at times he was even invited into the clerk's office to help with the accounts.

The last part of this certainly rings true. Even when he was writing up his diary, ill and exhausted in some wretched camp in Africa after a grueling day's march, Stanley's hand was always strikingly neat and clear. It is a matter of record, too, that at the age of thirteen he was presented with a Bible by the local bishop for "diligent application to his studies and good conduct." And indeed, for all his bitter condemnation of workhouse life, Stanley was to record his gratitude to "this strange institution" for teaching him to read and "to know God by faith, as the Father of the fatherless."

If Stanley is to be believed—and it would have to be a fairly substantial "if" but for corroborating workhouse records—it was in St. Asaph's, when he was twelve, that he had his first conscious encounter with his mother. Until then he had not realized that "a mother was indispensable to every child," and on being told that

Betsy Parry had been admitted to the workhouse with a son and daughter, his "first feeling was one of exultation . . . and the next one was of curiosity." In the brief account that follows, there is a poignancy which lends it credibility:

> Francis came up to me during the dinner hour, when all the inmates were assembled, and, pointing out a tall woman with an oval face, and a great coil of dark hair behind her head, asked me if I recognized her. "No, sir," I replied. "What, do you not know your own mother?" I started, with a burning face, and directed a shy glance at her, and perceived that she was glancing at me with a look of cool, critical scrutiny. I had expected to feel a gush of tenderness towards her, but her expression was so chilling that the valves of my heart closed, as with a snap.

After a few weeks, her circumstances having apparently improved, Betsy Parry left the workhouse, taking her younger boy-child with her and leaving the little girl behind. But Stanley's half-sister, Emma, remained a stranger to him.

Stanley's days in the workhouse came to an end when he was fifteen—suddenly and melodramatically if we are to believe him, routinely and respectably if we are to believe the workhouse records. As Stanley tells it, Francis was in the process of beating the entire senior class one by one over some trivial offense, but when it came Stanley's turn to lower his trousers and bend down, he rebelled.

> "Never again," I shouted, marvelling at my own audacity. The words had scarcely escaped me ere I found myself swung upwards into the air by the collar of my jacket and flung into a nerveless heap on the bench. Then the passionate brute pummelled me in the stomach until I fell backwards, gasping for breath. . . . Recovering my breath, finally, from the pounding in the stomach, I aimed a vigorous kick at the cruel Master as he stooped to me and, by chance, my booted foot smashed his glasses and almost blinded him with the splinters. Starting backward with the excruciating pain, he continued to stumble over a bench and the back of his head struck the stone floor; but as he was in the act of falling, I had bounded to my feet and possessed myself of his blackthorn. Armed with this, I rushed at the prostrate form and struck him at random over his body, until I was recalled to a sense of what I was doing by the stirless way he received the thrashing.

It would surely have been impossible for a man with only one hand to wield a blackthorn while at the same time flinging a bulky fifteen-year-old around, but in his fever of invention Stanley clearly failed to think about that. He went on to describe how he and another boy dragged the unconscious Francis down the corridor to his private room, while "some of the infants in the fourth room began to howl with unreasonable terror." Then, deciding that he must run away, Stanley "climbed over the garden wall and . . . hastened through the high corn as though pursued by bloodhounds."

But there were no bloodhounds, real or figurative, and if we can believe a correspondent who checked the workhouse books in 1889, the last entry against Rowlands' name, dated May 13, 1856, read simply: "Gone to his uncle at the National School, Holywell." That, as we shall see, is almost exactly what did happen.

As further evidence that his story of thrashing Francis and then fleeing was pure invention, we may note that elsewhere in the workhouse records, the words "run away" are inscribed against the names of absconders. No such entry is made in Stanley's case. And the boy whom he refers to as "Mose," and who he claims ran away with him, is almost certainly one Moses Roberts who, as the records disclose, absconded ten months before.

In the light of all this evidence, it can be said with certainty that Stanley's story of his escape from St. Asaph's was fantasy, most probably inspired by Dickens, with Stanley in the role of Nickleby, Francis playing the part of Squeers, and St. Asaph's standing in for Dotheboys Hall.

Stanley seemed to believe that his putative father, John Rowlands, had died within a few weeks of his birth—although the record shows that in fact he lived until 1854, when he succumbed to delirium tremens—and after quitting St. Asaph's the boy decided to seek the help of his putative paternal grandfather, also named John Rowlands. He was a well-to-do farmer in the village of Lys, and according to Stanley this encounter was "quite unforgettable."

Stanley found "a stern-looking, pink-complexioned, rather stout old gentleman . . . smoking a long clay pipe." He asked the boy who he was and what he wanted "in a lazy, indifferent way." When the boy blurted out his story, Rowlands took his pipe from his mouth, pointed at the door with the stem, and said: "You can go back the same way you came. I can do nothing for you and have nothing to give you."

Toward the end of his life Stanley would recall: "I have forgotten a million things, probably, but there are some few pictures and some few phrases that one can never forget. . . . If I have recalled that scene once, it has been recalled a thousand times."

The boy allegedly received an equally chilling reception from his uncles Moses and Thomas at Denbigh and then, hungry and exhausted, made his way to the village of Brynford, where his schoolmaster cousin Moses Owen, eldest son of Stanley's Aunt Mary, was in charge of the local Anglican church school. Here, after giving his young relative a brisk oral examination to evaluate his educational attainments, Owen offered him a job as pupil-teacher. Payment was to be in clothing, board, and lodging.

Stanley found that in some subjects a few of the senior boys were more advanced than he was, but he studied hard to close the gap and was "kept indoors to learn Euclid, Algebra, and Latin, and Grammar." If only out of self-interest Owen was determined to turn his young assistant into a thoroughgoing pedagogue. "At meal-times he was always cross-examining me on the subject of my tasks," wrote Stanley. "[H]is conversation was high scholastic, and, when out walking with him, I was treated to lectures. Fed by such methods and stimulated to think, I became infected with a passion for books, and for eighteen hours out of the twenty-four I was wholly engrossed with them."

But the boys were "uncongenial through their incurable loutishness," Stanley would recall, and "they all appeared to have become acquainted with my antecedents. . . . The gentlest retort was followed by expressions which reminded me of my ignoble origin. Often, they did not wait to be provoked but indulged their natural malice as if from divine privilege. The effect of it was to drive me within my own shell, and to impress the lesson on me that I was forever banned by having been an inmate of the workhouse."

After a while, we are told, Cousin Moses, too, turned against him, influenced—Stanley believed—by his domineering mother, who felt that on his meager salary he could not afford to give room and board to the family bastard.

"He did not stoop to the vulgar punishment of birching or caning," Stanley wrote, "but inflicted moral torture by a peculiar gift of language. His cutting words were more painful to bear than any amount of physical castigation. . . . With every spoonful of food I ate, I had to endure a worded sting that left a rankling sore. I was 'a dolt, a born imbecile, and incorrigible dunce.' "

Eventually, Owen told the boy to leave, and for a while young John was given room and board by the forbidding Aunt Mary in return for his help on her farm at the village of Fynnon Bueno. From Fynnon Bueno, the boy was shunted off to Liverpool, where his Aunt Mary's brother, Tom Morris, had rashly boasted that he could get him a job in an insurance office.

Morris was a man of fair education and sunny disposition who had fallen on hard times. He was supporting a large family on the one pound (five dollars) a week he earned in a cotton mill. As Stanley would recall, "his heart was altogether too expansive for one of his condition," and he welcomed the boy into his impoverished and overcrowded home, for all that he could ill afford to feed another mouth—especially since the job at the insurance company failed to materialize.

The first known photograph of the young Stanley dates from this period. It was obviously taken before Tom's wife, Maria, pawned his one good suit to help pay for his food, for the boy is importantly dressed in a high-collared style that would have been appropriate to the insurance office he never entered. But it is the eyes and the set of the mouth, not the clothes, that seize the attention. There is still the suggestion of baby fat about the face and body, but the gaze that fairly leaps out of the sepia oval prefigures the implacable and pugnacious man he was to become.

Young John walked the streets for weeks looking for work and eventually found employment in a haberdashery at five shillings a week, raising and lowering shutters, sweeping floors, trimming lamps and cleaning windows from seven in the morning until nine at night. The work was so heavy that after a couple of months the boy fell ill and was replaced by a stronger eighteen-year-old.

Meanwhile, things had turned sour at Uncle Tom's, where the boy's relatives were having second thoughts about their hospitality toward him. "The finances of the family had fallen very low," recalled Stanley. He was also having constant fights with his cousins, particularly a youngster named Teddy, whose side was invariably taken by his parents. "It had been evident that here, also, as at Fynnon Bueno, there was a wide distinction between children who had parents and those who were orphaned."

It was that bitter sense of rejection by his own flesh and blood that spurred the boy eventually to a snap decision that would change his life forever. Having at last found another job, as a delivery boy at a wholesale butcher's close to the docks, he was making a delivery to the packet ship *Windermere*, a Yankee merchantman lately arrived from New Orleans with a cargo of cotton. The master, Captain David Hardinge, appraised the boy as he looked wide-eyed at the rich fittings of the captain's cabin.

"How would you like to sail in this ship?" asked Hardinge.
    "But I know nothing of the sea, sir."

*John Rowlands, age 15. The workhouse rebel was really a teacher's pet. (The Autobiography of H. M. Stanley, 1908)*

"Sho! You will soon learn all that you have to do, and in time you may become a captain of as fine a ship."

The *Windermere* was sailing for New Orleans in three days; Hardinge offered five dollars a month and an outfit of sea clothes; Stanley made up his mind on the spot. "I will go with you, sir, if you think I will suit." When he got home that evening, the boy broke the news to his uncle and aunt. Tom Morris put up token resistance to his departure.

"But there rose up before me a great bulk of wretchedness," Stanley wrote, "my slavish dependence on relatives who could scarcely support themselves, my unfortunate employment, Teddy's exasperating insolence, family recriminations, my beggarly wardrobe, and daily diet of contumely; and I looked up from the introspection and, with fixed resolve, said: 'It's no use uncle. I must go.' "

*JOHN ROWLANDS,* now aged sixteen, spent the first three days of his career as a seafarer in the landlubber's customary way—below decks being violently sick. On the fourth day he was told in brisk and brutal fashion that he was not to enjoy the comparatively comfortable role of cabin boy, as he had been led to believe by Hardinge, but would have to endure the life of a deck hand, working before the mast. A second mate named Nelson bawled at him down the scuttle: "Now then, come out of that you ---- young Britisher! Step up here in a brace of shakes, or I'll come down and skin your ---- ---- carcass alive!"

Such properly Victorian dashes liberally bedeck Stanley's account of the *Windermere*'s seven-week voyage to the Gulf of Mexico. But while coy about the verbal brutality, he describes in considerable detail the sadistic use made by Nelson and a fellow mate named Waters of the rope's end, the belaying pin, the fist, and the boot:

> Just as Francis flogged, beat and pummelled the infants under his charge, so the ruffian mates stormed, swore, and struck or booted the full-grown wretches on board the Windermere. . . . Bully Waters, with awful energy and frantic malice, drew blood from "old salt" and "joskin" indiscriminately, with iron belaying pins, and kicked, and pounded, until I was sickened at the sound of the deadly thuds and the faces streaming with blood. . . .

Such brutalities, as we know from innumerable sources, were an inescapable feature of life at sea in the nineteenth century, but Stanley's vivid description of shipboard existence is at best quasi-realistic. He could not bring himself to allude, even obliquely, to the sexual abuse of the younger, greener crew members by the older and more senior hands that was virtually routine on merchant ships of the period. No less than the man o' war, the merchantman of the day ran—to quote Winston Churchill's memorable adumbration of the Royal Navy's guiding principles—on "rum, sodomy and the lash."

But Stanley, as any good Victorian was bound to, allows no hint to creep into his narrative of the carnal outrages he must either have witnessed or been subjected to.

# Chapter Two

*I*T WAS in the city of New Orleans that John Rowlands became Henry Stanley. This occurred, or so he claimed, when a merchant of that name adopted him, having seen in him the son he had never had but always wanted. As in Stanley's account of his childhood, the Dickensian resonances are striking; if the workhouse tyrant of his tender years is Wackford Squeers, the kindly benefactor of his adolescence is surely Mr. Brownlow. This can be seen as evidence of the hold that Dickens' fiction had over the popular imagination of his age. It also shows how assiduously Stanley interwove fact with fantasy in giving an account of his early life.

The New Orleans where he jumped ship in February 1859 was the world's greatest export center, handling almost $200 million worth of outgoing goods a year, mostly cotton for the insatiable mills of England and France. As a financial center the Louisianan metropolis rivaled New York, its thirteen banks holding deposits of $20 million in cash and $12 million in gold. It was also the New World's greatest slave market, although—anxious not to lose its position as the major export outlet of a unified and increasingly prosperous nation—its politics were not so rabidly secessionist as those of most of the antebellum South.

It was an extravagantly cosmopolitan city, with no fewer than thirty-two different nationalities represented in a white population of 155,000, of whom 41 per cent were foreign-born. It was splendidly licentious, boasting a citizenry unusually rich in pimps, crooks, whores, gamblers, cranks and confidence tricksters. Set on a crescent-shaped sweep of the Mississippi, this lusty metropolis was as noted for its elegance as for its squalor, for its gentility as for its violence, for its civic virtues as for its corruption. The impact all this must have had on the workhouse boy, John Rowlands, is not hard to imagine.

True, his months in Liverpool would have urbanized him to a certain extent, but the glum splendors of the city on the Mersey could not have prepared him for the "tumultuous sensation of pleasure, wonder, and curiosity" he experienced as the *Windermere* tied up at a pierhead where "the levee sloped down with a noble breadth to the river, and stretched for miles . . . crowded with the cargoes of the hundreds of vessels which lay broadside to it."

That evening, when he went ashore with an older ship's lad named Harry, young Rowlands fell more deeply under the spell of New Orleans and its "soft, balmy air, with its strange scents of fermenting molasses, semi-baked sugar, green coffee, pitch, Stockholm tar, brine of mess-beef, rum and whiskey drippings.".

At a boardinghouse in Poydras Street, Harry introduced him to the delights of Southern cuisine as they demolished "a spread of viands which were as excellent as they were novel—okra soup, grits, sweet potatoes, brinjalls, corn scones, mush-pudding and 'fixings.' " The next stop was "another house, the proprietress of which was extremely gracious." Lubricity jostles hypocrisy in high Victorian style in Stanley's description of what followed:

> Presently there bounced in four gay young ladies, in such scant clothing that I was speechless with amazement. My ignorance of their profession was profound, and I was willing enough to be enlightened; but when they proceeded to take liberties with my person, they seemed to me to be so appallingly wicked that I shook them off and fled out of the house. Harry followed me, and with all the arts he could use, tried to induce me to return; but I would as soon have jumped into the gruel-colored Mississippi as I would have looked into the eyes of those giggling wantons again. My disgust was so great that I never, in after years, could overcome my repugnance to females of that character.

It is, of course, not necessarily surprising that a boy just turned eighteen—even one who must have been given some disturbing insights by St. Asaph's and the *Windermere* into the sexual nature of man—should be shocked and embarrassed on his first visit to a brothel. What is arresting is that the mature Stanley should feel it necessary to cite the incident, four decades later, as the rationale for a chaste manhood. For it was not just "females of that character" who made him feel uncomfortable; as he would confess to a friend at the age of forty-three: "The fact is, I can't talk to women."

An intriguing and perhaps equally revealing incident from Stanley's New Orleans period, and one that sounds a lot more like fantasy than truth, concerns a case of mistaken sexual identity. The androgynous female like Sweet Polly Oliver who "lists for a soldier to follow my love" or runs away to sea as a cabin boy, was a familiar folkloric figure of the eighteenth and nineteenth centuries. But, if Stanley is to be believed, he was able to share a boardinghouse bed for some days with "a blue eyed and fair-haired lad of about my own age" before realizing that his sleeping partner was not what he claimed to be.

His bedmate went by the name of Dick Heaton and had, like young Rowlands, come from Liverpool as a hand aboard an American packet and jumped ship in New Orleans. In Stanley's account,

> He was so modest he would not retire by candle-light, and . . . when he got into bed he lay on the verge of it, far removed from contact with me. When I rose in the morning I found that he was not undressed, which he explained by saying that he had turned in thus from the habit of holding himself ready for a call. On beginning his voyage he had been so severely thrashed for a delay caused by dressing that he had scarcely dared to take off his boots during the whole voyage.

Rowlands was apparently satisfied by this explanation and by Dick's account of how he had padded the seat of his pants with cotton to deaden the blows of repeated beatings. "I cast a glance at his hips and remarked that he need have no fear of being thrashed at New Orleans." However, "a little later, it struck me that there was an unusual forward inclination of the body and a singular leanness of the shoulders, compared with the fullness below the waist in him; and I remarked that he walked more like a girl than a boy."

But it was not until a day or two later that, waking to find Dick fast asleep at his side, Rowlands was "amazed to see what I took to be two tumours on his breast. My ejaculation and start woke my companion. He asked what was the matter? Pointing to his open breast, I anxiously inquired if those were not painful?"

Dick reddened and told him to mind his own business. But the penny was beginning to drop, and eventually Rowlands "sat up triumphantly and cried out with the delight of a discoverer, 'I know! I know! Dick, you are a girl!' " At last Dick confessed: his real name was Alice. And "now that her sex was revealed I wondered that I had been so blind as not to perceive it before, for in every movement there was unmistakable femininity."

Alice's story was that she had cropped her hair and disguised her sex to get a job as cabin boy—her only way of getting to America and away from the ill-tempered grandmother with whom she had lived in Liverpool. By the time she had finished her explanation, Rowlands had to leave for his job as a warehouse clerk, and they parted company promising to meet that evening. But when he returned to the boardinghouse after work, Alice was gone.

"She was never seen, or heard of, by me again," recalled Stanley, adding piously: "I have hoped ever since that Fate was as propitious to her as I think it was wise in separating two young, simple creatures who might have been led, through excess of sentiment, into folly."

AFTER his unconsummated visit to the brothel on his first night in New Orleans, John Rowlands returned to the *Windermere* to sleep. In the morning, the brutal Nelson seemed surprised to find him aboard. Captain Hardinge and his mates were co-conspirators in a petty racket involving the wages of the naïve lads who were induced to sign on. The idea was—beyond the routine brutalities of shipboard life—to treat them so badly that they would jump ship at the first opportunity, leaving Hardinge to pocket their wages and then find fresh dupes for the return journey. Thus, when Nelson saw the lad next morning he greeted him with: "Hello! You here still? I thought you had vamoosed . . . well, sonny, we must see what we can do for you."

Good as his word, he put the boy to work cleaning brass fittings on deck, subjecting him to continuing verbal and physical assault until on the fifth day young Rowlands at last decided to "leave the floating hell forever." That night, taking only his best shore clothes and the Bible he had been given by the Bishop of St. Asaph, he crept ashore, walked along the levee for half a mile, and went to sleep in a pile of cotton bales.

Early next morning, the young deserter rose, picked the cotton from his hair and clothes, and began to saunter along Tchoupitoulas Street, the waterfront's main commercial thoroughfare. The bustle of New World humanity made a lifelong impression on him:

> They had a swing of the body wholly un-English and their facial expressions differed from those I had been accustomed to. I strove hard to give a name to what was so unusual. Now, of course, I know that it was the sense of equality and independence that made each face so different from what I had seen in Liverpool. These people knew no master, and had no more awe of their employers than they had of their fellow-employees.

The colored folk and certainly the black slaves, who must have been abroad that morning in at least equal numbers to the whites, could hardly have shared "the sense of equality and independence" which Stanley so admired. They seem to have been invisible to this otherwise superb reporter-to-be, even though it is quite possible that he had never before seen a black man, except for the occasional Lascar on the Liverpool docks.

But if he failed to notice the Negroes, his eyes were wide open in other respects, and in his autobiography Stanley tells how, on the porch of a warehouse at the end of Tchoupitoulas Street, he spotted a sympathetic white face—that of a middle-aged man, dressed in a dark alpaca suit and stovepipe hat, who was tipped back in a chair against the doorway of Speake and McCreary, Wholesale and Commission Merchants, enjoying the morning sun and reading a newspaper.

Taking him for the proprietor, the young Rowlands approached tentatively and, according to his autobiography, asked in true Dickensian style: "Do you want a boy, sir?"

> 'Eh?' he demanded with a start: 'what did you say?'
> 'I want some work, sir; I asked if you wanted a boy.'

Intrigued by the lad's mixture of boldness and timidity, impressed when shown the Bible with its commendatory inscription by the Bishop of St. Asaph, the man asked the boy to demonstrate his skill by marking some coffee sacks with brush and paint. Young John did the job so swiftly and neatly that the merchant took him in hand, treating him to breakfast and a haircut before recommending him to James Speake of Speake and McCreary, who in turn offered the lad a week's trial as a junior clerk. That done, the boy's benefactor, who had introduced himself as a cotton broker by the name of Stanley, left on a business trip upriver, promising to look up his young protégé on his return.

In his benefactor's absence the lad found lodgings at a boardinghouse on St. Thomas Street, and so pleased his employer by his hard work and willingness to learn that he was taken on permanently at twenty-five dollars a month. All this gave him a self-confidence he had never felt before, and "within a few weeks of arriving in America I had become different in temper and spirit. . . . The childish fear of authority had fled—for authority no longer wore its stern, relentless aspect, but was sweetly reasonable . . . and my new feeling of dignity made me stretch myself to my full height and revel luxuriously in fond ideas."

Stretching to his full height involved voracious reading. The availability of cheap editions of the classics at a nearby bookstore enabled young Rowlands to buy and devour a four-volume edition of Gibbon's *Decline and Fall,* Spenser's *Faerie Queen,* Pope's *Iliad,* Dryden's *Odyssey,* Milton's *Paradise Lost,* Plutarch's *Lives,* and "a big history of the United States which I badly needed, because of my utter ignorance of the country."

On his return to New Orleans four weeks later, the benevolent Mr. Stanley was so impressed with his protégé's reading list and his progress at Speake and McCreary's that he invited him to Sunday breakfast at the genteel lodging house in St. Charles Street where, we are told, he lived with his wife, "a fragile little lady who was the picture of refinement."

> Nothing could have been better calculated to conquer my shyness than the gracious welcome she accorded me. We took our respective places at once, she as motherly patroness and I as a devotedly grateful protégé. . . . The elaborateness and richness of dress, the purity and delicacy of her face, the exquisite modulations of her voice, the distinctness of her enunciation, and the sweet courtesy of her manner . . . kindled as much of reverence as ever I felt in my life. . . . The being beside me might command me to endure any torture, or dare any danger, for her sake. . . . It was at this hour that I made the discovery of the immense distance between a lady and a mere woman; and while I gazed at her clear, lustrous eyes, and noted the charms which played about her features, I was thinking that, if a lady could be so superior to an ordinary housewife . . . what a beautiful thing an angel must be!

As Stanley would tell it, after that first Sunday breakfast, relations between the couple and their young protégé grew ever warmer, while his conduct grew correspondingly more virtuous and diligent: "They took me to church, each Sabbath; and, in other ways, manifested a protective care. I resumed the custom of morning and evening prayer, my industry at the store was of a more thoughtful kind, my comings and goings were of more exemplary punctuality."

Stanley dips even deeper into the well of sticky self-righteousness as he recalls, in his autobiography, how, in his zeal on behalf of Speake and McCreary, he unmasked two ungrateful Negro slaves who had been systematically stealing syrup, wine, hams, cans of sardines and boxes of biscuits from the warehouse. As a result of his revelations "a constable was called in and Dan and Samuel were marched off to the watch-house, to receive on the next day such a flogging as only practiced State-officials know how to administer. Dan, a few days later, was reinstated at the store; but Samuel was disposed of to a planter, for field-work."

After this ingratiating episode, young Rowlands was more than ever in the good books of his employer. But fate, in the form of a yellow fever epidemic, was to thwart his upward progress in the world of commerce. His master, James Speake, caught the disease and died within a few days. Soon afterward, the firm was sold to a less congenial master and, as Stanley told it, some weeks after that, while his benefactor was upriver on business, the saintly Mrs. Stanley was also stricken.

Deeply concerned, the devoted John Rowlands asked his new boss, a Mr. Ellison, for a few days off to help the Stanleys' Irish maid Margaret in her round-the-clock sickbed duties. When Ellison refused his request, Rowlands resigned and hurried to the bedside of the woman he revered. But within days, we are told, the sickbed became a deathbed.

> Near midnight, Margaret, with a solemn and ghastly face, beckoned me into the sick lady's room. With my heart throbbing painfully . . . I entered on tiptoe. I saw a broad bed, curtained with white muslin, whereon lay the fragile figure of the patient, so frail and delicate that, in my rude health, it seemed insolence in me to be near her. . . . I saw by the dim light how awfully solemn a human face can be when in saintly peace. Slowly I understood how even the most timid woman could smilingly welcome Death, and willingly yield herself to its cold embrace.

But Mrs. Stanley was not quite ready to pass on. "She opened her mild eyes, and spoke words as from afar: 'Be a good boy. God bless you!' And, while I strained my hearing for more, there was an indistinct murmur, the eyes opened wide and became fixed, and a beautiful tranquility settled over the features. How strangely serene!"

A moving description, and another scene in which life seems to mimic the popular literature of the day. Indeed, for sheer sentimentality the death of Little Nell could hardly rival Stanley's description of the Grim Reaper, before bearing her away, allowing the gentle personification of Ideal Womanhood time to utter a few improving words. And like the death of Little Nell, that of the ethereal Mrs. Stanley was fiction: the woman whom Stanley dispatched with such glutinous reverence was, in fact, to live another nineteen years.

According to Stanley, the dead woman's brother-in-law arrived by coincidence from Havana the following day and took charge of things. He had the body embalmed, put into a lead-lined casket and sent upriver with Margaret to St. Louis, where the grieving widower, informed of his loss by telegram, was waiting to receive and bury it.

After a while, young Rowlands himself went upriver to St. Louis to find his benefactor, only to learn that he had returned to New

Orleans. So it was back to New Orleans, working his way downriver on a flatboat. And eventually the boy was reunited with Mr. Stanley, who had been searching for him and whose reception of him was "so paternal that the prodigal son could not have been more delighted." The widower, deeply moved by what he had learned of the lad's steadfast loyalty to his dying wife, climaxed the joyful reunion by declaring *with some emotion, that my future should be his charge!"*

"In my earliest dreams and fancies," Stanley would recall, "I had often imagined what kind of a boy I should be with a father or mother. What ecstasy it would be if my parent came to me, to offer a parent's love, as I had seen it bestowed on other children. . . . Before I could quite grasp all that this declaration meant for me he had risen, taken me by the hand, and folded me in a gentle embrace. My senses seemed to whirl about for a few half-minutes; and finally I broke down, sobbing from extreme emotion."

An impromptu christening followed in which, having declared that "in future you are to bear my name," the older Stanley "rose and, dipping his hands in a basin of water, he made the sign of the cross on my forehead, and went seriously through the formula of baptism, ending with a brief exhortation to bear my new name worthily."

There follows an idyllic account of how—the newly adopted Stanley having been lavishly outfitted and earnestly instructed by the older so as to be worthy of his new status—the two of them spent the next two years together, traveling up and down the Mississippi on business. During this period, we are told, the older Stanley imparted to his adopted son the acquired wisdom of his years in commerce, philosophy, religion and the liberal arts.

> With such a man, a river-voyage was no impediment to instruction. He set me an example of application . . . which, added to my own love of study, enabled me to cultivate indifference to what was passing outside our cabin. Our travelling library was constantly replenished at the larger cities with essays, memoirs, biographies, and general literature; but novels and romances were rigorously excluded. . . . [W]ith such a companion, these river voyages considerably advanced my education, as much so, indeed, as though I had been with a tutor. Nor, when we dropped our books, and promenaded the deck, was my mind left to stagnate in frivolity. He took advantage of every object worthy of notice to impress on me some useful, or moral, lesson—to warn me against errors of omission or commission.

Given the older man's reproving manner, it is not surprising that, from time to time, small clouds did appear in the impeccably blue skies of the father-son, tutor-pupil relationship. Stanley senior, we are told, would occasionally find it necessary to discipline his adopted son by "an unexpected sharpness of tone, or a denial of some liberty," and indeed our hero admits that "I was often erring or perverse, and at various times must have tried him sorely."

Eventually, Stanley tells us, fate brought about what was intended to be a temporary separation, but which sadly turned out to be permanent. As he describes events, the older Stanley had been talking for some time about giving up his interests in New Orleans and the vagrant life of a cotton broker, and instead going into business with his adopted son as a country storekeeper "at some place below Pine Bluff on the Arkansas [River]." The older Stanley at last took the first step toward acting on that wish after receiving news that his brother in Havana was sick and in need of help in looking after his affairs.

Before leaving for Havana, he sent young Stanley off to learn the business of country storekeeping from a German-Jewish acquaintance named Altschul, who was in trade at a settlement called Cypress Bend, about fifty miles from Little Rock. On his return from Havana, he told his protégé, he would go into the same kind of business, and the two of them would run the store together.

During his first nine weeks at Cypress Bend, says Stanley, he received three letters from his adoptive father in Havana: "Then month after month of absolute silence followed. . . . Until well into March, 1861, I was in daily expectation of hearing from him, or seeing him in person. But we were destined never to meet again. He died suddenly in 1861—I only heard of his death long after."

As baldly and briefly as that does Stanley recount the death of his adored adoptive father. But, in fact, like the demise of Mrs. Stanley, it was a fiction. Far from dying in Cuba in 1861, the older Stanley lived on in New Orleans until 1878, like his wife. What really happened? The question is difficult to answer; all we know for sure is what did not happen: Stanley's entire account of his adoption appears to be pure fantasy.

First, some facts about Stanley, senior: His full name was Henry Hope Stanley, and he was an Englishman. If it seems odd that despite their supposed intimacy the young Stanley never got to know his benefactor's middle name—or that, if he did, he chose not to mention it when writing of him—it is equally strange that he also never mentioned that his benefactor was not an American, as implied, but an Englishman.

Henry Hope Stanley had emigrated to America at the age of twenty-one from Cheshire, where he was born into a well-to-do family in 1815. Cheshire is the English county closest to North Wales, where John Rowlands was born and raised, and just as Henry Hope Stanley could not have failed to recognize the boy's Welsh accent, John Rowlands must surely have detected the English accent of his benefactor. Indeed, it seems quite possible that the boy's native lilt may have been instrumental in sparking the older man's interest. But none of this detail is given in the explorer's later reminiscences of this supposedly seminal relationship.

By the time he met young Rowlands, Henry Hope Stanley had been twice married. His first wife had been a Texan girl, her name lost to posterity, whom he met shortly after arriving in America. When they moved to New Orleans, soon after their wedding, she opened a boardinghouse in Dorsiere Street, in the commercial district, while he struggled to make his way in the cotton business.

In the summer of 1843 Mr. Stanley went on a lengthy business trip to the Red River. On returning at night, some months later, to Dorsiere Street, he found the house locked and deserted. Alarmed, he hammered on the front door of a neighbor, who broke the news to him that his wife had died some days previously of yellow fever and, as was customary to prevent the spread of infection, had already been buried. The circumstances are so similar to those of the second Mrs. Stanley's fictional death that one can only suppose John Rowlands heard of them—probably from his benefactor— and later adapted them to his own strange purposes. However, his autobiography never mentions the existence of the first Mrs. Stanley.

Henry Hope Stanley took a second wife in December 1847. She was a Miss Frances Mellor, also English-born, and aged nineteen when the marriage took place in New Orleans. This woman was the idealized figure of Henry Morton Stanley's reminiscences, a figure so divorced from reality that he never mentions her first name or provides any detail that would give her flesh-and-blood substance.

Like the first Mrs. Stanley, Frances bore no children, and to fill the gap in their lives the couple had adopted two girls by the time John Rowlands appeared on the scene—another detail that he significantly fails to mention.

He also fails, whether through memory lapse or with intent to mislead, to give anything like an accurate picture of the Stanleys' domestic arrangements. According to the New Orleans City Directory for 1859, they were not living in a lodging house on St. Charles Street, as he claimed, but in a house of their own, facing the then-fashionable Annunciation Square. Census information from the following year shows that a fourteen-year-old adopted daughter named Annie Stanley* was living there with them.

The same census, while listing no John Rowlands, does name one "J. Rolling," described as a clerk born in England, as a boarder, with a number of other clerks and cotton brokers, at a house in St. Thomas Street. This must certainly be the future Henry Morton Stanley.

By the late 1850s Henry Hope Stanley had risen to wealth and local prominence as the senior member of a partnership which owned two large cotton presses. In addition to his town house, he owned a country mansion at Arcola, in the countryside northwest of the city, where the summer air was more salubrious and the danger from yellow fever less acute.

Contemporary accounts describe him as a handsome man of florid complexion, always elegantly dressed, with a well-tended silky black beard. A former clerk of his said: "He was very kind to his employees. Often, when we had to work unusually hard and long, he waited till our tasks were completed and then took us to the theater and after the performance to supper. Everybody liked him. He was a good man to have for a friend."

A newspaper obituary shows that Henry Hope Stanley died "suddenly of heart disease" at Foley Plantation in Assumption Parish on the night of November 1, 1878. His wife predeceased him by a few months, and although no record of the precise date has been found, the inventory of her estate is dated June 22, 1878. Henry Hope Stanley left property valued at $130,000—a considerable fortune in those days. His half-brother, James Howard Brooks of Manchester, England, was the sole legatee.

For Henry Hope Stanley's purported adoption of John Rowlands, not a scrap of documentary evidence can be found, and indeed the explorer himself gives no account of any formal or legal measures having been taken in this direction, beyond the patently spurious "baptismal" ceremony described in his autobiography.

One final, obvious falsehood in Henry Morton Stanley's account is his claim that after the "death" of his benefactor's wife, he and his "father" spent two years together traveling up and down the river on business. This would have made the date of their parting some time in early 1862, but in fact—and by his own account—the young

---

* Of Annie, nothing is known beyond the fact of her existence at the time of the census, but the Stanleys' first adopted daughter, Johanna, had clearly been a disappointment. She eloped with their coachman, James Kemper, and subsequently made two further marriages—the last to a druggist—before her early death in 1874.

Stanley arrived in Cypress Bend at least a year earlier, in January 1861.

The most likely truth behind this tissue of omissions, evasions and downright falsehoods is that Henry Hope Stanley did, indeed, take an interest in the young Rowlands, but that it was not nearly so intense an interest as the lad had hoped for. It is easy to believe that after showing friendship and finding the boy a job (though not, we should note, in his own business) the older man was taken aback by the warmth and eagerness of his protégé's response.

The lad wanted more than a benefactor; he wanted a family, but that was not on offer. Henry Hope had, as a business associate put it, "a soft heart, but a hard head," and it seems all too likely that after a while he began to find the lad's doglike adoration and demands for affection altogether more than he could comfortably handle.

One can equally imagine that the angelic Mrs. Stanley was less taken with young Rowlands than the autobiographer would have us believe. One can envisage her telling her husband that she found the eighteen-year-old's mooning attentions embarrassing. She might even have tried to make that clear to the lad himself, which would explain the necessity for her to be killed off so that the imaginary adoption could be consummated.

Under these circumstances, it is all too easy to imagine Henry Hope Stanley inventing a pretext to rid himself of his clinging protégé. Certainly the suggestion that a successful cosmopolitan like Henry Hope would have considered exiling himself to a malarial Arkansas backwater is absurd. The only plausible explanation of his arranging for the lad to go to Arkansas to learn the trade of a country storekeeper was surely to get rid of him. The young Rowlands' rage and hurt at this rejection would certainly account for his symbolic murder of the older man.

Whatever its causes, the breach between Henry Morton Stanley and the man whose name he bore was absolute, with never an attempt at reconciliation on either side. By the time the now world-famous explorer found himself in New Orleans again, during a lecture tour in April 1891, both Henry Hope Stanley and his wife really were in their graves. But Mrs. Stanley's sister, a Mrs. Walter Nichol, was still living in the city, and Stanley made no attempt to look her up. Nor did he make contact with other acquaintances of his youth—some of them now prominent citizens—who were eager to meet him.

"He seems to have avoided his old friends as much as possible," reported a local historian with personal recollections of the Stanley visit. A story in the *New Orleans Daily States* gives some idea of the resentment this behavior caused. It was headlined

### STANLEY'S EARLY LIFE

A remarkable story that may
explain the explorer's queer
actions in refusing to see
old friends in New Orleans

The story featured an account given by "a lady of undoubted veracity" who, wishing to remain unnamed, said she had known Stanley as a youth named John Rollins in 1859. "He was always a boy of good habits," she said, "smart as a whip, and much given to bragging, big talk and telling stories."

She told how she met him again when he looked her up toward the end of the Civil War, by which time she was living in New York. She was puzzled because a friend who accompanied him called him Henry, whereas she had always known him as John. "I asked him whether he had two names," she recalled. "He said no, but that his mother had recently married again, and that the name of her second husband was Henry Stanley, and that he had taken this name."

No mention, then, of Henry Hope Stanley or of his adoption. Clearly, at this point Stanley had not yet settled on the authorized version of how he came by the name under which he would achieve world fame.

# Chapter Three

CYPRESS BEND was sheer misery for the young Stanley. Lonely and embittered by rejection, he was further reduced to a state of physical wretchedness by the swamp fever which "afflicted young and old in the bottom lands of Arkansas" and which laid him low within a week of his arrival.

Stanley had come to Altschul's store a sturdy, ruddy-complexioned youth, if anything a little overweight for his five-foot-five-inch frame. Before long the ague had reduced him to ninety-five pounds, and he was surviving on quinine and calomel. As he recorded, "the young physician of our neighbourhood, who boarded with Mr. Altschul . . . had known many cases to terminate fatally within a few hours. Blacks as well as whites were subject to it. Nothing availed to prevent an attack. The most abstemious, temperate, prudent habits no more prevented it than selfish indulgence or intemperance."

In his recurring misery Stanley found little to admire in the local plantocracy whom, "what with isolation on their wide estates, their life among obsequious slaves, indigestion and inflamed livers," he found neither amiable nor sociable. The sharp perceptions of Stanley's Cypress Bend reminiscences are in refreshing contrast to the sanctimonious implausibilities of his recollections of New Orleans. He skewers enduring clichés about Southern courtesy, gallantry and honor with a directness and realism worthy at times of a Zola:

> Several of the richer men owned domains of from six to ten square miles. They lived like princelings, were owners of hundreds of slaves, over whom they were absolute except as to life and limb, and all their environments catered to their egotism. . . . Such manners as they exhibited were not so much due to neighbourly good-feeling as to their dislike of consequences which might result from a wanton offishness. . . . Their general attitude was . . . stiff and constrained. Each slightly raised his hat as he came in, and their "Sirs" were more formal and punctilious than, as neighbours or fellow-citizens, they ought to have been. . . . The self-estimate of such men was sometimes colossal, and their vanities as sensitive as hair-triggers. . . . It is wonderful what trivial causes were sufficient to irritate them. A little preoccupation in one's own personal

affairs, a monosyllabic word, a look of doubt, or a hesitating answer, made them flare up hotly.

The rich planter was not the only target for Stanley's scorn.

The poor American settler, the Irish employee, the German-Jew store-keeper, in a brief time grew as liable to bursts of deadly passion, or fits of cold-blooded malignity, as the Virginia aristocrat. In New Orleans, and other great cities, the social rule was to give and take, to assert an opinion and hear it contradicted without resort to lethal weapons, but in Arkansas to refute a statement was tantamount to giving the lie direct, and was likely to be followed by an instant appeal to the revolver or bowie.

Still, Arkansas did much to prepare Stanley for his future vocation. Exposure to the local variety of malarial mosquito undoubtedly fore-armed his system against the later assaults of the African *anopheles*. And exposure to the code of honor of the Southern gentleman, and the Southern cult of the gun, drove him to acquire the sharpshooting skills which equally assured his survival in the Dark Continent. He devoted hours to target practice "until my proficiency was so great that I could sever a pack thread at twenty paces."

While he was learning the ways of the South, "astounding national events" were taking place, of which the young Stanley was only vaguely aware and in which, as a foreigner, he initially took little interest. But by March 1861, the talk of secession and war became so insistent that he could no longer ignore it. He was given a quick education in the politics of South versus North by Dan Goree, the son of a neighboring planter prominent in local affairs. As a result of Abe Lincoln's election, said young Dan, all slaveowners faced ruin.

"His father owned about 120 slaves," Stanley wrote, "worth from $500 to $1200 a head, and to deprive him of property that he had bought with cash was pure robbery. That was the reason that all the people of the South were rising against the Northern people. . . . [E]very man and boy would have to proceed to the war and drive those wretched Abolitionists back to their homes. . . ."

As an outsider, Stanley could not understand what all the fuss was about. He nursed "a secret scorn for people who could kill each other for the sake of African slaves. . . . Why a sooty-faced negro from a distant land should be an element of disturbance between white brothers was a puzzle to me." He also noted caustically how easily the pugnacious Southern gentleman let himself be egged on by his womenfolk:

The warlike fire that burned within [the men's] breasts was nothing to the intense heat that glowed within the bosoms of the women. No suggestion of compromise was possible in their presence. If every man did not hasten to the battle, they vowed they would themselves rush out and meet the Yankee vandals. In a land where women are worshipped by the men, such language made them war-mad.

The rabble-rousing fire of Southern womanhood would soon send Stanley himself off to war. He had for some time been secretly enamored of a girl named Margaret Goree, a cousin of Dan's. She had seemed more friendly and sympathetic, and quieter, than the other local girls, who would come into the store and attract his attention by shrill banter among themselves, then snub him if he ventured to join in.

Evidently, it did not occur to Stanley that Margaret would expect him to be as "patriotic" as the native-born young men and join the Dixie Greys, the company of volunteers that was being raised in the locality. When he showed no inclination to rush to the colors, Margaret did her bit for the South by sending him anonymously the equivalent of the white feather—a parcel containing a chemise and a petticoat. Stanley recalled,

I hastily hid it from view, and retired to the back room, that my burning cheeks might not betray me to some onlooker. In the afternoon, Dr. Goree called, and was excessively cordial and kind. He asked me if I did not intend to join the valiant children of Arkansas to fight? and I answered "Yes." . . . He praised my courage and my patriotism, and said I should win undying glory, and then he added, in a lower voice, "We shall see what we can do for you when you come back." What *did* he mean? Did he suspect my secret love for that sweet child. . . ? I believed he did and was, accordingly, ready to go anywhere for her sake.

It was the first of a number of betrayals Stanley was to suffer at the hands of women he fancied that he loved, and he soon had cause to regret allowing himself to be manipulated. "Enlisting in the Confederate service because I received a packet of female clothes was certainly a grave blunder," he conceded.

*A MAN'S* first experience of combat is a crucial rite of passage. In the chaos and terror of the battlefield he learns a lot about himself and, unless he is willfully blind or very stupid, some essential truths about the nature of his species. Participation in the Battle of Shiloh was just such an experience for Private Henry Stanley of the Dixie Greys, and a watershed in the development of his character. His ability to keep calm under fire served to strengthen his physical self-confidence, while the carnage he witnessed did something—if clearly not quite enough—to reduce his propensity for cant and hypocrisy.

He had been a member of the Confederate Army for nine months before the testing time came. The Dixie Greys had shipped out by riverboat from Cypress Bend to Little Rock to become part of the Sixth Regiment of Arkansas Volunteers. After several weeks of training they had been deemed ready for combat and marched through the streets of the Arkansas capital to board another riverboat with their silken company banner—hand-sewn by the lady patriots of their home district—flying bravely and the regimental band tootling "Dixie."

But the glory the Greys so ardently sought was not yet at hand. Soldiering, as Stanley was to learn, was a matter mainly of "commonplace marches and squalid camp life." While awaiting their opportunity to die for Dixie, the Greys submitted to savage and often senseless discipline and cold, inedible rations as they marched aimlessly to and fro across the South, bivouacking in muddy fields and—an alarmingly high proportion of them—falling victim to typhus, dysentery and malaria.

Finally, on April 4, 1862, they marched out of camp at Corinth, Mississippi, to do battle as part of a forty-thousand-strong army under the joint command of Generals Albert Johnston and Pierre Beauregard. Their orders were to confront fifty thousand Union troops under the command of Ulysses S. Grant and hurl them back across the Tennessee River.

The bloody clash of armies at Shiloh, the first major battle of the Civil War, began at daybreak on April 6. Against the Union soldiers' Enfield and Minié rifles, the Confederates were armed with obsolescent flintlock muskets whose ammunition consisted of rolls of cartridge paper containing powder, a ball and three buckshot. To load their guns they had to tear the paper with their teeth, pour some of the powder into the firing pan and lock it before pouring the rest into the barrel, pressing paper and ball into the muzzle and ramming it home.

As the cumbersomely armed Confederate infantry advanced in line toward the Union positions, Stanley noted that the locale "would have been a grand place for a picnic and I thought it strange that a Sunday should have been chosen to disturb the holy calm of those woods."

Taking the enemy by surprise at first light, the Southern troops advanced step by step, loading and firing as they went. As the Greys closed with the foe through a hail of bullets, they received the order to fix bayonets and rushed yelling for the first line of Union tents. The northern troops, still sleepy and disorganized by the shock of the surprise attack, fled, leaving behind their half-dressed dead and wounded. As the rebels pressed on to the second line of Union tents, the enemy, now thoroughly awake, opened up with everything they had of rifle, musket and cannon. To Stanley, "the world seemed bursting into fragments" as he took cover behind a fallen tree with a dozen comrades:

> How the cannon bellowed and their shells plunged and bounded, and flew with screeching hisses over us! Their sharp rending explosions and hurtling fragments made us shrink and cower. . . . I marvelled as I heard the unintermitting patter, snip, thud and hum of the bullets, how anyone could live under this raining death. . . . One here and there found its way under the log, and buried itself into a comrade's body. One man raised his chest as if to yawn and jostled me. I turned to him and saw that a bullet had gored his whole face and penetrated into his chest. Another ball struck a man a deadly rap on the head, and he turned on his back and showed his ghastly white face to the sky.

Ordered to break cover and resume their advance, Stanley and his comrades abandoned the doubtful shelter of the fallen log and rushed forward. As they gained the second line of Union tents, a bullet or shell fragment struck Stanley's belt buckle and threw him to the ground. Finding himself winded but unhurt, he crawled to the shelter of a tree to rest. Around him lay the fallen, and Stanley, like many a young man before and since, began to realize the horrid reality of war:

> I cannot forget that half-mile square of woodland, lighted brightly by the sun, and littered by the forms of about a thousand dead and wounded men, and by horses and military equipments. . . . It was the first Field of Glory I had seen in my May of life and the first time that Glory sickened me with its repulsive aspect, and made me suspect it was all a glittering lie. . . . Oh, for once I was beginning to know the real truth! Man was born for slaughter!

Catching up with his regiment, Stanley continued the advance toward the Tennessee River through scenes of continuing carnage. "Dead bodies, wounded men writhing in agony, and assuming every distressful attitude, were frequent sights; but what made us heart-sick was to see, now and then . . . a stray cavalry or artillery horse, galloping between the lines, snorting with terror, while his entrails, soiled with dust, trailed behind him."

By now, after twelve hours of continuous battle, both sides were exhausted, and having assaulted and taken another federal camp, the rebels stopped to eat and sleep. Before dawn the next day, they rose to continue their advance, unaware that during the night Grant had been reinforced by General Don Carlos Buell with twenty thousand fresh troops.

As they moved out in skirmishing order, the Dixie Greys now reduced to no more than 50 men, Stanley heard one of his officers call out, "Now Mr. Stanley, if you please, step briskly forward!" Stung by the implication that he was less than thirsty for the fray, Stanley moved more briskly than he should have, firing, loading and darting forward from one spot of cover to the next, until "to my speechless amazement I found myself a solitary grey in a line of blue skirmishers."

The next thing he knew, half a dozen Union soldiers surrounded him with leveled rifles, and a voice ordered him to drop his gun "or I'll drill a hole through you." Stanley quickly did as he was told. Then, "two men sprang at my collar and marched me unresisting into the ranks of the terrible Yankees. I was a *prisoner*!"

A few days later, Stanley found himself in a makeshift camp on the outskirts of Chicago, where he quickly discovered that the life of a prisoner of war was as precarious as that of a combat infantryman, and even more wretched.

The three thousand prisoners already incarcerated in Camp Douglas were "ragged and swarming with vermin . . . sickly and emaciated" with "ash-coloured faces." They were housed in "great wooden barns" with six-foot-wide sleeping platforms running down each side, on which each man was allowed thirty inches of space. Those for whom no space remained slept on the floor beneath the platforms. As Stanley wrote later:

> Within a week, our new draft commenced to succumb. . . . Our build-ings swarmed with vermin . . . dysentery and typhus began to rage. Day after day my company steadily diminished; and every morning I had to see them carried in their blankets to the hospital, whence none ever returned. . . . [E]ach time imperious nature compelled us to resort to [the latrines] we lost a little of that respect and consideration we owed to our fellow-creatures. For, on the way thither, we saw crowds of sick men who had fallen, prostrate from weakness, and given themselves wholly to

despair; and while they crawled or wallowed in their filth, they cursed and blasphemed as often as they groaned.

There was a way out of this hell. Within a few days of his arrival the camp commissary advised Stanley that he could gain his release by signing up with the Union army. At first, Stanley's response was negative. Although indifferent to the issues over which the war was being fought, he "could not take it upon me to do anything more than stand by my friends."

But after enduring six weeks of the camp's monstrous conditions, he came to his senses and, with several other prisoners, agreed to change sides. By early June he was wearing the blue uniform of the Illinois Light Artillery and on his way to do battle against his former comrades-in-arms.

But Stanley never made it to the battlefields of Virginia. After only two or three days' service in the war zone he finally fell victim to the dysentery that had carried off so many of his former fellow prisoners. Admitted to a military hospital at Harper's Ferry, West Virginia, he was found to be in such poor condition that, after about a fortnight, he was discharged from the service and turned out of the hospital to fend for himself.

"My condition at this time," he wrote, "was as low as it would be possible to reduce a human being to. . . . I had not a penny in my pocket . . . I knew not where to go; the seeds of disease were still in me, and I could not walk three hundred yards without stopping to gasp for breath."

Indeed, it took Stanley a week to walk nine miles from Harper's Ferry to a farm on the road to Hagerstown, Maryland, where a family named Baker took pity on him. After several days in a coma, he awoke to find himself bathed, in bed, and in clean clothes. The Bakers nursed him back to strength on a milk diet, and by early July he was sufficiently recovered to assist in the last part of the harvest and join in the harvest supper. He stayed with the Bakers until mid-August, when they drove him to Hagerstown, bought him a railway ticket, and put him on the train to Baltimore.*

It seems that Stanley chose to go to Baltimore because it was the nearest seaport and, weary and beaten, he wanted to return to his native Wales. For a few weeks—perhaps to gather strength before the Atlantic crossing—he worked as a hand on an oyster schooner in

---

* At this point in his story, Stanley's manuscript autobiography peters out, to be completed by his widow from his published works and unpublished notebooks and journals.

Chesapeake Bay. Then, some time in October 1862, he signed on with the schooner *E. Sherman,* bound for Liverpool, arriving a month later. He had been away almost four years and had little to show for it.

From Liverpool, Stanley made his way to the village of Glascoed, in Denbighshire, where he had learned that his mother was living, now respectably married to one Robert Jones, the father of her two youngest children. She and her husband were running an inn called The Cross Foxes and—predictably, given the indifference Betsy Parry had always displayed toward the illegitimate son of her wild youth— the arrival of the haggard, disheveled stranger was a thoroughly unwelcome surprise.

In a notebook entry written long after the event and seemingly intended for inclusion in his autobiography, Stanley recalls his bitter disappointment:

> With what pride I knocked at the door, buoyed up by the hope of being able to show what manliness I had acquired. . . . Like a bride arraying herself in her best for her lover, I had arranged my story to please one who would at last, I hoped, prove an affectionate mother! But I found no affection, and I never again sought for, or expected, what I discovered had never existed. I was told that "I was a disgrace to them in the eyes of their neighbours, and they desired me to leave as speedily as possible."

BY JANUARY 1863, Stanley was in New York, having crossed the Atlantic once more as a deck hand, this time on a ship called the *Ernestine.* For much of that year he served aboard merchantmen plying to and from the east coast of America. One of these was the 250-ton barque *Jehu,* which left Boston in May 1863, bound for Mediterranean ports. A cryptic retrospective journal entry tells of the loss of the *Jehu:* "Wrecked off Barcelona, Crew lost, in the night. Stripped naked, and swam to shore. Barrack of Carbineers. . . . demanded my papers!"

This was one of Stanley's fictions. If he did swim ashore, it was because he had jumped ship. Lloyds of London's records show that the *Jehu* arrived safely at Barcelona on June 25, 1863, leaving a fortnight later for Girgenti, Italy. Indeed, the *Jehu* remained in service until 1890. The fact of his entering such a pointless untruth in his private journal suggests that Stanley was by now a compulsive liar.

In October 1863, he took a shore job in Brooklyn, working as a clerk for Thomas Irwin Hughes, who described himself as a judge but was not quite that. The record shows that Hughes was a notary public and an "attorney for prosecuting government claims." One of Stanley's notebook entries characterizes Hughes as something of a wild character: "Boarding with Judge X——. Judge drunk; tried to kill his wife with hatchet; attempted three times.—I held him down all night. Next morning, exhausted; lighted cigar in parlour; wife came down—insulted and raved at me for smoking in her house!"

Stanley apparently remained in the judge's employ until the summer of 1864, when he suddenly and unaccountably decided to become involved once more in the Civil War, then nearing its end. Perhaps he was bored with life as a notary's clerk; perhaps he had become convinced of the justice of the federal cause; more likely, he merely yearned for a little adventure. On July 19 he signed up for three years in the federal navy, giving his age (falsely) as twenty and apparently concealing the fact that he had considerable experience as a merchant seaman, for he was marked down by the naval recruiting officer as a "landsman." This otherwise unaccountable deception may have been motivated by a reluctance to serve as a deck hand and, given his experience as a clerk, may have been instrumental in his being assigned as a ship's writer (clerk) to the frigate *Minnesota*.

In that role, he witnessed the first and second bombardments of Fort Fisher, North Carolina, one of the Confederates' last Atlantic coast strongholds, in December 1864 and January 1865. In the first bombardment, the Union forces tried to destroy Fort Fisher, which guarded the sea approaches to the vital Southern port of Wilmington, by blowing up a ship laden with explosives near the sea wall. This attempt failed, and the Union fleet was beaten off. A month later the federals returned, and this time achieved their objective in a two-pronged land and sea assault, hastening the collapse of the Confederacy three months later.

While serving on the *Minnesota,* Stanley struck up a friendship, despite the difference in their ages, with a fifteen-year-old boy sailor named Lewis Noe. "He was full of aspirations for adventure," Noe recalled some years later, "told marvellous tales of foreign countries, and urged that when we should leave the service I should accompany him on a proposed tour of Southern Europe. Being of a romantic turn of mind, I was pleased at the suggestion."

When the *Minnesota* put into Portsmouth, New Hampshire, after the Battle of Fort Fisher, Stanley persuaded Noe to jump ship with him. They left the dockyard on a pass forged by Stanley and once clear of the gates shed their uniforms, under which they were wearing civilian clothes. Together they headed for New York, where they temporarily parted company, intending to join forces later.

When Noe got to his parents' home in Long Island, they were horrified to learn of his desertion and ordered him to return to his ship before he got into serious trouble. Instead, he enlisted in the army, joining the Eighth New York Mounted Volunteers under the name—apparently suggested to him by Stanley—of Morton. With the Civil War coming to a close, Noe saw no action as a soldier, and he left the service with an honorable discharge when hostilities ended soon afterward.

By this time, Stanley had decided to heed Horace Greeley's advice—"Go West, young man." He wrote to Noe inviting him to come along, but his young friend declined.

Stanley went first to St. Louis, where he made his tentative entry into journalisn by persuading the editors of the *Missouri Democrat* to accept him as a freelance contributor from points farther west. From St. Louis he pushed on to St. Joseph, Missouri, before crossing the plains and the Rocky Mountains to California. He moved incessantly, from California to Salt Lake City, then back to San Francisco, then down to Denver and Central City, Colorado, sending back dispatches as he went.

Stanley soon found he could not earn enough to survive from freelance journalism, and to supplement his income he worked variously as a bookkeeper and an apprentice printer in Central City, and a gold-miner and smelting-works laborer at Black Hawk City, Colorado. During this period, he struck up a friendship with another young freelance reporter named William Harlow Cook, and they agreed to go adventuring together around the world.

As a first test of manhood they resolved to travel down the fast-flowing Platte River from Denver to Omaha—a distance of six hundred miles—in a flat-bottomed homemade boat. Provisioning the boat, and arming themselves for protection against Indians who might take potshots at them from the river banks, they set off downstream.

According to one of Stanley's notebook entries, they had "many adventures and narrow escapes" and capsized the boat twice before reaching their destination three weeks later. Cook recalled that the river banks "were infested with Indians, while the river itself was full of snags, eddies, and shallow spots." He added: "Several parties had gone down, but none had got through alive, they told us at Denver."

From Omaha, the adventurers took a riverboat to St. Louis and a train to New York, where they met up with Noe. Stanley had kept in touch with his former shipmate by letter while he was journeying in the West and had persuaded Noe, now aged seventeen, to join him and Cook in a new adventure—a trip that would take them around the world. The plan was to take ship to Turkey, trek overland across Anatolia to the Caucasus, thence to India and China, and eventually to return home via the Pacific and the West Coast of America.

Stanley—and presumably Cook, too—had saved enough from his freelance earnings to finance the trip. Also, they planned to cut their travel costs by working their passages across the Atlantic and to turn a profit on the adventure by freelance journalism en route and writing a book on their return.

Stanley seems also to have had some other ideas for making the adventure profitable. As Noe recalled: "He told me of diamonds and rubies and precious stones, and rich India shawls and other fabrics in Central Asia, [of] the real value of which the natives knew scarcely anything, which could be procured by us for insignificant sums of money, and could be sold at an enormous profit."

On July 10, 1866, the three sailed from Boston aboard the barque *E. H. Yarrington*, bound for Smyrna (now Izmir) on the west coast of Turkey, which they reached seven weeks later. A week after disembarking they struck out overland, intending to cross the Anatolian hinterland to Armenia.

They had not gone more than ten or twelve miles before they ran into trouble. On the second day out, as they camped close to a village, Noe set fire to some brush, apparently out of a misplaced sense of fun. The brush fire outraged the local peasantry, and Stanley and friends had to flee. Later Stanley punished Noe for causing so much trouble. According to Stanley, he gave the boy "a few strokes of a switch." According to Noe, Stanley tied him to a tree, stripped him to the waist, and "scourged me with a whip . . . until the blood ran from my wounds."

There was far worse trouble ahead, near a mountain village called Chi-Hissar, some three hundred miles from Smyrna, although what exactly happened there remains similarly a matter of controversy. According to Stanley, they were accosted by a band of ruffians whose leader made sexual advances to Noe. Stanley claimed that in response he struck the man with the flat of his sword, causing no serious injury, but that the ruffians, a dozen of them, seized him and his companions and dragged them off into captivity. They were tied up and beaten while xenophobic villagers crowded around to stone and spit at them as they lay helpless in their bonds.

Noe's version, as he recounted it six years later, was startlingly different, characterizing Stanley as being mainly, and criminally, responsible for the whole episode. Noe said that Stanley tried to murder a Turk whom they met on the highway in order to steal his two horses. He got the horses, said Noe, but the Turk escaped, soon afterward returning with a horde of clansmen who chased the young Americans into the mountains and took them prisoner.

Said Noe: "The first night of our imprisonment I was taken out by three of the Turks and treated in a shocking manner." This was Noe's delicate way of saying that he had been raped, and in this particular, at least, there is agreement between his version and Stanley's. A diary entry by Stanley shortly after the event, records that "Mr. Cook and myself were beaten. Louis [sic], a boy of 17, was ——." The final word had been scratched out. Later, in an unpublished manuscript entitled "Adventures of an American Traveller in Turkey," Stanley was a little more explicit. The Turks, he said, "had no pity or remorse but one by one they committed their diabolical crime which is, I think, or I hope, unknown to civilized nations, especially Christian America."

Stanley and his companions eventually gained their release when the provincial governor, learning of their plight and accepting Stanley's version of events, had the three westerners' captors clapped in irons and taken to the city of Bursa to stand trial for assault and robbery.

Bereft of money and possessions, Stanley and Noe made their way to Constantinople to report their plight to the American legation, leaving Cook in Bursa to press criminal charges. Long after the event, the American minister, Edward Jay Morris, recalled how Stanley and Noe turned up, without even shirts or socks, and were put up for the night at the embassy residence. "If ever the condition of men presented the traces of cruel treatment, theirs did," said Morris. "Mr. Stanley's own plight fully corroborated his story."

The following day, Morris loaned Stanley $600 without security, and Stanley, of his own volition, offered the ambassador in return a note for the same amount, which he said would be honored by his father. He gave the address of this fictitious parent as 20 Liberty Street, New York City. Morris later discovered that there was no such person. Noe alleged that Stanley kept the $600 for himself, but forced him under threat to sign a declaration that he had received one-third of it.

Without question, Stanley spent some of the money on deceptive self-adornment. He went to a tailor and ordered what Morris described as "a kind of semi-navy officer's coat and vest, with gold lace on the sleeves and Turkish buttons." Thus garbed, Stanley went next to Abdullah Brothers, Ottoman court photographers, to have his picture taken.

Soon after that, Stanley and Noe left Constantinople, and although Stanley did not bother to say farewell, Morris appears to have harbored no resentment. From Constantinople, Stanley and Noe went back to Bursa, where Cook, in the care of the Turkish authorities, was waiting to testify at the trial of their abductors. Stanley and Noe did not wait for the trial but left Cook, as Stanley put it, "at the base of Mount Olympus" and took ship to Marseilles.

Some weeks later, after the assailants had been tried and sentenced, Cook put in a claim for $2,000 in compensation and settled for $1,200. Out of this, the American envoy extracted the $600 he had lent Stanley, and Cook left for home with the balance.

While bearing in mind that Stanley and the truth were by no means always close acquaintances, one must remain skeptical about Noe's allegation that Stanley's criminal conduct was the cause of their plight at Chi-Hissar. Noe told his story as a partisan in the New York newspaper war that erupted in August 1872, after Stanley's discovery of Livingstone on assignment for the New York *Herald.* Stanley's achievement, a tremendous scoop for the *Herald,* had been sourly received by the *Herald*'s principal rival, the New York *Sun,* and Noe was quick to volunteer ammunition for the *Sun* to use in an attempt to blacken Stanley's character.

Noe's motives may have been mercenary, although there is no evidence that the *Sun* paid him for his revelations. More likely he was motivated by personal animus, and doubtless he had some genuine cause for grievance at Stanley's treatment of him. But the mere fact of Stanley's having been present when Noe was raped by the Turks may be sufficient to explain his vengeful outburst. What man can forgive another who, willingly or otherwise, has been witness to his utter degradation?

# Chapter Four

STANLEY headed back to America with the hapless Lewis in tow, breaking his journey in Britain where, leaving Noe with his uncle and aunt in Liverpool, he went alone to revisit the scenes of his unhappy childhood. Still seeking the approval if not the love of the mother who had so completely rejected him, and the respect of the purse-mouthed parish which had reared him as pauper and bastard, Stanley arrived in Denbigh in a hired coach and pair, wearing the fake naval uniform he had bought in Constantinople.

If anyone noticed the odd fact that its brass buttons bore the Ottoman star and crescent rather than the U.S. naval design of rope and anchor, there is no record that it was remarked upon. In the visitor's book at Denbigh Castle on December 14, 1866, Stanley signed himself by his baptismal name for the last known time. The entry reads: "John Rowlands, formerly of this parish, now ensign in the United States Navy in North America, belonging to the U.S. ship Ticonderoga, now at Constantinople, Turkey, absent on furlough."

Still in uniform, Stanley also visited the St. Asaph workhouse, where he was greeted as an honored alumnus whose current status reflected only credit upon the parish. The much-to-be-maligned James Francis was no longer there, having died in the North Wales Hospital for Nervous Diseases, otherwise the Denbigh Lunatic Asylum, a few months previously. The workhouse governors greeted Stanley warmly and treated the children to tea and cakes, while Stanley gave an improving lecture, saying how much he owed to St. Asaph's and the education he had received there. He told the children that they too should be grateful for the bounty of the parish and demonstrate their gratitude by showing what they could achieve in the great world outside. The governors were duly impressed, one of them commenting that Stanley had returned "gratefully, and, I may say, gracefully."

While in the district, the dashing "Ensign Rowlands" looked up his workhouse contemporary, Thomas Mumford, whom he tried to persuade to go back with him to America, promising to "make a man of you." When Mumford declined the invitation, Stanley asked the

*Stanley in his bogus naval uniform: the*
*buttons were wrong, but nobody noticed.*
(*The Geographical Review*, Vol. V, Jan.–June 1918)

workhouse governors to let him take one of the St. Asaph's boys under his wing, but "the boy's mother got wind of Stanley's intention and, becoming alarmed, refused her permission."

During this visit, well groomed, well nourished and in the guise of a U.S. naval officer, Stanley plainly made a better impression than before on his unloving mother. He appears to have spent Christmas and New Year's with her before returning to Liverpool on January 8 and taking ship for America.

Relations between him and Noe were still strained. Noe had signed a paper acknowledging receipt of "27 pounds (Turkish money) and 93 piastres" from Stanley, and before they sailed for the United States—on different ships—he signed another in which he renounced all claims on Stanley, "having made up my mind to work my passage home to New York, receiving clothes in exchange for passage money."

They were never to meet again, although for the next couple of years Stanley would continue to send cheery, if unreciprocated, greetings to his one-time friend and kept a photograph of the young Long Islander in his private papers until his death.

Once ashore in New York, Stanley took train for St. Louis, where, presenting himself to the editor of the *Missouri Democrat,* he got taken on as a reporter working on a linage basis to cover the state legislature in Jefferson City. Stanley also tried to cash in on his experiences in the Levant by lecturing. A printed handbill advertising what he had to offer is richly comedic.

---

The American Traveller,

HENRY STANLEY,

who was cruelly robbed by the Turks on September 18, 1866, and stripped, by overwhelming numbers, of his arms, passports, letter of credit, and over $4,000 in cash, will lecture on his

TRAVELS AND ADVENTURES IN TURKEY
AND
LIFE IN THE ORIENT!!

---

on _____ evening, at _____ in _____ the _____ inst.
Doors open at 7 o'clock. Lecture commences at 7 ½ o'clock.
Mr. Stanley has served in the American Navy from January 1862, till the fall of Wilmington, at which he was present, in January 1865.
He then took a grand tour through the interior of Asia Minor, from which he has just returned.

During his lecture he will appear in the costume of a Turkish naval officer.

He will also show to the audience a Saracenic coat of mail, needlework by a Turkish maiden, Turkish Fez, and the elegant cap of a Greek pirate, a Turkish Chibouque, a piece of skull from the tomb of Sultan Bajozetr, commonly called "Lightening" or "Thunderer," a whetstone from Mount Olympus, near the ancient city of Troy, of which Homer and Virgil sung 2,000 years ago.

There will also be on exhibition a Firman signed by the present Sultan of Turkey, Abdul Azziz. Also, a passport signed by our Secretary of State, William H. Seward.

Mr. Stanley will repeat the Moslem call to prayer after the manner of the Muezzin, in the sacred Arabic language used by 140,000,000 people.

The lecturer will close the exercise of the evening by singing a Turkish song á la Turque.

For all the wonders and delights offered by the intrepid traveler, the lecture series seems hardly to have been a success. A fellow journalist, reminiscing in a letter to Stanley four years later, recalled that he faced an audience of "four deadheads and four who had paid" on "that cold, bleak February night when you made your advent to the Tennessee House—full of your lecture on Turkey, and about twenty dollars worth of printed tickets of admission—most of which in a fit of disgust you consigned to the stove. . . ."

But although a flop as a lecturer, Stanley did better as a reporter. His accounts of the proceedings of the state legislature earned him a significant promotion when the *Democrat* assigned him in March 1867, as a special correspondent to cover Major General Winfield Scott Hancock's expedition to pacify the Plains Indians, who were resisting the westward march of the covered wagons across their hunting grounds.

In eight short months—covering first the Hancock expedition and later the activities of a peace commission sent out by Congress to conclude treaties with the tribes—Stanley established himself firmly in his chosen profession and set his feet on the path that would take him to Africa and world renown.

As Stanley would observe subsequently, his accounts of the Hancock campaign and the peace councils were "not without benefit to me in later years." Nor are they without benefit to the biographer trying to trace the development of a complex and contradictory character, emerging uncertainly from the chrysalis of a troubled youth. Though uneven in quality and, at their worst, decidedly flatulent, those dispatches reveal significantly maturing attitudes during Stanley's first experience of an unsophisticated native people confronted by the advance of western civilization.

Stanley was paid fifteen dollars a week plus expenses by the *Democrat,* but was able to stretch this occasionally to as much as ninety dollars a week by selling his dispatches to East Coast newspapers, including, most significantly for his future career, James Gordon Bennett's rambunctious New York *Herald.*

Hancock, a Civil War hero, was in command of fourteen hundred men, the largest force ever sent, up to that time, against the tribes of the southern plains. This force had taken the field in response to rumors that the Cheyenne, Kiowa and Arapaho tribes were about to go on the warpath to disrupt the whites' Arkansas River route to New Mexico and the Smoky Hill River route to Colorado. "This cannot be tolerated for a moment," said Hancock's superior, General William Sherman. "If not a state of war, it is the next thing to it."

Hancock's brief was to make peace with the Indians if they were so inclined and to fight if they were not. In the event, the Indians were unwilling to court the wrath of Hancock and his pony soldiers, and the expedition saw little or no action, killing only four Indians—two of them friendlies—in four months of campaigning.

Just the same, one of Stanley's dispatches, datelined "May 25, on the Platte Route," gave the impression that the entire region was about to erupt:

> The Indian War has at last been fairly inaugurated. The grass has at last appeared, and the Indians, true to their promises, true to their bloody instincts, to their savage hatred of the white race, to the lessons instilled in their bosoms by their progenitors, are on the warpath, all assertion of interested persons to the contrary notwithstanding.

Stanley professed scant respect for the wavering policies of the federal government and the ability of the regular troops, "though brave and noble men," to deal with the threat posed by the tribes. Echoing the prejudices of those who liked to assert that the only good Indian was a dead one, he fulminated:

> If the present suicidal policy of the Government is carried on, eventually the plains settlers must succumb to the unequal conflict or unite in bands to carry on the war after the manner of the Indians, which means to kill, burn, destroy Indian villages, innocent papooses and squaws, scalp the warriors, and mutilate the dead; in fact, follow in the same course as the red men, that their name will be a terror to all the Indians. Then, and not till then, may they hope for peace.

For the Stanley of this period, there were neither Hiawathas nor Minnehahas. Rejecting the romantic vision of the noble savage as portrayed by the likes of Longfellow, he disparaged Indian women: "coarse black hair, low foreheads, blazing coal-black eyes, faces of a dirty, greasy colour, who were not over-modestly dressed." He added: "Morality is hardly known among the Indians. . . . As a mother, the squaw ranks little above the lower animals. . . . Towels and soap are, of course, unknown luxuries."

However, he did feel that after being properly subdued the Indians could be civilized, and even at his most tendentious, he was no advocate of genocide. "Extermination is a long word, but a longer task," he wrote, "and civilization cannot sanction it."

Theodore Davis, an artist for *Harper's Weekly,* shared a tent with Stanley and described him as "methodical and indefatigable." He rode a big sorrel nag, using a simple snaffle bit and a short rein, and his outfit, "a thoroughly sensible one, made him a sufficiently characteristic figure to attract attention, but not to occasion remark." It consisted, recalled Davis, of a loose-fitting blue felt cap with a reversible band to protect the ears, stout rawhide boots, and an "ample blue-black overcoat with a cloak for a cape." Davis observed that Stanley had unusual stamina and was able to ride long hours without tiring.

As a writer, Stanley showed at this period a talent for vivid description marred by a tendency to moralize and a disastrous weakness—even by Victorian standards—for labored jocularity. In his first dispatch he assured his readers of "the deep respect we entertain for them as a body, and should anything else turn up in these hyperborean regions, they shall hear it." In a later report he described the effects of scalping, adding: "It is a horrible sight and the operation is one which we earnestly hope will never be performed on our worthy self. While writing, we assure you our scalp is intact, but how long it will remain so we cannot as yet inform you."

During Stanley's bouts of journalistic moralizing, he could be as censorious of the pioneering whites as he was of the Indians. He purported to be shocked by the "debauchery and dissipation" he found in the Colorado mining town of Julesburg. In the King of the Hills saloon there, "the women seemed the most reckless and the men seemed nothing loth to enter a whirlpool of sin. . . . There appears to be plenty of money here, and plenty of fools to squander it."

The sanctimonious tone, like the deeply prejudiced descriptions of the Indians, may merely have been Stanley's way of giving his readers what he thought they wanted. And he gave it to them with an acute eye for telling detail. "These women are expensive articles. . . .," he wrote. "In broad daylight they may be seen gliding through the sandy streets in Black Crook dresses, carrying fancy derringers slung to their waists, with which tools they are dangerously expert. . . ." As for the males, "I verily believe there are men here who would murder a fellow creature for five dollars. Nay, there are men who have done it, and who stalk abroad unwhipped of justice."

While deploring the immorality and violence of the mining towns, Stanley was schoolboyishly impressed by the dandified James Butler ("Wild Bill") Hickok, who was attached to the Hancock expedition as a scout and tracker and who boasted that he had killed "considerably over a hundred" men. According to Stanley's account of Wild Bill,

> He stands six feet one inch in his moccasins, and is as handsome a specimen of a man as could be found. . . . He was dressed in fancy shirt and leathern leggings. He held himself straight and had broad, compact shoulders, was large-chested, with small waist and well-formed, muscular limbs. A fine, handsome face, free from blemish, a light moustache, a thin, pointed nose, bluish-grey eyes with a calm look, a magnificent forehead, hair parted from the centre of the forehead, and hanging down behind the ears in wavy, silken curls made up a most picturesque figure. . . . He has none of the swaggering gait, or the barbaric jargon ascribed to the pioneer. . . . On the contrary, his language is as good as many a one that boasts "college larning."

Hancock's expedition ended in early July, and Stanley went back to St. Louis. But within a couple of weeks he was heading west again, this time to cover the proceedings of the Indian Peace Commissioners. And now, quite unexpectedly, we see a new Stanley, far more sympathetic to the Indians, no longer willing to project the worst prejudices of the pioneers.

What changed his point of view, and whether the change was sincere, one cannot say; neither his dispatches nor his private journals give any clue to the reasons for his conversion to the liberal camp. In a dispatch dated August 21, from Sioux City, Stanley offered a *mea culpa* for the tone of his earlier reports: "If we have been mistaken, we acknowledge it, and go back to first principles." The cause of the Indian troubles, he wrote, was "that the Indian was an outlaw, ranked with the wild beasts. If a white man shot an Indian, what law touched him—what power tried him for the offense and made him pay the penalty of his murderous deeds? It was as if he had shot a buffalo. Nothing was done, nothing was thought of it. . . ."

He went on to question the common assertion "that the Indian opposed himself to civilization, and that railroads would be destroyed, and that emigrants would be massacred":

> The Indian will accept civilization if it is offered to him with conditions that will make it worth his while to accept. Make him one of ourselves, bound by the same desires, possessing the same rights, and he will in time forget the savage pleasures of the past. . . . We know that if the red man could have been enslaved he would have been before this; but there was a free spirit in his nature which made it impossible. He could die, but he could not be enslaved. . . . [A]ll the evidence which can be furnished shows plainly that the Indian has ever been the wronged party, and that he fights because he believes that the white man was sworn to extirpate him. . . .

Stanley must have known that his newly liberal views were less likely than his previous bigotry to find favor among his readers. But in a dispatch dated August 26, he went even further, describing the Indians as "these wronged children of the soil."

Still, even in his new role as the sensitive champion of native rights, Stanley could not forgo the personal braggadocio that had marked his earlier dispatches. In one article he whimsically referred to himself as "your own inimitable 'Stanley.'" In another, he boasted of how "graphically and distinctly" he had covered the Hancock expedition. Subsequently, he made a great show of his knowledge of the wide world by praising a cup of camp coffee as "even excelling in my opinion the best Mocha I ever drank in an Egyptian khan." Up to that time, he had never been to Egypt. And in a further report he boasted childishly of the friendliness shown toward him by a much-feared Kiowa chief whom he had first encountered while on the march with Hancock.

> Satanta, or White Bear, seemed beside himself with joy on recognizing your correspondent, and gave him a gigantic bear's hug. He was introduced to other members of the press who looked upon him with some awe, having heard so much of his ferocity and boldness. . . . Agile and strong, he would certainly be a most formidable enemy to encounter alone on the prairie, especially with the words of "Wild Bill" ringing in the ears, "that man has killed more white men than any other Indian on the plains, and he boasts of it."

By Stanley's account, Satanta made one of the most impressive speeches of all those heard by the peace commissioners when they met the chiefs of the Comanches, Kiowas, Arapahos, Apaches, and Cheyennes at Medicine Lodge, Kansas, in late October. In return for a treaty binding the Indians to cease their marauding and attempts to disrupt the building of roads and railways across their hunting grounds, the commissioners offered "comfortable homes upon our richest agricultural lands" plus churches, schools and teachers, seed, agricultural implements, domestic livestock, doctors and veterinarians.

To these blandishments, Satanta replied: "I love the land and the buffalo and will not part with any. . . . I don't want any of these medicine homes [schools] built in the country; I want the papooses brought up just exactly as I am. . . . I don't want to settle [on the reservation]. I love to roam over the wild prairie, and when I do it I feel free and happy, but when we settle down we grow pale and die . . . my heart feels like bursting with sorrow. I have spoken."

For all his bold words, Satanta, like the other chiefs, signed a treaty with the commissioners the following day. Stanley and other reporters present added their signatures as witnesses. With that, Stanley's Western assignment was at an end.

Almost thirty years later, when any book bearing his byline was a guaranteed best seller, Stanley published a collection of his dispatches from the West. Recycled journalism rarely reads well, even to a generation still attuned to the literary conventions in which it was composed, and that of *My Early Travels,* with its pomposities, its elephantine attempts at humor, and its long passages lifted verbatim from other writings, is certainly no exception.

But Stanley's Western reporting, as reissued, is interesting because the dispatches were edited, sometimes quite heavily, to remove phrases and passages which one assumes the world-renowned Stanley of 1895 no longer wished to own. And among those omissions, sadly and unaccountably, are his comments on the injustices done to the Indians, including his *mea culpa* from Sioux City and his memorable description of them as "wronged children of the soil."

The reasons for another interesting omission are easier to understand. By 1895 Stanley was a British subject once more, having renounced his American citizenship so that he could accept a knighthood from Queen Victoria. Thus he was careful to excise an unflattering and really quite gratuitous comment on his native land. In a dispatch from Fort Laramie, Colorado, dated June 15, 1867, Stanley had reported a firm but conciliatory speech by General J. B. Sanborn to a group of chiefs responsible for an earlier massacre of American soldiers and added the comment: "Were these people on

English territory every reader could foresee their fate; but, forsooth, the leading civilized nation of the world must treat them with forbearance. So be it." In *My Early Travels* this passage has vanished.

In terms of his own development, Stanley's assignment to the Indian Wars was, as he said, "a kind of apprenticeship to the longer and more difficult one I was to continue into Unknown Africa." And in later years, by which time he was a world-famous figure and General Sherman was retired, he astonished the old soldier by quoting extensively from a speech Sherman had made to the plains Indians when he was a member of the Peace Commission. "I have had occasion to repeat your speech almost verbatim more than once to the Negroes of Central Africa," said Stanley.

# Chapter Five

WHILE he was out West, Stanley had earned well and spent little. As he would recall, with his unfortunate penchant for long-winded priggishness, he "practiced a rigid economy, punishing my appetites, and, little by little, the sums acquired through this abstinence began to impart a sense of security and gave a sense of independence to my bearing which, however I might try to conceal it, betrayed that I was delivered from the dependent state." In other words, having $3,000 in the bank, Stanley felt financially secure enough to throw up his job with the *Democrat* in December 1867, and try his luck in New York.

He called first at Horace Greeley's *Tribune* where—for all his having so fruitfully followed the editor-publisher's exhortation to go west—he was turned down. His next call was to the offices of the rival *Herald,* where he managed to obtain an interview with the publisher, James Gordon Bennett, Jr. This in itself was a feat, for Bennett was generally unapproachable, even by his own staff. But he had read Stanley's dispatches from the West and liked them well enough to spare a few minutes for their author.

At the age of twenty-six, five months younger than Stanley, Bennett was a monster in the making, a playboy sliding into degeneracy and megalomania. His frivolities were already legendary, but in truth his witless drinking, brawling and rutting represented the more agreeable side of his personality. The darker side showed itself in the ruthless way in which he manipulated the lives and careers of those who worked for him.

At the time his path and Stanley's crossed, Bennett, though not yet proprietor, was in effect editor-in-chief as well as publisher of the *Herald,* which his father, James Gordon Bennett, Sr., had founded in 1835 on a $500 loan and built into an organ wealthy enough to provide his son with an assured income of one million dollars a year.

The *Herald*'s raw vigor reflected perfectly the spirit of a turbulently well-endowed young America. As a later chronicler of the lives and work of the Bennetts would say, it "compelled support by its energy and won its way by force." Needless to say, that did not endear the *Herald* or its founder to Polite Society, which found him as brash and uncouth as his paper. Pained at his inability to buy his way into the drawing rooms of the elite, the older Bennett dismissed New York's upper crust as "the sons of bitches who are too snippety to invite me to dinner."

The son was to avenge the father in spectacular, if self-defeating, fashion. Himself accepted into society—as second-generation money invariably is, no matter how contemptible its origins—he resoundingly proved the original prejudices about the Gordon Bennetts to have been well founded. Turning up half-drunk at a party to celebrate his engagement to a daughter of one of the Four Hundred families, he quickly proceeded to total inebriation, and then brought the proceedings to a shocked and premature conclusion by urinating in the fireplace.

This in turn led to an inconclusive and bloodless duel with his fiancée's brother, the termination of his engagement, and his tactical retreat to Paris. There Bennett founded the European edition of the *Herald* (which survives to this day as the *International Herald-Tribune*), continuing to direct the fortunes of its New York parent by transatlantic telegram and frequent personal visitation.

"Young Jimmy's" spectacular display of ill-breeding was nine years in the future when the unknown and relatively untried Stanley knocked on his door in December 1867. The only account we have of their first meeting is Stanley's, and of course we have learned to regard his recollections with some caution; still, in this respect they read convincingly enough. After complimenting Stanley on his dispatches from the West, Bennett said there were no staff vacancies, although "I wish I could offer you something permanent, for we want active men like you." It was almost a stock reply in the newspaper business to job applicants—a test of resolve and persistence as much as anything else—and Stanley was ready for it. "You are very kind to say so," he countered, "and I am emboldened to ask you if I could not offer myself to you for this Abyssinian expedition."

"This Abyssinian expedition" was a punitive campaign which the British government was cranking up to launch against Theodore, the mad Emperor of Abyssinia, who—enraged at an imagined slight to his dignity by Queen Victoria*—had been holding a group of British diplomats and their families hostage for some years, ignoring all demands for their release. Bennett expressed doubts about the story's

---

* She had failed to reply to a fulsome letter, offering undying friendship, which some Foreign Office functionary had carelessly pigeonholed instead of having it passed on to the Palace.

news value to an American readership. Abyssinia was a long way off and more than geographically remote from the concerns of the *Herald*'s readers. Still, he asked, "On what terms would you go?"

Confident of his own abilities, and emboldened by the thought of the $3,000 he had saved, Stanley volunteered to go to Abyssinia at his own expense and be paid "by the letter," reserving the right to offer his work to other newspapers as well. Bennett countered that "we do not like to share our news that way, but we would be willing to pay well for exclusive intelligence." He added that if Stanley's letters were "up to the standard," prompt, and exclusive, he could expect a permanent position on his return from Abyssinia.

"Very well, sir," replied Stanley. "I am at your service, any way you like."

The deal struck, Bennett asked, "When do you intend to start?" and was no doubt impressed when Stanley replied that he would leave for Liverpool in two days aboard the express steamer *Hecla*. Bennett gave him a letter to the *Herald*'s agent in Britain, Colonel Finlay Anderson, and Stanley was on his way to glory.

He spent Christmas at sea and made his way to Suez—staging post for the Abyssinian expedition—via London, Paris and Marseilles. From Paris, on New Year's Day 1868, Stanley sent season's greetings to Lewis Noe, hailing him as "prince of boys and best of companions," and adding the exhortation: "In your rejoicings, forget not the exiled friend and brother. Henry."

At Suez, where the telegraph line to London and other European capitals terminated, Stanley shrewdly made the acquaintance of the chief telegraphist and tipped him generously to make sure that when dispatches arrived by sea from the correspondents covering the impending campaign, his would be cabled first. From Suez, now accompanied by a manservant and a fine Arabian thoroughbred, Stanley made his way by sea to the baking Red Sea coast of Eritrea, where General Sir Robert Napier and his expeditionary force had lately disembarked to begin an epic four-hundred-mile march through the wilds of Abyssinia to confront Theodore in his mountain fortress of Magdala.

Though now all but forgotten—and in any case a modest effort by the grandiose standards of Britain's imperial heyday—Napier's Abyssinian campaign was a remarkable display of military competence rare for that or any age. For once, a military operation was carefully thought through in advance, meticulously planned on the basis of sound intelligence, and set in motion with the coordinated efficiency and aplomb of a vast industrial undertaking. For this, Napier himself—no *beau sabreur,* but an engineer by training and temperament—must take the credit.

An advance party of engineers identified a ramshackle village named Zula, standing on an open plain in Annesley Bay, as the ideal point at which to land Napier's army. The derelict settlement had no port facilities, so, with typical Victorian bravura, the British built them, with two huge concrete piers, warehouses, lighthouses, and twenty miles of railroad track to facilitate the landing of a mountain of supplies and Napier's 13,000 troops, 20,000 camp followers—including water-carriers, prostitutes, and the vendors of other creature comforts—and 55,000 draft and pack animals. These included mules, camels and 44 elephants to carry the artillery, in the style of Hannibal crossing the Alps, over the invasion route's precipitous mountain passes and up and down the sides of its dramatic gorges. Men, beasts, weapons and materiel were brought—mainly from India, but some elements from Britain—in a fleet of 280 ships.

By the time Stanley himself arrived by steam packet from Suez, the advance guard of this army had climbed, scrambled and blasted their way up the side of the eight-thousand-foot-high Ethiopian plateau to Senafe, some forty miles inland. They had met no resistance, since this part of the country was under the control of Egypt, Abyssinia's traditional enemy. Indeed, the British would not have to fight until the end of their four-hundred-mile march, for most of the tribes whose territories they passed through had good reason to wish the overthrow of the tyrannical and capricious Theodore. Until they reached his stronghold at Magdala, the principal enemy of the British was not so much Theodore as the savage topography of his country.

When Stanley reached Senafe, he had the first of a number of encounters that left him "with feelings of no great love for Englishmen." As a brash American—which he appeared by now to be—and a journalist to boot, he evidently struck sparks off a certain kind of British officer, one of whom quickly summed him up as "a howling cad."

Arriving at Senafe with only a buffalo robe to shield him from the extreme cold of the nights, he went to the "sumptuous marquee" of a General M—— to apply for a tent. There, he would recall, "I had an interview, of which it will be sufficient to say that I left him with 'good evening' and an assurance that if ever I rested in his tent again it would be because he had sent for me."

He describes how one young officer to whom he bade a good morning merely stared at him through his monocle and rode on without a word, while another demanded to know coldly, "whom I have the pleasure of addressing." A third officer inquired, affably enough, "I say, old boy, how are you off for horseflesh and servants?" When Stanley replied that he had a horse, a mule and a servant, the officer replied: "Pooh, pooh, that will never do. You must have a cook, a hay-cutter, a cutcha wallah (groom), a panee wallah (water-carrier) to wait, and then you must have one horse for personal baggage, one horse for your cooking utensils, one horse to carry your rations, one horse to carry your tent, and two riding horses; for without these things, you know, egad, it is simply impossible to live in this country. . . ."

Later, when Napier ordered all officers to reduce their baggage to seventy-five pounds each for the final phase of the march on Magdala, Stanley recorded with malicious glee: "Oh, Anglo-Indian officers! dainty, heaven-born children! scions of patrician parents! had it come to this? Uneasy and wrathful were they in this extremity." And, describing a group of staff officers on the march, Stanley noted "a good deal of effeminacy" in their otherwise martial bearing. "One young lordling wore kid gloves and a green veil," he scoffed.

In all this, one can detect not just the justifiable scorn of the hardy, self-reliant campaigner proud of his ability to live rough and travel light, but also the suppressed rage and resentment of the illegitimate workhouse boy, cripplingly conscious of his own "base origins."

Stanley also encountered snobbery and standoffishness, real or imagined, among his British press corps colleagues. These included George A. Henty of the *Standard*, who would subsequently make his fortune as the author of "rattling good yarns" featuring intrepid heroes cast in what was popularly thought to be the Stanley mold. But for the moment, as Stanley confided bitterly to his diary, "I was made to feel that . . . an American journalist was not of such fine clay as a Briton of the same profession. There was no great harm that a number of English pressmen should make merry at my expense. . . ."

But when he came to publish his recollections of the campaign in book form five years later, Stanley gave a very different impression. "The English Press was very ably represented in Abyssinia," he wrote. ". . . I give them the credit of being the most sociable mess in the army, as well as the most loveable and good tempered."

For all the condescension and aloofness he encountered among the British, Stanley thought highly of the weathered and affable Napier, whom he described in his diary as "a charming old gentleman," and in his book as "not only a warrior chief, but a diplomat of the first rank." He doubted whether even "the vigorous Sherman" could have achieved "the happy consummation which finally rewarded" Napier's efforts to bring Theodore to book.

For all its interest, Stanley's account of the expedition does have its longueurs; he seems not to know what kind of detail to leave out and occasionally lays it on with numbing insistence. Still, his dispatches and subsequent book are redeemed by a lively grasp of military tactics and vivid descriptions of the toweringly dramatic terrain through which the army passed. And occasionally the plodding detail can fascinate, as in his description of a dinner in camp with Napier and his senior staff officers.

It was one of those stultifying Victorian blowouts, starting with "Indian patties, brain cutlets and veal pies, artistically gotten up," followed by "ragouts, potato cakes, vegetables and herbs of every description, cotelettes and fricasees . . . beefsteak pie, boiled hump, roast fowls and roast sirloin, cooked a l'Anglaise," in turn followed by chicken curry and rice. The whole was washed down with *tej,* an Abyssinian beer, and rounded off with "delicious blancmange and custards" and coffee and Havana cigars. That British gentlemen could march and fight on such a diet seems truly astonishing.

Still, Stanley conclusively dispels any idea that accompanying the expedition might have been any kind of a junket for the journalists. "After being in the saddle . . . for twelve to fifteen hours," he writes, ". . . it was no light task to sit down and hammer away at a letter. . . . Then to snatch a sleep of three hours, hastily swallow a cup of sugarless tea and dry, azinous bread, and mount saddle again at five o'clock in the morning to undergo the same experience was no joyous picnicking."

But his attempts at humor are leaden, his excursions into profundity embarrassing, and we see him at his flatulent worst when he is trying to be highfalutin. He shows off his knowledge of English literature by dubbing a loquacious and boastfully eccentric officer with whom he shares a tent "Captain Smelfungus," after a character in Sterne's *Sentimental Journey.* He displays the reach of his vocabulary when, seeking an adjective to attach to Napier for the measured pace of his march, he calls him "the cunctative English general." And he reveals his ponderous sense of style when, seeking a synonym for "tent," he offers us a "bell-shaped domicile," and elsewhere calls water the "potable element" and wine "the ruby cup that cheers."

The workhouse boy is desperately, and disastrously, determined to show himself the intellectual equal of any classically educated English gentleman. But for his pains, he is dismissed by the English officers as "a bounder." And, in turn, he displays an obsessive sense of grievance against the British ruling elite. Accompanying a certain Captain Speedy on a foraging mission, Stanley had helped to round up fifty-seven hundred pounds of flour, six thousand pounds of grain and other essentials. "Yet I regret to say that the magnanimous British Government has never even thanked me for it," he grumbled, "least of all have they given me a medal, such as all Abyssinian heroes obtained, which I consider to be a strange oversight on the part of the British Government, and deserving of gravest reproof."

In stately slow motion the British expeditionary force made its way south, up and down immense escarpments and ravines under a blazing equatorial sun, to where Theodore awaited it on the plateau before Magdala. In its measured inevitability and logistical virtuosity, Napier's march best resembles, by modern comparison, Britain's 1982 Falkland Islands campaign. In the last gasp of empire, as in its golden heyday, vast distances and seemingly insuperable physical obstacles were not permitted to deter Britannia when honor and prestige were put into question by an unhinged foreign tyrant.

And King Theodore, like the Argentinian generals, was no easy mark. For all his fits of madness, he was a skillful commander with a seasoned force of seven thousand warriors lying in wait for an advancing spearhead of no more than five thousand British and colonial troops. He had artillery, too, a battery of ten cannon plus an enormous mortar, built for him by German engineers.

The two armies finally clashed on Good Friday, April 10, 1868. With Stanley tagging along, the British vanguard had advanced somewhat overconfidently into a situation where ambush was easy, believing that "that fellow Theodore" and his men must have melted away into the mountains. Suddenly, a sergeant exclaimed: "There are men at the top of the hill, sir!"

"What?" bawled out Col. Penn; "aye, by Jove! I see them." "Egad, they line the whole summit from one end to the other!" said Col. Millward, aroused now to activity. "And, by Jove," added Penn, "Theodore has opened the ball! See you the puff? D'ye hear the music of chain-shot?" Two seconds of expectancy, "boom!" came the loud report, and half a second later a huge chain-shot flew over our heads, burying itself fifty feet in our rear. . . . It was life and death with them all now. Over 3,500 of the enemy were galloping—animated by fury—down the hill.

Napier and his staff, imprudently far ahead of the main column which was laboring up the slope behind them in a gathering thunderstorm, now faced the prospect of ignominious flight, death or certain capture as the enemy sped toward them, "caracoling and bounding joyously along." But the British commander "sat on his charger, serene and impassible." And, as seemed to happen so often in Victorian battle scenes, relief arrived in the nick of time—in the shape of a British rocket battery.

Rapidly, the rocketeers deployed and opened fire, so that "even in the act of launching their spears a stream of fire darted along the enemy's ranks, ploughing its way through their swaying masses" a mere fifty yards from where the imperturbable Napier sat his skittering horse.

When the Indian infantry of the threatened advance guard, armed only with ancient muzzle-loaders, were joined by British troops with breech-loading Snider rifles, the contest became unequal. "[The enemy] seemed to wish to fight hand to hand, but the Sniders gave them no chance," reported Stanley. "The fight became a battue—a massacre!" What the Sniders failed to achieve, Napier's Sikh and Punjabi troops did with the bayonet. "No mercy was asked . . . no puny blows were dealt; heads were chopped off, arms and limbs severed from trunks, and dead men lay stark and stiff plentifully. But they were all Abyssinians. . . ."

At five-thirty that afternoon, two hours after Theodore had "opened the ball," the battle was over. On the British side only 20 men had been wounded, of whom two died later; on the Abyssinian side the dead numbered at least 700, with another 1,200 wounded. Theodore had been unable to make effective use of his artillery because the British had advanced too rapidly to the base of the ridge on which the Abyssinian ordnance was positioned, making it impossible for the big guns to be depressed sufficiently to bear upon the enemy, 1,000 feet below.

As night fell on the rain- and blood-sodden field of battle, the British curled up to sleep in the open, their tents and provisions still en route. In the dark, they could hear the scavengers moving about, crunching the bones of the dead and dying enemy. Reported Stanley: "The last sounds our dulled ears caught were the jackals' shrill whelp [sic], the hyena's sonorous bay, mingling with the lichowl's mournful 'tu-whit-tu-whoo!' "

Theodore had watched the battle from the ridge where his artillery were deployed (and where his giant mortar exploded, killing many of his own people), raging—as Stanley solemnly reported—that "the English are not afraid of my chain-shot; they march up in spite of my big balls." A near-miss by a British rocket almost killed him, and that night he got drunk on arak and decided to send two of his hostages, a young British officer named Prideaux and a German missionary named Flad, to Napier's camp with an offer to make peace.

Prideaux, a lieutenant in the Bombay Army, was another of those monocled young sprigs of the aristocracy whose bearing so enraged Stanley. He had clearly spent much of the night preparing himself for his meeting with Napier, for his uniform was carefully brushed, his spurs polished and his black boots gleaming as he rode into camp under a white flag, in company with Flad and Theodore's brother-in-law, Dejach Alami. "With elegant insouciance and eyeglass fixed," reported Stanley sourly, Prideaux "sauntered up to the general-in-chief's tent twirling his cane."

Prideaux gave Napier Theodore's verbal message, seeking a "reconciliation." Napier sent Prideaux and his companions back with a written reply expressing his "desire that no more blood may be shed," and promising that if Theodore would surrender and hand over all his hostages unharmed he and his family would be guaranteed "honorable treatment." Theodore in turn sent Prideaux and Flad back with a rambling and inconclusive answer; he was flirting with the idea of renewing the battle, for despite the terrible casualties of the first day, he still had a formidable force at his disposal.

While he was in council of war with his chiefs, a sudden fit of madness seized Theodore, and putting a double-barreled pistol into his mouth, he pulled the trigger. Evidently he had cocked the wrong barrel, however, for the gun did not fire, and the pistol was wrested from his grasp by a loyal follower.

Not long after, on Theodore's instructions, all the hostages, except a handful who were too ill to be moved, were brought down from Magdala and told they were free to make their way to the British lines. Lest any of his followers should think he was going soft, and as if to compensate for letting the foreigners go, Theodore had 300 native prisoners thrown over a precipice.

With the safe return of the 61 hostages and their 187 servants, the objective of the campaign had been achieved. But Theodore could not be allowed to go unpunished. Spurning a peace offering of 1,000 cows and 500 sheep, Napier launched an attack on Magdala on Easter Monday, April 13. By that time, the bulk of Theodore's army had deserted, and only a loyal few remained to make a last stand with their crazed emperor.

They did not hold out for long against a determined assault by the Duke of Wellington's Own Irish Regiment. As the Irish burst into the fortress they found Theodore dying from a self-inflicted wound. He had shot himself with one of a pair of ornamental pistols sent to him as a present in happier days by Queen Victoria herself.

Stanley was quick to follow the Irish infantrymen into the captured stronghold, and a British press colleague who went in soon afterward saw him "waving a bloody rag which he averred was part of King Theodore's shirt." This correspondent said that he himself "saw the dead King almost immediately afterwards, and his shirt seemed to me to be intact." However, he added, Stanley and he became great friends, "and I became the recipient of many curious confidences of his early journalistic life."

Despite Bennett's initial skepticism about its newsworthiness, Stanley had the story of his career to date in the fall of Magdala and the death of Theodore. But, as any foreign correspondent whose career began in the pre-electronic age can attest, getting the story is only half the battle; the other, and often more difficult half, is getting it back ahead of the opposition.

Stanley's English colleagues handed their reports to Colonel Millward, who was hurrying to the coast with the official dispatches. Stanley, not about to entrust his copy to a British officer, followed on behind Millward with five servants and five horses, laden with baggage and trophies.

He reckoned on catching the next mail steamer to Suez without difficulty, but thirty miles from the coast he learned that sudden floods threatened to turn the road ahead into a raging torrent as it wound through a narrow ravine. Stanley was determined to press on, for the mailboat would leave Zula the next evening, and half a day's delay would mean missing it. Negotiating the flooded pass, Stanley and his party were almost swept away but managed to reach the safety of a rocky knoll. In his words:

> Onward adown the pass swirled the turbulent current, growing higher, ever higher, bearing everything before it but our own firm granite eyot, tearing the friable, gravelly soil away by tons, rioting around abrupt curves and angles in raging confluxes, foaming over obstructions, forming powerful rapids, whitened cascades and cataracts, which roared like ten thousand bass drums beating the battle call!

The corpses of drowned men and animals swept past them, together with uprooted trees, and the debris of a military camp upstream—carts, wheels, bales of hay and straw. The flood was level with the top of Stanley's refuge and still rising when the rain suddenly ceased and the sun came out. By the time the falling flood level was four feet from the top of his rock, Stanley decided he could wait no longer and, discarding all but the most essential baggage, urged his pack animals one by one into the stream. Getting his Arab charger, Sayed, to make the leap was more difficult. Stanley's personal servant Ali suggested that the "Yankee Sahib" should ride him in. Stanley reported:

> I urged Sayed gently to the edge of the rock, and permitted him to smell and snuff and snort as much as he pleased for three or four minutes. Then backing him two paces and setting myself well in the saddle, I dug my spurs simultaneously into each flank, lifting him up at the same time with the bridle. The effect of the spurs on the blooded horse was instantaneous; he couched himself for a spring for one-eighth of a second, and like a panther he bounded off the rock clean into the air and into the turgid water. Sayed, after flapping his ears, headed for the shore, half swimming.

Back on dry land, Stanley resumed his forced march to the coast, reaching Zula at noon the next day, in plenty of time to catch the mailboat to Suez. So far, it was level pegging between him and his British colleagues, whose dispatches were also aboard, in Millward's pouch. But when the ship reached Suez, Stanley's competitive foresight paid off.

First, the ship was put into quarantine because of the port authorities' fears of cholera aboard. Undeterred, Stanley smuggled his dispatch ashore with a covering note to the telegraph office manager to whom he had slipped baksheesh on his way to the war. By these means he scored an impressive world exclusive, decisively beating the British press to their own story. Indeed, his account of the fall of Magdala, the release of the hostages and the death of Theodore reached New York, via London, so far ahead of his colleagues'—and of the official dispatches—that at first it was widely disbelieved.

But even that was not the full extent of Stanley's scoop. Once the ship's quarantine was lifted, he went ashore with further details of the campaign, and the friendly telegraph manager saw to it that even his follow-up story was sent ahead of the English journalists' reports and Millward's official messages.

Then, guile and resourcefulness having kept Stanley ahead of the opposition, luck intervened to put him even farther in front. Hardly had his last page of copy been sent than the undersea cable broke somewhere between Alexandria and Malta, and the rival dispatches had to be taken to Malta by ship before they could be telegraphed to

London. By that time, Stanley was enjoying his ease and a good cigar in a Cairo hotel and savoring the news of his appointment to the *Herald*'s permanent staff as a roving foreign correspondent.

But in his moment of triumph he allowed himself no complacency. "I must keep a sharp lookout," he said, "that my second coup shall be as much a success as the first."

*AGED* twenty-seven, a successful if not yet celebrated journalist, and a seasoned world traveler, Stanley had by now all but completed the process of creating a definitive and commanding self out of the unpromising raw material of his origins, childhood and youth.

He was not yet Henry *Morton* Stanley, but was still groping to find exactly the right middle name that would set the cap on his emerging identity. Up to the time of Magdala, he had signed himself simply "Henry Stanley." Now he began to experiment with variations on a single theme, variously trying out Morley, Morelake, and Moreland before eventually settling for Morton.

One should, perhaps, not make too much of this nameplay. Those which Stanley tried on for size are, of course, all phonic variations on the Latin root word for death, and none approximates it more closely than Morton. Still, it would be rash to look for a death-wish lurking behind Stanley's final choice and his subsequent obsession with the life-threatening Dark Continent.

That he would return there time after time may suggest that he was courting self-destruction, but one can equally see an unquenchable life-wish at work in the way in which Stanley time and again dragged himself, by sheer will power, from the brink of death by malaria, dysentery and other tropical ailments. Stanley may have enjoyed flirting with death, but only the dubious evidence of his choice of a middle name suggests that it was his desire to give himself to her.

# Chapter Six

*IT WAS* in the winter of 1868 that Stanley had his first, fruitless brush with the story that was to bring him world fame. Persistent rumor had it that, after being unheard of for almost three years while on his third great trek into the African interior, David Livingstone—the most celebrated explorer of his day—was on his way out to civilization. The rumors did not specify whether he would emerge by way of the East African coast and the island of Zanzibar—the way he had gone in—or whether, having succeeded in finding the source of the Nile, somewhere deep in Central Africa, he could be expected to show up downstream, perhaps in the Sudan.

On the instructions of Finlay Anderson, the *Herald*'s European bureau chief in London, Stanley took himself off to Aden, roughly midway between Zanzibar and the Sudan, ready to move in either direction to secure the prized first interview with Livingstone. After some weeks, a British ship calling in from Zanzibar brought word that there was now considered to be no chance of Livingstone's coming out that way. So Stanley doubled back to Cairo, intending to organize an expedition to meet him on the Upper Nile. But before long word reached Cairo from Zanzibar, through the British consul, John Kirk, that the rumors of Livingstone's emergence from the interior by any route had proved to be unfounded.

With that, Stanley was recalled to London, glad to be relieved of an assignment that had brought him only boredom and frustration and that had given him far too much opportunity for dangerous introspection. New Year's Day in Aden had found him in a particularly dark mood:

> What a curious custom it is to take this day, above all others, to speak of happiness, when inwardly each must think in his soul that it admonishes him of the lapse of time.... The knowledge that every moment makes me older ... forever reminds me that happiness is not to be secured in this world, except for brief periods.... If I could find an island in mid-ocean, remote from the presence or reach of man, with a few

necessaries sufficient to sustain life, I might be happy yet; for then I could forget what reminds me of unhappiness and, when death came, I should accept it as a long sleep and rest.

At this time, Stanley seems to be struggling with sexual desire as well as existential despair; in the code language of his period, he upbraids himself for harboring "vile thoughts that stained the mind," and resolves "with God's help to be better, nobler, purer."

He also makes a New Year's resolution to break himself of his addiction to cigars, which by now he smoked almost incessantly. But he soon admits failure. "For six days I strove against the hankering, though the desire surged up strongly. Today I have yielded to it, as the effort to suppress it absorbed too much of my time, and now I promise myself that I shall be moderate. . . ." It sounds like the rationalization of the nicotine addict down the ages—and an endearing lapse in such a preternaturally iron-willed man.

After getting his orders to return to base, Stanley became more optimistic. On his way to London by sea "under a divine heaven," he reflected smugly on his transition from boy to man. But even in this happier frame of mind, he was conscious of the need for activity and movement to ward off the black moods that beset him. "[T]he more tasks I receive, the happier is my life," he wrote. "I want work, close, absorbing and congenial work, only so that there will be no time for regrets, and vain desires and morbid thoughts."

Constantly, it seems, he was experiencing slights and snubs, real or imagined, that reminded him of the shallowness and treachery of men, and of the "baseness" of his origins. While in Egypt, en route for Aden, he had found himself in a railway compartment with two young Englishmen, with whom he shared the water, sandwiches and oranges he had prudently brought along for the journey from Cairo to Suez. They had seemed grateful and friendly, and Stanley had spoken expansively about his travels in the Middle East, pointing out places of interest they were passing and delving into his richly stocked memory to inform them on the society, customs, history, economy and religion of the country.

He thought he had made a favorable impression, but clearly the two Englishmen regarded him as a pushy little Yankee know-all. Having arrived in Suez, he was washing for dinner when he overheard them discussing him through the thin partition wall of their adjoining room. He was shocked and bitterly wounded. "Had I been a leper or a pariah, I could not have been more foully and slanderously abused," he wrote. "This is the third time in fourteen months that I have known Englishmen who, after being polite to my face, had slandered me behind my back."

No doubt Stanley was not a man to everyone's taste. His gruff demeanor and physical build—five feet five, powerful shoulders, deep chest, strangely penetrating light-gray eyes—bespoke a rough-hewn pugnacity which many found unattractive. He also tended to be humorless, tactless, priggish and opinionated, and when he became excited his pronounced American accent lapsed disconcertingly into the singsong of his Welsh origins. He did not hide his impatience at the shortcomings of others, and in particular, his flamboyance grated on the aloof and laconic type of upper-class Englishman who took vacations in the Levant.

But to American acquaintances he seemed considerably more agreeable. Edward King, a Paris-based colleague who worked with him in Spain in 1869, found him "honest, original and wise. He had no unpleasant self-consciousness; his mind was as healthy as his body, as guiltless of vanity as was his frame of infirmity." And Edward Jay Morris, the American minister to Turkey who had first met Stanley after his ill-fated Anatolian trek with Lewis Noe and Harlow Cook in 1866, met him again at the end of 1869 and found that he had changed "wonderfully."

> The uncouth young man whom I first knew had grown into a perfect man of the world, possessing the appearance, the manners and the attributes of a perfect gentleman. . . . Instead of thinking he was a young man who had barely seen twenty-six summers [sic], you would imagine that he was thirty-five or forty years of age, so cultured and learned was he in all the ways of life.

On his way back to London after the abortive first Livingstone assignment, Stanley stopped over in Paris for a few days' break. There he became involved in another intense friendship with an adolescent male, suggestive of his odd relationship with Lewis Noe. The successor to Noe was one Edwin Swift Balch, the son of an American businessman whom Stanley had met in Cairo.

Armed with a letter of introduction, Stanley called on the cultivated and cosmopolitan Balch family and discovered in thirteen-year-old Edwin an avid audience for his tales of adventure and derring-do. In turn the precocious Edwin, a fluent French-speaker, was pleased and flattered to be able to take Stanley on conducted tours of Paris in all its late–Second Empire splendor.

Stanley would later confide to a colleague that he loathed Paris:

"The atmosphere . . . stifled him; he did not like so much brilliancy and fashion; he abominated the theatre and detested the boulevards." Nevertheless, he had young Edwin pick him up every morning in the lobby of the Hotel du Louvre, where he was staying, for a day of sightseeing. "The bill for our excursions was paid by the New York *Herald,*" Balch would recall, and Stanley was "especially interested in 'Le Stryge' [The Vampire] at Notre Dame." Other places they visited included the Louvre, Vincennes, and the palaces of Versailles and St. Cloud. One is bound to wonder whether it was Paris or Edwin that Stanley really wanted to see.

Like most boys of his age, young Balch was fascinated by the unfolding drama of African exploration which then held the attention of Europe and America, and when Stanley left Paris for London at the end of February, he gave Edwin a prophetic farewell gift—a copy of David Livingstone's *Missionary Travels,* a current best seller, and E. D. Young's *The Search After Livingstone.*

He inscribed the volume by Livingstone to "my dear young friend Edwin, from Henry Morelake Stanley." He also gave the boy a print of his photograph, taken in Constantinople three years before, wearing his pseudo–naval officer's uniform. In the months that followed he kept in touch by letter, and in October 1869, before setting off on a journey through the Levant and Persia to India, Stanley invited Edwin, then aged fourteen, to accompany him—a suggestion which the boy's parents very sensibly squelched.

None of this is evidence that Stanley's relationship with the boy was overtly homosexual. Such tendencies as he may have had he seems to have kept strictly submerged. And clearly, for all his awkwardness with women, he was not unattracted to the opposite sex. Two encounters with females during this period—one a Greek girl whom he wanted to marry in the summer of 1868, the other a Welsh girl to whom he proposed in 1869—attest to that.

Stanley met the Greek beauty on the Island of Syra, while reporting on the Cretan revolt against Turkish rule. As Stanley tells it, his interpreter Christos Evangelides, noticing him to be much taken by the good looks of the island girls, suggested that he should pick one as a wife. Stanley found the idea "delicious."

"A wife! My wife!" he gushed in a journal entry. "How grand the proprietorship of a fair woman appeared! To be loved with heart and soul above all else, for ever united in thought and sympathy with a fair and virtuous being, whose very touch gave strength and courage and confidence! Oh dear! How my warm imagination glows at the strange idea!"

Evangelides had a vested interest in setting the impressionable young reporter on fire with thoughts of a Greek bride; he hoped that Stanley might marry his nineteen-year-old daughter, Calliope. But, as Stanley observed, Calliope was no beauty, and consequently not "the one to thaw my reserve." Unfazed, Evangelides took him the following evening to visit a family named Ambella, whose daughter was a considerable improvement on his own so far as looks were concerned. Stanley was immediately smitten, finding the girl "as near as possible to the realisation of the ideal which my fancy had portrayed."

> Her name was Virginia and well it befitted her. Where had I seen her face, or whom did she recall? My memory fled over scores of faces and pictures, and instantly I bethought me of the Empress Eugenie [of France] when she was the Countess Montijo. A marvellous likeness in profile and style! She is about sixteen, and, if she can speak English, who knows?

In Stanley's version of events, they were no sooner introduced than the girl's parents and Evangelides launched into an embarrassingly pointed conversation about his single status and the desirability of his finding a wife, preferably Greek. "I am sure that if you look around you will find a young lady after your heart," said Mrs. Ambella, at which Stanley bowed. His "face was aflame," and Virginia too was "alternately crimson and pale."

Stanley's work took him away from Syra for two to three weeks, but in his absence he wrote to Virginia. When he returned he again visited the Ambellas. This time Virginia's two brothers and a younger sister were present, and it seemed to Stanley that the family were now seriously considering him as a son-in-law. Indeed, the following day a friend of the Ambellas called on him to say that he had "only to name the day." Stanley promptly did so, nominating the following Sunday.

That night, when he again visited the Ambellas, Stanley found that "whatever misgivings I may have had . . . were banished by the touch of [Virginia's] hand, and the trust visible in her eyes." But then, if Stanley's account is to be believed, the romantic idyll began to crumble; it seemed that Virginia's mother had been suddenly beset by second thoughts. "She said that I was quite a stranger . . . and she was therefore obliged to ask me to have patience until all reasonable assurances had been given that I was what I represented myself to be."

Stanley acquiesced while continuing to see the family, taking them to dinner the next night at the Hotel d'Amérique—where he found Virginia "lovelier than ever"—and dining at their home the night after that. On this occasion, Stanley recorded, "I had the honor to be seated next to [Virginia]."

> We exchanged regards but we both felt more than we spoke. We are convinced that we could be happy together. . . . Toasts were drunk, etc. Afterwards, Virginia exhibited her proficiency on the piano, and sang French and Greek sentimental songs. She is an accomplished musician, beautiful and amiable. She is in every way worthy.

But quite abruptly, the following day, Stanley sailed for Smyrna—presumably on assignment for the *Herald*—and that was effectively the end of the affair. From Smyrna, Stanley says, he wrote to the Ambellas to say that "they must not expect my return to Syra unless they all came to a positive decision, and expressly invited me." But no invitation ever came, and Stanley's travels never took him back to his "Sirens' Isle."

It is a strange story, quite lacking internal logic, and it seems clear that once again Stanley is hiding at least part of the truth. There would be no sense in the Ambella family's pushing him into a proposal of marriage, as he claims, only to turn him loose once hooked. And, in fact, there is evidence to suggest that Stanley was all along keener on the match than the Ambellas were. Why else would he have appealed to Hekekyan Bey, an Ottoman official he had met in Cairo, to pressure the family into permitting the marriage?

> Dear Sir, I want you to do me a favour. I am in love. The object is a Greek girl, steeped in poverty, but famous for her beauty. She is cursed with obnoxious parents, but I risk all and wish to marry her. . . . Upon receipt of this, will you be kind enough to write at once and state to them that by refusing me they have lost a most eligible offer and if any unhappiness is the result they have no one to blame but themselves.

With Hekekyan Bey, too, Stanley was less than entirely honest. A Greek island family "steeped in poverty" would scarcely have the social skills necessary to dine at the Hotel d'Amérique. Nor would they own a piano or be able to educate their daughter well enough to play it proficiently or to speak fluent French, as Stanley tells us Virginia did. Clearly, the Ambellas must have been of the prosperous, probably professional, middle class, and one can be sure that they would feel no need to hawk a well-endowed and beautiful daughter to an itinerant American journalist who would almost certainly take her from them forever.

Nor would a well-to-do Greek family of that period—or even this—be keen on their daughter's marrying outside the Orthodox faith. Perhaps the "obnoxiousness" of Virginia's parents lay in their unwillingness to allow the match; altogether, Stanley sounds more like a rejected suitor than a fugitive from a rigged marriage.

The second romance of this period in Stanley's life concerns a buxom Welsh beauty whom he met two or three months later when, during a brief trip to London, he made a flying visit to Denbigh to see his mother. Stanley was now received with respect—and some awe, no doubt—in her household, and was even accepted in Denbigh society, having made such a mark in the world. Thus, it was possible for the workhouse boy to be received in the home of his half-sister Emma's employer, a retired solicitor named Thomas Gough-Roberts.

There he met Gough-Roberts's nineteen-year-old daughter, Katie. It seems that his "warm imagination" still glowed at the idea of marriage to a beautiful girl. But, especially after his experience in Syra, he was not yet self-confident enough to declare himself, and nothing happened until Katie's father took action to speed things up.

This occurred just before Easter of 1869, when Gough-Roberts called on Stanley at the Langham Hotel, where he customarily stayed when in London. Gough-Roberts lost no time in letting Stanley know that he viewed him favorably as a prospective son-in-law and sweetened the offer by mentioning that Katie would bring a dowry of £1,000 to whoever was fortunate enough to win her hand.

Such attentions gave Stanley's fragile self-regard a considerable lift. "When a well-to-do solicitor of one's native town is so frank and good-natured as to be oblivious of St. Asaph," he wrote in his journal, "it must be that he thinks more highly of me than I can persuade myself to do." Still, he was not too far gone in gratitude at Gough-Roberts's approbation to fail to notice that his prospective father-in-law showed signs of heavy attentions to the bottle.

From his room at the Langham on Easter Sunday 1869, Stanley wrote Katie Gough-Roberts a remarkably self-revealing letter, fifteen pages long. He expressed delight that "arrangements had been made" whereby they could correspond openly and with her father's approval, and confessed that he had been struck with admiration the moment he first saw her. "This admiration begot something warmer," he wrote, "and this something warmer begot another deeper and more lasting feeling."

It is not certain how much the Gough-Robertses already knew of

Stanley's early history, and perhaps he was merely making a virtue of necessity by disclosing his illegitimacy. "I was a waif cast into the world," he wrote, "treated as circumstances developed themselves. Neither of my parents ever deigned to take the slightest notice of me."

He went on to give an account of his childhood in the workhouse and his young manhood in America, spicing it with his familiar, and frequently mendacious, braggadocio about his exploits under fire in the Confederate army and the U.S. navy and boasting of his present fame "over all America as a traveller, a gentleman and an author."

> This waif—this boy Rowlands—this Stanley, is he who addresses you now. I assure you that he is very ambitious and means, God willing, to rise to some notoriety before he dies. He could do better if he had a wife, not a pretty, doll-faced wife, but a woman educated, possessed of energy. . . . With her aid and encouraging presence . . . I would defy the world.

In a postscript, he added: "Tell me how I must address you. Miss Roberts is so formal, almost unkind. Address me by my name, Henry."

Although the letter reveals a continuing bitterness toward his mother, Stanley continued to court her favor, longing for her love or, if that were not forthcoming, at least for her approval. Shortly after his London meeting with Gough-Roberts he had found time to take Betsy, and Emma, on a brief vacation to Paris.

"Mother is in raptures with Paris," he wrote, "—the life on the boulevards, the Bois and the Imperial Palace." Paris, in the final days of the Second Empire, was indeed enchanting, and to an unsophisticated countrywoman like Mrs. Jones it must have been an overwhelming experience. For all that he disliked the place, one can imagine that Stanley took a keen pleasure in showing her the sights to which he had been introduced by Edwin Balch, if only that she should see how high her unloved and unwanted son had managed to climb without parental assistance.

While awaiting Katie Gough-Roberts's reply to his proposal, Stanley was sent to Madrid to cover the republican upheavals then convulsing Spain. While doing so, he managed to keep up his correspondence with Katie, sending her letters and signed photographs, often as frequently as twice a week. It seems that he intended to marry her as soon as the exigencies of his hyperactive career permitted.

Between spring and autumn of 1869, Stanley dashed about the Iberian peninsula, from one flare-up to another, as the civil war ran its bloody course. Stanley produced in those few months some of the finest reporting of his newspaper career up to that time. He had an eye for human interest, then a novel journalistic concept, writing not just about the generals and politicians on both sides of the conflict but about the ordinary soldiers and the civilians who were caught up in it.

He exposed himself to constant danger to give *Herald* readers firsthand accounts of the fighting and time and again showed himself master of the art of getting to where the story was despite the hazards of travel and the frequent obstructionism of the authorities. "I exclude all words like 'fail' and 'can't' from my vocabulary," he wrote.

Unable to reach Valencia by land, he chartered a boat to get him there by sea, arriving in time to witness the savage street fighting which was tearing the city apart. Wandering through the streets, he was constantly at risk of being shot or bayoneted as a spy by suspicious soldiers.

Perched on a rooftop in Saragossa, he watched for thirty-six hours without a break as rebels threw up barricades and defended them against repeated government assaults. There, he "witnessed personal instances of ferocity and courage which made me hold my breath." The fighting men on both sides of the barricade "appeared like characters suddenly called out to perform in some awful tragedy; and, so fascinated was I by the strange and dreadful spectacle, I could not look away."

Stanley's output was prodigious, so much so that in June a friend wrote to urge him to take a break. Stanley dismissed the suggestion. He was "at the beck and call of a chief whose will is imperious law," he wrote.

> The slightest inattention to business, the slightest forgetfulness of duty, the slightest laggardness, is punished severely; that is, you are sent about your business. . . . It is also my interest to do my duty well. . . . You do not—cannot—suppose that I have accepted this position merely for money. I can make plenty of money anywhere—it is that my future promotion to distinction hangs on it. . . . Stern duty commands me to stay. It is only by railway celerity that I can live.

*It is only by railway celerity that I can live.* But for the mode of transportation, that none-too-felicitous phrase could be the motto of the traveling media circus that nowadays flits from hotspot to hotspot by scheduled flight and charter plane, driven by a mixture of ambition, insecurity and hunger for the adrenalin high to which the roving correspondent becomes addicted. Stanley was a prime example of the breed. "Even if I had a month's holiday, I could not take it," he wrote. "I would be restless, dissatisfied, gloomy, morose. To the ———— with a vacation! I don't want it."

Eventually, it took a peremptory summons to meet Bennett in Paris to pry Stanley loose from his Spanish assignment.

That meeting was to pass into newspaper legend and the annals of African exploration as the moment when the visionary publisher secured himself a small niche in history by boldly assigning Stanley to his rendezvous with Livingstone and destiny. Yet Stanley's highly colored account is the only one we have of the meeting, and on close examination it lacks credibility.

As Stanley told it, the telegram that was handed to him at 10:00 A.M. on October 16, 1869, at his lodgings in Madrid read simply and briefly: COME TO PARIS ON IMPORTANT BUSINESS. BENNETT. According to Stanley, he immediately began packing up his entire apartment. This seems a curious response to such a summons; after all, the cable said nothing about leaving Spain for good, and it would surely have been more appropriate simply to pack an overnight bag. Nevertheless, "Down come my pictures from the walls . . . into my trunks go my books and souvenirs, my clothes are hastily collected, some half-washed, some from the clothes-line half dry, and after a couple of hours of hasty hard work my portmanteaus are strapped up, and labelled for 'Paris.' "

As Stanley would relate the incident for posterity, he caught a train from Madrid at three o'clock that very afternoon, spent the night in Bayonne on the French-Spanish frontier and reached Paris the following night. Railway celerity, indeed! One did not keep the great man waiting. He went straight to the Grand Hotel and knocked at the door of Bennett's room:

> "Come in," I heard a voice say.
> Entering, I found Mr. Bennett in bed.
> "Who are you?" he asked. "My name is Stanley," I answered.
> "Ah, yes; sit down. I have important business on hand for you."
> After throwing over his shoulders his robe-de-chambre, Mr. Bennett asked, "Where do you think Livingstone is?"
> "I really do not know, sir!"
> "Do you think he is alive?"
> "He may be and he may not be," I answered.

"Well. I think he is alive, and that he can be found, and I am going to send you to find him."

"What!" said I. "Do you really think I can find Dr. Livingstone? Do you mean me to go to Central Africa?"

"Yes; I mean that you shall go and find him wherever you may hear that he is, and to get what news you can of him, and perhaps"—delivering himself thoughtfully and deliberately—"the old man may be in want: take enough with you to help him should he require it. Of course, you will act according to your own plans, and do what you think best—BUT FIND LIVINGSTONE!"

And when Stanley draws his employer's attention to the expense of "this little journey," Bennett seems unconcerned. "Draw a thousand pounds now," he says, "and when you have gone through that, draw another thousand, and when that is spent draw another, and when you have finished that draw another thousand; and so on; but, FIND LIVINGSTONE."

Even up to this point, the strange business of his packing up his apartment on so cryptic a summons and the astonishing speed with which he got to Paris has made Stanley's account seem somewhat fanciful. From this point on, it strains credibility to the breaking point. For Stanley invites us to believe that Bennett, having ordered him so emphatically to spare no expense or effort to find Livingstone, would then reel off a bewildering list of other assignments—many of them scarcely newsworthy at all—that were to take priority over the search.

For a start, Stanley should go to Egypt to report on the opening of the Suez Canal. Then he should go to the Upper Nile and "describe whatever is interesting for tourists." After that, to Jerusalem to report on recent archaeological discoveries. Thence to Constantinople, for some "letters" about the Sultan's problems with the Khedive. "Then—let me see—you might as well visit the Crimea and those old battlegrounds. Then go across the Caucasus to the Caspian Sea. . . . From thence you may get through Persia to India; you could write an interesting letter from Persepolis."

And only if Livingstone were still missing when he had done all that should Stanley sail to Zanzibar and mount an expedition to look for him.

In journalistic terms, this set of instructions makes no sense at all. Admittedly, the opening of the Suez Canal was newsworthy, and for Stanley to cover it while en route for Africa was perfectly logical. But to have him then make a twelve-month detour by way of Turkey, the

Caucasus, Persia and India, just to produce a string of mere travel-ogues about old battlefields and archaeological discoveries defies reason. Megalomaniac and playboy Bennett may have been, idiot he was not.

Clearly, then, Stanley's account of his meeting with Bennett was in large part fictional. Even the date he ascribed to it was a lie. As an unpublished diary note reveals, he went to see Bennett with a good deal less celerity than he claimed, meeting him not on October 17, but on October 27. As if to conceal that mendacity, the pages for October 17 and the next eight days were at some point torn out of his journal.

*James Gordon Bennett, Jr. He gave Stanley the order "Find Livingstone" —but seemed in no hurry to see the mission accomplished. (Library of Congress)*

What really passed between the two men, and why should Stanley have lied about it? A plausible account may be deduced from a wealth of circumstantial evidence.

Stanley had already taken one run at the Livingstone story on the instruction of the *Herald*'s Finlay Anderson, who, based as he was in London, took a special interest in the matter. Anderson would have communicated that interest to Douglas A. Levien, who succeeded him as London bureau chief in the summer of 1869. Quite probably, Anderson also raised the matter directly with Bennett when he got back to New York. In fact, Bennett's biographer, Don C. Seitz, had "the distinct impression" that the idea of sending Stanley to find Livingstone originated with Anderson. "Indeed," wrote Seitz, "I recall [Anderson] making some such statement to me shortly before his death."

If we accept that the original idea was Anderson's, we may assume that he intended the assignment for Stanley, the star of his bureau, and that Stanley was aware of this. That would account for a letter Levien wrote to Stanley on July 12, 1869, reporting that Bennett was expected in London within a few days and that "I have then a proposition to make to him which I think you may like." Added Levien: "I will not mention it, however, until I have learnt his views, in case it should end in a disappointment."

But nothing to do with Bennett was ever straightforward. He was a compulsive player of power games, and the very fact that Anderson and Levien were so keen on sending Stanley to Africa would be quite enough to excite his megalomaniac spite. Why Stanley? he may have asked himself. And indeed, Seitz says that Bennett's first intention was to assign another of his roving foreign correspondents, the resonantly named De Benneville Randolph Keim. But Keim was beyond the reach of the electric telegraph at the moment and could not be otherwise contacted.

So Stanley it was who got the assignment. But was Bennett really very much interested in Livingstone and Africa? Any journalist reading Stanley's account of the briefing he received from Bennett must come to the conclusion that the *Herald* chief was far more interested in what was going on in the Levant than in the fate of a broken-down British explorer somewhere in Central Africa. How else to explain why he should order Stanley to make a Cook's tour of Egypt, the Caucasus, Persia and India before looking for Livingstone? The lost explorer appears to have been a mere afterthought, and perhaps a grudging one at that.

This would explain why it was that when Stanley did at last reach

Africa, fourteen months later, he found that Bennett had made no provision for the financing of the Livingstone expedition: he had either forgotten or no longer cared about it, if he ever did.

In fact, it was only because Stanley had some time before been given—as he put it—"carte blanche at the bankers," that he felt bold enough to sign drafts drawn on the *Herald* to outfit and equip the expedition. And even then, Bennett refused to honor those drafts until he learned that Stanley was on his way back from the interior, giving his newspaper the possibility of an historic scoop. Seen in that light, even Seitz's claim that, whoever had the original inspiration, "Bennett seized the chance and backed his man unflinchingly," sounds conspicuously hollow.

But if Bennett was as lukewarm as he seems to have been about the Livingstone assignment, why did Stanley choose to twist the truth and give his boss such a large share of the credit?

When he wrote his best-selling *How I Found Livingstone* and dedicated it to Bennett, Stanley was still in the *Herald*'s employ and hoping that the paper would finance a second expedition to Africa. He was no doubt also aware how resentful Bennett was that he should be basking in world celebrity while Bennett's own role was overlooked.

Add to this the crippling lack of self-esteem, lurking just behind the self-confident facade, which had left the young Stanley with altogether too much respect for authority and inherited status. As a *Herald* colleague would note, after coming back from Africa a hero, Stanley "exhibited for Mr. Bennett much the same respect as one might imagine Bismarck had for the Emperor he created." And while "it was the free and easy habit of the *Herald* staff to designate their chief as 'the young man' . . . Stanley never fell into this undignified habit. . . . Mr. Bennett was always given his name." In short, for all his courage, resolution and swagger, Stanley was something of a toady.

But if he flattered Bennett by flagrantly exaggerating his role in 1872, why did Stanley never put the record straight in later years, when he no longer depended on the man's beneficence? The most likely answer is that, having created the myth, he could not disown it without making himself look foolish.

# PART TWO

# THE SEARCH FOR LIVINGSTONE

I do not think I was made for an African
explorer, for I detest the land most heartily.

*H. M. STANLEY*

# Chapter Seven

*IF THE* wind is in the right quarter, the traveler by sea can often smell Zanzibar before he sees it; the island exudes a sweet *bouquet d'Afrique,* compounding cloves and copra, sweat and sewage, that will linger in the scent-memory for life. This was the introduction that Stanley received when, having completed the journalistic Cook's Tour on which Bennett had sent him and sailed from Bombay via Mauritius and the Seychelles, he arrived in Zanzibar on January 7, 1871, aboard the whaling ship *Falcon.*

He was immediately enchanted. "... the sky is one of cerulean tint," he wrote, "the sea is not troubled and scarcely rocks the ship; the shore is a mass of vivid green. ..."

Behind this lovely facade lived a cruel reality. The island of Zanzibar, for centuries the fiefdom of the Sultans of Muscat and Oman and since 1832 their capital, was the headquarters of the Central African slave trade. The Arabs conducted that commerce with a heartless insouciance, while the British were doing their best to stamp it out. But Stanley—seduced by the soft rhythms of the island and the wild poetry of the interior just over its western horizon—saw Zanzibar with the eyes of a heedless romantic. It was, he wrote,

> The Baghdad, Isfahan, the Istanbul if you like, of East Africa . . . the great mart which invites the ivory traders from the African interior. . . . Baghdad had great silk bazaars, Zanzibar has her ivory; Baghdad once traded in jewels, Zanzibar trades in gum-copal; Istanbul imported Circassian and Georgian slaves; Zanzibar black beauties from Uhiyo, Ugindo, Ugogo, Unyamwezi and Galla.

The classification of "black beauties" as trade goods, along with gum copal, suggests a certain moral myopia on Stanley's part, but it should be said in fairness that by the standards of his day he was not entirely insensitive on the subject of race. Having taken a stroll through the African quarters of Zanzibar, he wrote an admonition to any white stranger to "learn the necessity of admitting that negroes are men like himself . . . that they have passions and prejudices, likes and dislikes, sympathies and antipathies, tastes and feelings in common with all human nature." And the Zanzibari Blacks, or Wangwana, whom he hired as captains, guides and *askaris* (armed escorts) for his expedition, were "an exceedingly fine-looking body of men, far more intelligent in appearance than I could ever have believed African barbarians could be."

Condescending, no doubt, but Stanley's mind was clearly not so closed as those of many contemporary white travelers in Africa. The intellectually superior Richard Burton, for one, dismissed Africans as "one of those childish races which, never rising to man's estate, fall like worn-out links from the great chain of animated nature . . . befuddled, ignorant hopeless people." And Samuel Baker saw them as "a hopeless race of savages, for whom there is no prospect of civilisation."

Until ten years or so before Stanley's arrival in Zanzibar, its legitimate foreign commerce had been dominated by the Americans. Yankee traders from Boston and Salem brought to Zanzibar huge quantities of "Merikani"—the durable cotton cloth much valued by the tribes of the interior—and took back cargoes of hides, ivory and gum copal. In 1859, thirty-five of the sixty-five foreign ships which put into Zanzibar had been American, but in 1869 they numbered only eight out of fifty-three, and the U.S. dollar, once the common currency of Zanzibar and the coast, had been supplanted by the Austrian-minted Maria Theresa dollar.

The distractions of the Civil War and a vigorous blockade of Confederate ports had been largely to blame for the decline in American trade and influence, a process that was accelerated by the opening of the Suez Canal, giving America's European trading rivals dramatically easier access to the East African coast.

Both commercially and diplomatically, then, the most influential foreigners on the island by the time Stanley arrived were the British. And, partly because of residual trade rivalry and partly because of the ineffable snobbery of the colonial British, there was little love lost between the representatives in Zanzibar of the two great English-speaking nations.

The American consul was a Yankee ex–sea captain named Francis Webb, who had come to the island as the agent of a wealthy Salem merchant and shipowner. Because Webb was "in trade," his British opposite number, Dr. John Kirk, felt entitled to look down on him.

Webb was in the habit of putting animal skins destined for export to America out to dry on the flat roof of his residence; Kirk would speak of "the American stinking hides," and utter similar disparaging remarks, wrinkling his nose in patrician distaste as he passed. The cheerfully thick-skinned Webb had a word for such attitudes: "Kirkism."

Although he and Stanley had never met, they had corresponded a couple of years previously when Stanley was in Aden waiting for word of Livingstone's expected emergence from the interior. So after disembarking from the *Falcon* Stanley made one of his first stops at the U.S. consulate, where he made himself known to Webb.

Webb took an immediate liking to him, which was indeed fortunate, for Stanley discovered on his arrival, with only eighty dollars in his pocket, that Bennett had made absolutely no provision for the funding of his expedition. On the slightest of acquaintanceships Webb pledged his own word to the local merchants that his countryman's credit was good. As a result, Stanley was able to run up expenditures in excess of $20,000—$8,000 alone on the purchase of cloth, wire and beads to barter with the tribes of the interior for food and safe passage.

As Stanley would admit to Bennett later, after the publisher had belatedly honored the drafts his employee had signed, the expense incurred "frightened me considerably," but "I was too far from the telegraph to notify you of such expense or to receive further orders from you; the preparations for the expedition therefore went on."

Did Stanley ever doubt that his employer actually wanted him to press on with the search for Livingstone? If he did, he put the thought out of his mind. He knew that if he could pull it off he would put himself safely beyond criticism for overspending. And, in fact, his expedition was the most lavish and expensive ever mounted from Zanzibar up to that time. In all, he purchased six tons of supplies, which Webb and his wife allowed him to store in the courtyard of their house until he was ready to sail for the mainland.

At the outset, Stanley was "totally ignorant of the interior and it was difficult at first to know what I needed." He pored over the published accounts of his celebrated forerunners in Central African exploration, the Englishmen Burton, Speke and Grant, and Livingstone himself. But although "a good deal of geographical, ethnographical and other information appertaining to the study of Inner Africa was obtainable . . . information respecting the organisation of an expedition . . . was not in any book.''* So Stanley turned for advice to the Arab slave-traders, who knew the interior and its ways better than anyone.

The venerable, gray-bearded Sheikh Hashid told him that he would need 10 *doti*, or forty yards, of cloth per day to buy food for a hundred men. Hashid further advised Stanley that "Merikani" was the most popular cloth among the tribes, and Stanley accordingly ordered 2,000 doti of it. Of Kaniki, a blue jean manufactured in India, he bought 1,000 doti, at the same time purchasing 650 doti of other colored cloths, such as Barsati, which Hashid told him was favored by the cannibalistic Unyamwezi.

Among yet other tribes, Stanley was advised, beads took the place of cloth as currency. One tribe would prefer white beads, another black, and others, brown, red, yellow, green and so on. He purchased accordingly. Another essential trade commodity was copper wire— "numbers 5 and 6, almost the thickness of telegraph wire, were considered the best." Stanley bought 350 pounds of this.

Anxious to be away and on the trail of Livingstone, he defied the island languor to engage in a frenzy of acquisition: provisions, cooking utensils, rope, twine, tents, donkeys, canvas, tar, needles, tools, beddings and medicines—including many bottles of the indispensable Dr. Collis Brown's Chlorodyne, used by prudent tropical travelers to this day to soothe the savage bowel.

What he could not purchase he improvised. Finding no pack saddles available, Stanley designed one himself, to be made out of canvas, rope and cotton. He bought one large boat, capable of carrying twenty men, for $80, and a six-man boat for $40. To make them easier to carry, he had the outer boards removed and replaced with canvas.

Personnel had also to be acquired. Stanley had already taken on as his second-in-command a Scotsman named William Farquhar, first mate of the barque *Polly*, on which Stanley had sailed from Bombay to Mauritius. Once ashore in Zanzibar, he hired as his third-in-command a Cockney named John Shaw, lately third mate of the American merchantman *Nevada*. Shaw had been paid off after successfully disputing a charge of mutinous behavior and was hanging around the bars and brothels of the island when Stanley found him.

---

* Stanley seems not to have read Speke or Burton too closely. Both Speke's *Journal of the Discovery of the Sources of the Nile* (London, 1863) and the appendix to Burton's *The Lake Regions of Central Africa* (London, 1860) contain much information on this score.

Stanley noted that Farquhar was "a capital navigator and an excellent mathematician . . . strong, energetic and clever but, I am sorry to say, a hard drinker. Every day while we lived at Zanzibar, he was in a muddled condition, and the dissipated life he led at this place proved fatal to him . . . shortly after penetrating the interior."

He was less censorious of Shaw's equally conspicuous moral shortcomings, noting instead that "he possessed all the requirements of such a man as I needed, and was an experienced hand with the palm and needle, could cut canvas to fit anything, was a pretty good navigator, ready and willing. . . ." Farquhar's salary was set at $400 a year, and Shaw's at $300.

Next, Stanley hired as captain of his twenty-man escort of askaris "the famous Bombay," who had traveled with Burton and Speke on their 1856–58 expedition in search of the sources of the Nile. Bombay was a grizzled little villain, aged about fifty, with a smile that revealed a huge gap, caused when Speke knocked out three of his teeth for insubordination.

Bombay was taken on at $80 a year, and five other "faithfuls," including Grant's and Burton's former valets, were taken on at half Bombay's salary. Bombay himself hired the rest of the askaris. To arm them, himself, and his two white assistants, Stanley purchased "one double-barrel, breech-loading smooth bore gun, one Winchester rifle (16-shooter), two Starr's breech-loaders, one Jocelyn breech-loader, one elephant rifle, two breech-loading revolvers, 24 muskets, six single-barreled pistols, one battle axe, two swords, two daggers, one boar spear, two American axes, 24 hatchets and 24 butcher knives."

With the exception of Webb, Stanley told nobody the real purpose of his expedition. Competitive newspaperman that he was, he was not about to jeopardize a scoop by talking about it. Instead, he spread the word that he was planning to explore the upper reaches of the Rufiji River. And although some may have wondered why such an unsensational objective should be worth so much money to "that Yankee rag," nobody seems to have been openly skeptical.

Whether Consul Kirk was fooled when Stanley, in his elephantine way, pumped him for information about Livingstone is not clear. Kirk had been a member of one of Livingstone's previous expeditions, and he and Stanley met at one of the British consul's Tuesday evening receptions. It was, wrote Stanley, "the dreariest evening I ever passed, until Dr. Kirk . . . called me aside to submit to my inspection a magnificent elephant rifle. . . .

I heard anecdotes of jungle life, adventures experienced while hunting and incidents of his travels with Livingstone. "Ah, yes, Dr. Kirk," I asked carelessly, "about Livingstone—where is he, do you think, now?" "Well, really," he replied, "you know that is very difficult to answer; he may be dead; of one thing I am sure, nobody has heard anything definite of him for over two years. I should fancy, though, that he must be alive."

Kirk told Stanley that from time to time he sent supplies into the interior for Livingstone to be left at his last known location and that a small supply train was at that moment on its way. "I really think the old man should come home now," Kirk added. "He is growing old, you know, and if he died the world would lose the benefit of his discoveries." This, said Kirk, was because he kept "neither notes nor journals," seldom took astronomical observations to determine his exact position, and "simply makes a note or a dot or something on a map, which nobody could understand but himself."

Pressed further by Stanley, Kirk allowed that Livingstone was "a very difficult man to deal with," although he personally had never had a quarrel with him. Stanley ventured: "I am told he is a very modest man; is he?" Kirk replied in disparaging tones. "Oh, he knows the value of his own discoveries; no man better. He is not quite an angel."

Pursuing his objective with a characteristic lack of subtlety, Stanley pressed on. "Well, now, supposing I met him in my travels—I might possibly stumble across him if he travels anywhere in the direction I am going—how would he conduct himself towards me?" Replied Kirk: "To tell you the truth, I do not think he would like it very well. I know if Burton, or Grant, or Baker, or any of those fellows were going after him, and he heard of their coming, he would put a hundred miles of swamp in a very short time between himself and them."

Kirk was furious when Stanley later embarrassed him by publishing his less than admiring off-the-record remarks about Livingstone. But Kirk had delivered similar confidential judgments to others, and the comments in his private journals were even more caustic.

Before Stanley left Zanzibar for the mainland, the indispensable Webb arranged an audience for him with the Sultan, Sayed Barghash. Stanley so beguiled the devout ruler with tales of the Muslim countries he had visited that Barghash gave him a firman—virtually a passport—and letters of introduction to Arab merchants whom he might encounter in the interior. He also presented Stanley with a horse from his own stables, and with these acquisitions, plus an

*John Kirk, British consul in Zanzibar,*
*displayed a lordly disdain for Stanley*
*and a lack of concern for*
*Livingstone.*

American flag sewn by "that kind-hearted lady, Mrs. Webb," Stanley set sail for the mainland on February 4, 1871, exactly four weeks from the date of his arrival in Zanzibar.

He was impatient to strike into the interior before the onset of the rainy season—and before Livingstone should hear of his coming and make himself scarce—and noted testily that although it was only twenty-five miles from Zanzibar to Bagamoyo, on the mainland, "it took the dull and lazy dhows ten hours before they dropped anchor."

But when Stanley got to Bagamoyo he encountered vexations and delays he had not so far imagined. These were mostly connected with the business of hiring the 140 *pagazis,* or porters, that he required.

The supply of such essential labor had been cornered by a young Ismaili entrepreneur named Sewa Haji Paru, who kept Stanley waiting week after week, growing to a state of excruciating impatience, while he steadily notched up the price of his essential services. "Half a dozen times a day I found him in dishonesty," Stanley fumed.

> Each day he conceived a new system of roguery. Every instant of his time seemed to be devoted to devising how to plunder me, until I was at my wits' end. . . . I would prefer the three months' march, with all its horrors, anxieties swamps and fevers, to the two months' preparation for the expedition I had at Bagomoyo.

But Sewa Haji Paru gave Stanley one piece of invaluable advice: instead of traveling in one big caravan, conspicuous and liable to attract extortion and attack, he should split his expedition into five smaller parties, sending four on ahead and finally setting out himself at the head of the fifth.

While at Bagamoyo, Stanley had an unexpected further encounter with Kirk, of whom he had by now the lowest possible opinion. He had discovered that the small caravan of supplies and letters for Livingstone, sent from Zanzibar three months previously, was still loitering in Bagamoyo. It had been delayed by the same problem that was holding up Stanley, the shortage of pagazis, but clearly Kirk had made no attempt to expedite matters. The caravan only left Bagamoyo on February 15, when its leader received word that Kirk himself was on the way to the mainland. Even then, it seems, Kirk's main purpose was not to speed its departure but to go hunting.

He arrived in Bagamoyo from Zanzibar aboard the British gunboat *Columbine* and went ashore with some British officers. Stanley met Kirk and his naval friends that night at a dinner given by the French Catholic priests of the Holy Ghost Mission in Bagamoyo, where to Stanley's amazement champagne and other fine wines were served. The "vinuous influence," as Stanley called it, did little to ease the tension between the two. Stanley reproached Kirk for his lack of urgency over Livingstone's supplies; Kirk told Stanley tartly that he would soon find out what conditions in the interior were really like.

Kirk's lame official explanation was that he had heard "through a native" that the caravan was loitering in Bagamoyo and that "by using my influence with the Arabs I succeeded at once in sending off all but four loads, and followed inland one day's journey myself." Added Kirk: "Had I not gone in person they might have lingered yet several months." But when Stanley caught up with the Livingstone caravan at Unyanyembe, or Tabora, several hundred miles inland, its leader told him that he had not seen Kirk since leaving Zanzibar on November 1. In a dispatch from Tabora, Stanley put the knife in:

> Does it not appear to you that Dr. John Kirk . . . showed great unkindness, unfriendliness towards the old traveller, his former companion, in not pushing the caravan . . .? Does it not seem to you . . . that a small caravan of thirty-three men might have been despatched within a week or so after their arrival at Bagamoyo . . .?"

While waiting with mounting impatience to strike out for the interior, Stanley had time to write to a number of friends and acquaintances in America and Europe. One letter went to his young friend Edwin Balch in Paris. The most fervent went to Katie Gough-Roberts, in Denbigh. So far as Stanley was concerned, they were still betrothed. True, her father had refused permission for them to marry before Stanley's departure from England for Suez and beyond, saying that they should wait until his return. But Stanley had written to her regularly since, and would continue to do so while on the search for Livingstone.

Only on his return would he learn that she had thrown him over to marry a young Denbigh architect named Urban Bradshaw. Her faithlessness would reinforce the sense of rejection and betrayal that had haunted Stanley throughout his life, and which future events would only intensify.

# Chapter Eight

DAVID LIVINGSTONE was fifty-seven when Stanley set out to find him, a former Scottish mill hand turned medical missionary whose epic travels in the uncharted interior of Africa had made him a British national hero and an international celebrity. His two best-selling books about his expeditions, and scores of articles by others in the daily and the periodical press, had turned him into a figure as instantly recognizable as Queen Victoria herself. With his craggily mournful Caledonian features, drooping mustache, naval cap and ever-present walking stick, he was an icon and a perfect exemplar of muscular Christianity to an age sure in its faith and obsessed by African exploration.

To a less illusioned, less pious era, Livingstone seems a man of curiously mixed motivation and decidedly uneven temper if unquestionable goodness, and it is often difficult to discern a logical purpose in his meanderings across Africa between 1852 and his death in 1873.

He seems by turns the avid evangelist, impelled by the power of faith to bring the heathen to Christ; the earnest geographer, driven by scientific curiosity to fill the blank spaces on the map and solve the age-old riddle of the Nile's sources; the fervent humanitarian, inspired by love of his fellow man to destroy the Central African slave trade; the essential colonialist, asserting that Commerce, following in the footsteps of Christianity, will civilize the African by bringing him into prolonged contact with superior races; and the raging egocentric, concerned more with self-promotion than any of the above.

In his own day, the London Missionary Society, sponsors of Livingstone's 1852–56 expedition—in which, with a handful of black companions, he crossed the continent from west to east, traced the entire 1,700-mile length of the Zambezi and discovered the Victoria Falls—came to believe that his motives were more worldly than divine. In 1857, the elders of the society delivered the judgment that Livingstone's 4,300-mile journey had been "only remotely connected with the gospel," and he angrily severed his connections with them. He could afford to do so: his account of the expedition—*Missionary*

*Livingstone in England, with his daughter Agnes. "How I envy such a father," Stanley would tell her. (Library of Congress)*

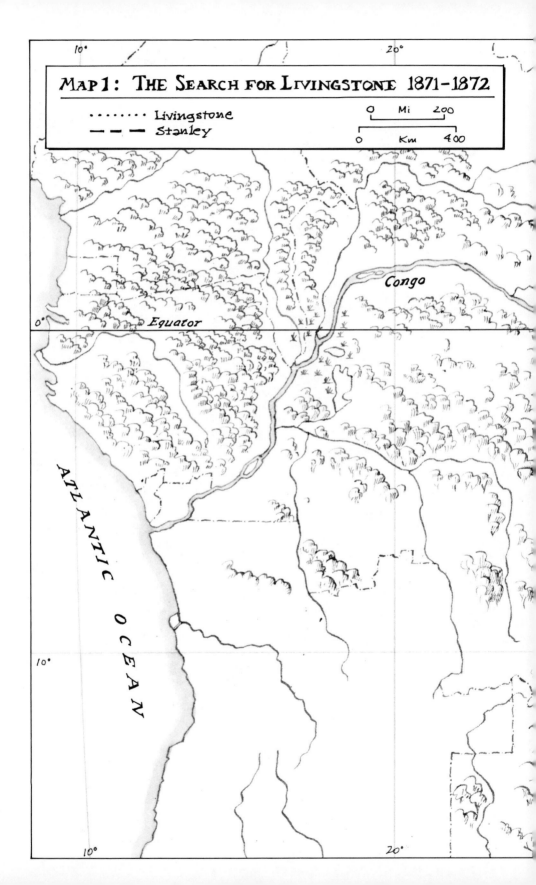

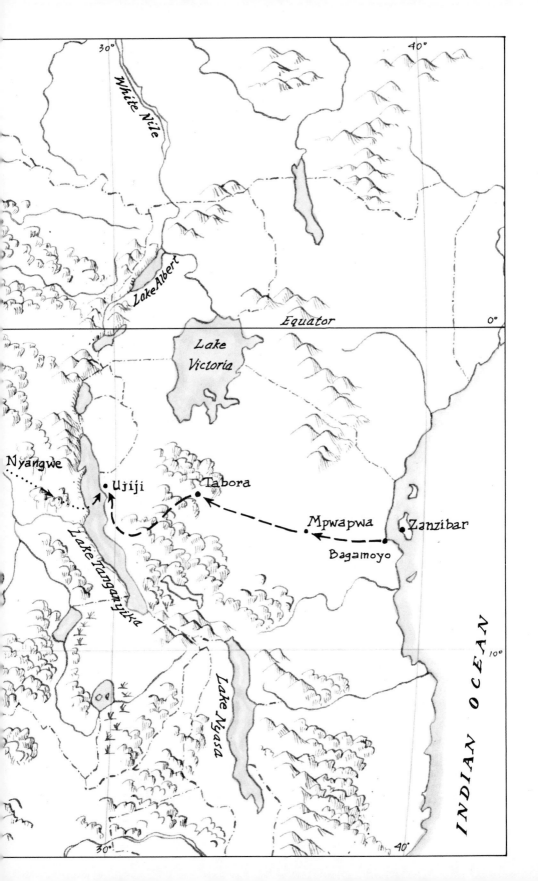

*Travels and Researches in South Africa*—had been a runaway success, bringing him financial independence.

In his personal relations, Livingstone was deeply loved by his African followers, but was to make himself bitterly resented by the whites who took part in his second expedition, from 1858 to 1863. While he showed fatherly solicitude for the Blacks, he seemed arrogant and disdainful to the half-dozen whites—including his younger brother Charles and the consul-to-be Kirk—who accompanied him, scorning to consult or even inform them about his plans and reveling in his superior ability to endure the hardships of the trek. Commented Kirk: "He knows how to come round niggers very well, but if his digestive system don't go all right, he loses his diplomatic power wonderfully."

Livingstone's second expedition, financed jointly by the British government and the Royal Geographical Society and much more lavishly equipped than the first, was concerned chiefly with mapping the Zambezi region and investigating its mineral and agricultural resources. Largely as a consequence of Livingstone's shortcomings as an organizer and his failure to get on with his British assistants, the expedition was a relative failure. But it kept public interest in Africa at a high pitch and was the basis for another Livingstone best seller, *The Zambezi and Its Tributaries.*

For a while, memories of the backbiting during the Zambezi expedition and the recriminations that followed it, soured Livingstone on exploration, and he vowed never to return to Africa. Then Sir Roderick Murchison, president of the Royal Geographical Society, urged him to go back, offering him the chance to succeed where Burton, Speke, Grant, Baker and the others had failed by finding the source of the Nile somewhere within the lake regions of Central Africa.

Livingstone—feeling ill at ease in Britain and nurturing unchristian disdain for the likes of Burton ("a beastly fellow," and a "moral idiot") and Speke ("a poor, misguided" man of "slender mental abilities")—agreed. Now aged fifty-two, he sailed for Zanzibar to put together a small expedition, modestly funded by the RGS and the Foreign Office, in which this time he would be the only white man.

He went "not simply as a geographer, but as a missionary and [to] do geography on the way," promising himself that, besides solving the ancient riddle of the Nile, he would establish a framework for a series of missionary outposts and formulate a strategy to destroy the slave trade. Arguably, it was Livingstone's intense moral revulsion for that trade which, more than any other factor, drew him back to

Africa. He considered its suppression to be "a greater matter by far than the discovery of all the Nile sources together."

In his previous journeyings, Livingstone had seen how the slavers depopulated and laid waste vast tracts of the interior. He had seen the long lines of men, women and children, chained together at the neck, on their Via Dolorosa to the coast. He had seen the burned villages, the uprooted fields, and the corpses littering the trail of slaves who had died on the march. With a compassion that went beyond the purple prosifying and moral posturing of the time, he had written: "The strangest disease I have seen in this country seems really to be broken-heartedness, and it attacks free men who have been captured and made slaves."

Urged on by political pressure from the churches and the influential Anti-Slavery Society, the British government had tried to stop the trade by coercing the Sultan of Zanzibar into signing an antislavery pact in 1845. But the results had been meager. The treaty did not interfere with the practice of slavery on the island itself or prohibit the collection of slaves from the African interior. It merely banned their export from Zanzibar to Oman and the other markets of the East, and the Zanzibar dhow masters found it easy enough to dodge the squadron of British warships, empowered to board them and seize their cargoes, that the Admiralty had sent to patrol the Indian Ocean sea lanes.

So when Livingstone arrived in Zanzibar in February 1866, to organize his last expedition, the traffic in slaves was running at between 80,000 and 100,000 souls a year. "It is the old, old way of living," sighed Livingstone, ". . . slave dhows coming and slave dhows going away. . . . On visiting the slave market, I found about 300 slaves exposed for sale. . . . The teeth are examined, the cloth lifted to examine the lower limbs, and a stick thrown for a slave to bring, and thus exhibit his paces. Some are dragged through the crowd by hand and the price called incessantly. . . ."

But if the power and prestige of Britain could not stop the trade, how could one crusty, conscience-driven Christian expect to pit himself successfully against such a deeply embedded and time-hallowed practice, especially when he might need the slavers' help for his very survival? Conceivably, Livingstone did not even ask himself that question. His faith in God—and himself—was limitless: somehow, the sheer moral force of his presence must suffice to end a commerce in human flesh that had flourished for generations.

In March 1866, he set off from Zanzibar with an armed escort of thirteen Indian sepoys, plus twenty-three Africans, four of them devoted personal servants with whom he had traveled before. With this modest expedition, accompanied by porters and pack animals, Livingstone would attempt to save bodies from slavery and souls from sin while exploring westward to ascertain whether the Nile originated to the south of lakes Victoria and Albert, as then seemed possible, or if it flowed out of Lake Tanganyika, as he suspected.

But though his faith was unshakable and his curiosity undiminished, the aging Livingstone's rugged constitution had been undermined by the host of ailments with which Africa punished intruders. Also, he seemed to have lost the knack of commanding the absolute loyalty of his Africans. Desertion, sickness, theft, accident, tribal hostility, and the difficulty of finding food in a landscape utterly ravaged by the slave trade all took their toll.

Still, there was no thought of turning back. Instead, he pushed ever deeper into the heart of the continent, by now obsessed with the idea that the Lualaba River, flowing westward out of Lake Bangweolo, turned north to become the Nile.

By the time Stanley set out from Zanzibar to search for him, Livingstone was "a mere ruckle of bones," having been on the march for almost six years. Immobilized by foot ulcers, racked by dysentery, and tended only by three faithful servants after the death or desertion of the rest of his expedition, Livingstone had been stranded for seven months in Bambarre, deep in cannibal country almost a thousand miles from Zanzibar.

Then, on February 4, the day before Stanley sailed from Zanzibar to the mainland, a small caravan arrived bringing supplies from Kirk and ten porters. And within a week the indomitable Livingstone was on the trail again—not heading east toward the coast and safety, but west toward the Lualaba.

*STANLEY* was in a buoyant, almost exalted mood when he at last left Bagamoyo* at the head of the last of his six caravans. The column, led by a stalwart guide who bore aloft the Stars and Stripes, included Stanley's Arabic interpreter—a Christian Palestinian named Selim whom he had hired in Jerusalem—two cooks, and the British seaman Shaw. Shaw rode a donkey and Stanley a bay horse given to him by one of Zanzibar's small American community. At his heels loped Omar, a dog that Stanley had acquired in Bombay.

---

* According to a dispatch dated July 4, this was on April 1; according to Stanley's book *How I Found Livingstone*, it was on March 21.

He had decided to head straight for Ujiji, on the eastern shore of Lake Tanganyika, where he had deduced from the best information available he was most likely to find Livingstone, or at least to receive up-to-date news of his whereabouts. Stanley appears to have set out with few misgivings. He wrote:

> We left Bagomoyo, the attraction of all the curious, with noisy eclat, and defiled up a narrow lane shaded to twilight by the dense umbrage of two parallel hedges of mimosas. We were all in the highest spirits—the soldiers sang extempore, the Kirangoze [guide] lifted his voice into a loud bellowing note, and fluttered the American flag . . . and my heart, I thought, palpitated much too quickly for the sobriety of a leader. But I could not help it. The enthusiasm of youth still clung to me, despite my travelled years, my pulses bounded with the full glow of staple health; behind me were the troubles which had harassed me for over two months . . . and before me glowed the sun of promise as we sped toward the Occident. . . .

Despite the onset of the rains and the death of Stanley's two riding horses on the third day out, the first couple of weeks of the march were relatively trouble-free. For much of the time they traversed scenery which Stanley found "as beautiful as that which many an English nobleman is proud to call his 'park' . . . lawn and sward with boscage sufficient to agreeably diversify it." But then they came to "the terrible Makata swamp," a five-day slog through knee-deep water and black mire, and "from here commenced the list of calamities which afterwards overtook me."

> First the white man Shaw caught the terrible fever of East Africa, then the Arab boy Selim, then myself, then the soldiers one by one, and smallpox and dysentery raged among us. As soon as I had recovered from the effects of the fever I was attacked by dysentery, which brought me to the verge of the grave. From a stout and fleshy person weighing 170 pounds, I was reduced to a skeleton, a mere frame of bone and skin weighing 130 pounds.

Stanley drove his men through the swamp with demonic determination and a liberal application of the lash. He had no sympathy at all for those he termed malingerers. "When mud and wet sapped the physical energy of the lazily-inclined," he wrote, "a dog-whip became their backs, restoring them to a sound—sometimes to an extravagant—activity." As a white man, Shaw was spared the lash of the dog whip but not that of his leader's tongue; he was "a chronic hypochondriac," said Stanley.

The caravan led by Farquhar, which preceded Stanley's through the swamp, had suffered similarly. When Stanley caught up with it he found the Scotsman in "a most miserable plight," suffering from dropsy or elephantiasis, and all his nine donkeys dead. Stanley seems to have felt little sympathy for Farquhar, who, he callously observed later, looked as though he had been fattened by cannibals "as we do geese and turkeys for the Christmas dinner—as interesting a case of hypertrophy as Barnum's fat woman."

Both Shaw and Farquhar were by now in a near-mutinous frame of mind and, concluding that their only hope for survival was to get rid of Stanley and turn the caravan back to Bagamoyo, they hatched a plot to kill him. As Stanley retired one night, a bullet tore through his tent, missing him by inches. He rushed out, revolver in hand, and confronted Shaw, by whose side lay a still-warm gun. Shaw stammered out a cock-and-bull story of having shot at a thief outside his tent. Stanley was unconvinced. "I would advise you in future," he warned, ". . . not to fire into my tent, or at least so near me. I might get hurt, you know, in which case ugly reports might get about. . . ."

A few days later he left Farquhar, with a servant to look after him, at a town called Mpwapwa and pushed on. Some time later news reached him that Farquhar had died and, with stunning insensitivity Stanley remarked to Shaw: "There is one of us gone, Shaw my boy! Who will be the next?" The question was rhetorical. Stanley had no doubt the next would be Shaw, whose dalliances with African women had "put the last finishing touches to his enfeebled frame." Indeed, Stanley reported that within a few hours of hearing of Farquhar's death, Shaw was "taken very ill, whether of fever or what I do not know. . . . I suspect it is a fierce attack of veneral affection [sic]."

It was during his grueling march westward, or so he tells us, that Stanley turned to the Bible, rereading it "with a higher and truer understanding than I had ever before conceived."

> Its powerful verses had a different meaning, a more penetrative influence, in the silence of the wilds. . . . Alone in my tent . . . I flung myself on my knees, and poured out my soul in utterly secret prayer to Him from whom I had been so long estranged, to Him who had led me here mysteriously into Africa, there to reveal Himself and His will. I became inspired with fresh desire to serve Him to the utmost. . . .

With this religious experience—if Stanley's autobiographical rec-ollections are truthful and not merely a nod towards the pietism of the time—came disillusionment with journalism and the correspondent's life that Stanley had formerly relished. The Bible "reminded me that, apart from God, my life was but a bubble of air," while newspapers merely "fostered arrogance and worldliness." Added Stanley: "[M]y black followers might have discerned, had they been capable of reflection, that Africa was changing me."

ON HIS WAY from Bambarre west to the Lualaba, Livingstone appears to have made a remarkable recovery from the sickness that had laid him low for so many months while he waited for supplies from Kirk. Passing through tree-covered hill country in early March 1871, he recorded in his journal a lyrical account of village life, one which reflects the deep affection he felt for the African people:

> The villages are very pretty, standing on slopes. The main street generally lies east and west, to allow the bright sun to stream his clear hot rays from one end to the other. . . . A little verandah is often made in front of the door, and here at dawn the family gathers round a fire . . . [to] inhale the delicious air and talk over their little domestic affairs. The various shaped leaves of the forest all around their village . . . are bespangled with dewdrops. The cocks crow rigorously, and strut and ogle; the kids gambol and leap on the backs of their dams quietly chewing the cud; other goats make believe fighting. Thrifty wives often bake their new clay pots in a fire, made by lighting a heap of grass roots. . . . The beauty of this morning scene of peaceful enjoyment is indescribable. . . .

But there was a dark shadow over this African Eden: often Livingstone found the villages deserted, their inhabitants having fled at his approach, believing his caravan was that of an Arab slaver.

At the end of March, he reached Nyangwe, on the Lualaba, but found his further progress impeded. His porters, fearful of penetrating farther, grew mutinous and made it impossible for him to acquire canoes by telling the local natives that Livingstone was secretly planning to make war. "It is excessively trying," complained Livingstone, "and so many difficulties have been put in my way I doubt whether the Divine favor and will is still on my side."

Nyangwe, like Bambarre, was in cannibal country, and as he waited with mounting impatience for the chance to take to the river, Livingstone commented matter-of-factly on this practice in his journal:

> The men here deny that cannibalism is common: they eat only those killed in war. . . . Some west of the Lualaba eat even those bought for the

purpose of a feast; but I am not quite positive on this point; all agree in saying that human flesh is saltish, and needs but little condiment. And yet they are a fine looking race. . . .

Whatever their dietary preferences, the people of Nyangwe showed no inclination to eat Livingstone, or to harm him in any way, and his sojourn there—though increasingly frustrating—was both comfortable and secure by the fragile norms of African travel.

ON JUNE 23 Stanley's ravaged and depleted caravan reached the village of Kwihara—in effect, a suburb of Tabora, the Arabs' Central African capital. He had made the march in record time, covering 525 miles in 84 days, a trek that had taken Burton and Speke 134 days and Speke and Grant 115 days.

Tabora was by no means the primitive settlement that popular imagination in Europe and America would expect to find in the deep interior of Africa. Estimating that it contained over a thousand houses known as *tembes* sheltering a population of five thousand Arabs and natives, Stanley was moved to exclaim: "On my honor, it was a comfortable place." He went on to describe the setting:

> The plain on which the settlement is situated is exceedingly fertile, though naked of trees; the rich pasturage it furnishes permits them to keep large herds of cattle and goats. . . . Rice is grown everywhere, sweet potatoes, yams, muhogo, holcus sorghum, maize or Indian corn, sesame, millet, field peas, or vetches called chiroko are cheap, and always procurable. Around their tembes the Arabs . . . have planted orange, lemon, pawpaw, and mangoes, which thrive here fairly well. Onions and garlic, chillies, cucumbers, tomatoes and binijalls, may be procured by the white visitor from the more important Arabs, who are undoubted epicureans in their way. The slaves convey to them from the coast once a year, at least, their stores of tea, coffee, sugar, spices, jellies, curries, wine, brandy, biscuits, sardines, salmon and such fine cloths and articles as they require for their own personal use. Almost every Arab of any eminence is able to show a wealth of Persian carpets, and most luxurious bedding, complete tea and coffee services, and magnificently carved dishes of tinned copper and brass lavers. Several of them sported gold watches and chains. . . . And, as in Persia, Afghanistan and Turkey, the harems form an essential feature of every Arab's household. . . .

Stanley had heard news of Livingstone from a number of Arab traders encountered en route. One claimed to have seen him at Ujiji the previous year—"he has a long, white mustache and beard, and was very fat. He was then about going to Marungu and Manyuema [the region of which Nyangwe was the principal town]." The second Arab, whom Stanley encountered five weeks later, confirmed that the *mzungu* (white man) had gone to Manyuema, adding that he had accidentally shot himself in the thigh while out shooting buffalo. A month later, Stanley's third Arab informant told him of a white man known to the natives as "Dochter Fellusteen" near to whom he had lived for three months in Ujiji. He too described Livingstone, curiously, as being very fat and with a long white beard. And a fourth informant brought word to Kwihara that Livingstone was now on his way back to Ujiji from Manyuema.

"Wherever he is," Stanley reported to the *Herald* with a flourish of characteristic bravado, "be sure I shall not give up the chase. If alive, you shall hear what he has to say; if dead I will find and bring his bones to you."

*LIVINGSTONE* was indeed on his way back to Ujiji at this point, broken in spirit and again in failing health after witnessing a terrible and apparently purposeless massacre of innocents at Nyangwe by Arab slavers.

The event climaxed more than three months of mounting frustration during which he had been stranded in Nyangwe, unable to go forward for want of the canoes he needed, unwilling to turn back without testing his now firm conviction that the Lualaba, on whose waters he gazed daily, ran into the upper reaches of the Nile.

He had struck up an uneasy relationship with Dugumbe, a half-caste Arab trader heading a large party with five hundred guns, who had lately arrived in the district intending to open up new areas for the collection of ivory and slaves. Although the Arabs suspected that "Daoud Felasteen," as they called him, was gathering evidence to damn the slave trade in the eyes of the world, they treated him with the respect due to his gray hairs and courage.

Dugumbe promised to get canoes for Livingstone, but like the native Manyuema chieftains who made similar promises, kept finding excuses for not delivering. Everyone, it seemed, including Livingstone's fearful and rebellious Banian porters, preferred for their own reasons to keep him bottled up in Nyangwe if they could not coerce him into turning back. "I am distressed and perplexed what to do so as not to be foiled," Livingstone wrote on July 14, 1871, "but all seems against me."

The following day dawned hot and sultry, and all morning the sound of gunfire from across the river bore evidence that Dugumbe's men were on the rampage. The usually cheerful atmosphere of the Nyangwe market, where natives from miles around came to buy and sell their fruit, vegetables and livestock, was tense and uneasy. With about fifteen hundred people present, the market was less crowded than usual, since, as Livingstone recorded, "many villages of those that usually came from the other side were now in flames."

Then Dugumbe's men appeared on the scene. One group remained by the creek, at one end of the marketplace, while others sauntered into the crowd. Livingstone "felt inclined to reprove them, as one of my men did, for bringing weapons into the market, but I attributed it to their ignorance." He was walking away from the scene when he saw one of the intruders seize a fowl from a protesting market woman.

> Before I had got thirty yards out, the discharge of two guns in the middle of the crowd told me that slaughter had begun: crowds dashed off from the place, and threw down their wares in confusion, and ran. At the same time . . . volleys were discharged from a party down near the creek on the panic-stricken women, who dashed at the canoes. These, some fifty or more, were jammed in the creek, and the men forgot their paddles in the terror that seized all. . . .

To escape the ensuing butchery, scores of natives tried to swim to safety to an island about a mile away. The slavers peppered the long line of bobbing heads, many of whom "disappeared quietly, while other poor creatures threw their arms high, as if appealing to the great Father above, and sank. . . . By and by, all the heads disappeared. . . ."

Livingstone was more deeply affected, perhaps, by the massacre at Nyangwe than by any of the horrors he had witnessed in his years of African exploration. "Oh, let Thy Kingdom come!" he wrote. "No one will ever know the exact loss on this bright sultry summer morning, it gave me the impression of being in Hell!"

Sick at heart over what he had seen, and realizing there was no chance now of acquiring the canoes he needed to trace the course of the Lualaba, Livingstone decided the next day, July 16, to retrace his steps to Ujiji. "I was laid up all yesterday afternoon," he wrote, "with the depression the bloodshed made—it filled me with unspeakable horror. 'Don't go away,' say the Manyuema chiefs to me; but I cannot stay here in agony."

\*     \*     \*

*AT KWIHARA,* as he prepared for the next leg of his journey to Ujiji, Stanley had learned that the way ahead was blocked by conflict between a native king called Mirambo and the Arab traders. Mirambo's territory lay astride the caravan routes to the west, and he had begun levying extortionate duties on all trying to pass. The Arabs, confident that they could easily defeat him, declared war and urged Stanley to join them as an ally.

Feeling he had a common interest in clearing the route to Ujiji as quickly as possible, Stanley agreed. He and the Arabs set out from Tabora with a force of two thousand men, and at first things appeared to be going well.

"On the first day," Stanley reported, "we burned three of his villages, captured, killed or drove away the inhabitants. On the second I was taken down with the ever-remitting fever of the country. On the third a detachment was sent out and audaciously attacked the fenced village where the King was, and after an hour's fighting entered it at one gate while Mirambo left it by another."

But Mirambo's withdrawal was a ruse. With four hundred of his men he lay in wait alongside the route the Arabs must take on their way back to their own camp. As the Arab force, including forty of Stanley's men, passed by they were ambushed, and a terrible slaughter ensued. "Seventeen Arab commanders were slain," Stanley reported to the *Herald* in a dispatch sent to the coast by native runner, "among them one or two personal friends of mine who had travelled with me from the coast. Five of the soldiers of the *Herald* expedition were killed."

The next day, utterly demoralized by their defeat and hearing that Mirambo was heading for their encampment, the Arabs took flight and headed back toward Tabora. Stanley's men—including Shaw, who tried to slip away as his fever-stricken leader lay helpless in his hammock—joined in the general panic. But for the steadfastness and loyalty of Selim, Stanley would have been abandoned to the mercies of Mirambo. Instead of fleeing like the others, the young Palestinian hauled his master to his feet, helped him to dress and, rounding up more help, got Stanley onto his donkey and out of immediate danger.

Despite Stanley's entreaties that they should stand and fight rather than lead Mirambo back to their homes, the Arabs fled headlong for Tabora. There, the governor and other Arab chiefs even considered retreating all the way to the coast, abandoning the entire district to

Mirambo. Whatever they might do, Stanley was determined to stand his ground and, as soon as possible, to push on.

To do otherwise would mean the end of his expedition and, as Stanley must have feared, the end of his career with the *Herald*. He knew the risk he had taken in signing those drafts in Zanzibar, and although Stanley could only have guessed it at this point, Bennett was adamantly refusing to honor them. Accordingly, Stanley hoisted the American flag over his *tembe,* turned the compound into a fortress and, fighting off intermittent bouts of malarial fever, awaited the arrival of Mirambo.

A week later, Mirambo's army attacked Tabora. From his flat roof Stanley could easily see the smoke and flames as the tribal warriors fought their way in, looting and killing, mutilating and burning. With his own men, plus a number of Arab fugitives, totaling 150 armed men altogether, Stanley waited for Mirambo to come his way. "I hope to God he will come," he wrote, "and if he comes within range of an American rifle, I shall see what virtue lies in American lead." But the attack never materialized. After five days, Mirambo and his men melted into the bush, satisfied with their booty from the sack of Tabora.

"After this event," Stanley reported, "I informed the Arabs that I could not assist them any more, for if they ran away once they would run away again, and declared my intention to travel at once to Ujiji by another road. They all advised me to wait until the war was over; that I was going straight to death by travelling during war time. But I was obstinate and they looked on me as a lost man."

Most of Stanley's porters deserted rather than push on, and it was only with considerable difficulty that he was able to hire replacements. He also hired guides who claimed to know an alternative route to Ujiji, taking a long detour to the south to skirt Mirambo's territory. Taking Kirk's small supply caravan for Livingstone under his wing, he stripped his own of all but the barest essentials to ensure a speedy march. As the moment for departure drew near, many of his new recruits lost courage, and their reluctance to risk the dangerous onward journey brought them close to mutiny.

Among them was Shaw, who begged to be left behind. But Stanley would not hear of it. As the only other white man in the party, he insisted, Shaw had to set an example to the blacks.

*WITHIN* a few days of starting his march back to Ujiji, Livingstone again fell victim to the foot ulcers which had immobilized him some months previously. His morale was in scarcely better condition than his feet. Believing his party to be Arab slavers, the local natives fled at his approach, adding to Livingstone's depression. "To a village, ill and almost every step in pain," reads a journal entry dated August 7, 1871. "The people all ran away, and appeared in the distance armed, and refused to come near—then came and threw stones at us, and afterwards tried to kill those who went for water. We sleep uncomfortably, the natives watching us all round. Sent men to see if the way was clear."

The following day, as they were passing through dense forest along a trail so narrow that branches brushed them on both sides, Livingstone's party was ambushed. He was a short distance behind the main body, who were allowed to pass; Livingstone, wearing a distinctive red jacket and mistaken by the tribesmen for a notorious slave-trader named Mohammed Bogharib, was the target, and "a large spear from my right hand [side] lunged past and almost grazed my back."

> The two men from whom it came appeared in an opening in the forest only ten yards off and bolted, one looking back over his shoulder as he ran. As they are expert with the spear I don't know how it missed, except that he was too sure of his aim and the good hand of God was upon me.

A few moments later a second spear missed Livingstone by about a foot. His men opened fire blindly into the forest, but to no effect. They could hear the ambushers jeering and shouting imprecations but could find no target at which to aim. In reply, more spears were thrown from behind the protective wall of vegetation. The party struggled on into a clearing, where Livingstone had his third brush with death that day.

A large tree, growing out of a twenty-foot anthill, had been weakened by a fire set close to its roots, and as Livingstone approached he heard a warning crack and saw the tree falling straight for him. He turned and ran "and down it came to the ground one yard behind me. . . . Had the branches not previously been rotted off, I could scarcely have escaped."

Livingstone took this third narrow escape as a further sign that he was under the protection of God. His party pressed on through the jungle gauntlet for another five hours.

> From each hole in the tangled mass, we looked for a spear; and each moment expected to hear the rustle which told of deadly weapons hurled

at us. I became weary with the constant strain of danger, and—as, I suppose, happens with soldiers on the field of battle—not courageous, but perfectly indifferent whether I was killed or not.

When they at last got out of the forest into cultivated countryside, having lost two men, Livingstone came under the protection of a friendly cannibal chief named Monanbonda, who offered to send a party back into the forest to wreak revenge on Livingstone's attackers, the Moezia tribe. Livingstone replied that the Moezia had mistaken him for the slaver Bogharib, and that he "had no wish to kill men: to join in his old feud would only make matters worse."

Leading Livingstone's party through his bailiwick, Monanbonda pointed out a spot where trampled grass indicated a skirmish had recently been fought. "Here we killed a man of Moezia and ate his body," said Monanbonda. Observed Livingstone, in a diary entry that night: "They seem to eat their foes to inspire courage, or in revenge. It is not want that has led to the custom, for the country is full of food."

Livingstone rested and marched, rested and marched, "very ill with bowels," until he came to Bambarre, from where he had set out for Nyangwe seven months before. He felt he must press on to Ujiji, where he expected supplies from Kirk would be awaiting him and where he could rest and recuperate in comparative security. But he was growing weaker by the day:

> In the latter part of [the march] I felt as if dying on my feet. Almost every step was in pain, the appetite failed, and a little bit of meat caused violent diarrhoea, whilst the mind, sorely depressed, reacted on the body. All the traders were returning successful: I alone had failed. . . .

STANLEY, too, was weak from fever as he prepared to set out from Kwihara. But not too weak to impose a harsh discipline on backsliders among his reluctant party. The first to incur his wrath was his captain of askaris, Bombay, who vanished on the eve of departure. Stanley sent a searcher, who found Bombay "weeping in the arms of his Delilah." Stanley thrashed Bombay and three other "black laggards" with his dog whip "as a gentle intimation that I was not to be baulked."

Then it was the turn of the hapless Shaw, still begging to be allowed to stay behind. Stanley gave him short shrift. "Now, Mr.

Shaw," he said, "I am waiting, sir. Mount your donkey if you cannot walk." Five hundred yards out, Shaw fell from his mount and pleaded to be allowed to turn back. In reply, Stanley called some of his men to put Shaw back onto his donkey, and the caravan moved on.

That night, as they camped a few miles from Kwihara, Stanley had another violent attack of fever, which did not help him to accept with equanimity the next morning's news that twenty of his men had deserted. He dispatched a party of loyal bearers back to Kwihara to look for them and sent Selim to borrow or buy a long slave chain. When most of the deserters had been rounded up and brought back, Stanley displayed the chain and warned that anyone who tried to decamp in future would march all the way to Ujiji with it around his neck.

But even this dire warning did not prevent two more attempted desertions the following night. This time Stanley made good on his promise, "had them tied up and flogged and then adorned their stubborn necks with the chain." With evident satisfaction, Stanley commented in a dispatch to the *Herald* that this was the best method of dealing with deserters and that he would "never travel again in Africa without a good long chain."

The following day, Stanley decided that he had been wrong to force Shaw to make the journey. But it was not compassion that changed his mind. Shaw had again fallen from his donkey, and Stanley had forbidden anyone to go to his help, leaving "the foolish fellow" to lie in the sun for an hour until, "when I coldly asked him if he did not feel rather uncomfortable he sat up and wept like a child."

Telling Shaw that he only imagined himself to be sick, Stanley warned him that "if you return you DIE!" But Shaw begged to be allowed to go back, and Stanley, at last realizing that he would be better off without him, arranged for four porters to carry Shaw back to Kwihara. Before turning in that night, Shaw—his spirits improved by the prospect of leaving his demanding employer—played some tunes on an accordion which Stanley had bought him in Zanzibar.

"Although it was only a miserable ten-dollar affair," wrote Stanley, "I thought the homely tunes evoked from the instrument that night were divine melodies. The last tune played before retiring was 'Home Sweet Home;' and I fancy that before it ended we had mutually softened towards each other."

The next morning, having seen Shaw off and given "a sound flogging" to some more runaways, Stanley drove his men on into an immense forest where, he reported, "the poison of the dead and corrupting vegetation is inhaled into the system with often . . . fatal results." It was a constant theme of Stanley's, and of other explorers of his time, that swamp and jungle vapors were to blame for the malaria—literally, "bad air"—that plagued and often killed them. But though ignorant of its origins, Stanley described malaria's symptoms accurately enough:

> The tongue has a sickly yellow hue, or is colored almost to blackness; even the teeth assume a yellow color and become coated with an offensive matter. [The fever] will rage through the system and lay the sufferer prostrate, quivering with agony. . . . It is succeeded by an unusually severe headache, with excessive pains about the loins and spinal column. . . .

Those were the agonies of the less dangerous, "intermittent" form of the illness. In the most toxic "remittent" form, reported Stanley, "the patient is at once seized with excessive heat, throbbing temples, loins and spinal aches: a raging thirst takes possession of him, and the brain becomes crowded with strange fancies, which sometimes assume most hideous shapes."

Thus plagued, and additionally troubled by rumors of war ahead and by the extortionate demands of the African chiefs through whose territory he passed, Stanley pushed on, keeping his party together by threats, beatings, and the sheer supremacy of his will. "Oh!" he wrote, "the racking anguish of body that a traveller in Africa must undergo! "

A couple of weeks later, the recalcitrance of Stanley's men turned to open mutiny. The caravan came to a halt and, bringing up the rear, Stanley found the guides and porters standing around in groups, talking angrily together, with their loads thrown onto the ground. Reaching his double-barreled shotgun from Selim's shoulder, Stanley advanced. One of the guides, a six-foot-four-inch giant named Asmani, "came on in a sidelong way with a smirking smile on his face, but in his eyes shone the lurid light of murder. . . ."

Asmani's brother Mabruki sneaked to Stanley's rear, "but sweeping the gun sharply round, I planted the muzzle of it at about two feet from his wicked-looking face and ordered him to drop his gun instantly. He let it fall from his hand quickly, and giving him a vigorous poke in the breast with my gun, which sent him reeling away a few feet from me, I faced round to Asmani and ordered him to put his gun down. . . . Never was a man nearer his death than was Asmani in those few moments. I was reluctant to shed his blood . . . but if I did not succeed in cowing this ruffian, authority was at an end. . . ."

But for the intervention of Mabruki, who swept Asmani's gun aside to save him from certain death, the affair would have ended in bloodshed. "Ask the master's pardon, man," urged Mabruki, and Asmani did as he was bidden. The march continued, but not before Stanley had delivered a flogging—not to Asmani, but, "with such vigor that [his] back will long bear traces," to Bombay, whom Stanley blamed for not having anticipated and pre-empted such mutinous behavior.

Although all his energy and resolve were concentrated on reaching Ujiji and Livingstone, Stanley also allowed his thoughts to dwell occasionally on the potential for white settlement of the "unpeopled country"—by no means all desert, forest and swamp—through which he traveled. "What a settlement one could have in this valley!" he wrote enthusiastically at one point:

> See, it is broad enough to support a large population. Fancy a church spire rising where that tamarind rears its dark crown of foliage, and think how well a score or two of pretty cottages would look instead of those thorn clumps and gum trees! Fancy this lovely valley teeming with herds of cattle and fields of corn, spreading to the right and left of this stream! . . . But be hopeful. The day will come . . . when happier lands have become crowded and . . . have no room to turn about. It only needs an Abraham or a Lot, an Alaric or an Attila to lead their hosts to this land which, perhaps, has been wisely reserved for such a time.

*LIVINGSTONE* had been "reduced to a skeleton" by the time he reached Ujiji on October 23. Here, he expected to take possession of supplies, sent up from the coast, which had arrived over a year previously. But to his consternation he found that Shereef, the Arab in charge of the supply caravan, had sold the goods, claiming to have divined through the Koran that Livingstone was dead and would therefore have no need of them. This was too much even for the saintly doctor to bear with Christian composure.

"Shereef was evidently a moral idiot," he wrote in his journal, "for he came without shame to shake hands with me, and when I refused, assumed an air of displeasure, as having been badly treated. . . . I told him that were I an Arab, his hand and both ears would be cut off for thieving, as he knew, and I wanted no salutations from him."

Sick, without medicines, and forced "to wait in beggary," dependent on the grudging charity of the Arabs of Ujiji, Livingstone nursed a growing grievance against Kirk for sending his supplies by such unreliable and corrupt means and hoped against hope that some other form of relief would arrive from the coast. Mercifully, he had not long to wait. "When my spirits were at their lowest ebb," he wrote, "the good Samaritan was close at hand, for one morning Susi came rushing at the top of his speed and gasped out, 'An Englishman! I see him' and off he darted to meet him."

*A WEEK'S MARCH* from Lake Tanganyika, Stanley had received news from a caravan traveling in the opposite direction that a white man had arrived in Ujiji a few days previously from the far side of the inland sea. "He is old," said the natives. "He has white hair on his face, and is sick." Stanley was exultant. That night, he wrote in his diary: "Hurrah! This is Livingstone! He must be Livingstone! He can be no other. . . . But we must now march quick, lest he hears we are coming, and runs away."

Stanley pushed on with all possible haste. To avoid extortionate demands for tribute which would have left him perilously low on essential supplies and trade goods, he abandoned the trail and traveled by night on a parallel path through forest and grassland. On November 10, according to his journal,* he woke in a euphoric mood, conscious that Ujiji lay only a few hours' march away, and dressed as for a momentous occasion, in white flannels and well-oiled boots, with his pith helmet well chalked and a new pugaree folded around it, "so that I might have paraded the streets of Bombay without attracting any great attention."

It was "a happy glorious morning," gushed Stanley, on which "the sky lovingly smiles on the earth and her children. The deep woods are crowned in bright green leafage. We are all . . . looking as spruce, as neat, and happy as when we embarked on the dhows at Zanzibar. . . . I almost vent the feelings of my heart in cries!"

Reaching a mountaintop a few hours later, Stanley had his first view of Lake Tanganyika—"an immense broad sheet, a burnished bed of silver," laid out at his feet—and rejoiced. A couple of hours more and Ujiji lay below "embowered in the palms, only five hundred yards from us! At this grand moment we do not think of the

---

* His dispatch to the *Herald* gives the date as November 3. Constant attacks of fever had played havoc with Stanley's personal calendar.

hundreds of miles we have marched. . . . At last the sublime hour has arrived!"

Stanley's caravan marched down to the sleepy little port firing their guns into the air in announcement of their approach. Arabs and Africans, aroused from their midday torpor, rushed out of their huts and *tembes,* at first fearful that the gunfire signaled a raid by Mirambo's warriors. Those fears were rapidly allayed by the sight of a white man in a pith helmet leading the group, at whose head flew the flags of Zanzibar and the United States. Gleefully, the inhabitants of Ujiji flocked to surround and greet the newcomers to a cacophony of horns and drums.

One man elbowed his way through the excited crowd to address Stanley in English: "Good morning, sir!" "Who the mischief are you?" asked Stanley. It was Susi, who dashed off to tell his master of Stanley's arrival.

Within minutes, Livingstone was hobbling from his *tembe,* overlooking the town square, to greet Stanley's caravan. Selim saw him coming. "Oh, what an old man!" he exclaimed. "He has got a white beard." Stanley made an enormous effort to suppress his feelings.

> What would I not have given for a bit of friendly wilderness where, unseen, I might vent my joy in some mad freak, such as idiotically biting my hand, turning a somersault, or slashing at trees. . . . My heart beats fast, but I must not let my face betray my emotions, lest it shall detract from the dignity of a white man appearing under such extraordinary circumstances.

So, maintaining an appearance of perfect sang-froid, Stanley walked down the living avenue of people who crowded in from each side, to where Livingstone stood in front of a semicircle of Arab dignitaries. Then, raising his hat, he uttered the greeting that would bring him undying fame and an almost equal measure of ridicule.

"*DR. LIVINGSTONE,* I presume?" The phrase was to haunt Stanley for the rest of his life and define him after his death for millions who might otherwise never have heard of him. Even in his own time it seemed either a display of absurdly overdone stiff-upper-lippery, or else an attempt by a loud Yankee to ape the manner of an English gentleman.

Music-hall comedians soon learned that as a catch phrase it was good for an easy laugh. Errand boys would sing it out to each other as their paths crossed. With ponderous waggishness, suburban Milquetoasts would intone it when they met while out walking the dog. Twenty years later, when Stanley was receiving an honorary doctorate at Oxford, an irreverent student would mar the solemnity of the occasion by calling out "Dr. Stanley, I presume." In a later era it would be a boon to flippant headline writers, while it would also seem somehow sophisticated to use Stanley's unfortunate greeting as the title of a jazz composition, a cocktail, a fashion boutique, a discotheque.

Poor Stanley. It dawned on him soon enough that in the moment of his greatest triumph he had bared his throat to the knife of derision. Having reported his own words in a dispatch to the *Herald* that was already on its way back to the coast, he could not disown them. Instead, he sought to explain himself in subsequent accounts.

His first report of his meeting with Livingstone, in a dispatch dated November 10, 1871, reflected the prevailing psychology of racial superiority, pure and simple:

*The memorable meeting at Ujiji: Stanley "couldn't
think of what else to say."*
(How I Found Livingstone, 1873)

It was the dignity that a white man and leader of an expedition ought to possess that prevented me from running to shake hands with the venerable traveller; but when I caught sight of him . . . so far away from civilization, it was very tempting. False pride and the presence of the grave-looking Arab dignitaries* of Ujiji restrained me. . . .

In a subsequent dispatch, dated December 26, Stanley's crippling sense of social inferiority, and the recollection of past snubs delivered by monocled Englishmen—compounded by Kirk's warning that Livingstone did not like the company of strangers—appear to have been the determinants:

> . . . I looked upon Livingstone as an Englishman, and I feared that if I showed any unusual joy at meeting with him he might conduct himself very much like another Englishman did once whom I met in the interior of another foreign and strange land wherein we were the only two English-speaking people to be found within the area of two hundred miles square, and who, upon my greeting him with a cordial "Good morning," would not answer me, but screwed on a large eye glass in a manner which must have been as painful to him as it was to me, and then deliberately viewed my horse and myself for the space of about thirty seconds, and passed on his way with as much insouciance as if he had seen me a thousand times and there was nothing at all in the meeting to justify him coming out of that shell of imperturbability with which he had covered himself.

By the time he got around to writing his book *How I Found Livingstone*, in 1872, Stanley added the rather appealing—and surely authentic—detail of his secretly wishing to "vent my joy in some mad freak" at the sight of Livingstone, and appended a footnote citing an incident from Alexander Kinglake's *Eothen* in which two English travelers encountering one other in the Arabian desert merely touch their hats "as if we had passed in Bond Street."

But when Stanley began putting together his autobiography in the mid-1890s, neither racial superiority nor social inferiority figured in his explanation. Instead, he tried to suggest he was not certain that the man he addressed on that famous day in Ujiji was Livingstone at all:

* Burton, for one, felt that if Stanley believed his reserve would impress the Arab onlookers he was hopelessly misguided. "Had the travellers fallen upon one another's bosoms and embraced, they would have acted like Arabs from the days of Esau and Jacob till A.D. 1873," Burton commented. "Far from impressing Arabs with a sense of dignity [his demeanor] would only draw forth some such comment (to put it in a complimentary form) as "Wallah! What manner of greeting is this!"

Up to this moment my mind had verged upon non-belief in his existence, and now a nagging doubt intruded itself into my mind that this
white man could not be the subject of my quest. . . . Consequently . . .
when the moment of discovery came, and the man himself stood revealed
before me, this constantly recurring doubt contributed not a little to
make me unprepared for it. . . . Under all these circumstances I could do
no more than exercise some restraint and reserve. . . .

Toward the end of his life, when "Dr. Livingstone, I presume" had
passed into the common culture, and Stanley himself had passed into
legend, there were those who wondered whether he really had uttered the phrase. A young curate named Tovey who came to tea
when the prematurely aged Sir Henry Stanley was living in Surrey,
dared to put the question to him: "You didn't really say it, did you?"
    Stanley fixed the clergyman with his disconcertingly steady gaze
and remained silent for what seemed like minutes. Finally, he answered.
    "Yes," he said. "I couldn't think what else to say."

# Chapter Nine

UNTIL he met Livingstone, Stanley was essentially a reporter—more ruthless and driven, perhaps, than most—on the trail of a scoop; the unlovable in pursuit of the unreadable, as his contemporary Oscar Wilde might have said. But once he encountered the formidable doctor, he began to undergo a change.

Stanley had steeled himself for a hostile or at best cool reception, and had intended to snatch his interview and head back for the coast, with or without his quarry, as quickly as he decently could. The adventurer who had faced the hazards and hardships of the trail so fearlessly had been terrified of a rebuff. But Livingstone received him with such unaffected warmth and lack of pretension that, almost from the moment they began to talk on the verandah of his *tembe*, Stanley fell under his spell and, complete professional though he was, even found himself "too much engrossed to take my note-book out."

It was not simply that Livingstone was pleased to see another white man after more than five and a half years, and to have the sorely needed supplies he brought with him. He also appeared to value his providential visitor for his own sake. He insisted on hearing Stanley's news of the outside world before diving into the bag of mail from family and friends which the younger man had delivered to him.

"There we sat, the man, the myth, and I," as Stanley would say after his return from Africa, and Livingstone listened while Stanley sketched in the events of the past few years—the opening of the Suez Canal, the fall of the Second Empire, the election of Grant, the revolution in Spain. In return, Livingstone began telling the story of his own epic wanderings far deeper into the interior of Africa than any white man had gone before. "The man's heart was gushing out," wrote Stanley, "not in hurried sentences, in rapid utterances, in quick relations—but in still and deep words."

They broke off for a meal prepared jointly by their respective cooks, and Stanley remembered that he had brought with him a bottle of Sillery champagne to celebrate the occasion. He sent for it and, without a trace of the sanctimoniousness that might have been expected from a missionary, Livingstone drank "a silver goblet full of the exhilarating wine" as they toasted each other.

Over and over, Livingstone repeated: "You have brought me new life. You have brought me new life." Stanley was captivated. In the bowed but rugged older man, he perceived none of the faults that Kirk had mentioned. The consul "must have been a sad student of human nature or a most malicious person," Stanley commented in a dispatch to the *Herald*. And in a later judgment, based on four months in Livingstone's company, in camp and on the march, he wrote:

> I grant he is not an angel, but he approaches to that being as near as the nature of a living man will allow. I never saw any spleen or misanthropy in him. . . . He is sensitive, I know; but so is any man of a high mind and generous nature. . . . His gentleness never forsakes him; his hopefulness never deserts him. . . . Whenever he began to laugh, there was a contagion about it, that compelled me to imitate him. . . .

If Livingstone's love of laughter was unexpected ("Underneath that well-worn exterior lay an endless fund of high spirits and inexhaustible humour."), Stanley also found Kirk's assertion that he was deficient as a geographer, taking no notes and making no detailed observations, to be quite untrue. Livingstone kept a big diary containing twenty pages of observations which he had taken on his trip to Manyuema, and "in the middle of the book there is sheet after sheet, column after column, carefully written, of figures alone." Also, Stanley recorded admiringly, "During the four months I was with him, I noticed him every evening making careful notes; and a large tin box that he has with him contains numbers of field notebooks. . . . His maps also evince great care and industry."

Stanley was equally impressed by Livingstone's "wonderfully retentive memory," noting that he could recite entire poems by Byron, Burns, Tennyson, Longfellow, Whittier and Lowell. But, above all, he was impressed by the man's unostentatious, practical Christianity.

> His religion is not of the theoretical mind, but it is a constant, earnest, sincere practice. It is neither demonstrative nor loud, but manifests itself in a quiet, practical way, and is always at work. . . . In him, religion exhibits its loveliest features; it governs his conduct not only towards his servants, but towards the natives, the bigoted Mohammedans, and all who come in contact with him.

Stanley's reportage and reminiscence frequently drip with a treacly religiosity, but in writing of Livingstone's spiritual qualities he seems sincere and unaffected. And in tracing the sequence of events that had led him from a hotel room in Paris to the *tembe* in Ujiji, he claimed to see "the hand of an overruling and kindly Providence."

Viewed in this light, the profane Bennett becomes the unlikely instrument of God's will, for had he sent Stanley straight to Africa in 1869, instead of via the Levant and India, Stanley would most likely never have found Livingstone. By this reasoning, even the "black Napoleon," Mirambo, and the "cowardly and bigoted Mohammedans" at Tabora were agents of the Christian God, for had they not been at war, delaying Stanley three months, the two white men would almost certainly have failed to connect. That they should have converged on Ujiji within a few days of each other, Stanley felt, was surely more than coincidence.

On their first meeting, he did not reveal to Livingstone that he was a newspaperman, and Livingstone failed to enquire what had brought him to Ujiji. Only on their second day together did Stanley find the courage to admit that he was a special correspondent of the New York *Herald* and ask, with some trepidation, whether Livingstone had heard of that publication. He had, indeed. Remote though his concerns were from such matters, Livingstone was well enough informed to blurt out: "Oh—who has not heard of that despicable newspaper?"*

But his disdain for the *Herald* did not extend to its special correspondent. As a good Christian, Livingstone hated the sin but loved the sinner; Stanley's presence was no less welcome than before, and the following day Livingstone wrote a personal letter of gratitude to Bennett for having sent him.

Within a few days, Stanley had committed the story of Livingstone's "wonderful travels" to his notebook and, had he been the man he was before, would promptly have been on his way back to the coast with his scoop. But he could not bear to part from Livingstone so soon. It requires no great insight to see that in him Stanley had found the father he never had, and Livingstone seems to have reciprocated the feeling. "I am very happy, you have brought me my child," he told Uledi, one of Stanley's Zanzibari stalwarts. And in a letter to a friend, Livingstone would describe Stanley's behavior to-

---

* Stanley recorded Livingstone's use of the word "despicable" in his diary, but in his published account of the conversation, he tactfully deleted the adjective.

ward him as that of "a son to a father—truly overflowing in kindness."

On his side, Stanley found Livingstone to be "benevolently paternal . . . almost tender, though I don't know much about tenderness." Basking in the sun of such benevolence, Stanley added, "I have come to entertain an immense respect for myself and begin to think myself somebody, though I never suspected it before. . . . I get as proud as can be, as though I had some great honor thrust on me."

No doubt to delay the moment of parting, Stanley suggested to Livingstone that they now explore Lake Tanganyika together. Nothing could have been more pleasing to a father's heart. In his determination to find out whether the Nile originated in Lake Tanganyika, Livingstone needed to establish whether the Ruzizi River, at the northern end of the lake, flowed into or out of it. And now this splendid young man whom God had sent to succor him was suggesting a side expedition to find the answer.

No more than a week after Stanley's arrival in Ujiji, then, they set off by canoe with twenty men. Livingstone was in good form. The nourishing fresh food Stanley was able to purchase from the locals, the medicines he brought with him, and the tonic provided by his company had enabled the doctor to make a remarkable recovery. As for Stanley, he even welcomed the attack of fever that felled him a few days out, "since I became the recipient of the very tender and fatherly kindness of the good man whose companion I now found myself."

A few days after that they reached the head of the lake and, confirming that the Ruzizi River flowed into and not out of it, finally scotched the notion that Tanganyika was the reservoir from which sprang the mighty Nile. Back in Ujiji, after a twenty-eight-day, three-hundred-mile round trip that Livingstone described as "a picnic," they allowed themselves two weeks to rest, write up their diaries, letters and dispatches, and prepare for the trek back to Tabora. There they were to part company, Stanley for the coast with his dispatches and Livingstone to gather his strength and resources for a return to the Lualaba.

They left for Tabora on December 27. And because the war between the Arabs and Mirambo continued to keep the direct route closed, Stanley decided, with Livingstone's concurrence, to travel south by lake to Urimba, about eighty miles as the crow flies, before marching east and then north to their destination. They set out in two canoes—Stanley's flying the Stars and Stripes and Livingstone's the Union Jack—while a land party under Asmani and Bombay carried their heavy goods along the shoreline.

On the difficult, fifty-three-day overland stage of the journey from Urimba, Stanley suffered grievously from recurrent fevers, while Livingstone was in agony with his ulcerated feet. To make matters worse it was the season of heavy rains, which made the going arduous. But despite his malaria and the hardships of the march, the luxuriant growth of the Ukawendi forest through which they passed—and no doubt the continuing joy he found in Livingstone's company—moved Stanley to raptures of descriptive writing:

> Beautiful, bewitching Ukawendi! By what shall I gauge the loveliness of the wild, free, luxuriant, spontaneous nature within its boundaries? . . . In Ukawendi you can almost behold the growth of vegetation; the earth is so generous, nature so kind and loving, that . . . one feels insensibly drawn towards it. . . . Even while staggering under the pressure of the awful sickness, with mind getting more and more embittered, brain sometimes reeling with the shock of the constantly recurring fevers . . . I regarded the alluring face of the land with a fatuous love. . . .

But Stanley's guides could not find their way through this dangerously seductive sylvan paradise. Food ran low, game was scarce, and the porters were growing exhausted. Stanley resolved to lead them out of the jungle by chart and compass alone, ignoring the protests of his men that he was heading in the wrong direction:

> No sun shone upon us as we threaded our way through the primeval forest, by clumps of jungle, across streams, up steep ridges, and down into deep valleys. A thick haze covered the forests; rain often pelted us; the firmament was an unfathomable depth of grey vapor. The Doctor had perfect confidence in me, and I held on my way.

Alternating threats with cajolery, Stanley dragged his reluctant guides and porters behind him day after day, putting on an appearance of confidence he did not fully feel. As he observed, to appear at all doubtful would be dangerous, if not suicidal, "and though they demurred in plaintive terms and with pinched faces, they followed my footsteps with a trustfulness which quite affected me." At their lowest point in the forest, when it seemed that they might all perish, Stanley carved his initials on a tree together with Livingstone's, as if fashioning a joint memorial.

But at last they were clear and, in the plains, they were able to replenish their food supplies with grain, fruit and vegetables purchased from native villages and game shot by Stanley. Livingstone's feet were blistered and bleeding; Stanley was feverish. But after a brief rest they pushed on, at one point running into a fresh hazard—a swarm of wild bees. Stanley was not badly hurt, but Livingstone was "stung dreadfully in the head and in the face; the bees had settled in handfuls in his hair."

Halfway to Tabora they encountered a caravan traveling in the opposite direction and learned of the death of Shaw at Kwihara a month after Stanley had sent him back. "Ah, Doctor," said Stanley, "there are two of us gone. I shall be the third, if this fever lasts much longer." Livingstone replied that if Stanley was going to die of fever he would have done so at Ujiji, when he had had a severe attack of remittent, the most serious form. "Don't think of it," he urged. "Your fever now is only the result of exposure to wet."

To cheer him further, he reminded Stanley of all the good things awaiting them in Tabora—"jellies and crackers, soups, fish and potted ham, besides cheese"—and, joining in this food fantasy, Stanley "pictured myself devouring the hams and crackers and jellies like a madman. I lived on my raving fancies."

Conversation between Stanley and Livingstone turned often to the subject of death. Livingstone said he could never pass through an African forest without wishing to be "buried under the dead leaves, where he would be sure to rest undisturbed." Ever since he had buried his wife in the woods of Shupanga, in Southern Africa, he had "sighed for just such a spot, where his weary bones would receive the eternal rest they coveted."

Livingstone also spoke wistfully of the death of his son Robert in the American Civil War. Under the assumed name of Rupert Vincent, the young man had enlisted in the Union army and had died in battle before Richmond, Virginia. The fact that Stanley had also served and suffered in the Civil War forged an extra bond between him and Livingstone.

As they neared Tabora, they received their first intimations of the world beyond their enclosed universe. While they were in camp at a village four days' march from the Arab capital, two couriers, whom Stanley had sent to Zanzibar some months before with a dispatch for the *Herald*, turned up with a bag full of mail and newspapers. The first letter Stanley opened contained a rude shock. It was from Webb, the United States consul in Zanzibar, complaining that Bennett had disclaimed responsibility for the expedition and was refusing to honor Stanley's draft. Stanley was thunderstruck. Ruin and dismissal stared him in the face. "There was not a doubt of it! Bennett was about to treat me as I had heard he had treated others of his unfortunate correspondents."

He felt so despondent that for a while he could not bring himself to open the rest of his mail. When he finally did so, he found a later letter from the *Herald* superseding the first. Bennett would, after all, honor his debts. Stanley's relief can be imagined. As for Livingstone, he had been so immersed in his letters from home that he never noticed his companion's passing anguish.

After reading the rest of his mail, Stanley turned to the newspapers. In them he read of the merciless slaughter of men, women, and children that had accompanied the suppression of the Paris Commune by the French army. "Oh, France! Oh, Frenchmen!" commented Stanley. "Such things are unknown even in the heart of barbarous Central Africa." For light relief, he and Livingstone turned to "the innocent pages of 'Punch.' " "Good-hearted, kindly-natured 'Punch!' " Stanley gushed, "a traveller's benison on thee! Thy jokes were as physic; thy innocent satire was provocative of hysteric mirth."

Four days later, February 18, they marched into Kwihara, flags flying and guns firing. Stanley led Livingstone by the arm to his old *tembe* and said: "Doctor, we are at last at HOME!"

The trek from Urimba had if anything increased Stanley's admiration for his traveling companion. "Livingstone, with all his frankness, does not unfold himself at once," he noted, and "had I left him at Ujiji, I should have lost the chance of viewing him on the march, and obtaining that more detailed knowledge I have."

True, along with his deepening understanding of Livingstone, had come the suspicion "that he was not of such an angelic temper as I believed him to be during my first month with him." Nevertheless, Stanley had become "steeped in Livingstonian ideas upon everything that is African," and in the older man's company he curbed his own explosive temper, either in emulation of the doctor's example or in fear of his disapproval. His diaries contain no more accounts of chaining deserters and flogging recalcitrants, and more than once a disapproving look from Livingstone was enough to stop him from opening fire on natives who seemed about to turn belligerent.

Stanley frequently urged Livingstone to return with him to civilization, but the older man stubbornly insisted on continuing his mission. Before they parted company, he gave Stanley a large box containing his journals and letters for delivery in London. In return Stanley made over to Livingstone 697 lengths of cloth, totaling 2,788 yards, 992 pounds of beads, and 350 pounds of copper wire for barter or for hongo (tribute), plus clothing, tools, medicines, rifles and some 4,000 rounds of ammunition. Added to the belated supplies from Kirk, which had been awaiting him in Tabora, Livingstone now had enough by Stanley's reckoning to keep himself and fifty porters—whom Stanley undertook to recruit and send back from the coast—going for four years.

Just the same, he found it necessary to reassure himself of Livingstone's fitness to continue his wanderings across Africa.

"Though now going on sixty years of age," he wrote, "he looks but forty-five or fifty—quite hale and hearty. He has an enormous appetite, which has abated nothing of its powers since I have known him. He is in need of no rest . . . he is now fleshy and stoutish, and must weigh about one hundred and eighty pounds. . . . I have not the slightest fears about his health or of any danger coming to him from the natives."

For his part, Livingstone tried to persuade Stanley to go with him to the Lualaba, a remarkable concession from a man who was egocentrically loath to share his discoveries with others. But Stanley knew that he must march to a different drummer, one named Bennett. As the moment of parting drew near, he became ever more emotional. On March 13, the night before his departure, he confided to his diary that "the regret I feel now is greater than any pains I have endured. . . . I sobbed, as one only can in uncommon grief. . . ." Equally affected, Livingstone tried to put off the moment of parting. "Had you not better stop until after the rains, which are now nearly over?" he asked. But Stanley steeled himself and demurred.

The next morning, Livingstone accompanied him as far as the crest of a ridge, a few miles from Kwihara. As they marched side by side, Stanley "took long looks at Livingstone, to impress his features thoroughly on my memory." And Livingstone wept as they said their farewells, belying his self-description, in his letter of thanks to Bennett, as a man "as cold and non-demonstrative as we islanders are usually reputed to be." As Stanley recalled: "We wrung each other's hands, our faces flushed with emotion, tears rushing up and blinding the eyes."

Then, setting aside such sentimental self-indulgence, Stanley turned his face to the east and barked out an order to his men:

'MARCH! Why do you stop? Go on! Are you not going home?' And my people were driven before me. No more weakness. I shall show them such marching as will make them remember me. In forty days I shall do what took me three months to perform before.

In the event, they reached Bagamoyo not in forty but in thirty-five days.

# Chapter Ten

*E*VEN before he reached the coast, Stanley had a foretaste of what was awaiting him on his return to civilization. Acclaim, yes, but also skepticism, spite, jealousy and ridicule. For the brooding and hypersensitive Stanley, it would often seem that the slurs outweighed the plaudits.

On May 2, four days' march from Bagamoyo, three of his men who had gone on ahead with letters and dispatches met him on their way back from Zanzibar with "a few bottles of champagne, a few pots of jam and two boxes of Boston crackers," sent by the American consul, Webb.

Webb also sent four copies of the *Herald*, one of which, dated December 22, 1871, contained Stanley's first dispatch, sent from Tabora five and a half months previously. As well, there were clippings from other American newspapers, and to his rising anger Stanley gathered from these that "many editors regard the expedition into Africa as a myth." One paper, published in Tennessee, indulged in "humorous banter" at his expense and ended: "We need never expect to hear from that *Herald* commissioner again. He'll get into some other big Makata swamp, and go the way of his hapless dog, Omar."

Stanley was outraged: "While I was travelling in Africa, upon an errand that I supposed, in my innocence, would have commended itself to most Christians, there were people praying for my failure. . . . The sentiment embodied in the above extract proves to me what I may expect when I reach home. . . ."

He did not have to wait that long.

At sunset on May 6, when Stanley and his party entered Bagamoyo, firing off their guns and shouting hurrahs, Stanley was surprised to encounter a young British naval officer, Lieutenant William Henn, who belonged to an expedition that had been belatedly organized by the Royal Geographical Society to find and relieve Livingstone.

With the extraordinary complacency that seems to afflict Britain's most venerable institutions down the ages, the society had managed to remain unperturbed about Livingstone's fate until the end of 1871. For this complacency, Kirk, the British consul in Zanzibar, was at least partly to blame. He had assured the society that supplies were reaching Livingstone, and as Sir Henry Rawlinson, president of the RGS after the death of Murchison, would put it: "We never doubted of [Livingstone's] well-being . . . since continuous native reports of his wanderings in Manyuema were transmitted to us by Dr. Kirk."

However, public agitation and the awful suspicion that a reporter from that "damned Yankee scandal-sheet" might shame them by getting to Livingstone first, eventually spurred the RGS into action. Five hundred pounds was obtained from the Foreign Office and another four thousand raised by hastily organized public subscription, while two adventurous naval officers and a missionary were selected to organize and lead a relief column from Zanzibar. They were at Bagamoyo, and waiting for monsoon floods in the coastal plain to subside before leaving for the interior, when word reached them via Stanley's messengers that Livingstone had already been relieved.

They were not pleased. By the time Stanley himself turned up at Bagamoyo, the leader of the RGS expedition, Lieutenant Lewellyn Dawson, had gone back to Zanzibar and resigned in a huff. Henn, his second-in-command, had remained in Bagamoyo to wait for Stanley and ascertain Livingstone's material needs, if any. And though he now welcomed Stanley warmly enough—offering him a drink of beer and congratulating him on "your splendid success"—he, too, clearly nursed some resentment. This was not lost on Stanley. "Splendid success!" he exploded. "Is that the view they take of it?"

With Henn at Bagamoyo was Livingstone's second son, Oswell. He expressed determination to press on to Tabora to meet his father, although he would later beg off, claiming poor health. But Henn did not even make a show of willingness to continue after Stanley told him that Livingstone needed "nothing more than a few canned meats."

"You have taken the wind out of our sails completely," he told Stanley in deciding to return to Zanzibar and, following Dawson's example, relinquish his mission.

Meanwhile, news of Stanley's arrival at Bagamoyo had reached Zanzibar, so that when he sailed in the next day, with the Stars and Stripes flying at the mast of his dhow, the roofs and wharves overlooking the harbor were crowded with spectators. He appeared "fearfully" worn, said an eyewitness. "His hair was quite grey. His body was wasted and emaciated, and he looked more like a man of forty-five than twenty-six [sic]."

Webb was the first to greet him as he stepped ashore, but Kirk was conspicuously absent. The British consul was brooding over a letter from Livingstone—sent on ahead by Stanley's messengers—which took him coldly to task for having entrusted his vital supply caravans to slaves and "moral idiots" like Shereef.

Kirk was particularly hurt at having been addressed by Livingstone as "Sir," instead of "My dear Kirk," as of yore. As he would make quite clear, he was convinced that Stanley had turned Livingstone against him. He studiously avoided mentioning the matter when he called to congratulate Stanley at the U.S. consulate the next day. But a couple of weeks later, when Stanley, about to leave for home, asked Kirk's help in embarking the fifty porters he had recruited for Livingstone, the British consul refused. "I am not going to expose myself to needless insult again," he said. "I am not going to do anything more for Dr. Livingstone in a private capacity."

While in Zanzibar, Stanley also received the somewhat stiff congratulations of Lieutenant Dawson, and here too there was an undercurrent of mutual hostility. Dawson was obviously worried about how his precipitate decision to abandon his mission would be received at home. Oddly, he sought reassurance from Stanley, asking him repeatedly if he thought he had done the right thing. Stanley told him bluntly that he had indeed been "rather too hasty," even though it was true that Livingstone no longer needed relief.

As they talked, it transpired that the office-holders of the RGS had given Dawson no instructions about what to do if his expedition met Stanley on the march. Stanley grew indignant, all his feelings of inferiority flaring up. "Why did they not mention my name?" he demanded. "They knew that I was in the country and no matter how poor a traveller I may have been, it was a contingency that might arise." In reply, Dawson blurted out: "The truth is, they didn't want you to find him. You cannot imagine how jealous they are at home about this Expedition of yours."

Dawson evidently shared their jealousy, choosing to return to England on an American freighter via the Cape rather than travel with Stanley and his erstwhile companions. "Though I do not grudge Mr. Stanley his well-earned success," said Dawson in a letter to the RGS, "it would be distasteful to me, if not to both of us, to travel in company."

*STANLEY* returned to Europe via the Seychelles, Bombay, Aden and the Suez Canal, bringing with him his gun-bearer Kalulu, an African slave boy who had been presented to him by an Arab merchant in Tabora and whom he informally adopted. Selim, Stanley's loyal Palestinian translator, also traveled with his master as far as Egypt, before breaking off to return home to Jerusalem. He scarcely returned rich: Stanley had paid him a mere one pound, or five dollars, a month—a pittance even by the standards of the time.

At Aden, Stanley found a cable awaiting him from Bennett, via the new head of the *Herald*'s London bureau, George Hosmer: YOU ARE NOW FAMOUS AS LIVINGSTONE HAVING DISCOVERED THE DISCOVERER. ACCEPT MY THANKS, AND WHOLE WORLD. Hosmer added on his own account [the] ASSURANCE [of a] FELLOW CORRESPONDENT THAT MORE SPLENDID ACHIEVEMENT, ENERGETIC DEVOTION AND GENEROUS GALLANTRY NOT IN HISTORY HUMAN ENDEAVOUR. But already, on both sides of the Atlantic, the knives, as well as the "welcome back" bunting, were out for the returning hero.

The Royal Geographical Society and a significant section of the British press could not, or would not, bring themselves to believe the truth of Stanley's claims. In his first presidential address to the RGS in May, Rawlinson had delivered himself on the subject in tones which for silky spitefulness would be hard to match:

> There is one point on which a little *éclaircissement* is desirable, because a belief seems to prevail that Mr. Stanley has discovered and relieved Dr. Livingstone; whereas, without any disparagement to Mr. Stanley's energy, activity and loyalty, if there has been any discovery and relief it is Dr. Livingstone who has discovered and relieved Mr. Stanley. Dr. Livingstone, indeed, is in clover while Mr. Stanley is nearly destitute. . . .

The hostility of the British Establishment was heightened by what it considered to be the spiteful tone of Stanley's complaints against Kirk. The consul had friends and relatives in high places, and even those who did not know him felt that Stanley's allegations somehow constituted an American attack on the British professional and upper classes as a whole. They closed ranks in defense of their own.

In New York, Bennett—while relishing the notoriety all this was giving the *Herald*—felt that it was time to cool things off and cabled Stanley an instruction to "stop talking." But far from holding his tongue, Stanley gave it even freer rein. In Paris, at a dinner given in his honor by the American ambassador, he accused Kirk of a good deal more than complacency and incompetence. Made reckless, perhaps, by French newspaper comments comparing his feat with Hannibal's march on Rome, Napoleon's crossing of the Alps and Sherman's march from Atlanta to the sea—and perhaps a little tipsy as a consequence of the wine he had consumed at dinner—Stanley declared: "I have a mission from Dr. Livingstone to describe Kirk as a traitor."

He awoke on the morning after to the realization that he had gone too far. "I must endeavour to restrain myself," he wrote in his diary, "for though I do think Kirk has behaved abominably . . . it does not do to run a-tilt at anybody in a mixed assemblage of this kind."

Later that day, he took the boat train to London and was appalled to find, waiting to greet him on the dock at Dover, his half-brother, Robert, and his uncle Moses, both of them well oiled. "What a welcome!" he exploded. "Had these stupid newspapers not mentioned my [real] name, the vanity of my poor relations would not have been kindled. . . . I never felt so ashamed, and would have given all I was worth to have been back in Central Africa."

The embarrassment of the moment was soon forgotten when he reached London, where he found interest in his exploit at fever pitch. "I have seldom if ever, known anything create so widespread and intense an interest throughout the country," a friend wrote to Livingstone.

The interest was of a mixed kind, though. Stanley found invitations to dine and to lecture piled up waiting for him at the London bureau of the *Herald*. But a section of the press was against him, and in some cases cruelly so. The *Spectator* found "something of the comic" in contemplation of "the newspaper correspondent who, in the regular exercise of his profession, moved neither by pity, nor love of knowledge, nor by desire of adventure, but by an order from Mr. Bennett, coolly plunges into the unknown continent to interview a lost geographer."

Some newspapers and periodicals even implied that the letters of Livingstone's which Stanley had brought out from the interior were forgeries. That slur was quickly disposed of, the Foreign Office vouching for the letters' authenticity and Livingstone's eldest son, Tom, confirming that the diary handed over to the family by Stanley was also genuine.

But even that did not deter the more malicious of Stanley's critics, who now floated the rumor that he had appropriated Livingstone's letters and diaries from a messenger he encountered on the march. According to this slanderous suggestion, Stanley never actually met Livingstone but, with the letters in his possession, turned back and concocted the story of their meeting. And, all the more wounding for being the truth, reports circulated that the supposedly American Stanley was in reality a bastard Welshman named Rowlands. Stanley's anger and bitterness need not be left to the imagination. To a letter from a sympathizer he responded:

First they would sneer at the fact of an American having gone to Central Africa, then they sneered at the idea of his being successful—then when they heard my name they tried to rob me of it—in one paper I was Smith, in another I was Jones, in another Thomas, and now they have changed it to Rowlands. . . . [A]fter decently burying Livingstone in forgetfulness they hate to be told he is yet alive. What a country!

While the controversy raged, the RGS studiously ignored Stanley's very presence in England. Rawlinson, having taken the precaution of leaving London for the country shortly after Stanley's arrival, refused to call a special meeting of the society to hear a report from him. But in the face of insistent public demands that Stanley be given a hearing, Rawlinson authorized a statement suggesting that, since the RGS did not hold public functions during the summer, Stanley might address the geographical section of the British Association, which would shortly hold its annual conference in Brighton.

*Punch*, one of Stanley's supporters among the daily and periodical press of London, had some fun with this: "The President of the Royal Geographical Society, who discovered that Livingstone discovered Stanley and not Stanley Livingstone, has at last discovered that Stanley is in England. This is not a bad discovery. It seems, however, to have been accomplished only after a severe effort."

How severe may be judged from the stiff tone of a belated letter from Rawlinson to Stanley, offering "our best thanks for the transmission of direct intelligence from Dr. Livingstone" and "our most cordial acknowledgements for the timely succour rendered" to him.

Stanley's appearance before the British Association in Brighton drew an overflow crowd of distinguished guests, including the exiled French Emperor, Napoleon III, and his Empress, Eugénie, to whom Stanley bowed as he was accompanied to the dais by Rawlinson. Somewhat overawed by the size and status of his audience, Stanley tried to read from a prepared text that dealt, in suitably dry language, with his and Livingstone's joint exploration of the northern end of Lake Tanganyika. After several false starts he gave up the attempt and instead delivered a theatrically extempore account of his discovery of Livingstone.

"I consider myself in the light of a troubadour, to relate to you the tale of an old man who is tramping onwards to discover the source of the Nile," he began. Neither in content nor in style was this the kind of thing the learned geographers wished to hear, and when he had finished the president of the association's geographical section, Francis Galton, acknowledged Stanley's efforts by commenting that "we don't want sensational stories, we want facts."

Galton proved himself even more hostile and insensitive during the question period by calling on Stanley to answer the rumors which

*Stanley with Kalulu and Selim: He returned from the wilds to a different kind of jungle.*
(Courtesy of Mrs. Richard Stanley)

had been circulating about his origins. Was it true, for example, that he was Welsh and not American? Stanley angrily scorned to answer, saying that such a question "could only proceed from idle curiosity." Later he noted in his diary that "a person like myself, with such a miserable, unfortunate past, cannot possibly find pleasure in speaking before people who have wined and eaten to the full about his poverty-stricken childhood."

Brighton was to provide further humiliation. The following evening Stanley was invited to a formal dinner given by the Sussex Medical Society. He was evidently in a state of high tension—possibly he drank too much, to steady his nerves—and almost gabbled as he responded to a toast to "the health of the visitors." Some of the doctors close to the top table began to smirk and exchange whispered remarks as he described his meeting with Livingstone. In outraged reaction, Stanley stopped in midflight, drew a sovereign from his pocket and threw it down on the table before bowing curtly to the chairman and stalking out.

Stanley's understandable bitterness at the skepticism and scorn he seemed everywhere to encounter spilled over onto the pages of the book describing his expedition which, with prodigious energy, he was now close to finishing. Addressing the "gentlemen geographers," he raged rhetorically: "You caused the world to believe that you were anxious about your great Associate. You wished men to believe . . . that you craved to know what had become of him. Without aid or comfort from you, the mission to find him was begun, carried through and ended." And, addressing the press, he railed: "Some of you first doubted the truth of my narrative; then suspected that the letters I produced as coming from [Livingstone] were forgeries; then accused me of sensationalism; then quibbled at the facts I published, and snarled at me as if I had committed a crime."

But Stanley had his supporters and sympathizers, among them the very highest in the land. When it seemed that the rancorous controversy would never end, Queen Victoria herself intervened. On August 27, to his amazement and delight, Stanley received a magnificent gift from her—a gold snuff box studded with exquisite jewels and adorned with the royal cipher. An accompanying letter from the Foreign Secretary, Lord Granville, which was published prominently in *The Times*, conveyed the Queen's "high appreciation" of Stanley's "prudence and zeal in opening a communication with Dr. Livingstone and relieving Her Majesty from the anxiety which, in common with her subjects, she had felt."

This was vindication indeed, and within a couple of weeks Victoria sent an even stronger signal to the "gentlemen geographers" by commanding Rawlinson to bring Stanley to meet her in audience at Dunrobin Castle in Scotland. In the train north, no doubt seething silently, Rawlinson condescendingly instructed Stanley on how he should behave in the royal presence. Above all, said Rawlinson, he was not to write or talk about the audience afterward. "I almost laughed in his face when he charged me with the last," Stanley reminisced many years later. "Poor blind Sir Henry to think that I would venture to write or speak about this lady, whom in my heart of hearts, next to God, I worshipped!"

Fortunately for his fragile self-esteem, Stanley never found out that his feelings for the Queen were scarcely reciprocated. Writing within hours of the audience to her daughter Vickie, the Crown Princess of Prussia, Victoria described him dismissively as "a determined, ugly little man—with a strong American twang."

Still, publicly he had been given the royal seal of approval, and the RGS could no longer withhold the honor that was due to him. Despite the objections of a few diehards, who insisted that he was no geographer, not a true explorer, and decidedly not a gentleman, it was decided that Stanley should be awarded the society's gold medal at a testimonial dinner on October 21.

In his speech, Rawlinson attempted to make amends, apologizing for his jibe about Livingstone's having found Stanley and claiming that this had been based on "incorrect information." Stanley replied by saying that the time had come for "everything to be forgiven and forgotten." He even held out the hand of reconciliation to Kirk, saying that he was glad to hear that the consul had received a friendly letter from Livingstone. "As long as Livingstone thought he was injured by Kirk, he would think so also," reported *The Times*, "and if Livingstone would think Kirk was his friend he would think so too (laughter)."

Rawlinson said the last word on the controversy at the RGS annual meeting in November, by which time Stanley was back in New York. Referring to the "unjustifiable sneers and doubts" first entertained about Stanley "in some quarters," Rawlinson declared: "Let it be understood then, once and for all, that there is not the remotest ground for questioning the accuracy of Mr. Stanley's statement."*

---

* In the same speech, Rawlinson announced a formal reprimand of Dawson of his "lamentable error of judgment" in breaking up the RGS relief expedition. "He seems to have retired from the field owing to a wrong impression of Dr. Livingstone's character," said Rawlinson.

Meanwhile, on the other side of the Atlantic, rancor and controversy over Stanley's feat had been fueled by motives as spiteful as, and even more petty than, those that had been displayed in London. Some of the *Herald*'s competitors—led by the New York *Sun*, whose publisher, Charles A. Dana, bore a personal as well as a professional grudge against the Bennetts—were only too willing to cast doubts on Stanley's character. And in Lewis Noe they found a willing instrument.

On August 24, the *Sun* published a long letter from Noe in which he asked to be allowed to "express a little incredulity in reference to the story of Henry Stanley, Dr. Livingstone's alleged discoverer." Noe then proceeded to characterize his former friend as an unprincipled confidence trickster at best and a psychopathic killer at worst.

Quite possibly the letter was written for Noe's signature by a *Sun* reporter, for it seems far too fluent and well constructed for a man of such little education. The letter was followed up by an interview with a *Sun* reporter in which Noe enlarged on his charges.

Harking back to their Anatolian adventure in company with Harlow Cook, Noe said that "each day Stanley made new revelations of his character. They convinced me that he was capable, if a sufficient inducement existed, of any crime." He thought of running away, said Noe, "but escape in such a country, from such a man, for a boy of seventeen, penniless and friendless, ignorant of the language, manners and customs of the people, seemed like an impossibility."

Noe added: "More than once he has threatened to kill me if I exposed him. With his cruel and vengeful nature I believe he would not hesitate to carry his threat into execution if a favorable opportunity occurred. . . ." But he, and the *Sun*, seemed to reveal the real purpose of his disclosures by saying that he had postponed making them "until, by the prominence [Stanley] should give himself, I could make the exposure more effectual."

The *Sun* reporter who conducted a follow-up interview with Noe a few days later made little pretense of objectivity. He described a photograph of Stanley shown to him by Noe as revealing "gray eyes, having a cold, sinister and even vicious look." In contrast, he had been "most favorably impressed with [Noe's] respectability, honesty and candor."

But Harlow Cook soon gave the lie to Noe. In an interview with the Chicago *Times*—which was neutral in the war between the *Herald* and the *Sun*—he said Stanley had been "basely slandered," dismissing Noe as "a whining little pup," and "a weak, dish-water kind of boy . . . no backbone to him, no character at all."

Then Ambassador Edward Jay Morris, who had helped Stanley in Constantinople, and was by now retired and living in Atlantic City, New Jersey, weighed in. He told the *Herald* he had nothing but admiration for Stanley—"a man I am proud to call my friend"—and declared himself "shocked that any attempt had been made to diminish the laurels [he] has so justly earned." Morris called Noe's allegations "entirely too absurd to be believed" and said of Stanley: "I regarded him as a young man of great courage and determination; his countenance showed this, being stern, almost to serenity,* but with nothing sinister about it."

In a subsequent interview, the *Sun* tried to make what it could of the fraudulent draft for $600 which Stanley had given to Morris. But the ex-ambassador dismissed it as a matter of little importance, pointing out that he had been reimbursed out of the compensation paid by the Turkish government and revealing that, while in Constantinople in late 1869, Stanley had called on him to apologize.

Stanley himself entered the controversy in a letter to the *Herald* from London. It expressed "profound astonishment at the discovery of so debased a character as this wretched young man, Noe, turns out to be." Said Stanley: "He proclaims himself the victim of a foul and unnatural outrage, gives his name in full, with his present address; he dwells fondly on the disgusting details which unmanned him;† offers himself up voluntarily to public scorn and contempt, and deliberately stamps himself as the greatest moral idiot‡ in existence."

To enter on a detailed refutation of Noe's "most atrocious falsehoods," said Stanley, would be "undignified and unworthy of me" and would "bring the contemptible newspaper and its unmanly correspondent into greater prominence than they deserve."

Perhaps so, but some of Noe's "falsehoods" could not be refuted, such as his revelation that Stanley was not a native-born American, as he claimed, but a Welshman. This question of nationality mattered to the *Herald*, which, in the brashly chauvinistic spirit of the age, had been parading Stanley's discovery of Livingstone, and its publisher's enterprise in sponsoring it, as an all-American triumph.

Clearly, the question of his nationality was important to Stanley, too, if for more complex reasons, among them the understandable desire to hide his illegitimacy. In his letter to Bennett he dealt with the

---

* Probably a misprint for "severity."

† He didn't. Noe's only reference to the rape was his oblique statement that he was "treated in a shocking manner."

‡ A revealing use of one of Livingstone's favorite terms of opprobrium.

issue by ducking it. But in a preface—later deleted—to his soon-to-be-published book, he declared: "I claim to be an American; nothing can force me to deny it." Indeed, throughout his life Stanley would angrily turn aside questions about his origins, should anyone dare to raise the matter. As a British friend and colleague, Henry Lucy, would comment: "The subject being a curiously sore one with Stanley, I never heard it alluded to in his presence."

But, Lucy added, "those who are intimately acquainted with him will know that his tongue betrayed him. . . . In private company, talking at ease with familiar friends, he inevitably lapses into the peculiar rapid high intonation peculiar to one of Welsh birth."

And yet, for all his desire to obliterate his past, Stanley could not bring himself to sever altogether his ties to North Wales. During the hectic summer of 1872—when he was embroiled in controversy, traveling about Britain to lecture, finishing his seven-hundred-page account of the Livingstone expedition, and all the while insisting on his American-ness—he still found time to make a side trip to Denbigh, where he visited his mother and also called in at the St. Asaph Workhouse, to praise once more the education he had received there.

Indeed, Stanley appeared to have a compelling need to reveal the truth about his origins to someone he could trust, and that October he met just such a person—Emilia Webb, an upper-crust English-woman who, with her husband, was a friend of Livingstone's. The doctor had written to the Webbs commending Stanley and they invited him to visit them at Newstead Abbey, their home near Nottingham.

At first, Mrs. Webb found Stanley rather rough, boorish, and pugnacious, "a perfect porcupine with all your quills out," as she told him. But as they became better acquainted, she warmed to him, as he did to her, despite the privileged, fox-hunting, English–country-house existence she and her old Etonian husband enjoyed. And before long, Stanley was confiding to her the details of his early life which he so doggedly withheld from others.

For Emilia Webb, Stanley's best side was most noticeable when he was in the company of her six children, the youngest of whom was six. He would play games with them on the grounds, pretending he was leading them on an African expedition, and promising that on a later visit he would bring Kalulu, who had achieved some fame as the great man's loyal little black shadow.

The oldest child, Augusta, recognized both sides of Stanley's personality. "He was always at his best with children," she would recall many years later, ". . . gentle both in speech and manner. He had so much the heart of a boy . . . that he played not with them but as one of themselves." On the other hand, she noted that "I have never seen eyes like those of Stanley when he was angry. They seemed to scorch and shrivel up all he looked at." His whole personality gave "the impression of overwhelming and concentrated force, a human explosive power that only required a mere chance to turn towards good or evil."

Mrs. Webb herself recognized Stanley's need for love. "He has under all his roughness one of the most affectionate natures I have ever met with," she told a friend. "He needs a good woman to marry him, for the right wife could make anything of him, only she would have to care for him enough."

Soon after his visit to the Webbs, Stanley would have a painful reminder of the faithlessness of the woman who had *not* cared for him enough—Katie Gough-Roberts, who had jilted him to marry an architect and was now living in Manchester as Mrs. Katie Bradshaw. She was still in possession of his letters, and he wanted them back, especially the one in which he had written at length about his early life. But from either mercenary or other motives, she insisted that she would only hand the correspondence over to him in person.

For his part, Stanley would not, or could not, contemplate a face-to-face encounter. But when he went to Manchester to lecture at the Free Trade Hall in October, Katie and her husband were in the audience, along with a number of Stanley's relatives from North Wales. After the lecture, Mrs. Bradshaw followed him to the home of the local worthy whose house guest he was. She rang the door bell and sent in, via the butler, a note saying that she had the "biography letter" with her. Stanley sent the butler back to collect it, but Katie refused to hand it over, saying that Stanley must come for it in person. He refused to do so, and she left, taking the letter with her.

From Manchester it was a short trip to Liverpool, where a few days later Stanley boarded the steamship *Cuba*, bound for New York, with his mascot Kalulu in tow. "Welcome Home Henry Stanley," read the huge banner which adorned the dock when the *Cuba* arrived on November 20, 1872. A boatload of press colleagues had sailed out to meet the ship and drink champagne toasts to Stanley, while an official delegation from the *Herald*, headed by his friend and mentor Finlay Anderson, was at the dockside to bear him off in triumph to the office. A later generation would have given him a ticker-tape parade down Broadway.

But James Gordon Bennett, Jr., was conspicuously absent from the dockside and from the *Herald* library, where virtually the entire editorial staff gathered to honor the returning hero. Instead, Bennett remained in his private office, waiting for his editor, Thomas Connery, to bring Stanley to him for an interview which lasted a mere ten minutes.

The megalomaniac publisher was nursing a bitter resentment of his too-successful special correspondent's celebrity, having thoroughly convinced himself that the idea of going after Livingstone had been his and his alone. Quite forgotten was his initial lack of urgency, his refusal to fund the expedition, and Stanley's overgenerous tributes to his visionary genius, including the dedication of *How I Found Livingstone* to Bennett in recognition of "the generosity and liberality which originated, sustained, and crowned this enterprise." As Bennett's biographer would say, "There sprang into his bosom a jealousy of Stanley that almost approached the dignity of hatred. That his hired man, whom he had sent on an errand, should, as a result, reach at one bound the summit of eminence was too much to be borne. . . ."

Bennett was fond of saying that "I will have no indispensable men in my employ," and more than once proved that he meant it by firing some of his most effective reporters and editors for no reason other than to demonstrate his ability to do so. But Stanley's celebrity had made him fireproof, and this can only have increased Bennett's resentment. Those who were in his confidence at the time said later that he would break out into fury when Stanley's name was mentioned. "Who was Stanley before I discovered him?" he demanded. "Who thought of hunting Livingstone? Who paid the bills?"

When Stanley's book was published in New York, some critics criticized his lumbering literary style, and although the *Herald* ran a favorable review, "Bennett let Stanley know he echoed the slighting attacks of some other papers." When Stanley delivered what was to be the first of a series of lectures at New York's Steinway Hall on December 3, the *Herald*'s George O. Seilhammer managed to damn his performance with faint praise. And indeed that first lecture was deadly dull, lacking in color, incident or humor, and quite dry enough to have satisfied the most exacting of the "gentlemen geographers" at Brighton.

For his second night's performance, Stanley tried to liven up his content and delivery, but with little more success, and this time Seilhammer dropped all restraint and gave him a thorough drubbing. He was "intolerably dull," wrote Seilhammer, his "elocution was bad," he "talked commonplaces," and delivered them in "a singsong and doleful monotone."

Seilhammer was one of Bennett's chief sycophants and would never have treated a *Herald* colleague so without the approval, implied or stated, of his boss, and as he confessed to *Herald* night editor Joseph I. C. Clarke, he "sensed" that such "raw truth" would not displease the front office. "When Bennett sent for me the next day to reproach me severely, as he did, I could see that he was really gratified," said Seilhammer.

The rest of the New York press, of course, were equally savage. When the lecture series was canceled after a dismal third night, the *Sun* gleefully quoted no less an authority than the janitor of Steinway Hall. "Stanley's played out," he said. "There will be no lecture tonight or any other night, as Mr. Stanley's receipts do not meet expenses." And the *Sunday Mercury* commented that "the discoverer of Livingstone is reported to have been dispatched by the *Herald* at an immense expense in search of an audience. 'On! Stanley, on!' "

Meanwhile Stanley's famous greeting to Livingstone had already become a vaudeville catch phrase, to be greeted with roars of laughter by New York audiences. A musical comedy entitled *Africa*, featuring the vaudeville team of Harrigan and Hart, played to packed houses at the Theatre Comique on Broadway. Its climax came in a comic scene in which Stanley and his men stride back and forth across the stage before, pushing aside a huge cactus, Stanley spots his quarry, tips his hat and declaims the well-known words.

Stanley was either too obtuse to realize Bennett's hostility toward him or else too shrewd to show that he was aware of it. A *Herald* colleague noted: "Next to himself, he apparently recognized but one claim to his allegiance. This was that of the owner of the paper which had sent him on his now immortal quest." This same colleague gives an intriguing glimpse of the mixed emotions of dislike, puzzlement and reluctant admiration which Stanley inspired in his fellow *Herald* staffers:

> His egotism was attractive in its frankness. It disarmed resentment and baffled sarcasm for . . . what would have been egregious vanity in a commonplace nature, was in him the expression of a strong-willed man's confidence and belief in himself. . . . The chilled personal relations which would have distressed a more sensitive man lost their chilliness against his panoply of self-esteem. . . . He went his way disdainful of any adverse feeling he might arouse, ascribing it, I have no doubt, rather to envy of

his professional position than to any personal cause for which he might be individually responsible.

Compensating for his failure as a lecturer, Stanley's book had already made him a wealthy man. On both sides of the Atlantic it was a conspicuous best seller. Edward Marston, a partner in the London publishing house which produced it, declared that the book had received "an ovation seldom, perhaps never before, accorded a book of travel." But professional geographers, ethnographers and rival explorers, of course, found fault and split hairs on obscure points of detail, and the revered Florence Nightingale went so far as to dismiss it as "the very worst book on the very best subject."

That comment bit deep and was hardly fair criticism. Though frequently clumsy and occasionally stagy, Stanley was a meticulously thorough travel writer and, relieved by his heroic achievements of the need to indulge in Mittyesque fantasies, a reliable if subjective reporter. He was capable of absorbing and communicating an immense amount of detailed and exotic information and putting it into context. Even the formidable Burton, who had cause to resent Stanley's comments about his own book of African exploration,* felt bound to concede that his rival could "see things as they are, and he can describe in forcible language what he sees. Briefly, he wants only study and discipline to make him a first-rate traveller."

But Stanley's paranoid perspective discounted praise and battened on criticism. Nor did it allow him to perceive that the hostility he found so hurtful might be in any way provoked by his own self-defensively harsh and boastful behavior. Looking back in later years, Stanley wrote: "All the actions of my life, and I may say all my thoughts since 1872, have been strongly colored by the storm of abuse and the wholly unjustified reports circulated about me then." Quite forgotten was the fact that for every critic there were a dozen admirers and that many among the world's powerful—not least Queen Victoria herself—had given him unstinting praise.

In a later journal entry, reflecting on the bitter aftermath to his discovery of Livingstone, Stanley indulged to the full his tendency toward self-pity and sticky self-righteousness:

> It was owing to repeated attacks of the Public and Press that I lost the elastic hope of my youth, the hope and belief that toil, generosity, devo-

---

*The Lake Regions of Central Africa, of which Stanley had commented, inter alia, that it was "wonderfully clever and truthful" but had given him "many eccentric ideas" about African travel and had a "wormwood and fever tone" which he regarded as "the result of African disease."

tion to duty, righteous doing, would receive recognition at the hands of my fellow creatures who had been more happily born, more fortunately endowed, more honored by circumstances and fate than I . . . . It seemed as though the years of patient watchfulness, the long periods of frugality, the painstaking self-teaching in lessons of manliness, had ended disastrously in failure.

# Chapter Eleven

*F*OR Stanley, the months following his return to America were bitter and frustrating. With the collapse of his plans for a lecture tour, from which he estimated he might have earned as much as $50,000, there was little for him to do except attend a seemingly endless round of dinners as guest of honor.

He derived little pleasure from these, for he never felt at ease in white-tie society. Also, he was afraid that all the rich food and drink would undermine his constitution, which was only now recovering fully from the ravages of his trek to Ujiji and back. Wisely, he always made sure his wine was well watered and never ate more than three courses.

On such occasions he was often accompanied by Kalulu, an exotic mascot and living souvenir of his master's great exploit, who would obligingly perform parlor tricks, such as imitating a Muslim at prayer, performing tribal dances, and singing in Swahili. As an outlet for his explosive energies, Stanley dashed off *My Kalulu*, an adventure novel for boys based loosely on the personal history of his young protégé. Such was Stanley's renown that any book he wrote was assured of a good sale, but *My Kalulu*, a sentimentalized hodgepodge of African folk tales and jungle exploits—Stanley's first and only venture into fiction—proved only that he did better to stick to journalism.

Meanwhile, although he remained on full pay, there was no work for him at the *Herald*. A reporter of Stanley's renown could hardly be sent out on routine domestic assignments. Impatiently he waited for Bennett to assign him to his next big story, but the publisher, now back in Paris, seemed to be in no hurry. He no doubt enjoyed keeping his jumped-up employee dangling for a few months.

To make matters worse, Stanley suffered—more than most, perhaps—from the crushing sense of anticlimax which, like the post-coital tristesse of a seasoned libertine, typically afflicts the reporter on returning to the everyday world from a demanding assignment in distant parts. "When a man returns home and finds for the moment nothing to struggle against," he wrote, "the vast resolve which has sustained him through a long and difficult enterprise dies away . . . and then the greatest successes are often accompanied by a peculiar melancholy."

At last, in April 1873, Bennett summoned him to Paris. Stanley sailed for Europe, stopping in England to put Kalulu into a boarding school on the outskirts of London, before reporting to his imperious boss at the Hotel des Deux Mondes. But to Stanley's chagrin, Bennett had sent for him only to order him back to his pre-Livingstone assignment in Spain, where the civil war dragged on.

Stanley felt that his career had returned to square one, and the "peculiar melancholy" remained with him for five months until, to his great relief, the British decided to send another punitive expedition to Africa, and Bennett, remembering Stanley's great success in Abyssinia, assigned him to cover it.

The focus of Britain's imperial wrath this time was the truculent West African kingdom of Ashanti, whose warriors had ill-advisedly tugged the lion's tail once too often. Since the beginning of the nineteenth century the Ashanti had been in the habit of undermining British prestige by invading and pillaging their neighbors the Fanti, who lived under the Union Jack in Britain's Gold Coast protectorate. Now, like the Abyssinian Emperor Theodore, the Ashanti king had kidnapped a number of white missionaries and was demanding a ransom for their release. It was time to teach the upstart black kingdom a lesson, and the task had been given to one of Britain's most brilliant young soldiers, Sir Garnet Wolseley, who had been promoted to the rank of general while still in his thirties after putting down Canada's Red River rebellion without the loss of a single man.

Stanley arrived on the fever-ridden Gold Coast, widely termed "the White Man's Grave," in late October to find that the campaign had not yet begun. Wolseley was there with his headquarters staff, but the main body of troops was still at sea. Bored and impatient for action, Stanley spent his time filing interminably dull dispatches, including lengthy speculations on the causes and cure of malaria,* a detailed history of Ashanti ("a strangely original people") and their enemies, the Fanti ("worthless" and "fearful"), and a critique of Britain's torpid administration of the Gold Coast.

But if Stanley found the way Britain ran its protectorate unimpressive, he held the young commander who had been sent to defend it in

---

* He came to the bold conclusion that malaria was caused by a lack of ozone and could be cured by moving the patient to an area where there was more of it in the atmosphere. Failing that, Stanley believed, twenty grains of quinine should do the trick.

great esteem, despite Wolseley's bias against the press, which he had notoriously called "the curse of modern armies." Stanley described Wolseley as a "stately little gentleman of proud military bearing, quick bright eye, broad high forehead, ardent temperament, a sparkling vivacious intelligence animating every feature." Indeed, he paid Wolseley the ultimate compliment of saying that if he had not been a soldier he would have made a "first-class special correspondent, just the man to have seized an item and dared a general-in-chief to lay hands on him, just the man to be sent to any part of the world to collect news."

For his part, Wolseley did not at first take to Stanley, finding him too "self assured and cool." So when Stanley tried to ingratiate himself, the young general gave him a cold rebuff. "I told him to go to the proper officer who had charge of the correspondents," Wolseley recalled.

With his customary foresight, and lavish expenditure of his employer's funds, Stanley had equipped himself with a small, coal-burning launch, brought from England as deck cargo, to enable him to get upriver to the site of anticipated battles. When the time came, he was to abandon the boat and accompany Wolseley's invading column on foot, like his British colleagues, but to relieve the tedium while waiting for the campaign proper to begin, he took the little launch, *Dauntless*, on a hazardous sea voyage, braving the heavy Atlantic surf, from Wolseley's headquarters on Cape Coast Castle, and hugging the coast to the mouth of the Volta River, 120 miles away.

There he interviewed the commander of a secondary British force which was to make a synchronized flanking march on the Ashanti capital, Kumasi. Stanley had invited his British press colleagues to accompany him on this trip, but only the *Standard* correspondent, George A. Henty, was rash enough to accept the invitation. Later, Henty commented that he would never have done so had he realized how small the *Dauntless* really was.

When the main force of twenty-five hundred British troops—the Black Watch, the Rifle Brigade and the Royal Welsh Fusiliers—at last arrived to link up with the two battalions of West Indians, battalion of marines and sailors, artillery battery and company of engineers that awaited them, the campaign got under way.

In many ways, and allowing for the great differences in climate and topography, Wolseley's march on Kumasi paralleled Napier's advance through the rugged Abyssinian highlands to Magdala, and had an equally successful outcome. Wolseley's plan was to march his

force 140 miles to the Ashanti king Kofi's stronghold along jungle
trails blazed by his engineers, and on arrival to raze Kumasi to the
ground by fire and gunpowder.

As the British column moved inexorably toward the Ashanti capital, brushing aside whatever slight resistance it met, Kofi began sending messages offering to settle his dispute with Britain peacefully by
freeing his hostages and paying an indemnity. At one point it seemed
that Wolseley might be prepared to accept the offer, and Stanley was
"swayed by fears that the expedition is destined to terminate peacefully." But he need not have worried; Wolseley was even more determined than he was to derive the maximum in glory and prestige
from the campaign.

At the approaches to Kumasi, the invading and defending armies
at last clashed head-on. The British, with their breech-loading Snider
rifles and rocket batteries, had a clear technological advantage over
the Ashantis, armed only with ancient muzzle-loaders, spears and
swords. But the Ashantis, having greater experience of jungle warfare
and greatly outnumbering the British, fought resolutely. Stanley reported that

> The firing at such close quarters to us waxes terrific. The line of the
> fighting . . . is not fifty yards away from us, and we are plentifully touched
> and tapped, lightly it is true, by the hail of slugs.* Men with whom I am
> conversing abruptly spin round as they feel the blows. . . . Every man of
> the right column feels that this is a critical moment, and that he must roll
> back the tide of attack, or be driven himself in hot haste to infamous
> flight, and so he plies his Snider with that nervous rapidity born of
> desperate necessity.

What Stanley failed to report—for then as now convention required that war correspondents take no direct part in the fighting—
was that he too fell to plying a Snider, perhaps out of "desperate
necessity," but more likely for the pleasure of the fray. In conversation with the celebrated journalist Frank Harris, and in his memoirs
many years after the event, Wolseley recalled admiringly that, although surrounded and in "the utmost danger" during an ambush by
the Ashanti, Stanley "looked as cool and self-possessed as if he had
been at target practice."

> Time after time, as I turned in his direction, I saw him go down to a
> kneeling position to steady his rifle, as he plied the most daring of the

---

* The effective range of the Ashantis' muzzle-loaders was about forty yards.

enemy with a never-failing aim. It is nearly thirty years ago and I can still see before me the close-shut lips, and determined expression of his manly face. . . . I had previously been somewhat prejudiced against him, but . . . ever since I have been proud to reckon him amongst the bravest of my brave comrades. . . .

For all the barbarity of some of their customs, Stanley found the Ashantis to be a people of surprisingly advanced culture. As the British column entered a subcapital he discovered that "it was not by any means a despicable village." Describing the interior of a house which he and other correspondents examined, Stanley reported being "astonished at the immaculate cleanliness of it, and the elaborate ideas of ornamentation which they possessed."

> Many little things which we see about us evince the taste and industry of the Ashantis. . . . An artisan has chiseled and shaped a beautiful stool which any drawing room might possess for its unique shape, design and perfection of workmanship. . . . There is art in this stool and whether it is original with the Ashantis, or borrowed from strangers, it is certainly a most interesting specimen of woodwork, the whole of which is cut from a solid block of wood. . . . Take again this soup, or water ladle, and regard the designs which ornament the handle. A European turner would be proud of the work. . . .

Kumasi contained even more impressive evidence that the Ashantis were a good deal more than mere savages: "The streets were numerous, some half a dozen were broad and uniform. The main avenue . . . was about seventy yards wide, and here and there along its length a great patriarchal tree spread wide its branches. The houses in the principal streets . . . were wattled structures, with alcoves and stuccoed facades, embellished with Mauresque patterns. . . ."

But behind this facade of cleanliness, order, esthetic sensitivity and refined craftsmanship, lay a vast charnel house emitting "foul smells so suffocating that we were glad to produce our handkerchiefs to prevent the intolerable and almost palpable odor from mounting into the brain and overpowering." Stanley and his colleagues had found a "Golgotha" in a grove at the back of the town where for generations Ashanti kings had been in the habit of ritually slaughtering recalcitrant slaves, enemies and other undesirables.

"We saw some thirty or forty decapitated bodies in the last stages of corruption," Stanley wrote, "and countless skulls which lay piled in heaps and scattered over a wide extent. The stoniest heart and the most stoical mind might have been appalled. . . . At the rate of a thousand victims a year, it would be no exaggeration to say that over 120,000 people must have been slain for 'custom' since the Ashantis became a kingdom!"

After the British had put the capital to the torch and blown up Kofi's huge stone-built palace, thus implanting what Wolseley called "a wholesome fear of British power" in the hearts of the Ashanti, he ordered an immediate withdrawal to the coast, hoping to reach there before the onset of the rains. "The campaign has been a success," reported Stanley before leaving the Gold Coast for London, "and the brave and deserving have been rewarded by their Queen and the nation."

In Stanley's reporting of the Ashanti campaign, it is striking that this time there is not a single monocled fop, effete lordling or arrogant swell to be seen. The celebrated discoverer of Livingstone is no longer to be snubbed as a pushy little Yankee, and consequently Wolseley's officers are brave, splendid fellows all.

ON HIS way back to London, when his ship called into St. Vincent, Cape Verde Islands, on February 25, 1874, Stanley received news that affected him deeply: Livingstone had died nine months previously, deep in the jungle of the Lualaba River basin.

His loyal followers, Chuma and Susi, had removed Livingstone's heart and buried it under a tree. Then they had reverently eviscerated and sun-dried his body for two weeks before wrapping it in calico and carrying it a thousand miles to the coast. There it had been put aboard a British mail steamer for transshipment to England and a state funeral.

"Dear Livingstone!" wrote Stanley, "another sacrifice to Africa! His mission, however, must not be allowed to cease; others must go forward and fill the gap. 'Close up, boys! close up! Death must find us everywhere.' May I be selected to succeed him in opening up Africa to the shining light of Christianity!"

That diary entry, stagy and pietistic as it sounds to modern ears, may in fact denote the exact moment when a growing intention to abandon journalism as a career and devote his energies exclusively to African exploration crystallized in Stanley's mind. Besides his filial reverence for Livingstone, he was still bitter over the way the world had treated him on his return. "I have a spur to goad me on," he wrote. "My tale of the discovery of Livingstone has been doubted. What I have already endured in that accursed Africa amounts to nothing in men's estimation. Here, then, is an opportunity for me to prove my veracity, and the genuineness of my narrative!"

But, as much as he revered the memory of his mentor, Stanley had no intention of continuing Livingstone's work by Livingstone's methods. His efforts would be much tougher, much better financed, much more methodically organized. "Each man has his own way," Stanley wrote. Livingstone's had been "almost Christ-like for goodness, patience and self-sacrifice." But as Stanley saw it, "the selfish and wooden-headed world requires mastering, as well as loving charity. . . ."

On reaching London in mid-March, Stanley hastened to send a five-page letter of condolence to Livingstone's daughter, Agnes.

> I was stricken dumb and cannot give you a description of the misery I feel. How I envy such a father! The richest inheritance a father can give his children is an honoured name. What man ever left a nobler name than Livingstone? . . . I loved him as a son, and would have done for him anything of the most filial. The image of him will never be obliterated from my memory. . . .

A month later, Livingstone's body arrived at Southampton, where a twenty-one-gun salute was fired and a special train took the coffin to London for a state funeral at Westminster Abbey. Stanley was one of the eight pallbearers, occupying the foremost position at the right-hand front of the coffin. In the second row was Kirk, on leave from Zanzibar at the time. Behind the coffin walked Kalulu, wearing a smart new gray suit. With Livingstone's interment among the heroes of England, a new chapter opened in the life of Henry Morton Stanley.

# PART THREE

# QUEEN OF AFRICA
# SUBDUED

Oho Congo, stretched upon thy bed of forests,
Queen of Africa subdued.

*LEOPOLD SENGHOR*

# Chapter Twelve

*A*MONG the nine hundred distinguished mourners who packed the Abbey to lay Livingstone to rest on April 18, 1874, was Edwin Arnold, editor of the *Daily Telegraph*, one of the papers that had *not* seen fit to pour doubt and scorn on Stanley on his return to England two years before. Like Stanley himself, Arnold believed fervently that Livingstone's work should go on, and was convinced that while Stanley might lack the vocation to open up the continent to "the shining light of Christianity," he was in all other respects the very man for the job. Within days of the funeral they met in Arnold's office.

"Could you, and would you, complete the work?" Arnold asked Stanley, offering the bait that the *Telegraph* was willing to foot the bill for a new expedition. And Stanley, springing from his chair and holding out both hands to his questioner, cried, "Will I! Will I!"

There was one complication: Bennett and the New York *Herald* still had first call on Stanley's services. Also the *Telegraph*'s proprietor, Edward Levy-Lawson, was not so keen as Arnold imagined to bear the full cost of the expedition. Accordingly, he cabled New York asking if Bennett would bear half the expense. Within twenty-four hours a curt reply was on Levy-Lawson's desk: YES. BENNETT.

Stanley immediately plunged into preparations for the expedition, which would be the biggest yet sent into the African interior. Its objectives were simply enough stated, yet staggering in scope. Completing Livingstone's work meant, in effect, testing Livingstone's belief about the sources of the Nile against Speke's. Stanley must therefore circumnavigate Lake Victoria to verify or disprove once and for all Speke's assertion that the Nile flowed out of the lake's northern extremity, and then follow the Lualaba to the sea to disprove or verify Livingstone's conflicting theory that the Lualaba was the source of the Nile.

Yet even as he busied himself with the details of this enormously ambitious and perilous undertaking, the hyperactive Stanley also found time for the luxury of falling in love. The object of his passion was a pert and pretty American heiress named Alice Pike, half his age, whom he met while she was vacationing in London with her widowed mother and sisters.

There are two distinct versions of the romance that followed their meeting. One is told by Stanley in a series of diary entries and letters which, until quite recently, remained undiscovered in the copious Stanley family archives; the other version is provided by Alice in a highly colored memoir which she dictated to an amanuensis in the late 1920s. It was never published, and remained undiscovered until 1988.

Given Stanley's notorious evasiveness and at times downright mendacity about his personal life, his version must be regarded with some caution. Still, it seems more reliable than Alice's account, which, written more than fifty years after the event, bristles with evidence of a colorful and self-infatuated, if decidedly commonplace, imagination.

Alice was the youngest daughter of Samuel Pike, an entrepreneur of German-Jewish extraction who made a fortune as a distiller of whisky in Cincinnati before moving with his family to New York City in 1866. There he increased his millions through real-estate speculation and built a grandiose mansion alongside the Vanderbilts' and Astors' on the site now occupied by the famous department store Saks Fifth Avenue. Unusual for a robber baron of his time, Sam Pike was a man of considerable culture; he wrote poetry, played the flute and—a passionate opera lover—spent half a million dollars to give Cincinnati a replica of Milan's La Scala.

In the summer of 1873, this admirable man dropped dead of a heart attack at his office in Wall Street. The following spring his forty-five-year-old widow sailed to England with her diamonds, her vast wardrobe and her three daughters, Alice, Nettie and Hessie, en route for Paris, where Hessie was to be married to a wealthy Frenchman. The Pikes were staying at London's newly built Langham Hotel, a favorite haunt of rich American tourists, when they made the acquaintance of Stanley, who lodged there whenever he was in London.

Exactly how they met is a matter of dispute between Stanley's and Alice's versions. He recorded being introduced to Mrs. Pike—a "good looking, stout and exceedingly good-tempered" woman—by a fellow American and being invited to join the family at dinner. Stanley found Nettie "rather fast," with a "disagreeably loud" voice. Alice seemed more subdued. Stanley noted in his diary that she had a "soft, girlish profile," a "large but well formed" mouth and a nose that "had a certain Jewish fullness at the point." She wore rather too many diamonds, but her figure, clad in black silk, was "very elegant." Added Stanley: "The carriage of her head indicated that if she does not know much of society she had a lower opinion of society than she had of herself."

The Pike women were obviously thrilled to find themselves in the company of the most celebrated man in London. Unlike Queen Victoria, they did not find him ugly. Nor was he. At thirty-three, Stanley was a powerfully compact man, five feet five inches tall, barrel-chested, and quite compelling. He had wavy black hair, gray-flecked as a result of his African hardships, a firm mouth, determined chin, and blue-gray eyes of startling directness and intensity. As Americans, the Pike women were not at all put off by the cigar-chomping brashness which the English upper crust found so tasteless.

After dinner Alice and Nettie questioned Stanley about his African travels. He obviously found their company charming, even though, as he recorded afterward, "they are both very ignorant of African geography, and I fear of everything else."

For all the disapproving tone of that diary entry, Stanley seized every opportunity to spend time in the company of the younger sister. She responded flirtatiously, thrilled and flattered by the attentions of so celebrated a man. Within days of their first meeting, Stanley was hooked in spite of himself. "I fear that if Miss Alice gives me . . . encouragement," he wrote, "I shall fall in love with her, which may not perhaps be very conducive to my happiness, for she is the very opposite of my ideal wife."

But although her behavior convinced him she was "heartless and a confirmed flirt," he could not keep away from her. Busy as he was, he made sure they met daily, taking outings together to Hyde Park, and once to Windsor. Alice decided that "Henry" was too mundane a first name for him and began calling him by his middle name. He went along with this quite happily.

All too soon Alice had to leave London for Paris and her sister's wedding, followed by a lightning tour of the more fashionable of Europe's watering places. Stanley, immersed in preparations for his new expedition, could not accompany her, but wrote longingly, almost daily, signing himself "Your loving Morton." She returned to London for a few days before leaving for America, and when it was time for her to embark for New York with her family, Stanley took the train with them to Liverpool to see her off. "She has sworn undying fidelity to me and our parting was very tender," he wrote.

Two weeks later, Stanley himself sailed to New York, ostensibly to see Bennett but really because he was desperate to see Alice. He proposed to her and she accepted. Stanley wanted to get married immediately, but Mrs. Pike insisted they wait. Stanley would be away for two years or more, she pointed out, and besides, Alice was too young to marry; let them at least wait until his return from Africa. Stanley had no choice but to agree, but in his diary he lamented: "Two years is such a long time to wait, and I have so much to do, such a weary, weary journey to make before I can ever return. No man had ever to work harder than I have for a wife."

Thwarted for the time being, the two lovers drew up and signed a marriage pact: "We solemnly pledge ourselves to be faithful to each other and to be married to one another on the return of Henry Morton Stanley from Africa. We call God to witness this our pledge in writing."

Five days later they spent their last evening together, dining and then walking hand in hand near Central Park before returning to her home at 613 Fifth Avenue. There, in the parlor, "she raised her lips in tempting proximity to mine and I kissed her on her lips, on her eyes, on her cheeks and her neck, and she kissed me in return." As a parting gift Stanley gave Alice a copy of *How I Found Livingstone* which he playfully inscribed in pencil with a version of the gladiatorial farewell: *"Ave Alice! Morituri te Salutant"*—Hail, Alice! We who are about to die salute you.

The next morning Alice went to Pier 42 to see Stanley off to Liverpool aboard the S.S. *Celtic*. They promised to write regularly to each other, and she gave him two photographs of herself, one a portrait, the other a full-length picture in which she wore a tightly-waisted silk outfit with a full, embroidered skirt.

"She repeated her vows to me as we stood together," wrote Stanley, "and as I clasped her hands to bid her goodbye, she gave me such a look—a long, earnest, wide-eyed look—during which I thought she was striving to pierce the dark, gloomy picture, but I turned away—and the spell broke."

So much for Stanley's version of the romance. Alice's account differs in several important details, and contains a number of wild improbabilities. In dictating her memoir, the elderly Alice used the third person, as if to relieve herself of false modesty and any obligation to be truthful. As she told it, she and Stanley met not at the Langham but at a royal charity gala, where he was the star attraction as "the lion of London," and she was on hand to sing operatic selections.

She starts off with a little lie, claiming to have been only fifteen at the time and describing the devastating first impression she made on

*Alice Pike at seventeen. They vowed
to marry, "but two years is such a long
time to wait." (National Museum of
American Art, and Smithsonian
Institution)*

Stanley, with "her lovely white arms raised slightly . . . her lovely
face a petal whiteness" as she sang "Ritorna Vincitor" from *Aida*.

"This young girl in her tight, pointed taffeta bodice," she wrote,
"her bewildering tulle skirt, black as night and trimmed with long jet
fringe . . . made his pulses chase in a confusion that bewildered
him. . . . The rich, dramatic voice. . . . What depth and range of feeling she encompassed. . . . Stanley was caught, in the fullest sense of
the word, and he knew it."

And a few nights later he stands entranced as she dances in the
moonlight, just for him, in the garden of one of London's great
houses. She wrote:

> Alice's lips parted, showing the small, white teeth. She was no longer
> a child, but an alluring woman, calling to her mate. Fascinated and
> completely under her spell, Stanley's blood grew hot in his veins as never
> before. His soul and body wanted and begged for her. "Alice, most
> beautiful, stop! Stop! I can't bear it! You've made me mad, nymph-of-
> the-moon! I love you!" He madly caught her to him and she looked up,
> wide-eyed with surprise. "Don't! Don't! You'll spoil everything," she
> whispered. . . .

In more than four hundred pages of typescript, Alice rarely rises
above that novelettish level. She goes on to tell how, instead of
waiting for Stanley, she foolishly and unhappily married Albert Clif-
ford Barney, the son of a wealthy industrialist from Dayton, Ohio,
bore him two daughters, became a leading light in the artistic and
social life of Paris and Washington, and spent the rest of her life
regretting having thrown away the chance to become Mrs. Henry
Morton Stanley.

> Why had she been so stupid? . . . [Stanley] had come too soon. She had
> been too young, too full of the frolic of play days, carefree, irresponsible
> and gay. Altogether lovely, yes, and so he had loved her. Oh! why did he
> not just kidnap her and say 'Now you belong to me'? But no. He had
> been the gentleman, one of Nature's gentlemen to be sure, and he had
> accepted her decision and gone with sorrow. . . .

Alice Pike Barney's panting prose might best be left in decent
obscurity but for what it tells us, indirectly, about the emotional
maturity of the man whose romantic inspiration she was throughout
the most difficult, dangerous and extended expedition in the history
of African exploration.

Stanley would carry her photograph, carefully wrapped in oilskin, next to his heart through jungle, swamp and bush, over mountain and cataract, and in numberless fights against hostile tribes. And her given name would adorn the prow of the forty-foot boat in which he was to circumnavigate two of Central Africa's greatest lakes and sail the entire length of the Congo River.

He would write Alice regularly and passionately as he tamed the savage continent, and not until he got back to civilization after almost three years would he discover that, like Katie Gough-Roberts before her, she had thrown him over to marry another. Bitterly hurt by her betrayal, he resolved never to speak her name again or to reveal why he had named his boat the *Lady Alice.*

History is, of course, replete with examples of exceptional men making utter fools of themselves over banal if beautiful women. But the story of Henry Stanley and Alice Pike is surely a minor classic of the genre.

# Chapter Thirteen

$D$URING his visit to New York, Stanley did see Bennett, but only once, and only after the proprietor of the *Herald* had kept him waiting several days for an appointment. It was not a cordial meeting. Bennett gave him short shrift and passed him on to the editor, Connery. "This is rather an unkind way," complained Stanley, "to receive one he is about to send to complete the discoveries of so many great travelers in Central Africa."

But Stanley should not have been surprised. Bennett was still envious of his celebrity and piqued at having been forced into collaboration with the *Telegraph*, quite overlooking the fact that he had been notably reluctant to pay for the last expedition and would possibly have balked at footing the entire bill for the next. Hence the terseness of Bennett's one-word reply to Levy-Lawson's cable and the tetchiness which throughout marked the *Herald*'s partnership with the *Telegraph*. Bennett even refused to sign a contract, instead lodging his $30,000 half share of the agreed expenses in a special bank account, to be drawn upon as needed.

There was a marked difference of emphasis between the two newspapers when, the day before Stanley left New York for England to wrap up preparations for his great trek across Africa, the *Telegraph* and the *Herald* separately announced details of the expedition. Bennett's announcement made a point of stressing how much the *Herald* had already spent on sending Stanley to find Livingstone and how much more it was investing in the new venture. Arnold laid more emphasis on the example of co-operation between two nations with a "common interest in the re-generation of Africa" and on the hope that "very important results will accrue ... to the advantage of science, humanity and civilisation."

The twin announcements unleashed a torrent of applications from an astonishing variety of would-be adventurers applying to join the expedition. On both sides of the Atlantic, African exploration excited a popular fervor of crusaderlike intensity, and the raw enthusiasm of the volunteers, their diversity and sheer numbers inspired one of Stanley's few successful attempts at humor:

Over 1200 letters were received from "generals," "colonels," "captains," "lieutenants," "midshipmen," "engineers," "commissioners of hotels," mechanics, waiters, cooks, servants, somebodies and nobodies, spiritual mediums, and magnetizers, etc., etc. They all knew Africa, were perfectly acclimatized, were quite sure they would please me, would do important services, save me from any number of troubles by their ingenuity and resources, take me up in balloons or by flying carriages, make us all invisible by their magic arts, or by "the science of magnetism" would cause all savages to fall asleep while we might pass anywhere without trouble. . . .

In fact, Stanley had already picked the three European assistants he needed for his expedition. The brothers Frank and Edward Pocock, rugged young fishermen from the Kentish village of Upnor, had been recommended to him by Arnold, whose yacht they had used to crew, and Stanley himself had spotted a promising third man in Frederick Barker, a zealous and energetic young clerk at the Langham Hotel.

Stanley turned to a boatbuilder at Teddington, on the Thames, for construction of the *Lady Alice*. He stipulated that it should be made of Spanish cedar in eight 5-foot sections, each small and light enough to be man-carried along narrow trails through brush and jungle. When fully assembled it would be 40 feet long, 6 feet at the beam and 2½ feet deep. Given his meticulous requirements, the *Lady Alice* could not be finished in time for Stanley's departure for Zanzibar on August 15, 1874, and had to be shipped out on the next available vessel.

Much had changed on Zanzibar by the time Stanley arrived on September 21, 1874, after an absence of twenty-eight months. His old friend the U.S. consul Webb had retired to his hometown of Salem, Massachusetts, and his old enemy, the British consul Kirk, still on home leave, had been temporarily replaced by the same Captain William Prideaux whose monocle and "elegant insouciance" had so irritated Stanley when they met during the Abyssinian campaign.

More important, the practice of slavery on the island had been officially abolished. In the wake of Livingstone's shocking account of the massacre at Nyangwe, the British government had sent Sir Bartle Frere, backed by an impressive show of naval might, to persuade Sultan Barghash to ban the trade once and for all. As a result, by the time of Stanley's return the infamous slave market had been closed down, and its site was being prepared for the construction, appropriately enough, of a massive Anglican church.

Word of Stanley's return soon spread among the Wangwana, as the free blacks of Zanzibar and the coast were called, and they rushed to volunteer for his latest expedition. Bombay was away in the interior with another explorer, but the remaining "faithfuls" of the search for Livingstone—Mabruki Speke, Manwa Sera, Chowpereh and Uledi among them—appeared happy to see their former master. Stanley gave them handsome presents, signed them on as captains and followed their advice in selecting three hundred others to act as porters, guides and askaris.

It is striking that despite Stanley's repute as a leader who drove his men to the limits of endurance and punished idlers and rebels without mercy, there was no shortage of eager applicants. It may be that he could not inspire the love of the Wangwana, as Livingstone had, but he could command their respect. And Stanley, after his fashion, seems to have reciprocated. He claimed that he considered the Zanzibaris—and indeed "a large proportion of the negro tribes of the continent"—to be "capable of great love and affection, and possessed of gratitude and other noble traits of human nature.

"I know too," wrote Stanley, "that they can be made good, obedient servants, that many are clever, honest, industrious, docile, enterprising, brave and moral; that they are, in short, equal to any other race or color on the face of the globe, in all the attributes of manhood."

Also, in case his readers should think him too generous in his opinion of the black man, Stanley admonished them to remember "the condition of the Briton before St. Augustine visited this country," and "the original circumstances and surroundings of the Primitive Man." So, he urged, "let us leave off this impotent bewailing of [the Africans'] vices and endeavour to discover some of the virtues they possess as men, for it must be with the aid of their virtues, and not by their vices, that the missionary of civilization can ever hope to assist them."

Nowadays, such comments sound merely patronizing, but Stanley's admonition seems spontaneous enough to belie, once again, the racist label that his detractors have stuck on him. Still, there is no denying that Stanley would show little compunction in using the bull whip and the slave chain to punish recalcitrance, mutiny, theft or desertion. His justification would be that if Africa was to be charted and tamed it would not be by the methods of the rectory drawing room. And, unarguably, Stanley drove himself as relentlessly as he drove the Wangwana.

The lash he applied to his own back was his obsessive thirst for vindication. No matter that he was now laden with honors, lionized and lauded wherever he went; no matter that the scoffers had long since been shamed into apology and silence and that he was independently wealthy thanks to phenomenal sales of his book. His "paramount idea" as he set out was "that if I lived to return with good results my unjust enemies would be silenced forever."

On November 12, after the end of Ramadan, the Muslim month of fasting, he was ready to leave for the mainland, and the biggest and costliest expedition ever mounted from Zanzibar sailed in six dhows for Bagamoyo. Its stay there was brief; Stanley's men, flush with advance wages and keen to spend them in the rum shops and brothels of the coast, made themselves such a nuisance to the local forces of law and order that he judged it wise to move them into the interior as quickly as possible.

So, in the predawn light of November 17, Ted Pocock sounded his bugle, the porters hoisted their burdens, and the caravan moved off in a line stretching half a mile.

"In this manner," wrote Stanley, "we begin our long journey, full of hopes. There is noise and laughter along the ranks, and a hum of gay voices murmuring through the fields. . . . We had an intensely bright and fervid sun shining above us, the path was dry, hard and admirably fit for travel . . . and nothing could be conceived in better order than the lengthy thin column about to confront the wilderness."

Such an ideal state of affairs, of course, could not last long. The sun became altogether too fervid as they descended into the valley of the Kingani River, and "The ranks become broken and disordered; stragglers are many; the men complain of the terrible heat; the dogs pant in agony. Even we ourselves . . . would fain rest, were it not that the sun-bleached levels of the tawny, thirsty valley offer no inducements. . . ."

Of the five dogs accompanying the expedition—one a magnificent prize mastiff named Castor, given to Stanley by the wealthy Baroness Angela Burdett-Coutts—two died of heat stroke that first day. And after a night's rest two porters were found to be so sick that they were discharged and sent back to Bagamoyo. Stanley had the premonition that this was only the beginning of his troubles. Within the next few weeks, he predicted, "scores will have deserted, the strong will have become weak, the robust sick, the leader will be ready to despair and to wish that he had never ventured a second time into the sea of mishaps and troubles which beset the traveler in Africa!"

And so it proved. By the time they reached Mpwapwa, some 160 miles from the coast, fifty men had deserted, others had been recaptured and put into slave chains, and the white men had all suffered debilitating bouts of fever. Recalling that Mpwapwa was where Farquhar, his assistant on the Livingstone expedition, had died, Stanley noted feeling "a sharp throb of regret" and a "sorrowful foreboding . . . that perhaps one, if not all, of the white men on this expedition might find similar unhonored graves in this strange land." Still, despite all their travails, the march from the Indian Ocean had been "unprecedentedly successful," taking only twenty-five days, or less than half his previous time.

From Mpwapwa, Stanley's caravan abandoned the traditional route, due west to Tabora and Ujiji, and struck northwest through unknown territory toward Lake Victoria. It was a route harsher by far than anything they had encountered to date, taking them across the forbidding Merenga Mkali (bitter water) desert.

> The heat was intense, the earth fervid, the thorny jungle a constant impediment, and a sore trouble, and its exhalations nauseating. Had an enemy lurked in the jungle of sufficient audacity and power to withstand a few Snyders [sic], the Expedition might have been ruined there and then, but a kind Providence watched over us and permitted us to straggle into camp, a wretched and most demoralized caravan.

The next day, "added to the torments of great thirst and heat, both Frank Pocock and I suffered from fever." Another day on, and both Pocock brothers were ill with fever, but Stanley had to rise from his litter to pay *hongo* to the chief of the Chikombo tribe, through whose territory they were passing. The day after that, another of the dogs died.

From desiccating heat and drought, the expedition passed next to a region of "furious rainy tempests," where "some days both nature and man warred against us . . . the expedition seemed to melt away; men died from fatigue and famine, many were left behind sick, while many, again, deserted. Promises of reward, kindness, threats, punishments, had no effect. The expedition seemed doomed." But on this expedition, at least, Stanley consoled himself that he had white assistants of higher caliber than Shaw and Farquhar:

> Though selected out of the ordinary class of Englishmen, [Barker and the Pococks] did their work bravely—nay, I may say heroically. Though suffering from fever and dysentery, insulted by natives, marching under

the heat and tropical rain-storms, they at all times proved themselves of noble, manful natures, stout hearted, brave men, and—better than all—true Christians.

Christmas found Stanley encamped under a downpour in famine-stricken Ugogo and, as a diary entry records, "a more cheerless Christmas Day was seldom passed by me." He weighed a mere 134 pounds, having left Zanzibar at 180, it was miserably cold, and he had nothing to eat but boiled rice. The rest of his party were in like condition, and "unless we reach some more flourishing country . . . we must soon become mere skeletons."

In his misery, Stanley's thoughts turned to Alice, and he took up his pen to write to her. "How your kind woman's heart would pity me and mine," he exclaimed.

> I am in a centre-pole tent, seven by eight. As it rained all day yesterday, the tent was set over wet ground which, by the passing in and out of the servants, was soon trampled into a thick pasty mud. . . . The tent walls are disfigured by large patches of mud, and the tent corners hang down, limp and languid, and there is such an air of forlornness and misery about its very set that it increases my own misery. . . . I sit on a bed raised about a foot above the sludge, mournfully reflecting on my misery. . . . Outside my tent things are worse. The camp is in the extreme of misery and the people appear as if they were making up their minds to commit suicide or to sit still inert until death relieves them. . . .

But if Alice's letters to Stanley are any guide, she was quite incapable of imagining the hardships he was undergoing, and totally wrapped up in the frivolities of her own existence. "I do love dancing so much," she wrote merrily in a letter which Stanley mercifully never saw until his return to Zanzibar two years later. "Honest, I would rather go to an opera, though, than a party. . . . Almost every evening some fellows come in—I get awfully tired of them."

As the caravan marched on after Christmas, north toward the lake, its misfortunes continued. Rapacious tribal chiefs demanded ever more in *hongo*, there were daily desertions, the guides and porters increasingly squabbled among themselves, twenty men were sick, as were the Pocock brothers and Barker. To cap it all, Stanley discovered a conspiracy by some fifty of his men to desert en masse. He does not record how he put down the incipient mutiny, except to remark tersely in his diary that "the ringleaders were clapped in chains and flogged."

A few days later, Stanley's column encountered hundreds of ref-ugees fleeing from the scene of a battle in the seemingly endless war being waged by Mirambo, the "black Napoleon," against the tribes of the region. The expedition pushed on, only to find its way strad-dled by an equally formidable foe—a trackless and barely penetrable thicket of stunted acacia, euphorbia and thorn trees which tore at their flesh as they hacked their way through it. "It sickens me almost to write of this day's experience," wrote Stanley. "Though our march was but ten miles, it occupied us as many hours of labor, elbowing and thrusting our way to the injury of our bodies and detriment of our clothing."

The next day was a repetition of these miseries, and "still we saw no limit to this immense bushfield." To make matters worse, the column's guide had lost the way, and Stanley had recourse to his compass, leading his party ever northward. There was no game to be found, and the food situation was growing hourly more critical. Stanley dispatched twenty of his strongest men to a village some thirty miles away where he thought food might be purchased and sent twenty other men under Manwa Sera to look for stragglers in the dense bush. Stanley himself left camp in a vain search for game, while his men scoured the stunted forest for edible roots and berries.

Death by starvation seemed inevitable when Stanley and Frank Pocock found a ten-pound pound sack of oatmeal and three tins of revalenta, or lentil flour, hidden away among the medical supplies. Emptying a sheet-iron trunk of its contents to make a caldron, Stan-ley filled it with water, added the mixture of oatmeal and revalenta, and cooked up a mess of thin gruel. "How inexpressibly satisfied they seemed," wrote Stanley, "and with what fervor they thanked 'God' for his mercies!"

The morning after this feast, Stanley's foraging party returned with sacks of millet they had been able to purchase, and the column ate heartily before resuming the march north, although "two more poor fellows breathed their last before we left camp."

After four agonizing days, they at last broke out of "this fatal jungle" into a broad plain where "we discovered a people remark-able for their manly beauty, noble proportions and nakedness." Sadly, this tribe—the nomadic Masai—proved to be as suspicious and inhospitable as they were good-looking. Stanley's men, mean-while, were so weakened by their sufferings that six died, while thirty more were on the sick list with dysentery, ulcerated feet, diarrhea, and various chest ailments. In addition, Ted Pocock appeared to have typhoid fever, and although Stanley would have preferred to rest his porters and nurse the sick, he felt obliged to move on "to more auspicious lands, where the natives were less suspicious, where food was more abundant, and where cattle were numerous."

Ted Pocock was in a bad way. "His tongue was thickly coated with a dark fur, his face fearfully pallid, and he complained of wandering pains in his back and knees, of giddiness and great thirst." Soon he sank into delirium, and as the column made camp on the evening of January 17, 1875, Stanley was called to his side "only in time to see the young man breathe his last."

> Frank gave a shriek of sorrow when he realized that the spirit of his brother had fled forever and . . . bent over the corpse and wailed in a paroxysm of agony. We excavated a grave four feet deep at the foot of a hoary acacia with wide-spreading branches, and on its ancient trunk Frank engraved a deep cross. . . . When the last solemn prayer had been read, we retired to our tents to brood in sorrow and silence over our irreparable loss.

Stanley had left the coast with 347 men and was now reduced to 229. Twenty-one were dead, 89 had deserted, and 8 had been left behind sick, yet the stupendous journey had scarcely begun. Stanley knew he could not hope to complete it if he continued to lose men at this rate, but within days another 24 would die in battle with a hostile tribe.

The trouble began with the murder of Kaif Halleck, one of the "faithfuls" of the 1871 expedition, who, having fallen behind the main party, was later discovered hacked to pieces on the edge of a wood at the entrance to the territory of the Waturu tribe. Although there was little doubt that the Waturu were responsible for the murder, Stanley decided to take no action. "We can mourn for him, but we cannot avenge him," he counseled his men.

But restraint brought no rewards. Soon Stanley and his men heard war cries and saw a large body of Waturu warriors armed with spears, shields, bows and arrows mustering on high ground near the camp. He sent two messengers to inquire the reason for this show of hostility and was told that one of his men had stolen milk from a village the night before. Stanley atoned for this real or invented offense by sending the tribesmen a handsome tribute of cloth, with which they were apparently satisfied. But soon afterward two of Stanley's men were attacked, one fatally, when they went into the forest to cut wood.

As Stanley told it in a dispatch to the *Herald* and *Telegraph*, and later in his book *Through the Dark Continent*,* he even then urged restraint, bearing in mind the forbearance taught him by Livingstone. " 'Keep silence,' I said; 'even for this last murder I shall not fight; when they attack the camp it will be time enough then.' "

The massed Waturu warriors seemed to be divided over whether or not to attack, the young warriors urging an immediate assault, the elders counseling restraint. As he waited to see which faction would prevail, Stanley told Pocock to distribute twenty rounds of ammunition to each man. Then the warriors began to advance slowly on the camp, shouting jibes and insults: "Ye are women, ye are women. Go ask Mirambo how he fared in Ituru."

The Waturu had reached within fifty yards of the camp when Stanley unleashed his men, sixty of whom rushed out to give battle, driving the Waturu back with heavy losses in a running fight that lasted an hour. As the two sides fought, Stanley strengthened the defenses of the camp by ordering his noncombatants to build a strong stockade and erecting marksmen's nests at each corner.

While the Waturu licked their wounds and buried their dead, Stanley and his men hunkered down inside the stockade, "in a mood," as Stanley put it, "to pray that we might not be attacked, but permitted to leave the camp in safety." But next morning the Waturu turned up in greater force than before. Again they were driven off, but now Stanley decided to take the offensive rather than remain bottled up inside his stockade in a war of attrition and starvation that he was eventually bound to lose.

Dividing his askaris into four groups, each under a seasoned campaigner, with two more groups in reserve, he sent them to fan out across the valley, killing and burning as they went. Although they were overwhelmingly outnumbered, their Sniders and muskets more than redressed the balance, and at dusk Stanley's soldiers returned to camp with an abundance of captured grain and cattle. They had lost twenty-one dead and three wounded, but dozens of Waturu villages were burning, and at least thirty-five Waturu warriors were dead.

The fighting resumed on the third day, though whether it was the Waturu who reinitiated it is unclear. In *Through the Dark Continent*,

---

* Though not in his exploration diary, where he gives a slightly different version, saying that the Waturu made a simultaneous rush on the camp as the wounded survivor of the latest attack staggered in and that "the men hitherto restrained by me were then ordered to go out and meet them. . . ." Whichever version is correct, it seems clear that Stanley did initially react with restraint, if only because his sick and depleted numbers gave him good reason to avoid battle.

Stanley says they again advanced on his camp, in greater numbers than before. In his diary he says that none came, and in a dispatch to the *Herald* and the *Telegraph* he leaves the question moot. What is clear from his own account is that, provoked or not, he sent his men out in force to "burn what had been left the previous day."

> Long before noon it was clearly seen that the savages had had enough of war and were demoralized and our people returned through the now silent and blackened valley without molestation. Just before daybreak on the fourth day we left our camp and continued our journey northwest, with provisions to last six days, leaving the people of Ituru to ponder on the harsh fate they had drawn on themselves by their greed, treachery, and wanton murder, and attack on peaceful strangers.

So ended the first of many battles that Stanley would wage on his epic journey across Africa. His conduct would give rise to much criticism in Britain, where those of clerical and liberal mind felt that Christian precepts of peace and love should suffice to guide him safely through the wilderness. But Stanley saw no reason to apologize. On his return to Britain he remarked defiantly that "I am happy to say we did not leave that place [Ituru] until we had perfectly sickened them."

The expedition's relief at their delivery was short-lived. "No sooner are we out of one danger," Stanley lamented, "than we are near another. We have escaped the [Waturu] only to find ourselves constantly thinning in numbers by disease, war and desertion. On mustering the Expedition, I found it numbered only 173 souls, 174 less than the number I led from Bagomoyo. . . . This is terrible, but God's will be done."

Only when they reached Lake Victoria, Stanley thought, would his men be able to feed and rest sufficiently to recover their strength. But the lake was still far off, "and before we reach it many a stout fellow will have been left behind."

His gloomy prognostication seemed justified. In the next few days five more of his porters deserted, and Stanley sent ten trackers—"detectives" as he called them—to find and bring them back, dead or alive. "To permit such rapid thinning of my already scant numbers without making an effort to capture them would have been unwise," he rationalized, "as others might attempt to imitate their example."

A day later, the "detectives" returned with three of the runaways, one of whom had absconded with a box of ammunition. He was court-martialed, and it was left to his comrades to decide his punishment by majority vote. "Fifty-one were for hanging him off hand," recorded Stanley, "while 80 pleaded that he should be chained until the termination of the Expedition and flogged."

Despite Stanley's earlier pessimism, conditions improved considerably when the column reached the plain of the Luwamberri River, which was found to be teeming with game. Stanley counted large numbers of giraffe, zebra, gnu, buffalo, springbok, waterbuck, kudu, hartebeest, wild boar, "and several varieties of smaller antelope," and shot so many of them that "inordinate feasting and festive rejoicings have been the order of the day."

While they feasted they rested, and it was three days before Stanley resumed the march. But on the second day out he lost another of his most valued men to typhoid fever, a "faithful" who had accompanied Livingstone on his last journey and to whom Livingstone had given the name Gardner. "We conveyed the body to camp," wrote Stanley, "and having buried him, raised a cairn of stones over his grave at the junction of two roads. . . . In honour of this faithful, the camp is called after his name—Camp Gardner."

As they marched on toward the lake, they were reminded constantly of the proximity of Mirambo and his marauding warriors, at one point only a day's march away. Frequently they were themselves mistaken for Mirambo's column, and only the white skins of Stanley, Pocock and Barker convinced the suspicious locals that they had nothing to fear and saved the expedition from attack.

Finally, on February 27, the advance guard of the caravan at last sighted their goal.

"On a sudden hurrahing in front," wrote Stanley, ". . . Frank Pocock impetuously strode forward until he gained the brow of the hill. He took a long, sweeping look at something, waved his hat, and came down towards us, his face beaming with joy as he shouted out enthusiastically with the fervor of youth and high spirits, 'I have seen the Lake, Sir, and it is grand!' "

The entire expedition halted on the brow of the hill to feast their eyes on the vast inland sea—the world's second largest freshwater lake*—"which a dazzling sun transformed into silver, some 600 feet below us, at the distance of three miles." Then as they marched down toward the village of Kagehyi, 100 yards from the water's edge, the porters, guides and askaris broke into an extemporized song of triumph.

* Only North America's Lake Superior is bigger.

Sing, O friends, sing; the journey is ended:
Sing aloud, O friends; sing to the great Nyanza.
Sing all, sing loud, O friends, sing to the great sea.

After they had made camp at Kagehyi, Stanley offered up heartfelt thanks to "Almighty God, who has wonderfully preserved us through manifold dangers." Then, meticulous as ever, he consulted his two rated pedometers to calculate that they had traveled 720 statute miles in 103 days, a journey which he reckoned would have taken an Arab trading caravan nine months to a year.

# Chapter Fourteen

STANLEY allowed himself a mere week to rest, recover his strength, write letters and newspaper dispatches, and assemble the *Lady Alice*, before setting out on the next phase of his expedition—a circumnavigation of Victoria Nyanza. He begrudged even that much delay. "As I look upon [the lake's] dancing waters, I long to launch the Lady Alice and venture out to explore its mysteries," he wrote in a dispatch.

One of his letters was addressed to "My darling Alice," and signed "Morton." It was in part a factual account of his journey so far, in part a passionate avowal of love and longing:

> The very hour I land in England I should like to marry you, but such a long time must elapse before I see you, that even to see your dear face again appears to me as a most improbable thing. . . . I have often wondered how you pass your time. I suppose it is in one constant round of gaieties? What a contrast to yours are my surroundings. . . . My present abode is a dark hut; through the chinks of the mud I can but faintly see these lines as I write. Outside naked men and women create a furious jangle and noise, bartering with my people for beads.

Stanley's surmise was correct. Alice was enjoying "a constant round of gaieties"—and the flattering attentions of a league of young suitors. By her own account, she was already putting Stanley out of her mind, "for she realized fully after the poignancy of their last meeting that it were far better if she never saw him again." Their final evening together in New York had been "too devastating, for the intensity of his ardor and the strain of being with him had been altogether too enervating. . . . She had not asked for this love, and so consoled herself with a complete denial of responsibility."

Obviously Alice was already regretting, if she had not actually forgotten, her marriage pact with Stanley. Within a few months she would meet and become engaged to Albert Barney of Dayton, and after that—although letters continued to arrive from Stanley—she "did not read them; she feared to do so." Exotic gifts, sent by Stanley before leaving Zanzibar, also kept coming to her door. One was "a bunch of ostrich feathers, large, stiff and ungainly—sixty of them," noted Alice. "The duty on these was sixty dollars. Well, the moths enjoyed them."

Despite Stanley's close questioning of the local tribesmen, none of them could say for sure whether Victoria Nyanza was one lake or a string of smaller ones. But while hard information was at a premium, the natives had a vast store of fantasy on which to draw.

"There were, they said," wrote Stanley, "a people dwelling on its shores who were gifted with tails; another who trained enormous and fierce dogs for war; another a tribe of cannibals, who preferred human flesh to all other kinds of meat. The lake was so large it would take years to trace its sources, and who then at the end of that time would remain alive?"

Stanley was robustly skeptical of such tales, but not so his men. Not one of them stepped forward when he called for volunteers to sail with him on the *Lady Alice*. "Where are the brave fellows who are to be my companions?" demanded Stanley, but "there was a dead silence; the men gazed at one another and stupidly scratched their hips." In the absence of volunteers, Stanley simply press-ganged eleven of his best men, all with some experience of the sea. Pocock and Barker stayed behind with the bulk of the expedition to await Stanley's return, and on March 8, 1875, the *Lady Alice*, fully assembled with oars, masts, sails and spars, flying the Union Jack and the Stars and Stripes and laden to the gunwales with provisions, gifts and trade goods, moved out into a broad arm of the lake, named after its discoverer, Speke Gulf.

By the second day out, the worst fears of the Wangwana seemed about to come true; they were overtaken by a storm that was "wild beyond description." But the day after that was beautiful, and "the wild waters of yesterday were calm as those of a pond." Virtually the entire fifty-seven-day journey, counterclockwise around the lake for over a thousand miles, followed a similar pattern: furious storms followed by periods of idyllic calm, fat days when Stanley and his men ate their fill followed by lean periods when they came close to starvation, cheerful exchanges with friendly tribes followed by tense encounters with hostiles. And, more than once, a bloody battle.

The first of those occurred when a fleet of thirteen canoes, containing 100 Wavuma warriors, encircled them between the mainland and the island of Bugeyeya off the northeastern shore of the lake. At first, the Wavuma held out sweet potatoes, as if to trade, but it soon became clear that their intentions were not innocently mercantile.

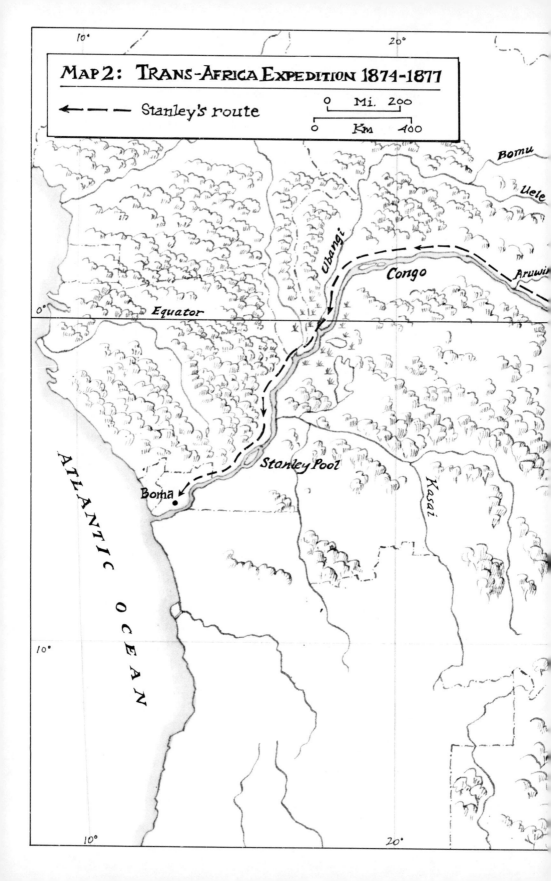

MAP 2: TRANS-AFRICA EXPEDITION 1874-1877

← – – – Stanley's route

0    Mi.  200

0    Km   400

Bomu

Uele

Ubangi

Congo

Aruwi

Equator

Stanley Pool

Kasai

Boma

ATLANTIC OCEAN

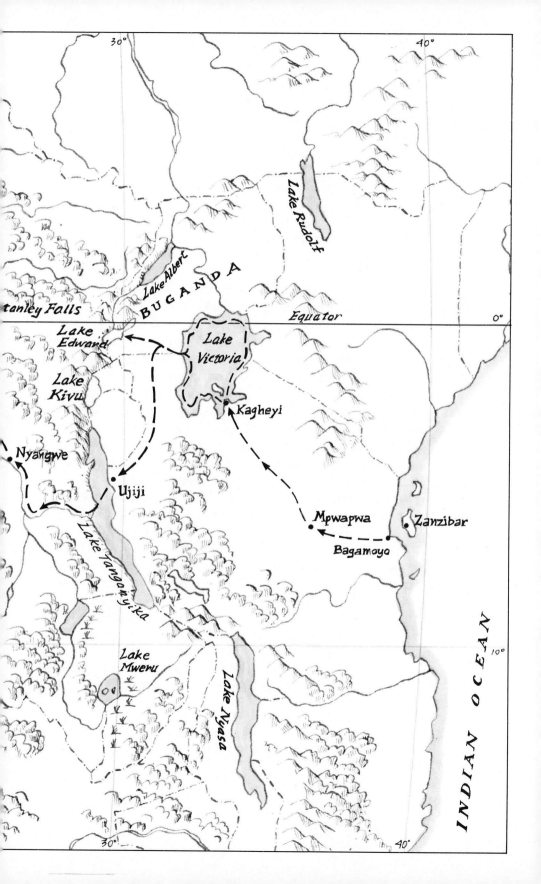

In his initial account of what followed, as published in the *Herald* and the *Telegraph*, Stanley told how he tolerated the threats and taunts of the Wavuma until one of them snatched a handful of beads from the *Lady Alice*, held them up and dared him to try to get them back. For Stanley this was one provocation too many: "I fired and the man fell dead in his canoe." In a later version of this incident, no doubt influenced by the criticism that greeted him on his return to England, Stanley said that before shooting to kill he first "fired over their heads; and as they fell back from the boat I bade my men pull away." Either way, in the ensuing battle he shot dead three more of the Wavuma and sank three of their canoes by blasting them along the waterline with his elephant gun.

The day after this encounter, the *Lady Alice* sailed past the Ripon Falls, first discovered and named* by Speke almost thirteen years previously, and identified by him as the true source of the Nile. This finding, based more on supposition than on meticulous investigation, remained fiercely disputed until it was confirmed once and for all by Stanley's circumnavigation, which proved Victoria Nyanza to be one lake, not several, with the Ripon Falls as its only major outlet.

Passing the falls and heading west, Stanley entered into the domain of Mutesa I, the Kabaka (king) of Buganda, Central Africa's most powerful monarch. Stanley sent ahead a message to tell of his coming, and Mutesa dispatched an envoy to meet and escort this white stranger—the fourth[†] he had ever seen—claiming that Stanley's arrival had been foreseen by his mother in a dream a few nights before. With the envoy's escort of six canoes leading the way, the *Lady Alice* made her way to Usavara, where the all-powerful Kabaka had set up a magnificent camp for the occasion.

Mutesa ruled a kingdom which for wealth, power and political sophistication was superior to any Stanley had yet encountered in mainland Central Africa. The explorer stepped ashore "amid a concourse of 2,000 people, who saluted me with a deafening volley of musketry and waving of flags" and was "very much amazed at all this ceremonious and pompous greeting." He was welcomed by a resplendently attired official who introduced himself as Mutesa's *katikiro* (prime minister), and conducted to comfortable quarters to

---

* In honor of the first Marquess of Ripon, president of the Royal Geographical Society in Speke's day. The Ripon Falls no longer exist, having been submerged since the construction of the Owen Falls hydroelectric dam, close to the town of Jinja, in 1954.

† Stanley's forerunners were Speke, Speke's fellow English gentleman-explorer Grant, and Charles Chaille-Long, an American officer in the service of the Khedive of Egypt.

eat, rest and await the pleasure of the king. After some hours, the call came. Stanley described his audience:

> Issuing out of my quarters I found myself in a broad street eighty feet wide and half a mile long, which was lined by [the Kabaka's] personal guards and attendants, his captains and their respective retinues, to the number of about 3,000. At the extreme end of this street and fronting it was the king's audience house. . . . As I advanced towards him the soldiers continued to fire their guns. The drums, sixteen in number, beat a fearful tempest of sound and the flags waved.

Again, Stanley was enormously impressed by the ceremonial. He was even more impressed by Mutesa himself when, after a solemn and silent handshake, he was invited to sit in the royal presence while a hundred of the Kabaka's "great captains" looked on. Mutesa appeared to be about thirty-four years old and, Stanley noted, was "tall and slender . . . but with broad shoulders" and a face which was "very agreeable and pleasant and indicates intelligence and mildness. . . . As soon as Mutesa began to speak I became captivated by his manner, for there was much of the polish of the true gentleman about it. . . ."

For a normally sharp-eyed reporter—one, moreover, whom life had taught to view his fellow man with deep suspicion—Stanley seems to have been far too easily taken in by Mutesa. Into his diary that same day he delivered a wildly extravagant encomium upon this monarch whom others, on far better evidence, considered "a murderous despot":

> I have seen in Mutesa a most intelligent, humane and distinguished prince, a man who if aided timely by virtuous philanthropists will yet do more for Central Africa and civilization what fifty years of gospel teaching unaided by such authority cannot [sic] do. I see in him the light that shall lighten the darkness of this benighted region. . . . In this man I see the possible fruition of Livingstone's hopes. . . .

This was a very different being from Mutesa the homicidal clown—weirdly reminiscent of a Ugandan despot of our own era, Idi Amin—whom Speke had described thirteen years before. The young monarch who welcomed Stanley's forerunner to his court had affected the stiff-legged gait of a prowling lion, "but the outward sweep of the legs, intended to represent the stride of the noble beast, appeared [to Speke] only to realize a very ludicrous kind of wad-dle. . . ."

Speke had given the Kabaka a gift of three rifles, one of which Mutesa promptly handed to a page, with orders to go out and shoot someone at random. The page did so and "returned to announce his success with a look of glee." But so hardened was Mutesa's court to casual homicide that no one paid much attention. "The affair created hardly any interest," noted Speke. "I never heard, and there appeared no curiosity to know, what individual human being the urchin had deprived of his life."

Such offhand atrocities were clearly an everyday occurrence. In a further journal entry while Mutesa's guest, Speke noted that "nearly every day . . . I have seen one, two, or three of the wretched palace women led away to execution, crying out as she went to premature death . . . in the utmost despair and lamentation, yet there was not a soul who dared lift a hand to save any of them."

Could Mutesa have become a totally reformed character by the time Stanley came on the scene? It seems unlikely. History teaches that the murderous impulses of absolute despots become more, not less, insatiable with age and indulgence. And we have it on good authority that at the time of Stanley's visit Mutesa kept his court executioners so busy that "the capital was nicknamed *Ndabiraako ddala* ('see me for the last time') because when two men met they did not know whether they would ever see each other again." Nor, ap-parently, did Mutesa have any compunction about selling his own people into slavery. As the same authority has recorded: "He allowed the Arabs to carry on slaving so that they might give him large quantities of cloth in exchange."

Stanley was well aware of Speke's opinion of Mutesa, but attrib-uted the king's reformed behavior to his conversion to Islam by an emissary of the Sultan of Zanzibar. "False and contemptible as these [Muslim] doctrines are," he wrote in his diary, "they are preferable to the ruthless instincts of a savage despot, whom Speke and Grant left wallowing in the blood of women. . . ."

Improbably fancying himself as a missionary manqué, Stanley now set out to take Mutesa's spiritual elevation a step further by persuad-ing him to abandon Islam for Christianity. Mutesa responded by assuming the role of an earnest seeker after truth and light, and soon Stanley felt able to inform the world, through a joint dispatch to the *Herald* and the *Telegraph*, that "by one conversation" he had con-vinced Mutesa of the superiority of the Christian faith. "If it were only followed by the arrival of a Christian mission here," he assured his readers, "the conversion of Mutesa and his Court to Christianity would be complete." In a direct appeal to "the leading philanthropists and the pious people of England," Stanley exhorted:

> Here, gentlemen, is your opportunity—embrace it! The people on the shores of the Nyanza call upon you. Obey your own generous instincts and listen to them, and I assure you that in one year you will have more converts to Christianity than all other missionaries united can number.

Stanley's inflated rhetoric would have an electrifying effect in Europe, setting off a theological scramble for Africa analogous to the territorial scramble which was soon to follow. First in the field would be the Anglicans of the Church Missionary Society. Close behind would come the White Fathers of Catholic France. By their joint, but far from coordinated, efforts the Christian missionaries would all but drive the mullahs from the scene. But their fierce mutual competition would also cause endless mischief and eventually civil war between followers of the rival Christian confessions. In later years, British colonials, muttering into their gin-and-tonics about complaining wives and squabbling native Christians, would say that "white women and White Fathers" were the source of all Uganda's problems.

In fact, Mutesa had never been a Muslim and would never become a Christian. Although at the time he met Stanley, he observed many of the outward rituals of Islam and obliged his court to do likewise, he could not bring himself to undergo the painful ritual of circumcision required for formal conversion. Nor, for rather different reasons, could he ever bring himself later to take the decisive plunge into Christianity. The idea of monogamy was as repugnant to Mutesa as the prospect of penile mutilation, and so he resisted baptism, realizing that once he submitted the missionaries would insist on his shedding all but one of his many hundreds of wives.

He also soon tired of the missionaries' constant complaints about his habit of putting his subjects to death on the whim of the moment. Consequently, Mutesa remained a pagan until his death in 1884.* In sum, the display of gentle good behavior and eagerness to embrace Christianity which so impressed Stanley was an act put on by the wily Mutesa for reasons of *realpolitik*. He wanted the support of Christian Europe as a counterpoise to the Khedive of Egypt, whose

---

* And in the following year, his son and successor, Mwanga I, would demonstrate his own respect for the Christian faith by murdering the first Anglican Bishop of East Africa, the Right Reverend James Hannington, as he arrived to take up his episcopal duties.

representatives were pushing southward into his territory from the Sudan.

Later events would prove Mutesa to have been too clever by half: distant Europe was far more a threat to his sovereign power than neighboring Egypt, which lost all interest in controlling the Nile's Ugandan headwaters after the spendthrift Khedive Ismail was deposed in 1879. On the other hand, the Christian missionaries whom Mutesa summoned up by gulling Stanley were to be the advance guard of white rule. The Victorian aphorism had it that "Trade follows the Flag." Just as surely the Flag followed the Cross.

Quite coincidentally, and underscoring the reasons for Mutesa's fears of Egyptian expansion, one of the Khedive's foreign officers, the French colonel Linant de Bellefonds, turned up with an escort of forty Sudanese soldiers within days of Stanley's arrival at Mutesa's court. Despite the element of rivalry inherent in their situation, the two white men struck up an instant friendship. "Each one of us," wrote de Bellefonds, "found in the other a brother and opened his heart to him." For his part, Stanley found de Bellefonds "extremely well informed, energetic and a great traveller."

When de Bellefonds left to return down the Nile to Khartoum, Stanley entrusted his letters and newspaper dispatches to him. From the Sudanese capital de Bellefonds faithfully forwarded Stanley's papers to Cairo, whence the dispatches were telegraphed to London. Shortly after discharging this duty, de Bellefonds was killed in a skirmish with rebellious Sudanese tribesmen, leading to the popular legend that Stanley's dispatches had reached Cairo caked with de Bellefonds' blood—a legend which lent additional drama to Stanley's clarion call for missionaries to lighten the African darkness.

Having dispatched his news about the lake and Buganda, Stanley was anxious to be on his way, complete his circumnavigation, and rejoin the rest of his expedition, for whose safety he was beginning to feel some concern. So, after ten days as a pampered and flattered guest, he took his leave of the Kabaka. Mutesa had promised him an escort of thirty canoes and warriors, but Magassa, the admiral designated to command the escort fleet, kept finding excuses to delay his departure. Tired of waiting for him, Stanley decided to push on unescorted—a decision that was to prove fateful.

Sailing south along the west coast of the lake, the *Lady Alice* came within a week to a large island called Bumbireh. The islanders seemed menacing, but Stanley and his men—hungry and near-desperate to replenish their foodstocks—approached the shore in the hope of placating them by gifts and diplomacy. As they neared the shore, dozens of the islanders waded out to meet them; up close, they seemed less menacing than from a distance.

"No sooner, however," wrote Stanley, "had the keel of the boat grounded than the apparently friendly natives rushed in a body and seized the boat and dragged her high and dry on land, with all on board. . . . Twice I raised my revolvers to kill and be killed but the crew restrained me, saying it was premature to fight. . . . Accordingly I sat down in the stern sheets and waited patiently for the decisive moment."

Although Stanley's boat was now surrounded by furious hostiles brandishing spears, bows and arrows, and battle clubs, his interpreters remained admirably calm, placating the islanders with assurances of friendly intent and offers of cloth and beads. The chief of Bumbireh, Shekka, eventually agreed to allow Stanley and his men to leave in peace in return for four cloth dotis and ten necklaces. But on receipt of this *hongo* Shekka reneged and ordered his men to seize the oars of the *Lady Alice*. Then, confident that Stanley and his crew could not escape, the islanders retired to their village to eat and make merry.

A couple of hours later, having dined and drunk to the full, Shekka and his warriors returned to the beach with the obvious intention, as Stanley said, "to cut our throats." Stanley was still sitting in the stern, elephant gun at the ready, and as the warriors approached he muttered urgent instructions to his men. Then "with one desperate effort my crew of eleven men seized the boat as if she had been a mere toy and shot her into the water." As they clambered aboard, Stanley kept the islanders at bay with volleys from his elephant rifle and a double-barreled shotgun.

As the enemy fell back from the shoreline, Stanley's men ripped up the seats and footboards of the *Lady Alice*, using them as crude paddles to get farther out into the lake. The islanders tried to launch their canoes to give chase, but withering fire from Stanley's guns prevented them. He dropped two men with two shots, and with a third he killed a subchief and his wife and child who were standing a few paces behind him. This "extraordinary result," reported Stanley, "had more effect on the superstitious minds of the natives than all previous or subsequent shots."

As Stanley's men paddled frantically out of the cove toward open water, two canoes came out in pursuit from another direction. Stanley waited until they were within a hundred yards, then opened up with the elephant gun again, this time firing explosive shot.

"Four shots killed five men and sank the canoes," he recorded.

"This decisive affair disheartened the enemy, and we were left to pursue our way unmolested, not, however, without hearing a ringing voice shouting out to us 'Go and die in the Nyanza!' When the savages counted their losses they found fourteen dead and eight wounded. . . ."

Stanley and his men very nearly did die in the Nyanza. That night a fierce gale blew up and, "owing to the loss of our oars, we could not keep the boat before the wind." Helpless, they "resigned ourselves to the wind and waves, the furious rain and the horror of the tempest. . . . If our boat capsized, the crocodiles of the lake would make short work of us; if we were driven on an uninhabited mainland death by starvation awaited us. Yet with all these terrors we were so worn out with hunger, fatigue and anxiety that, excepting the watchman, we all fell asleep, though awakened now and then by his voice calling to the men to bale the boat out."

At dawn, the storm abated. Later that day they found an uninhabited island where bananas and a cherrylike fruit grew, and where Stanley shot two brace of large, fat ducks. Five days later, after weathering another furious storm, they sighted Kagehyi and, with much firing of musketry and waving of flags, rejoined their comrades.

Stanley's joy and relief subsided quickly enough when he learned that, twelve days before, Fred Barker had died of a sudden fever. In addition, half a dozen of his best Zanzibaris—among them Mabruki Speke, who had marched with Burton, Speke, Grant and Livingstone, as well as with Stanley—had succumbed to dysentery. In a letter of condolence to Barker's mother, Stanley called him "a rare young man, mettlesome, manly, and thoroughly English in his good qualities." Of Mabruki Speke, Stanley wrote in his diary: "Could an epitaph be written over his grave: Here lies the most faithful and true servant."

Once rested, and recovered from a fresh attack of intermittent fever, Stanley was anxious to march westward around the southern end of the lake to carry out the next phase of his expedition—an exploration of the territory between Lake Victoria and the smaller Lake Albert (now called Lake Edward) and a circumnavigation of Lake Albert itself. But, as during his search for Livingstone, the overland route was blocked by the ubiquitous Mirambo. Stanley's best recourse, therefore, was to go by water to a disembarkation point well north of Mirambo. But for that he would need a great number of canoes, and there followed a month of difficult and tedious haggling with local chiefs to obtain the loan of sufficient boats to carry the expedition.

Thus, it was not until June 19 that Stanley was able to set out with twenty-three canoes, bound for a halfway point which he called Refuge Island. There he set up a well-fortified headquarters, leaving Frank Pocock in command while he returned to Kagehyi to collect the rest of his men and supplies. It was July 11 before he completed the round trip and had his expedition together in one place again.

Refuge Island was not far south of Bumbireh Island, which lay athwart the route Stanley would take northward. And now that he was in full force—and reinforced by a number of Mutesa's war canoes that had been sent out in search of him—Stanley decided that he was in a position to take revenge on "the hated island, the savage ferocity of whose people I have seldom seen equalled."

The *Lady Alice* led the way, followed by six large canoes carrying 250 men. By a feinting movement, Stanley lured the Bumbireh warriors to open ground at the head of a westward-facing bay, where they had the afternoon sun in their eyes. He described the action that followed:

> After approaching within 100 yards of the shore I formed my line of battle, the American and English flags waving as our ensigns. Having anchored each canoe so as to turn its broadside to the shore I ordered a volley to be fired at one group which numbered about fifty, and the result was ten killed and thirty wounded. The savages . . . advanced to the water's edge slinging stones and shooting arrows. I then ordered the canoes to advance within fifty yards of the shore, and to fire as if they were shooting birds. After an hour the savages . . . retreated up the hill slope, where they continued still exposed to our bullets.

By the time Stanley's "work of punishment was consummated" and the Bumbireh warriors finally fled the scene of battle, they had lost thirty-three dead and at least a hundred wounded for the cost of only two men slightly injured on Stanley's side. As Stanley told it, Mutesa's warriors wanted to go ashore, mutilate the dead and massacre the survivors, "but I refused, saying that I had not come to destroy the island, but to punish them for their treachery. . . ."

Stanley felt he had struck an important blow for the right of innocent passage on the lake and that he had acted with Christian restraint in holding back Mutesa's warriors. But that was not how many at home saw it when his account of the battle reached the

*Herald* and the *Telegraph*, about a year after the event. The outcry was especially loud in England, where liberals were shocked and indignant editorials were penned, protesting at "this outrage on a peaceful and comparatively unarmed people."

Even the unabashedly racist old Africa hand "Ruffian Dick" Burton was critical. He "still shoots negroes as if they were monkeys," he commented in a letter to Kirk. "That young man will be getting into a row—and serve him right." Another noted African explorer, James Grant, lamented in a letter to the Royal Geographical Society that "even Stanley's best friends cannot but regret his pugnacity and want of discretion." And the philanthropists of the Aborigines Protection Society and the Anti-Slavery Society jointly urged the British government to take drastic action against Stanley for his "act of blind and ruthless vengeance." One reverend gentleman even suggested that Stanley should be sent back to Bumbireh "and there in the presence of the people he has so grossly outraged hanged with impartial justice as other murderers are."

Lord Derby, the British Foreign Secretary, pointed out that he could not order action against an American citizen, especially in an area well beyond British jurisdiction. But he did offer to send a message advising Stanley that he was not authorized to fly the Union Jack. That message was telegraphed to Kirk, now back at his post in Zanzibar, who in turn asked the American consul to forward it. There is no evidence that Stanley ever received it.

In New York, meanwhile, Bennett was reveling in the controversy, which only helped promote his newspaper. The *Herald* gleefully reprinted the anti-Stanley articles of its rivals and defended its man in characteristic knock-down, drag-out style. One editorial called Stanley's liberal critics "the howling dervishes of civilization," and when Stanley finally returned safely, the *Herald* sneered that no doubt "the philanthropists of London" would be greatly distressed:

> Their humane but rather impractical view is that a leader in such a position should permit his men to be slaughtered by the natives and should be slaughtered himself and let discovery go to the dogs, but should never pull a trigger against this species of human vermin that puts its uncompromising savagery in the way of all progress and all increase of knowledge.

From this distance in time, it seems that Stanley's punitive raid at Bumbireh, however ill-advised, was more opportunistic than premeditated, and that the opportunity would not have arisen at all had he not been forced by Mirambo's marauders to take the lake route to his next destination. As he noted in a news dispatch dated August 15, 1875, it was after reaching an island five miles south of Bumbireh that, "remembering the bitter injuries I had received . . . the death by violence and starvation we had so narrowly escaped, I resolved, unless the natives made amends for their cruelty and treachery, to make war on them. . . ."

But plainly Stanley brought a lot of controversy down on his own head by the colorful way he described the battle in his dispatches. Some felt he would have been wise not to have mentioned an event which would otherwise have remained unknown. But sensitivity was never Stanley's long suit, and far from remaining silent, he appears to have exaggerated to make the story more exciting: in his diary he noted the number of enemy killed as thirty-three, but when writing his account for the *Herald* and *Telegraph* he inflated the total to forty-two.

Stanley tried to undo the damage by the time he came to write his two-volume account of the expedition in 1877. Now he refrained from giving any casualty figures at all, merely recording that "the result was several killed and wounded." And he altered his account to make it seem that he resorted to arms only after the islanders tried to bar his expedition's passage northward. "Weakness and irresolution . . . had proved harmful on several previous occasions," pleaded Stanley. "The savage only respects force, power, boldness and decision." He even quoted from Livingstone's *Last Journals* to justify his behavior: "It may have been for the best that the English are thus known as people who can hit hard when unjustly attacked, as we on this occasion most certainly were."

In a private letter to his old friend Edward King, Stanley sought to dispel the idea that "peaceful and comparatively unarmed" natives, as his detractors called them, had no chance against modern firearms. The letter was written after Stanley's first battle with the Bumbireh warriors, but before his punitive expedition, and so perhaps was not intended as public justification of his strong-arm methods.

"As God is my judge," he wrote, "I would prefer paying tribute and making these savages friends rather than enemies. . . . They attack in such numbers and so sudden that our repeating rifles and Snyders [*sic*] have to be handled with such nervous rapidity as will force them back before we are forced to death; for if we allow them to come within forty yards their spears are as fatal as bullets."

That was no doubt so, but it does not excuse or explain the punitive raid on Bumbireh. The hostile islanders had already been severely mauled in their first encounter with him, and all that the subsequent raid accomplished was to satisfy Stanley's need to "teach the natives a lesson" and enhance his growing if exaggerated reputation as a ruthless conquistador to whom human life—especially black life—meant little.

# Chapter Fifteen

NEWS of the punishment meted out to the Bumbireh islanders preceded Stanley as he, his men and their Baganda escort paddled north, five hundred strong, in the *Lady Alice* and thirty-seven canoes, "to the sound of sonorous drums and the cheery tones of the bugle." Wherever they passed, the natives hastened to certify their friendship with gifts of fruit, vegetables, chickens, goats and oxen. "Thus," noted Stanley, "was our victory . . . productive of great good and plenty to us."

Some sixty miles up the coast, at a place called Dumo, Stanley chose a campsite. There, under the command of Frank Pocock, the expedition was to rest while Stanley and a handful of trusties went on to Mutesa's court to extract from the king the guides and warriors he had promised for the next phase of the journey—the exploration of the unmapped region west of Lake Victoria.

Stanley hoped to spend no more than a few days on his mission to Mutesa, but, as always, Africa marched to its own rhythms. Mutesa had gone to war with the neighboring Wavuma and was encamped with an army of 150,000 men and 400 canoes at Jinja, on the eastern side of the Ripon Falls. And when Stanley joined him there, to be "received with joy and honour by King and chiefs," the Kabaka demanded that he stay until the war was over, which, he assured his guest, would not be long.

But the Wavuma were redoubtable foes. "They fight desperately," Stanley noted, "and are expert divers, attack their enemy in the open lake, dive under the canoes and cut the vegetable cords which fasten the boat." After a series of battles in which the Wavuma acquitted themselves well, Stanley found himself revising his earlier high opinion of the Baganda and their king. "Mutesa is like a child," he confided to his diary. "It is useless to advise him. . . . The Wavuma deserve all praise for their hardihood and courage, while the Baganda to me make themselves objects of contempt."

After two months, the war ended in stalemate, and Stanley marched back with Mutesa and his army to Ulagalla, the old capital, where he was obliged to remain until mid-November before his es-

cort was arranged and he was allowed to return to his expedition at
Dumo. By the time he was reunited with his men, Stanley had been
away three months and five days and was in a fever of impatience to
be back on the trail.

Like Admiral Magassa before him, General Sambuzi—the officer
designated by Mutesa to command Stanley's escort across Bunyoro
to Lake Albert—was laggardly, and Stanley set off without him. He
and his men had marched eighty-six miles toward the lake before
Sambuzi and his force of two thousand warriors caught up with
them. Ten days later they passed out of friendly Buganda and into the
territory of Kabba Rega, king of the hostile Banyoro.*

As they advanced noisily across the uplands of Bunyoro, the natives took flight and hid, but on the intruding column's flanks and at
its rear an unseen army was gathering. One day, when Stanley and
his escort were encamped on a plateau overlooking the precipitous
descent to Lake Albert, a large force of natives gathered on the crest
of a hill to the east of the camp.

"The great war drum was at once sounded," wrote Stanley, "and
the camps summoned to prepare for war. Sambuzi himself headed a
large party and sallied out to meet them to see if their presence meant
hostility, while I with 50 rifles took position on a hill to observe the
field and act as circumstances would demand."

As Stanley looked on, Sambuzi and the leader of the Banyoro war
party parleyed. To the intruders' protestations that they had come in
peace, the Banyoro leader replied, "No, no, you are liars, you are bad
men. You Baganda have brought the White Man to eat the country."
Then, warning of their intention to join battle with the intruders the
next day, the Banyoro leader added ominously: "Tell us how you
will get away from here. Can you fly in the air? If not, think of
tomorrow and sleep on what we have told you."

The warning had its effect. In a panic, Sambuzi called his chiefs
and Stanley into conference that night. Stanley insisted on holding
them to their duty to escort him to the lake and wait there for him
while he sailed around it. The chiefs said they would all be killed if
they did as he demanded. Stanley made a compromise suggestion:
they should escort him to the lake, stand guard while he assembled
and launched the *Lady Alice*, and then leave for Uganda. Sambuzi
and his chiefs agreed to this, but that evening Stanley saw them
bundling up their provisions as if to steal away after dark.

* The people are the *Banyoro*, their land *Bunyoro*, just as the country named *Buganda* was
populated by the *Baganda*.

At this, Stanley's own men lost heart. Even the "gallant and ever faithful Kacheche" wanted to turn back. "Remaining here alone to fight all these people is certain death," he said. The other veterans of the expedition agreed, and Stanley had to bow to the inevitable. The next morning they started back, expecting to have to fight their way out of the trap into which they had marched. But the Banyoro let them leave unmolested, their warriors following at a discreet distance to see them off.

Five days later Stanley and his escort re-entered Buganda, and in a dispatch to his newspapers Stanley confessed that the whole excursion had been a "great folly." Still, he was able to console himself with the thought that "the geographical knowledge we have been able to acquire . . . is considerable."

After a couple of days' rest, Stanley marched his men south and west toward Lake Tanganyika, and on this leg of his journey he at last—though not by choice—came face to face with the dreaded Mirambo. The encounter took place at a town called Serombo, which Mirambo and his men entered to the beat of drums, the ululation of women and a fusillade of welcoming musket fire. The next day, when Mirambo visited Stanley's camp, Stanley was amazed to find him "so different from all I ever conceived of such a redoubtable chieftain and a bandit of such terrible reputation." Mirambo was, Stanley wrote,

> handsome, regular-featured, mild, soft spoken, with what you would call a meek demeanour, generous, open-handed with nothing of the small cent ideas of narrow mean-minded men. Indeed I did not let myself readily believe that this could possibly be the ferocious chief of the terrible Ruga-Ruga. . . . [He] indicated nothing of the Napoleonic genius which he has for five years displayed in the heart of Africa . . . except the eyes. . . . Unlike all other Africans I have met, they met your own and steadily and calmly confronted them [sic].

In Mirambo's tent that night, Stanley and the brigand chief underwent the ceremony of blood brotherhood and exchanged presents. The next morning Stanley pushed on toward Lake Tanganyika. Thirty-four days and 294 miles later, he found himself once more standing in the dusty town square at Ujiji, where he had met Livingstone four and a half years previously.

Stanley had been looking forward to finding some letters, sent up from the coast, waiting for him there. In particular, he had been hoping to hear from Alice.

"I daily fed and lived on that hope," he wrote. ". . . You may imagine how I felt when after enquiry about letters, I was met with 'There are none.' . . . What would you have done, oh my Alice? Tear your hair, clothes, and shriek distractedly, run about and curse the Fates? I did not do anything so undignified, but I soberly grieved and felt discouraged. . . ."

He told Alice that he was in good health, but "awfully thin," having lost sixty pounds. "My cheeks are sunk," he added, "my eyes large and sickly, my bones feel sore, even lying on two blankets. . . . Yet the same heart still throbs with deepest love, as it did long ago. . . ." Had he but known it, Alice's heart, if it was throbbing at all, was doing so for her young husband, by whom she was now four months pregnant.

A week or so later, having reassembled the *Lady Alice*, Stanley left Ujiji, sailing south along the eastern coast to make his clockwise circumnavigation of the lake. He had heard from Arab traders that Lieutenant Verney Lovett Cameron, a rival explorer commissioned by the RGS, had sailed west across the lake eighteen months before, hoping to become the first white man to cross the continent east to west.* Stanley wanted that honor for himself, but attached even higher priority to the task of following the Livingstone River, as he called the Lualaba/Congo, all the way to the sea.

He was accordingly glad to learn that Cameron, having reached the Lualaba, had turned westward toward Angola, leaving "the question of the Lualaba where Livingstone left it." That is to say, it was still not established whether—as Livingstone had believed, but Stanley strongly doubted—the Lualaba was an upper reach of the Nile or a headwater of the Congo, or perhaps even the Niger.

On July 31, the *Lady Alice* returned to Ujiji, having completed the 810-mile circumnavigation in fifty-one days. Stanley found the town ravaged by a smallpox epidemic, but the men he had left behind under the command of Pocock had largely escaped, thanks to the vaccinations Stanley had himself administered before leaving Bagamoyo. Only a handful of men who had dodged Stanley's needle had succumbed to the disease.

Since Ujiji was the last place from which it would be possible to send mail down to the coast with any realistic hope of its arriving, Stanley set himself to writing a series of detailed dispatches on his geographical discoveries around the lake. He also wrote a number of personal letters, among them one to Alice. After bemoaning the fact

---

* He succeeded. Starting from Bagamoyo in March 1873, he reached the Atlantic at Benguela in November 1875.

that he had "not received one encouraging word from you or any living friendly soul" since leaving Zanzibar, he went on:

> But I do not blame you, the letters were no doubt detained somewhere on the road. Then, my own Darling, if by that name I may call you, let us hope cheerfully that a happy termination to this long period of trial of your constancy and my health and courage await us both, that the time may come when we can both laugh at these silent, gloomy days to be, both be amused at our experiences, various and different as they are, and that [*sic*] our lives will never be marred by such a long separation. . . . For you, my own Alice, what treasures of love would I pour out before you if I could see you. . . . What means have I to convey my heart's load of love to you, but this letter which must go through a thousand miles of savages, exposed to all dangers of flood and fire and battle until it reaches the sea? And to go well it must be light, not heavy. I thus am prevented from enlarging on my love, and perhaps properly, lest too much would render its declaration insipid. . . . Grant then that my love towards you is unchanged, that you are my dream, my stay and my hope, and my beacon, and believe that I shall still cherish you in this light until I meet you, or death meets me. This is the last you will get, I fear, for a long time. Then, my darling, accept this letter with one last and loving farewell.

Stanley had finished his letters and reports and was ready to strike camp when a severe bout of malaria gripped him. For seven days he lay in his *tembe* alternately chattering with cold and burning with fever. On the eighth day, recovering but still weak, he rose to commence the march only to find that 38 of his 170 men had deserted rather than face the terrors of the trail ahead, which passed through the notorious cannibal country of Manyuema.

Keenly conscious that desertions at this rate could wreck the entire expedition, Stanley mustered his men and had thirty-two of the least reliable clapped in irons and marched under armed guard to the waiting transport canoes. Of his remaining men, Stanley considered only thirty loyal enough to be entrusted with guns as they made their way to the western side of the lake.

Stanley was bitterly disappointed by the desertions, complaining that his "faith in the stability of the Wangwana [was] utterly destroyed." When they encamped on the western shore of the lake he sent Pocock and his faithful "detective" Kacheche back to Ujiji to hunt for the deserters. Soon after he again succumbed to fever. He felt "terribly weak," and the heat was "terrible—138 F in the sun."

When Pocock and Kacheche returned after eight days, they

brought only four deserters with them. A day later, Stanley received another blow when Kalulu, the boy he had taken to Europe and America and considered almost a son, also deserted. He sent Kacheche after him, and when the boy was brought back the next day Stanley paid Kacheche a reward of five doti and had Kalulu put into slave chains, like the other deserters.

Stanley considered desertion to be one of the greatest hazards of exploration. "Unless the traveller in Africa exerts himself to keep his force intact, he cannot hope to perform satisfactory service," he wrote. ". . . Livingstone lost at least six years of his time, and finally his life, by permitting his people to desert." But, Stanley added, "over-severity is as bad as over-gentleness" in dealing with deserters. "What is required is pure, simple justice between man and man."

On his journey around Lake Tanganyika, Stanley had seen grim evidence of the slave trade which, despite the treaty forced by Britain upon the Sultan of Zanzibar, continued unabated. Camping at the mouth of a river on the western side of the lake, Stanley had observed a caravan of more than a thousand slaves, mainly women and children, who were in an appalling state from lack of food.

> The surviving children were in a condition ill-resembling humanity. The chests jutted out with the protuberance of a skeleton frame, while the poor bellies were in such a fearfully attenuated state, like an empty bladder; ribs and bones glared out; legs were mere sticks of bone, resembling weak supports to the large head and large chest. . . . The elders were in chains, but the number was so great that heavy bark cords had been made, to which the slaves were strung by the neck a few foot apart. Even children a few years old were subjected to the same treatment, probably because it was easier to count the list by gangs than one by one. Many of the older males were quite new to this servile treatment, as was evinced by downcast heads and abashed faces when strangers looked at them.

Now, during his forty-day march from the lake to the Lualaba, Stanley saw more such scenes and other evidence which inspired him to write a powerful dispatch on the slave trade after his arrival at Nyangwe, the town on the banks of the Lualaba where Livingstone had witnessed the massacre that shocked the civilized world three years before. Stanley was, of course, already well acquainted with the ramifications of the slave trade, as any traveler in Africa must be. Yet only now, near the limits of Arab penetration into the heart of the continent, did its full enormity strike home. "The slave trade elsewhere," Stanley commented, "is mostly confined to small private retail dealings in human flesh between Arab and Arab. Two or three, or half a dozen, or a dozen slaves are exchanged quietly between traders, as the exigencies of business or currency require. These few slaves are perhaps accepted in payment of a long-standing debt, or are purchased to complete the number of domestic servants. The buying or selling of them in such a quiet, orderly manner does not strike one as being specially repulsive—rather more as an exchange from one domestic service to another."

But here—at the wholesale end of the business, as it were—the trade provided sights to curdle the conscience even of the hard-boiled Stanley. Unable to sustain a promise "not to indulge my personal feelings, but to be cool, precise and literal," he raged that "it must be assuredly owing to the deep wiles of hell and its inhabitants that the people of a small island like Zanzibar are permitted to commit crimes such as no European State understands."

The natives were regarded by the slavers and their African mercenaries as if they were cattle, to be left to graze until required for the slaughterhouse, wrote Stanley. Then, when slaves were needed to satisfy the demands of the market, the Arab traders would "invite their friends and dependants for a few days' sport, just as an English nobleman invites his friends to grouse or deer shooting."

All men found carrying spears would be shot out of hand and dismembered. Women, children and submissive adult males who were too valuable to kill became slaves. "The murder of people on this scale is called a war," Stanley reported, adding that when he asked an Arab acquaintance if such "wars" were frequent, he received the reply: "Frequent! Sometimes six times and ten times a month. We cannot teach these pagans to be quiet. They are always kicking up trouble. . . ."

The extent of the devastation wrought by the slave trade was illustrated in a conversation Stanley had with Wadi Safeni, one of his captains, as they passed through "an uninhabited wilderness" beyond the western shore of Lake Tanganyika. "Master," said Safeni, "all this plain lying between Mwana Mamba and Nyangwe, when I first came here eight years ago, was populated so thickly that we travelled through gardens and fields and villages every quarter of an hour. There were flocks of goats and droves of black pigs round every village. A bunch of bananas could be purchased for one cowrie. You can see what the country is now for yourself."

Stanley blamed the continuation of the slave trade, in contravention of the recent pact between Zanzibar and Britain, on the weakness and inefficiency of his old acquaintance, Sultan Barghash, who either could not or would not stop his agents and officers from pursuing it. But Stanley had no illusions that his revelations would change anything. The action the British had taken, he wrote, "makes no more impression upon this appalling and desperate trade than what this letter will make."

One senses genuine outrage in Stanley's lengthy and admirably detailed dispatch—an honest outrage which carries far more conviction than the stale and conventional Victorian pieties he so often felt obliged to parade before his readers. But he blunted the impact of his revelations and inevitably cast doubt on his own sincerity by enlisting the help of the most notorious of all the Arab slavers—Hamed bin Mohammed, alias Tippu-Tib—for the next phase of his perilous journey across Africa.

Had Stanley been willing to abandon his plan to follow the Lualaba, pushing into regions which even the Arab slave- and ivory traders had not so far penetrated, he might have done without the services of Tippu-Tib. But, driven by his own imperatives, he felt no option but to join forces with this particular devil, and in so doing to provide more ammunition for those who would dismiss him as a mere freebooter, without principle or scruple.

That judgment was not entirely fair; even the irreproachable Livingstone had been forced to seek the assistance of Arab slavers to survive. Still, it has to be said that neither in the privacy of his diary nor in his public writings does Stanley reveal any signs of a struggle with his conscience over the hiring of Tippu-Tib.

Indeed, what Stanley had to say on first acquaintance about this man, the most adventurous and ruthless of all the Zanzibari merchant-warlords, was on the whole admiring. The diary entry recording their first meeting, en route between Bambarre and Nyangwe, describes him as "the redoubted . . . Tippu-Tib, a fine handsome dark man of Arab extraction* in the prime of life, who next to Sayid bin Habib† is the first of African explorers." A corresponding passage in Stanley's book *Through the Dark Continent* is no less devoid of moral judgment:

> He was . . . straight and quick in his movements, a picture of energy and strength. He had a fine intelligent face, with a nervous twitching of the eyes, and gleaming white and perfectly formed teeth. . . . With the air of a well-bred Arab, and almost courtier-like in his manner, he welcomed

* He was a half-caste, the son of an Arab father and an African mother.
† In his youth, Habib had traveled from Bagamoyo across the continent as far as Luanda, the Angolan capital.

me . . . while a buzz of admiration of his style was perceptible from the on-lookers. After regarding him for a few minutes, I came to the conclusion that this Arab was . . . the most remarkable man I had met among the Arabs, Waswahili [coastal natives] and the half-castes in Africa.

Yet Stanley was in no doubt about Tippu-Tib's slaving activities. He knew that Tagomoyo, perpetrator of the massacre which Livingstone had witnessed, was one of his trusted lieutenants. And Tippu-Tib at one point said to him: "Slaves cost nothing, they only require to be gathered."

From Tippu-Tib and other members of his entourage Stanley learned why Cameron had turned west toward Angola instead of following the Lualaba. Like Livingstone, he had been unable to beg, borrow, steal or hire canoes from the natives, and his men, like Livingstone's, had balked at the perils of following the river's course

*Tippu-Tib in middle age. The king of the Zanzibar slave traders, he carved an empire from the bush. (The Illustrated London News, Vol. 95, 1889)*

by land through "an eternal forest" occupied by "terrible dwarfs" and "ferocious cannibals." But for Stanley, the Lualaba represented a challenge that could not be avoided.

> If I merely struck direct west . . . how could I prove that the Lualaba is the Congo, or that it is not the Congo but the Nile or the Niger— whichever it may be? I should forfeit all right to be heard upon the subject. . . . My opinion about the Lualaba is that it . . . is too mighty a river here to be the Nile. I have crossed it, sounded it, tested its current, taken its altitude . . . and my conviction is that there is sufficient water in it to make three rivers such as the Nile. . . . But as neither conjectures, dreams, theories nor opinion will make one positive geographical fact, I propose to stick to the Lualaba, come fair or foul, fortune or misfortune. . . .

Thus determined, Stanley put a proposition to Tippu-Tib. For $5,000 he and 200 or more of his men should escort Stanley's 150-strong expedition for 60 marches of four hours' duration each in any direction Stanley chose. Stanley's hope was to get through the worst part of the forest under the protection of Tippu-Tib's guns and to find himself at a point on the river where he would stand a better chance of obtaining canoes for his onward journey to the sea. Stanley and the slaver haggled for three days before the deal was struck.

They marched on together to Nyangwe to prepare for departure, but at the last moment Stanley seems to have wavered momentarily. He called Pocock into his *tembe* for a conference and posed the question: "Was it right attempting a task so desperate?" Pocock suggested tossing a coin—heads they would follow the Lualaba, tails they would head south for Katanga. They spun and the coin landed tail side up. Unwilling to accept the verdict, they spun twice more, and it came down tails each time.

> Yet neither of us liked the idea of being thus ordered south by destiny. . . . [and] finally it was decided between us to take advantage of the Arabs' escort to get clear of Nyangwe and then to go on alone and never to return, no matter what opposed us. . . .

Before setting off with his escort on November 5, Stanley wrote to his friend Edward King. "I can die, but I will not go back. I anticipate trouble and many disagreeable things—possibly the digestion of myself in some cannibal's stomach—but I cannot picture to myself the idea of me standing, hat in hand, explaining personally to the proprietor of the New York Herald why I came back without fulfilling my promise."

The rain forest began one day's march from Nyangwe, and the combined column, numbering over seven hundred including women, children and slaves, entered it "bidding farewell to sunshine and brightness." Overhead, branches and thick leaves shut out the daylight, while the trees shed dew like rain in heavy drops. Vapor rose from the sticky clay beneath their feet, settling like a gray cloud above their heads and creating the atmosphere of a steam bath. They had "a fearful time of it," wrote Stanley, "crawling, scrambling, tearing through the damp, dank jungles."

Soon, Stanley's caravan was "no longer the tight compact force which was my pride, but utterly disorganized." The jungle path was "so slippery that every muscle is employed to assist our progress. The toes grasp the path, the heads bear the load, the hands clear the obstructing bush, the elbow puts aside the sapling." The men carrying the dismantled Lady Alice were the worst off, for the boat sections "had to be driven like blunted ploughs through the depths of foliage." Under these conditions, it took the boat-carriers all day to march six and a half miles.

Tippu-Tib quickly began to show signs of an intention to renege on his contract, and Stanley's high opinion of him began to dissipate accordingly. The slaver "seemed bent on making the marches as short as possible by delays and needless waits on the road, so that the 60 marches would not indeed amount to more than 30 ordinary marches." As well, he wanted Stanley to promise to give him thirty or thirty-five of his guns and men for the return journey to reduce the chance of his being attacked by the suspicious tribes who were now fleeing at their approach. Stanley rejected that suggestion as "sheer nonsense."

When they were eleven days out, Tippu-Tib threatened to abandon Stanley altogether. "I never was in this forest before and had no idea there was such a place in the world," he told Stanley. "The air is killing my people, it is insufferable. You will kill your own people if you go on." Stanley argued with him for two hours, appealing to his manhood and his honor, before the slaver grudgingly agreed to accompany him for twenty more marches on condition that they cross to the left bank of the Lualaba, where, although the natives were reputedly more hostile, the terrain was more open.

The joint force—now reduced to 450, following the departure of some 250 of Tippu-Tib's people—crossed the Lualaba four days later, using the Lady Alice and commandeered native canoes. At this point, Stanley decided it was time to give his men a morale-boosting speech.

"This great river," he told them, "has flowed on thus since the beginning through the dark wild lands before us, and no man, either white or black, knows whither it flows; but I tell you solemnly that I believe the one God has willed it that this year it shall be opened throughout its whole length and become known to all the world. . . . I am not going to leave this river until I reach the sea."

As Stanley told it, his words had an electrifying effect on the younger of his men, who called out: "Inshallah, Master, we will follow you and reach the sea." But the older men could not hide their misgivings and "shook their heads gravely."-

# Chapter Sixteen

So FAR, the size and strength of the joint force had made it immune from attack, but the tension along their line of march was palpable. Stanley tried in vain to lure the cannibalistic Wenya tribesmen of the left bank into blood brotherhood, but word of the slave-traders' ravages upstream had spread to this region, making the natives incurably fearful and implacably hostile.

The first clash occurred when Kacheche and another of Stanley's men ventured out of camp to buy food and were surrounded by hostiles. "One of them threw a spear at Kacheche, who shot him dead," wrote Stanley. After this incident the Wenya fled deep into the forest until, as Stanley noted, "there is not a native within 10 miles of us."

The joint force was now split into two parties, Stanley and thirty-two of his best men going by river in the *Lady Alice*, while Pocock led the rest of the expedition by land, accompanied by Tippu-Tib at the head of four hundred askaris, porters and auxiliaries, plus wives and concubines. As the land and river parties advanced northward, the drums warned of their coming, and the Wenya continued to flee, leaving their villages deserted. One riverine settlement whose inhabitants failed to get out in time stampeded when the *Lady Alice* hove into view. Cries of fear arose, and "everybody in a panic flew into the jungle, like a herd of buffaloes stung to frenzy by a fly pest."

But gradually the Wenya became emboldened to fight. The land party was repeatedly showered with spears and poison arrows as it hacked its way through the forest. To make matters worse, smallpox and dysentery broke out, and many of the marchers were disabled by thorns which penetrated the feet and legs, causing crippling ulceration. Afloat, conditions were little better. Rapids and whirlpools added to the hazards posed by Wenya ambushes, which began to take a steady toll of men and guns.

As conditions worsened Tippu-Tib repeatedly urged Stanley to turn back, becoming even more insistent after two of his favorite concubines died of smallpox. Finally, Stanley saw no choice but to release the slaver from his contract. He gave him a draft for $2,500—

half the original price—and a number of presents, including a silver goblet and 6,300 rounds of ammunition. On December 28, 1876, he and the slave-trader parted company amicably enough, Tippu-Tib providing a feast of roast sheep the night before Stanley and his people took to the river in the *Lady Alice*, followed by a fleet of twenty-three canoes, most of them stolen.

Before they set off, Stanley delivered another morale-boosting message to his men. "Sons of Zanzibar," he shouted, ". . . lift up your heads and be men. What is there to fear? . . . Strike your paddles deep, cry out Bismillah! and let us forward." But the "poor fellows" responded only with wan smiles and feeble strokes of their paddles, for now the expedition truly was venturing into the unknown. The way ahead was entirely unmapped and unexplored, and only Stanley's relentless determination, and the realization that they had gone too far to turn back, drove his men on.

The effort of keeping his reluctant fleet from straggling quickly reduced Stanley from inspirational rhetoric to angry curses. It was "one protracted torture," he wrote, "chest aches with violent shouting and upbraiding them for their foolish cowardice, voice becomes hoarse with giving orders which in a few seconds are entirely forgotten."

Out of the 143 souls under his command, he noted, 107 were enlisted men and the rest women and children. Of the 107 men, only 48 had guns, and of those 48, Stanley reckoned, only 32 were "effective men who would be able to make a tolerable resistance. Add to these 32 men, myself and Frank Pocock, and we are 34 fighting men, 109 are mere dummies which serve to frighten off savages deterred by a show of heads. . . ."

Warming to his theme, Stanley gave vent in his journal to a litany of complaints about the quality of his men. They were "terribly dull people to lead across Africa," in a semistupor from smoking *banghi* (cannabis) and hopelessly incompetent despite the two years' instruction he had given them in such matters as boatmanship and weapon-handling. One man had "loaded his gun with paper and a bullet and was surprised that his gun did not fire." Another, when ordered to seize the branches of a tree to stop his boat drifting past a landing, had jumped ashore to do so, allowing the boat to be swept away. And so on.

His irritability was understandable. As he said himself, the western half of the continent they were about to penetrate was "one wide enormous blank" on the map, "a region of fable and mystery—a continent of dwarfs and cannibals and gorillas." But even though he feared that he was leading his men to "almost certain death," he could not bring himself to turn back: "My fate drove me on. . . ."

On New Year's Day 1877, the expedition had the first of a series of armed clashes that would continue for over a thousand miles downriver. As they paddled past a riverine settlement, they called out *Seneneh*—peace—and made other pacific overtures.

> [But] our gentle and quiet behaviour was regarded by them as cowardice and their wooden war drums were beaten and immediately 14 canoes well manned dashed out. . . . I aimed at the nearmost canoe and fortunately struck two with the first bullet, at the sight of which they all precipitated themselves into the water. . . .

Similar incidents occurred on each of the following three days. The river also took its toll. Two men were drowned and four muskets lost when a violent storm swamped two canoes in midstream. Four more guns—breech-loading Sniders, this time—were lost when Manwa Sera capsized his canoe while negotiating some rapids. Then, on January 6, the expedition encountered the first of a chain of seven cataracts and innumerable rapids that were to punctuate the river for the next fifty miles.*

At each cataract, and at the more difficult of the rapids, the boats had to be hauled out of the water and, after paths had been cut through the forest, dragged laboriously overland. Many of the canoes were hollowed-out tree trunks, over fifty feet long and enormously heavy. While hauling them, or steering them through the rapids with rattan hawsers attached, the expedition frequently had to fight off attacking tribesmen. And all the time the river roared with a brain-numbing intensity that Stanley compared to "the thunder of an express train through a rock tunnel." To speak to the man next to him he had to bawl in his ear.

January 11, in particular, was "a terribly trying day." One of Stanley's men drowned when a canoe capsized, then another canoe was smashed by rocks in the same rapids, and a crewman named Zaidi only saved himself from being swept over the next cataract by clinging desperately to a rock that jutted up near the brink.

From the shore, Stanley and his men hurriedly lashed a rattan

---

*Despite the Africanization of place names which followed Congolese independence in 1960, this chain of cataracts is still known as Stanley Falls.

cable to a canoe and tried to float it out to the stranded man. But the cable snapped "like pack thread" under the force of the current, and the canoe was swept away. Stanley had a second canoe secured, this time with three cables made of rattan and tent rope, and asked for two volunteers to paddle it toward the stranded man. Uledi, the sturdy coxswain of the *Lady Alice*, stepped forward and was joined by a boat-boy named Marzouk.

Seven attempts were made before Uledi got close enough to Zaidi to throw him a line, but in grasping it Zaidi slipped from his rock and vanished over the brink. For thirty seconds there was no sign of him, and it seemed certain that he was lost. Then slowly his head appeared as he hauled himself back over the edge. "Pull away!" shouted Stanley, but as his men hauled to bring the canoe to shore, the cables snapped one by one. Before the last cable parted, Uledi and Marzouk, paddling frantically, managed to reach a small island in midstream, dragging Zaidi behind them. Stanley and his men "hurrahed with relieved hearts," but the three men were still in acute danger.

"A Fall 50 yards in width separated the island from us," wrote Stanley, "and to the right was a Fall about 300 yards wide, and below them was half a mile of Falls and Rapids and great whirlpools and waves rising like hills in the middle of the terrible stream, and below these were the cannibals of Mane-Mukwa."

Stanley had a stone attached to a length of whipcord and thrown across to the stranded trio. Another cable made of creepers and tent rope was attached to the whipcord, pulled across the raging waters, and made fast to a rock. But just as the first of the three, Uledi, began to haul himself across, the cable parted like its predecessors, and he only just managed to scramble back to safety.

Now night was falling, and Stanley decided that the next attempt must wait until morning. At first light he sent a party of men into the forest under armed protection to cut more lengths of rattan creeper. Three new cables were made of these, hauled across to the island, and made fast. Then, one by one and uttering fervent prayers to Allah, the three Zanzibaris pulled themselves across to the river bank, keeping their heads above the leaping waves only with great effort. Once the last man was safely ashore "the cheers we gave were heard far above the roar of the waters, and the camp heard it and knew that the three most gallant lads of the Expedition had been saved."

If the rescue of Zaidi was the most dramatic incident of the expedition's struggle through the Stanley Falls, it was scarcely the last. Day after day, they had to drive off attacking tribesmen, as Stanley's diary entries disclose:

January 27—The Wenya planned to attack us by two points . . . while our working parties were scattered over a length of two miles dragging heavy canoes over the rock terraces. Thirteen guns and a few successful well placed shots sent them flying. . . .

January 29—Today we have had three fights. . . . In the last . . . Muftah Rufigi of the Mgindo was killed by a desperate savage who attacked him with a knife 18 inches long which cut him on the head, almost severed the right arm from the shoulder, and then was buried up to the hilt in his chest.

January 30—We were assaulted in the most determined manner by the natives of the populous Yangambi. . . . They were the bravest we met.

Amid the lethal distractions of battle, Stanley at least had the satisfaction of knowing that his surmise about the Lualaba was proving well founded. After the expedition passed beyond the seventh and last cataract, the river made a decisive turn to the west, beginning the enormous arc toward the Atlantic that finally ruled out any possibility that the Lualaba could flow into the Nile. But the gratification of being proved right was short-lived. On February 1, Stanley had to lead his people in a battle fiercer than anything yet experienced.

This occurred at the confluence of the Congo and Aruwimi rivers where, looking upstream, they saw "a sight that sends the blood tingling through every nerve and fibre . . .—a flotilla of giant canoes bearing down upon us which both in size and numbers eclipses anything encountered hitherto!"

Stanley had time to count the number of canoes in the enemy fleet. "There are fifty-four of them! A monster canoe leads the way, with . . . forty men on a side, their bodies bending and swaying in unison as with a swelling barbarous chorus they drive her down towards us. . . . The crashing sound of large drums, a hundred blasts from ivory horns, and a thrilling chant from two thousand human throats, do not tend to soothe our nerves. . . . We have no time to pray."

Stanley called out to his men, "Don't think of running away, for only your guns can save you." And battle was joined. Despite the vast disparity in numbers, Stanley's superior tactics and weaponry quickly routed the attackers. His boats were anchored in line ahead, their occupants protected from spears and arrows by a wall of stout shields stretching from bow to stern of each vessel. And as the enemy swept by, withering fire from Stanley's repeating rifles left dozens of them "groaning and dying" in the bottoms of their canoes. "For five minutes we are so absorbed in firing that we take no note of anything else," wrote Stanley. Then, as the smoke of battle cleared, they saw the enemy in flight, and pursued them upstream to their village.

"Our blood is up now," wrote Stanley. "It is a murderous world, and we feel for the first time that we hate the filthy, vulturous ghouls who inhabit it. . . . We continue the fight in the village streets with those who have landed, hunt them out into the woods, and there only sound the retreat. . . ."

Before re-embarking, Stanley's men looted the village thoroughly for food and, noticing a religious shrine of some sort, made of 33 ivory tusks supporting a circular roof, they helped themselves to the tusks, too, together with 100 other pieces of ivory carved into a variety of shapes and forms. Before withdrawing with his loot, Stanley found time to notice and admire the workmanship of these and other artifacts in the village which "proved the people on the banks of this river to be clever, intelligent, and more advanced in the arts than any hitherto observed. . . ."

But his appreciation of native craftsmanship was tempered by revulsion at the evidence that lay all around of their cannibalistic habits—"the human and 'soko' [gorilla] skulls that grinned on many poles, and the bones that were freely scattered in the neighborhood, near the village garbage heaps and the river banks, where one might suppose hungry canoemen to have enjoyed a cold collation of an ancient matron's arm."

Stanley conceded that such evidence was "circumstantial," but accepted it as "indubitable proof" of cannibalism. Besides, he noted, the hostiles all along the river taunted them with cries of "*niama, niama!*"—meat, meat!—and gestures that made it gruesomely plain that they were to be eaten once killed.

After the Aruwimi River battle, and despite its victorious outcome, even the tireless, fearless Stanley was beginning to flag. "Livingstone called floating down the Lualaba a foolhardy feat," he noted in his diary on February 3. "So it is, and were I to do it again I would not attempt [it] without 200 guns. . . . I pen these lines with half a feeling that they will never be read by any other white person. . . ."

On February 7 they had a day without battle, and Stanley thanked God for it, adding that "twenty-six fights on this river have reduced my ammunition so low, and we are still so far from the coast, that I began to fear we should find ourselves hemmed by savage enemies without means of resistance." The respite seems to have been so welcome that Stanley mentions only briefly, and without comment, that this day he has for the first time heard the "Livingstone River," as he had named it, referred to by natives as the Congo. "River called Ikuta Yacongo," reads the entry in his diary.

The next day, too, was tranquil and, halting at an island called

Rubunga, where they were able to buy food that was both "cheap and abundant," Stanley noted that "a hearty geniality pervaded the market." There followed two more peaceful days, in which the worst terrors were provided by *tsetse* and gadflies of "hitherto unseen voracity." But on February 11 they again came under attack—first from a combined force of eighty canoes, which they put to flight "with great loss to the savages," and two hours later from another battle group which chased them downriver until the expedition "opened fire on them, killed two or three and drove them back."

In this engagement Manwa Sera dropped a Snider into the river, the fourth breech-loader he had lost in this fashion and the eighth to go to the river bottom so far. Such losses were not to be borne lightly, for the expedition was beginning to encounter tribes armed with muskets as well as spears and bows and arrows. The muskets constituted a back-handed kind of encouragement as a sure sign of commerce with European traders on the Atlantic coast, but were decidedly dispiriting given the expedition's ever-dwindling armory of repeating rifles. Stanley noted grimly that of the 100 guns with which they had left the coast, there were now only 52 left.

Still, the journey had its pleasures as well as its terrors. The next day brought some of each. Stanley was in a lyrical mood as he wrote: "We glide down narrow streams between palmy and spicy islands, whose sweet fragrance and vernal colour cause us to forget for a moment our dangerous life. We have before us the winding shores of islands, crowned with eternal spring life and verdure. . . ."

But he had barely finished jotting that description into his journal, "when lo! we came in sight of a village, and immediately war drums and horns sounded their defiance." A dozen large canoes came out and, despite the expedition's "friendly greetings," followed them downstream with muskets leveled.

> [S]uddenly I heard a musket shot and then another, and as I turned my head, I saw shot skipping over water towards us. Of course, we replied quick and sharp and fatal, and [they] were driven back in a panic with three or four killed, while we, thank God, had not suffered a scratch. . . .

The following day brought "the fight of fights," a running battle lasting five hours over ten miles of river, between Stanley's men and a fleet of fifty-four canoes, each carrying between ten and twenty Bangala warriors. There were no casualties on Stanley's side, but the attackers showed "great courage and aptitude for war," refusing to turn tail despite heavy losses. Again Stanley registered surprise and irritation at the animosity of the natives. "The hostility which these people bear for us is most strange," he wrote, "for as soon as they see us, without a word being spoken on either side, they man their canoes and fire away at us as if we were lawful game."

Once the expedition passed beyond the boundaries of the Bangala, there was a lengthy respite, and Stanley recorded no fights from February 15 to March 9. The lull was broken when, "without any cause further than the savage wilfulness of the natives," they were involved in a clash in which four of Stanley's men were wounded. This was the expedition's thirty-second battle, but also its last. Four uneventful days later, where the river "widened until it resembled a lake," Stanley and his men found themselves among "very peaceable people in canoes who spoke kindly and came near, unsuspicious and confident."

After 128 days on the river, in which they had traveled 1,235 miles, the fighting was done, and reveling in the peace of the lacustrine stretch, 15 miles wide by 17 miles long, where they now took their ease and ate their fill, Stanley conferred his name on it, calling it Stanley Pool. On opposite shores of that pool the Belgian Congo capital, Léopoldville, and the French Congo capital, Brazzaville, would one day stand.*

But if the fighting was over, the dangers and hardships were not. Immediately below Stanley Pool lay the first of a new series of cataracts and rapids—Livingstone Falls, as Stanley named them—over which the Congo, constricted within a cliff-lined gorge, plunges and boils for another 155 miles before broadening out and slowing down for its placid final approach to the South Atlantic. Friendly natives warned Stanley that the falls were impossible to descend, but he disregarded them. After all, on the Upper Congo they had fought their way past cataracts, rapids and hostile cannibals. Now, Stanley thought, in a region where trade had tamed the natural ferocity of the natives, he would encounter no enemy but the river herself. This was true, but he completely underestimated the brute power of that enemy and the number of cataracts—thirty-two in all—that lay ahead.

The expedition began its descent on March 15, and Stanley soon found that it was "horrible and slow work." In the first thirty-seven days they progressed only thirty-four miles and lost three canoes in the process. On two occasions, rattan cables used to slow the boats'

---

*Stanley Pool became Malebo Pool, and Leopoldville became Kinshasa after the Belgian Congo achieved independence. That the eponymous Brazzaville retained its colonial name may be taken as some kind of a compliment to the French.

descent snapped, allowing the craft to be swept away. In a third disaster, young Kalulu and five older men were drowned when the steersman, instead of clinging to the right bank as instructed, allowed his eighty-foot craft to drift to midstream where it was swept away like a straw. The loss of Kalulu, and other favorites who were in the canoe with him, cast Stanley into deep gloom.

"My heart aches sorely," he wrote, ". . . but it is such a dangerous career we now run, accidents are so numerous and daily, and I myself run daily three or four startling adventures, that we scarcely have space or time to wail or weep. Peace to them, and I pray we may have it (for it is a sad life) when we die."

Many more of Stanley's men might have drowned during the descent but for the life-saving efforts of Uledi, hero of the Zaidi rescue operation, who was a magnificent swimmer. And two weeks after Kalulu's death, Stanley himself came perilously close to drowning as he was descending the rapids in the *Lady Alice*. Six men on the shore were checking his rate of descent by hauling on rattan cables, fixed bow and stern, when a sudden surge of current pulled them off their feet, and the boat was swept away, "borne on the crests of great waves, whirled around like a spinning top, diving into threatening troughs, and swirling pits, then jostled aside, uplifted by another wave and tossed upon the summit of another. . . ."

> As we began to feel that it was useless to contend with the current, a sudden terrible rumbling noise caused us to look below, and we saw the river almost heaved bodily upward, as if a volcano had burst under it. It took the form of a low shapeless mound, and presently half of the mass approached us in lines of white breakers, gurgling bodies separated by so many whirling pools, one of which caught and embraced our poor shattered and way-worn boat, by which we were spun around and around with the stern threatening each moment to drop into the centre of the wide pit, until finally we were spun out of it into the ebb tide and so were saved.

Over stretches where the river was obviously too dangerous to be negotiated or where there was no foothold along the bank for the use of restraining cables, the boats were hauled ashore and dragged overland along paths cut through the bush or over cushions of undergrowth laboriously cut and then laid down to protect the boats' bottoms from damage. If the boats had to be hauled uphill, Stanley had his men lay down "tramways" made of timber sleepers and rollers. At one point the canoes were pulled up the side of a 1,200-foot mountain by this method, then dragged three miles across a plateau before being lowered again to a spot where the river was again negotiable.

As they made their way slowly and painfully downriver, Stanley and Pocock noticed increasing evidence of commerce between the natives and European traders at the Atlantic coast. "Gunpowder was abundant ... and every male capable of carrying a gun possessed one, often more." As well, the natives had British crockery, cutlery, glass and ironware and cloth of such quality that it became increasing difficult to barter successfully for food with the inferior trade goods they had brought from Zanzibar.

At this point, Stanley was almost as concerned about footwear as food. His last pair of boots were on the point of disintegration, and Pocock was reduced to wearing sandals made out of strips cut from a leather portmanteau. These were soon torn to shreds by the rocky terrain lining the river, and Pocock would as soon have gone barefoot. But Stanley was insistent that this would be inappropriate for a white man:

> Frequently, on suddenly arriving in camp from my wearying labours, I would discover [Pocock] with naked feet, and would reprove him for shamelessly exposing his white feet to the vulgar gaze of the aborigines! In Europe this would not be considered indelicate, but in barbarous Africa the feet should be covered as much as the body; for there is a small modicum of superiority shown even in clothing the feet.

There was a more practical reason why shoes should be worn—the presence of *jiggas*, a worm which bores into the soles of the feet where it lays its eggs, producing crippling ulcers that often turn gangrenous if not effectively treated. Pocock would in due course fall victim to this parasite and be unable to walk, a disability that was to be an indirect cause of his death.

On June 3, unable to carry out his usual task of leading the bulk of the expedition overland while Stanley supervised the river work, the immobilized Pocock was told by Stanley to wait for a hammock to carry him to where a new camp was being set up. Instead, while Stanley was occupied downstream, Pocock insisted on traveling in a canoe skippered by Uledi.

The canoe successfully negotiated some small rapids but, approaching a cataract farther downstream, Uledi steered into a little cove to reconnoiter before venturing farther. From a vantage point on top of a large rock Uledi was able to judge that it was impossible to shoot the falls and live. But Pocock would not accept this—

probably because pride made him refuse to submit to the humiliation of being carried in a hammock.

For whatever reason, he goaded Uledi back into the rapids by accusing him of cowardice. They had not gone much farther downstream before, as Uledi had feared, the current seized the canoe which, turning broadside on, was dragged remorsely toward the most precipitous midstream section of the cataract. Pocock was stripping off his shirt, ready to swim for his life, when the canoe plunged over the cataract and was carried down to the whirlpools which yawned below.

When at last the canoe came to the surface, eight men including Uledi were clinging to it, barely alive. Three were missing, among them Pocock. A few seconds later he came to the surface, floating face upward and clearly unconscious. Uledi swam after him, but both men were sucked into another whirlpool. Uledi surfaced, but Pocock did not. Later his body emerged again, but was swept away downstream.

Stanley was shattered by Pocock's death. Although chronically inclined to be hypercritical of his white assistants, he had become genuinely fond of him for "his many inestimable qualities, his extraordinary gentleness, his patient temper, his industry, his cheerfulness and tender love of me. . . ."

The diary entry recording Pocock's death begins with the words "A BLACK WOEFUL DAY!" and in contrast to Stanley's normal controlled style and notably neat handwriting is almost incoherent in places.

> Alas, my brave, honest, kindly-natured, good Frank, thy many faithful services to me have only found thee a grave in the wild waters of the Congo. . . . Thou Noble Son of Nature, would that I could have suffered instead of thee for I am weary, Oh so weary of this constant tale of woes and death. . . . I shall weep for my dear lost friend. "And weep the more because I weep in vain."

Stanley was not alone in his undoubtedly genuine grief. The Zanzibaris were so deeply affected by the loss of their *bwana kidogo*—little master—that they never fully recovered their morale. The incident "stupefied" them, Stanley wrote, "benumbing their faculties of feeling, of hope and of action. From this date began that exhibition of apathetic sullenness and lack of feeling for themselves and for their comrades, which distinguished their afterlife in the cataracts."

Pocock's death was followed by a string of lesser mishaps. The very next day, as Stanley camped at Zinga Falls with eleven of his men, separated by many miles and two cataracts from the rest of the expedition, the hitherto friendly Mowa tribesmen turned hostile. They had seen Stanley writing in his journal and decided that this was a form of magic that could endanger them all. As a result the Mowa chief demanded that Stanley's men should fetch "that white medicine paper which your King wrote, and tear and burn it before our eyes" or else the whole party would be killed.

Rather than sacrifice his irreplaceable notes, Stanley handed over "a sheet of paper scribbled over carelessly to satisfy them" and after this was torn up and burned, the Mowa chiefs were all smiles, allowing their people to sell food and visit the camp again.

The following day brought another crisis. From the rear party came news of a threatened mass mutiny. Stanley's men had decided that "they would prefer living and hoeing for the heathen than follow the White man longer, for his wages were but the wages of death." Meanwhile the Mowa were again becoming restive, saying that the strangers had angered the spirits of the falls by failing to offer a sacrifice. And indeed, it did begin to seem that there was a curse on the expedition. Stanley found himself immobilized for the next twenty-five days as he tried alternately to cajole and bully his rebellious rear party into bringing up the boats, beyond the Massassa Falls and the Bolo-Bolo Basin, where Pocock had died.

The diaries give some idea of Stanley's own low and confused morale during this period:

> June 10—The [Zanzibaris] try me exceedingly. Since I have lost Frank, I am unable to leave camp to superintend the men at their work. . . . How can I enforce them to their duty when they are so far from me? I have publicly expressed a desire to die by a quick sharp death, which I think just now would be a mercy compared to what I endure daily. . . . Ah Frank! You are happy, my friend. Out of this dreadful mess, out of this pit of misery in which I am plunged neck deep.
>
> June 15—Crossed over hills to Massassa Falls. Work is fearfully slow, useless to preach, talk, beg, threaten or punish. The people seem to be vowed to indolence and apathy. Goods diminished so fast that I am fear-stricken and weighed down with anxiety. To save myself and a brave few I must sacrifice about 110 lives [the rear party] and even at the last moment I do not think I could be capable of it. Better, far better to die as we have lived together and share fate, even the most fearful. Yet my people anger me, oh so much, and yet I pity and love them. . . .

On June 21, thirty-one of his men made good their threat to mutiny by deserting en masse. Stanley sent messengers to beg them, for their own sake, to return. "They have no money. They could speak no language. They had no arms to defend themselves from any tribe who might be induced by their helplessness to enslave them." At first the deserters spurned Stanley's entreaties, but two days later saw the force of his argument and returned. Stanley "did not reprove them." He lost another man by drowning the next day.

On June 27, the expedition was at last all together again and able to continue its weary, hazardous way downstream. A July 18 diary entry reflected something of Stanley's old pugnacity, but now mixed with the despairing self-doubt that had afflicted him since Pocock's death. It was a balance sheet of what the expedition had accomplished since leaving Nyangwe, reading in part like the progress of a conquistador and in part like the confession of a man who knows he has made a terrible miscalculation.

The expedition, he boasted, had "attacked and destroyed 28 large towns and three or four score villages, fought 32 battles on land and water, contended with 52 Falls and Rapids, constructed about 30 miles of tramway through Forests, hauled our canoes and boat up a mountain 1,500 feet high, then over mountains 6 miles, then lowered them down the slope to the river, lifted by rough mechanical skill our canoes up gigantic boulders, 12, 15 and 20 feet high . . . [and] obtained as booty in wars over $50,000 worth of ivory. . . ."

On the other hand, Stanley noted, they had lost twelve canoes and thirteen lives, nearly all the ivory and "our monies, beads, cloth etc. were wasted in the same manner. . . . Had I the least suspicion that such a terrible series of Falls were before us, I should never have risked so many lives and such amount of money. . . ."

Still more rapids and cataracts lay ahead, and more men were to be lost, four of them as prisoners to local tribes from whom they were caught stealing food. Their captors offered to ransom them, but the expedition's stock of trade goods was now so depleted that Stanley decided in consultation with his chiefs that the few must be abandoned to safeguard the survival of the many.

Toward the end of July, one of Stanley's best men, the "clever and cheerful" captain Wadi Safeni, went mad as a result of his privations. Stanley had his hands tied to stop him from harming himself, but he broke loose and "after embracing me in a most pathetic manner, he left. I immediately sent two men to follow him and bring him back but he could not be found. He had only a parrot with him which he carried on a stick. Poor Safeni, how will he fare now! I cannot stay as my goods are terribly short. I must haste, haste away from this hateful region of death, terror and barbarism. . . ."

On July 31, Stanley learned that Boma, the European trading station farthest upriver from the Atlantic coast, was now only six days away by water. But also learning that there were four more cataracts ahead of them, he decided at last to abandon the boats and finish the journey on foot. He had the *Lady Alice* lifted out of the water and carried to some rocks overlooking the next cataract where he left her "to bleach and to rot to dust!"

The expedition grew steadily weaker as they marched for three days, covering twenty-five miles, over territory in which little food was to be found. On the fourth day, as they camped outside "a miserable little village of about 50 souls" called Nsdanda, Stanley sent four of his strongest and most reliable men, including Uledi and Kacheche, ahead to Boma with a letter addressed to "any Gentleman who speaks English."

> Dear Sir I have arrived at this place from Zanzibar with 115 souls, men, women and children. We are now in a state of imminent starvation. We can buy nothing from the natives, for they laugh at our kinds of cloth, beads and wire. . . . I therefore, have made bold to despatch . . . this letter, craving relief from you. . . . I beg you not to disregard my request. . . . I want three hundred cloths, each four yards long, of such quality as you trade with, which is very different from what we have; but better than all would be ten or fifteen man-loads of rice or grain to fill their pinched bellies immediately, as even with the cloths it would require time to purchase food, and starving people cannot wait. The supplies must arrive within two days or I may have a fearful time of it among the dying. Of course I hold myself responsible for any expense you may incur in this business. . . . For myself, it you have such little luxuries as tea, coffee, sugar, and biscuits by you, such as one man can easily carry, I beg you on my own behalf that you will send a small supply, and add to the debt of gratitude due to you. . . .

After signing the letter, Stanley added a revealing, and surely superfluous, postscript: "You may not know me by name; I therefore add, I am the person that discovered Livingstone in 1871."

Three days later, having marched another twenty-one miles toward Boma, Stanley and his people were encamped, starving and apathetic, at a village called N'lamba N'lamba when one of the expedition children called out that he saw Uledi and Kacheche leading a file of porters toward the camp. They brought with them four sacks of rice, two sacks of potatoes, three large loads of fish, a bag of tobacco, five gallons of rum and "one load of sundry small things for [Stanley] such as tea, sugar, bread, butter, fish, jam, fruit in tin,

English shag [tobacco] and cigarette paper and three bottles of India Pale-Ale.

"Ye Gods! Just think, three bottles of pale ale . . . ," exclaimed Stanley. Two days later he led his straggling column into the little port, where he was met on the outskirts by a handful of European traders and the captain of a British steamship. It was exactly 1,000 days since the expedition had set out from Zanzibar.

AFTER they had rested for two days at Boma, Stanley and his people were taken by steamship to Cabinda, on the coast just north of the Congo estuary. There, Stanley sent a lengthy dispatch to his newspapers, telling of his safe arrival but begging his readers "not to exact too much from your willing servant, but to give him a week's breath." The trials and hardships of the journey had made him "an old man in my thirty-fifth year," said Stanley. "But the gracious God be thanked, who has delivered us from 'the mouth of hell and the jaws of death!' "

But despite his plea for a week's respite, and exhausted though he was—skeletal, hollow-eyed and with his hair turned white—Stanley found the energy to compose an article promoting the Congo River as "the great highway of commerce to broad Africa" and to describe in detail the landscape and the people he had encountered on his way down it.

After eight days in Cabinda, a Portuguese gunboat took the weary travelers south to Luanda, the Angolan capital, where they were all put up at the colony's expense and where the governor offered Stanley passage to Lisbon on another warship. Stanley declined the offer, feeling that he must see his people home to Zanzibar before himself returning to Europe and the acclaim which awaited him. Sixty of his Wangwana were suffering from scurvy, dropsy, dysentery and other physical ailments, and almost all had fallen into "a state of torpid brooding from which it was impossible to arouse them."

Stanley attributed the death of eight of his people directly to "this strange malady." Indeed, he felt that he might himself have fallen victim to despondency had he not been so busy. In Luanda he composed three very long press dispatches, describing the journey from Nyangwe to the coast. He also sent a fifteen-hundred-word letter of condolence to Frank Pocock's father:

I feel his loss as keenly as though he were my brother. Sorrow is difficult to measure and is expressed by different people in different ways.

*Stanley, gray and emaciated after his
epic trans-Africa trek. "Poor Stanley,"
wrote Alice, "how much you
have lost."*

My tears are over; the indescribable grief I felt when I was assured that I should see my amiable, faithful Frank no more has lost its intensity; but even now, whenever my mind recurs to those days of danger, despair and death, I feel my heart sinking. . . . There was not a finer, braver, better young man in the world than your son. . . .

From Luanda, Stanley and his people were taken to Zanzibar, via Capetown and Durban, aboard the British warship H.M.S. *Industry*. After seeing the survivors of his party ashore—eighty-eight men, thirteen women and six children—Stanley went to the home of his friend Augustus Sparhawk, an American merchant who had been holding his mail for him. There were dozens of letters awaiting his attention, but the only news of Alice was a press cutting telling of her marriage to Albert Barney almost eighteen months previously.

Stanley's feelings can only be guessed at. He makes no mention of the matter in any of his surviving diaries or letters, and the only clue we have is to be found in the recollections of his publisher, Edward Marston, who met him in Paris where he stopped over for a round of fetes and banquets on his way back to London. Stanley seemed "very lonely and depressed," Marston recalled. "He was evidently suffering acutely from a bitter disappointment; what that was, I could well guess, but need not disclose. 'What is the good of all this pomp and show?' were his words. 'It only makes me more miserable and unhappy.' It was not easy to arouse him from this unhappy mood."

On his return to London, Stanley found a letter awaiting him from Alice, dated a few days after the New York *Herald* had published the news of his safe arrival at Boma:

Dear Morton, Among the many congratulations and praises showered on you, receive my humble rejoicings also, of all you have accomplished. I am proud to know how bravely you have borne your many hard trials.

Poor Stanley! How much you have lost, but your gain has been great indeed. I shed tears when I read the fate of Kalulu and the "Lady Alice." I had hoped she would have proven a truer friend than the Alice she was named after, for you must know, by this time, I have done what millions of women have done before me, not been true to my promise. But you are so great, so honoured and so sought after, that you will scarcely miss your once true friend and always devoted admirer of your heroism. For indeed you are the hero of the day. That alone should console you for my loss. No doubt before long you will think it a gain, for Stanley can easily find a wife all his heart could desire to grace his high position and deservedly great name. . . .

If you can forgive me, tell me so; if not, do please remain silent.

Destroy my letters, as I have burnt all yours. Adieu, Morton, I will not say farewell, for I hope in some future time we may meet—shall it be as friends?

Alice Barney

That letter displays a good deal more common sense and dignity than do the memoirs in which the elderly Alice Barney—having in imagination transformed her shallow flirtation into the great lost love of her life—depicted herself as the inspiration for Stanley's triumph. "She made it possible for him," she boasted. "Without her spirit animating him, he would never have accomplished it, not even had the desire to penetrate those abysmal darknesses again. . . . 'Lady Alice' had conquered Africa!"

# PART FOUR

# THE SMASHER
# OF ROCKS

Civilisation never looks more lovely than when
surrounded by barbarism; and yet, strange to
say, barbarism never looks more inviting to me
[than] when I am surrounded by civilisation

*HENRY MORTON STANLEY*

# Chapter Seventeen

*A*MONG the newspaper-reading public of the civilized world, no one had monitored Stanley's progress across Africa more avidly or greeted the news of his emergence from the wilderness with more satisfaction than Leopold II, King of the Belgians. It was an interest more passionate by far than the scientific curiosity, humanitarian concern or armchair adventurism that animated the less exalted; Stanley's dispatches had inspired the king to wild dreams of empire.

Since his young manhood, Leopold had been seized of the idea that—to quote the legend he had ordered carved onto a piece of marble from the Acropolis—*Il faut à la Belgique une Colonie*. And from the moment of his ascent to the throne in December 1865, he had been actively scouting the possibilities of colonial acquisition, scanning the globe from the Caribbean to Indochina.

In the summer of 1875, impressed by Cameron's trans-African trek and his stories of the interior's natural riches, Leopold narrowed the focus of his attention and set himself to "find out discreetly whether there may not be something doing in Africa."

Discretion in such an undertaking was dictated as much by Leopold's own nature as by a shrewd acknowledgment of Belgium's insignificance relative to the industrial and military power of its neighbors. Rising Germany, acquisitive France, imperially gorged Britain, could each have slapped him down effortlessly had he sought to acquire any piece of territory they had an eye on. But, in cunning, the Belgian monarch was more than a match for the Great Powers.

"Leopold is subtle and sly," his father had once told a courtier. "He never takes a chance. The other day . . . I watched a fox that wanted to cross a stream unobserved: first he dipped in a paw to see how deep it was and then, taking a thousand precautions, he made his way very slowly across. That is Leopold's way." The recipient of that confidence, Interior Minister Alphonse Vandenpeereboom, would give an even less flattering reading of Leopold's character soon after the son succeeded the father: "He is artful and deceitful, if not two-faced at times."

Under the cloak of philanthropy and the spirit of scientific inquiry,

Leopold's first move in the game of empire was to convene an international geographical conference on Africa in Brussels in September 1876. Leopold considered it safe to proceed, though always with the greatest caution, because by that time Britain had demonstrated its own lack of interest in the Congo by repudiating Cameron's overzealous annexation of that territory on behalf of the Crown.

*King Leopold II. "Subtle and sly," said his father, "that is Leopold's way." (Library of Congress)*

In an opening speech, Leopold assured the delegates that he was "in no way motivated by selfish designs." ("No, gentlemen," he declared, "if Belgium is small, she is also happy and contented with her lot.") Rather, Leopold proposed the establishment of an international committee, buttressed by a number of supporting national committees, to set up a string of operational bases between Bagamoyo in the east and Boma in the west. From these, he proposed, the enlightened nations of Europe should fan out in a concerted effort to crush the slave trade and in the process open up the interior to scientific exploration, peaceful commerce and economic development.

The conference was a personal triumph for Leopold. The delegates agreed to the creation of an International African Association (AIA by its French initials) with the Belgian king at its head and the presidents of the main national geographical societies as its officers. Leopold, modestly accepting the presidency of the AIA for one year only, was widely praised for a noble and altruistic initiative. What he had really achieved, of course—as he said in a letter to Baron Solvyns, his ambassador in London—was "a fine chance to secure for ourselves a slice of this magnificent African cake."

Having erected the respectable screen for his ambitions, Leopold now cast about for the men to carry out his design. Belgium had no shortage of bureaucrats to do the paperwork, but where was the man with the proven experience, enterprise, courage and resolve to direct operations in the field? He was, at that moment, battling his way down the Congo River, past rapids and cataracts, running the gauntlet of cannibal attacks, spurring his men onward, ever onward to the sea. And when news of his arrival at Boma reached Europe, Leopold told Solvyns that Stanley was "the great traveller whom I dream of making the Belgian Gordon Pasha."

Leopold's first impulse was to sound Stanley out as soon as he reached London, but impatience overcame him, and he sent two high-powered emissaries to intercept him en route and invite him to a meeting in Brussels. So it was that, arriving by train in Marseilles in January 1878, to attend a banquet in his honor, Stanley was waylaid on the platform by Baron Jules Greindl and General Henry B. Sanford, a former United States consul in Brussels who was now in Leopold's employ as a propagandist and lobbyist for the African venture.

But Greindl and Sanford were to be disappointed. Stanley hoped to persuade the British to reverse their previous decision and this time agree to annex the Congo. So he fobbed the king's men off with the excuse that he was "so sick and weary that . . . at present I cannot think of anything more than a long rest and sleep."

In London, as had been the case in Milan, Marseilles and Paris, Stanley was treated as a returning hero. The voices protesting at the rough justice he had meted out to the natives of Bumbireh and other hostiles were drowned under a chorus of cheers. This time no one was suggesting that he was a fraud; the learned societies, and gentleman travelers like Baker, Burton and Grant, were now unanimous in their praises.

The Royal Geographical Society hastened to lay on a banquet in his honor and arranged a lecture at Burlington House in which Stanley would relate his experiences and findings to an eagerly waiting public. Since there was no map in existence showing the details of the interior, the *Telegraph*'s editor, Edwin Arnold, enlisted his young son and daughter to sew together four large bed sheets and paint an outline of Africa on it. Then, under Stanley's direction, the children painted in the rivers, lakes, mountains, plains and forests he had discovered.

The map hung behind Stanley as he spoke at Burlington House that night. The capacity audience gave him an ecstatic reception and, greatly encouraged by his new-found success as a public speaker, Stanley embarked on a determined campaign to persuade the British government to claim the vast and potentially wealthy territory he had traversed. As always, Stanley went about his work with prodigious energy, laboring over the manuscript of his book *Through the Dark Continent* by day, then dressing up in white tie and tails at night for the endless round of banquets and private dinner parties at which he seized every opportunity to promote his plan to set the Union Jack flying over the Congo Basin.

But in vain. For the moment, British officialdom had no interest in Africa south of the Sudan. Even the merchants of London, Liverpool and Manchester seemed quite satisfied with the profits they were making from the existing colonies. Also, for all his epic achievements and demonstrations of love for his mother country, Stanley was still not quite enough of a gentleman for Establishment tastes. Twice he had the opportunity to press his case with no less a personage than the Prince of Wales. The first time, "Bertie" listened without comment; the second time, he heard Stanley out and then responded by telling him he was wearing his decorations in the wrong order. For Stanley, it was another bitter experience of rejection.

I had hoped to have inspired Englishmen with something of my own belief in the future of the Congo. I delivered addresses, after-dinner speeches, and in private have spoken earnestly to try and rouse them. . . . I continued trying to impress upon them that some day they would regret not taking action, but it was of no use. I do not understand Englishmen at all. Either they suspect me of some self-interest or they do not believe me. My reward has been to be called a mere penny-a-liner.

He had, in fact, been called something a good deal worse than that, and officially if confidentially so, by his nemesis in Zanzibar. At the end of February, Kirk had been instructed by the Foreign Office to investigate allegations made by a missionary named Farler about Stanley's conduct during the trans-Africa expedition. On May 1 Kirk submitted his findings to the Foreign Secretary, Lord Derby. They were damning:

All that Mr. Farler has stated is, I am sorry to say, fully supported by reports that reached me at the time, and since I received Your Lordship's orders I have conversed with some of Mr. Stanley's principal followers, especially with Manwa Sera, a headman of the Expedition, and Kacheche, a *kirangosi,* or guide, and from these men and the statements of others I have been led to form the opinion that the doings of Mr. Stanley in this Expedition were a disgrace to humanity, and that his proceedings will prove one of the principal obstacles that future explorers and Missionaries will have to meet when following his track.*

One of Farler's most serious charges had been that Stanley had sold captured natives into slavery. Kirk's informants told him that nine prisoners had indeed been "bartered in exchange for food" by some of Stanley's men. But so far as Stanley himself was concerned, the most Kirk could say was that "I have not found [the allegation] denied by any of those with whom I have spoken." Regarding Stanley's belligerent behavior toward the tribes he encountered on his way down the Congo, Kirk was again unable to present any positive corroboration of unprovoked aggression against peaceful natives. Still, he adduced as evidence of the unbridled use of firepower against "defenceless" natives the fact that only two of Stanley's men had died in battle.

More convincingly, Kirk blamed much of the hostility and suspicion the expedition encountered on Stanley's practice of raiding na-

* Punctuation added and spellings amended.

tive villages to obtain food and canoes and to seize prisoners as guides or hostages. Said Kirk: "The expedition would seem to have subsisted, when among defenceless tribes, in a large measure on plunder." Kirk also relayed allegations of sexual misconduct, calculated to offend Victorian sensitivities at the Foreign Office:

> While descending the River they [Stanley's men] say that a village on an island was attacked and plundered and that there a young girl was seized and carried off by Pocock . . . and used by Pocock as his mistress. Soon after his death, she had a child of which it is said he was the father. . . . Mr. Stanley gave this slave girl to Kacheche, one of my informants, who lives now in Zanzibar with the woman and Pocock's half-caste child, which he is desirous to get rid of as Mr. Stanley left nothing out of Pocock's wages for its maintenance.

Stanley, too, was accused of having kept a native woman as his concubine before passing her on to one of his (un-named) Zanzibaris at the end of the expedition. This woman was said to have been one of a number of slaves given to Stanley as a present—presumably by Mutesa—in Buganda. According to Kirk's information, all those slaves except Stanley's woman subsequently ran away.

Other charges against Stanley concerned his treatment of his own men, which, said Kirk, "would appear on many occasions to have been very cruel." On one occasion a man, whom Kirk again failed to name, was allegedly kicked and beaten to death by Stanley. Also, "the chain gang was seldom empty on the march." In relaying this hearsay evidence, Kirk did have the grace to concede that "severe discipline among [Stanley's] attendants can be explained and understood."

Kirk's report had something to add to the controversy over Bumbireh. Stanley's account of the first battle largely corresponded with his men's, but they called the revenge raid—in Kirk's words—"wholly uncalled for and impolitic," and the taking of hostages before the attack "an act of foul treachery." Regarding those hostages, Kirk added, his informants had said that they were taken on to Buganda, "where the greater part of them were killed in cold blood in Mr. Stanley's presence."

Summing up, Kirk said he felt "forced to confess that I believe [the allegations] are substantially true and that if the story of this expedition were known it would stand on the annals of African discovery unequalled for the reckless use of power that modern weapons placed in his [Stanley's] hands over natives who never before had heard a gun fired."

Stanley was never given a chance to see, let alone rebut, this confidential report, in which Kirk's personal animus is evident throughout. No doubt Stanley's behavior on the march was frequently—if necessarily—less than gentlemanly. But Kirk makes no allowance for the possibility that his informants may have exaggerated or told him what they thought he might want to hear, possibly in the expectation of monetary reward.* He is vague on sources, names, dates and places, and injudicious, even reckless, in his use of language. As the Congo missionary W. Holman Bentley would point out: "Anyone who knows the people can have but one opinion; being there, [Stanley] had either to fight in self-defence, or walk quietly to their cooking pots."

But Kirk was highly regarded by the Foreign Office, and on receiving his report Lord Derby observed that Stanley's conduct did appear to have been, "to say the least, discreditable." Any hope that Stanley might have been listened to seriously by the Foreign Office mandarins and their political masters was effectively scotched. Thus, when Leopold sounded a new siren call Stanley was more responsive.

Disgusted by the British government's lack of interest and "more and more unfit," as he said, "for what my neighbours call polite society," he yearned to return to an Africa whose perils he found less daunting than London's. Accepting an invitation to Brussels in June 1878, he engaged in preliminary discussions with the king and his aides.

Leopold, still afraid of provoking British intervention, had in mind "a purely exploratory mission" at this point. This would "offend no one and provide us with stations, staffed and equipped, which we will put to good use once they have got used, both in Europe and Africa, to our being on the Congo." Stanley, wanting to make a bolder beginning, urged Leopold to sponsor a company to finance the building of a railway from the Lower Congo to Stanley Pool, circumventing the cataracts. Leopold liked the idea in principle, but believed that it was too soon to raise the considerable funds needed for such an undertaking. He insisted, gently and persuasively, that the first priority was to set up the river stations.

There were more talks between Stanley and Leopold's aides in Paris that August, and in November "this able and enterprising American," as Leopold called him, was again summoned to the royal

---

* Stanley's friend, the American merchant Augustus Sparhawk, noticed that Manwa Sera made frequent visits to Kirk's residence, traveling furtively by back streets, and concluded that he was "a big rascal and too fond of money."

palace in Brussels. There he met Leopold and "various persons of more or less note in the commercial and monetary world" who had clubbed together to form the high-sounding Comité d'Études du Haut-Congo. They voted $100,000 to equip and launch an expedition, and Stanley accepted a contract to head it for five years at $5,000 a year.

Ostensibly, the "study committee," or CEHC, was a syndicate of Belgian, Dutch and British entrepreneurs. Hiding behind a Belgian banker, Leopold was its principal subscriber and guiding spirit, acting through a colorless Belgian Army colonel named Maximilien Strauch, whom he appointed president of the committee. The CEHC's terms of reference were never published, and its true objective was not spelled out to Stanley. But he was not fooled. "It has been pretty evident," he noted, "that under the guise of an international association [Leopold] hopes to make a Belgian dependency of the Congo Basin."

In fact, Stanley had perceived only the half of it: Leopold's plan was not for a *Belgian* colony but for a personal fiefdom over the entire Congo Basin—almost a million square miles and eighty times the size of Belgium. In setting up the CEHC to supersede the moribund AIA, without informing the AIA's various national committees, Leopold had taken a long stride toward fulfilling that audacious objective. A year later, after his Dutch backers went bankrupt, he moved again, quietly buying out the remaining foreign investors before killing off the committee and replacing it with the Association Internationale du Congo (AIC).

All this juggling with confusing sets of initials was designed to make it seem that the AIC was the successor to the AIA and a truly international undertaking. In fact, it was entirely under Leopold's control, and its aims were far from international or altruistic. "Care must be taken not to let it be obvious that the Association du Congo and the Association Africaine are two different things," he enjoined Strauch. "The public doesn't grasp that."

Leopold's continuing insistence on secrecy was prudent. He had good reason to fear not only that at any point great-power suspicions might scotch his scheme, but also that liberal Belgian politicians might raise a fatal hue and cry if they caught wind of it. "Belgium does not need a colony," Prime Minister Walther Frère-Orban had said. "Belgians are not drawn towards overseas enterprises." So a cloud of obfuscation accompanied Stanley's departure from Brussels, Africa-bound, in early February 1879.

Traveling as "M. Henri," he sailed from Marseilles to Suez, and thence on a specially chartered steamer to Zanzibar to recruit captains, askaris and porters for the new expedition from among his old traveling companions. Meanwhile a freighter carrying supplies and equipment for the expedition—including building materials and four small river steamboats—secretly prepared to sail from Antwerp to rendezvous with Stanley at the mouth of the Congo.

Stanley's unheralded arrival in Zanzibar caused something of a stir. "We don't know for what reason he is here, but presume it has some concern with some grand commercial scheme," the U.S. consul, William Hathorne, wrote to a friend in America. Stanley and Kirk prudently avoided each other, though Stanley infuriated his enemy by disparaging British intentions toward Zanzibar during an audience with Sultan Barghash.

While on the island, Stanley recruited sixty-eight Zanzibaris for his expedition, and it is striking that despite Kirk's charges of Stanley's cruelty toward his men, forty who had been with him on the epic 1874–77 transcontinental trek signed on again. These included the lion-hearted Uledi and Susi, the faithful servant of Livingstone who had first greeted Stanley as he marched into Ujiji looking for his master. Stanley also persuaded Sparhawk to come along to command one of the stations he planned to set up, and in July he embarked again, heading for the Congo via the Suez Canal and the Mediterranean.

At Aden, a message was waiting from Strauch, summoning him to Brussels for consultations. Stanley replied that he could not leave his Zanzibaris, who might take fright and rebel if he abandoned them even temporarily. Strauch compromised by arranging to meet the ship at Gibraltar. There he informed Stanley that Leopold had evolved a grandiose new objective for his activities in the Congo—the creation of a "confederation of free negro republics," which would ostensibly be an independent black state like Liberia, the West African nation founded in 1822 by freed American slaves. However, said Strauch,

> It is clearly understood that in this project there is no question of granting the slightest political power to negroes. That would be absurd. The white men, heads of the stations, would retain all power. . . . Every station would regard itself as a little republic. Its leader, the white man in charge, would himself be responsible to the Director-General of Stations, who in turn would be responsible to the President of the Confederation. . . .

Stanley was not enthusiastic about this scheme, "It would be madness for one in my position to attempt it," he told Strauch, "except so far as one course might follow another in the natural order of things." Essentially, he was not concerned with the politics of the business at hand, only the practical problems involved.

On August 14, 1879, just over two years from his last sight of the mighty river, Stanley's ship sailed into the estuary of the Congo and headed for Boma. "I am devoured with a wish to set my foot on terra firma and begin the great work," he wrote to Strauch.

That great work effectively began 110 miles from the sea, at the foot of Yellalla Falls, the first cataract. There, having recruited 170 local blacks, to give him a total force of 240 Africans and 14 Europeans, Stanley established his first station, at Vivi. Then, leaving Sparhawk in charge of Vivi, he began the herculean task of building a road and hauling his riverboats and heavy equipment along it to the site of the next station, Isangila, fifty miles upstream.

It was during the making of this roadway, cut by hand and dynamite through savagely rocky terrain and in blistering heat, that he earned from his awestruck Zanzibaris the soubriquet he was to prize for the rest of his life: Bula Matari—Smasher of Rocks.

# Chapter Eighteen

ONE thing Stanley had not bargained for when he set out for the Congo was that Leopold and a French rival would try to turn his mission into a race. But as he slowly and painfully pushed uphill alongside the cataracts, an Italian-born French naval officer, Pierre Savorgnan de Brazza, was hurrying down from Gabon in the north, with the intention of hoisting the Tricolor over both banks of Stanley Pool before Stanley got there to run up the colors of the AIA.

Brazza was traveling light, and having no obligation to set up stations or build roads, was able to move a good deal faster than this rival. Stanley's sponsors in Brussels grew alarmed. "The interest of the enterprise demands that you should not tarry," Strauch told Stanley. "Rivals whom we cannot disregard threaten, in fact, to forestall us on the Upper Congo . . . We have no time to lose."

At this point, the end of December 1879, Stanley had painfully completed only 22 miles of the 235 miles of road needed to haul his riverboats and heavy equipment, in separate consignments, from Vivi to the Upper Congo. He replied stiffly: "I am not a party in a race for the Stanley Pool, as I have already been in that locality just two and a half years ago and I do not intend to visit it again until I can arrive with my 50 tons* of goods, boats and other property, and after finishing the second station."

Strauch and Leopold could only fume. Try as they would, they could not force Stanley's pace. Building roads and hauling heavy equipment uphill in the fearful heat, his men were dropping one by one, many dying of sickness and sheer exhaustion. Stanley himself remained for the moment in good health, and Leopold realized that he could not afford to alienate him. So the hapless Strauch was stuck in the middle, trying to please his royal master who wanted speedier progress while placating his prickly subordinate, who would not be rushed.

This was the state of affairs when, to Stanley's great surprise,

---

* In a later letter, Stanley spoke of eighty tons of goods, etc. Which the correct figure is not clear.

Brazza made a personal appearance at his camp. It happened while Stanley was en route between his first station, Vivi, and his second, Isangila, fifty miles farther upstream. He was resting in his tent when the Frenchman—an imposingly handsome figure wearing a blue naval coat and white pith helmet, and with "a brown leather bandage" on his feet—marched in at the head of fifteen Senegalese sailors and Gabonese interpreters.

"The gentleman is tall in appearance, of very dark complexion, and looks thoroughly fatigued," Stanley noted. "He is welcome, and I invite him into the tent, and a *dejeuner* is prepared for him, to which he is invited. I speak French abominably, and his English is not of the best, but between us we contrive to understand one another. . . ."

Brazza was on his way down to the coast, and thence back to France. He told Stanley that he had recently been at Stanley Pool, but concealed the fact that while there he had signed a treaty with a paramount chief named Makoko, ceding the north shore to France. Brazza had left a Senegalese sergeant in charge of the post he had set up at the pool and was on his way home with the treaty in his baggage, hoping to persuade the French government to ratify it and take formal possession.

On saying farewell after a two-day stay, Brazza looked at a mountain which obstructed Stanley's road-building efforts and remarked complacently: "It will take you six months to pass that mountain. . . . You should have at least 500 men." The implied challenge only strengthened Stanley's resolve, and with renewed determination he blasted, pickaxed, sledgehammered and shoveled his way past the mountain in seven weeks.

By February 1881, he had set up the Isangila station, 140 miles from the Pool, having lost six Europeans and twenty-two Africans to disease and exhaustion since leaving Vivi. In the process he had trekked 2,300 miles back and forth along 38 miles of road, built three bridges, "filled a score of ravines and gullies, [and] cut through two thick forests of hard wood." Ahead of him and his surviving officers and men lay 90 miles of navigable river before the spot where they must build the next station, Manyanga.

Despite the hardships of the advance, Stanley was meticulous about his standards of hygiene and personal appearance, lamp-blacking his mustache and shaving daily. He was less scrupulous in his treatment of his officers. One of them, an engineer named Paul Nève, gave a splendidly sardonic impression of Stanley's leadership style in a letter from his sickbed at Isangila:

> Mr. Stanley has taken great care of me during these bad days . . . the sort of care a blacksmith applies to repair an instrument that is most essential and has broken down through too rough usage. . . . Teeth clenched in anger, he smites it again and again on the anvil. . . .

A few weeks later, Nève died, and soon Stanley himself came close to death when malaria laid him low just before the assault on the last cataract below Stanley Pool. Day by day the fever grew more intense, and day by day Stanley increased the dosage of quinine that he took in a draft of hydrobromic acid. The combined effect of the fever and the cure made Stanley feel "as though I was pressed down by a crate. The lower part of my back seemed to be palsied; large tumours and bed sores afflicted me. . . ."

After two weeks, he was taking fifty grains of quinine a day and was too weak to lift his arms. Feeling close to death, he ordered his servant to increase the dosage to sixty grains, dissolved in a glass of Madeira. His black employees and European officers gathered around the sickbed. Stanley tried to give instructions in case of his death, which now seemed inevitable.

"Again and again, I strove strenuously to utter the words that my lips would not frame," Stanley wrote. A Danish officer named Christophersen held his hand. "Look well on me, Albert," whispered Stanley. "Do not move. Fasten your eyes on me that I may tell you." But at this point, as Stanley later recalled, he had a sudden presentiment that the crisis was past. "I am saved!" he cried, and fell back senseless.

It was two weeks before Stanley was strong enough to walk. His weight was down to 100 pounds. But he summoned the energy to deal with the pile of mail—much of it from Strauch—that was awaiting his attention. In a lengthy letter he replied with considerable asperity to a number of suggestions Strauch had made about the conduct of the expedition:

> Always something new, always by each mail some new divergence from the straight, direct, simple path, some new change of plan, some additional weight to carry—new instructions impossible to carry out—new arrivals of inexperienced officers, who absolutely know nothing of practical life—who appear even never to have been instructed in the simplest camp duties, who are always weak and ailing in health, who have to be carried about and instructed like little children, but who have nevertheless stomachs to feed and are encumbered with baggage, who are

jealous of their rank and each of whom wants a separate station, or post, or duties, apart from another's influence.

Stanley's letters to Strauch were virtually all couched in the same bilious tone—justified, no doubt, but sharpened by the side effects of malaria. This constant snappishness was also in evidence in his dealings with his white officers. He was hypercritical and acerbic to a degree that led many of them to quit, including his one-time friend Sparhawk. To his Zanzibaris he was more lenient, because they "accepted the reproaches they deserved with such good-nature that, however stupid they were, I could not help forgiving and forgetting."

Stanley's officers, of course, were subject to the lash only of his tongue, while his blacks risked physical punishment for poor performance or breach of regulations. Still, if Stanley is to be believed, such punishments were not nearly as harsh as his detractors have made out. Whipping or caning was "repulsive if inflicted with severity," he told Strauch. "It wounds, disfigures and renders disgusting the very person in whom you wish to implant self-respect and invest with a certain dignity. . . . The best punishment is that of irons, because without wounding, disfiguring or torturing the body, it inflicts shame and discomfort. . . ."

And to an inexperienced colleague leading an expedition on the eastern side of the continent, he gave advice similarly, suggesting that, if stern, he tried always to be scrupulously fair. "Be kind to your blacks," he admonished, "do not tease or worry them with unnecessary orders. . . ." In the same letter he seems also to refute the often-heard criticism that he was trigger-happy:

> Rush not into danger by any overweening confidence in your breechloading rifles and military knowledge. Be calm in all contentions with native chiefs; and one gold rule which you should remember is 'Do not fire the first shot' whatever may be the provocation.

Stanley's constant complaints to Strauch about the quality of the officers he sent out drew from Strauch the countercomplaint that Stanley seemed to have a prejudice against Belgians. Certainly, Stanley found the Belgians wanting by comparison with the British. "In sheer despair," he asked Strauch why young English missionaries, fresh from college, were able to succeed where his officers failed. "There is no zeal, intelligence, thoughtfulness or industry [in them]," he wrote.

Still, he spoke well of a German officer named Lindner, whom he characterized as "good at business, practical, clever, quick to learn." Perhaps he saw something of himself in the young German. He could have been describing himself when he told Strauch that, for all his good qualities, Lindner was so quick-tempered that he "soon gets into a white heat" and that he was "too imperious for his size, and ambitious for his state, stubborn, capricious and variable. . . ."

When Leopold learned that Brazza had raised the French flag over the north shore of Stanley Pool, he was far from pleased. According to Ambassador Solvyns, he held Stanley to have been "stupid to the highest degree" in allowing Brazza to get there first. "He ought to have begun by securing the most important part of the Congo," wrote Solvyns, ". . . and one wonders why, as a Californian [sic], he did not think to lay his rival low with a rifle shot. He proved as gentle and tractable as those wretched savages that have to be civilized."

For his part, Leopold seems to be writing with teeth clenched when he instructs Stanley by letter, on New Year's Eve of 1881, that "it is indispensable that you should purchase for the Comité d'Études as much land as you can obtain, and that you should successfully place under the sovereignty of the Comité, as soon as possible and without losing a minute, all the chiefs from the mouth of the Congo to Stanley Falls.

"Brazza in a very short time has placed under his dependence the chiefs around the Stanley Pool," the king went on. "Should we not do the same for the Comité? Others will do it for themselves, and against us, and our whole work, our whole expenses, would be absolutely lost. If you let me know that you are going to execute these instructions without delay I will send you more people and more material. Perhaps Chinese coolies."

The king, beginning to worry about the cost of the enterprise, also ordered Stanley to defray the expenses of his expedition by setting up toll gates on the road he had built. "It is but fair and in accordance with the custom of every country that those who make use of our roads should pay us something," wrote Leopold. Stanley was appalled. The idea, he replied, was "impossible of realisation."

> The mere rumour of such a course in Europe would bring general condemnation on our heads, and I beg that the utmost caution be taken to prevent such ideas getting abroad. Portugal, Holland, France and England would at once start up in affected horror. . . . I dare not obey your orders unless you repeat them after this caution.

It seems odd that the blunt, bull-at-a-gate Stanley should have to give a necessary lesson in diplomacy to the crafty, sinuous Leopold, but his new responsibilities had forced him to become less the free-booter, more the diplomat. And Leopold took his point and dropped the idea of exacting tolls.

Stanley had encountered a good deal of hostility and suspicion on reaching the Pool, largely because Brazza had successfully poisoned the native chiefs' minds against him. "You know the white brother who came here and with whom you fought,"* Brazza had told them. "Well, others will come and stronger than he. If you hoist the symbol [the French flag] which I am going to hand over to you, they will not get a footing in your land without your permission and they will never fire a shot at your subjects."

Malamine, the shrewd and intelligent Senegalese sergeant Brazza had left behind to mind the fort and safeguard French interests, had gone Brazza one further, persuading the local chiefs not to sell food to Stanley's expedition when it turned up.

Under these circumstances, Stanley made a tactical withdrawal from the north shore and directed his attentions to the south, where the hostility was less intense. Here, the man he must win over at all costs was a powerful chief named Ngalyema, a shifty and unpredictable brute who had enriched himself as a middleman for trade between the Europeans at the coast and the tribes farther upstream. Stanley described him as "covetous and grasping in disposition, and, like all other lawless barbarians, prone to be cruel and sanguinary."

With a thousand musket-armed warriors at his command, Ngalyema controlled the approaches to the Upper Congo, and Stanley could advance no farther without his goodwill. Negotiations were long and difficult and to grease the wheels Stanley forwarded a bizarre request to Strauch:

> Ngalyema . . . has desired me to ask you if you will be kind enough to send him a thing of which he will by and by—when it pleases God—make his coffin. It is to be of sheet iron, painted black or Japanned black, and the dimensions as he gave them to me yesterday are a circle 42 inches diameter at top, 21 inches deep. In short, it is to be something like a long and deep sponge bath, with cover. He is very anxious for it, and whatever the bill will be, he will pay for it. I have promised in your name that it will be here in five months.

That winning over Ngalyema was a task requiring both guile and daring is illustrated by one of the most colorful passages in Stanley's

* In fact, Stanley had not fought any battles with the tribes around the Pool. See Chapter 16.

account of his colony-building expedition. He probably touched up the details here and there, after his usual fashion, but his correspondence bears out the essence of the story.

Ngalyema had undergone the ceremony of blood brotherhood with Stanley and exchanged presents with him, but was soon persuaded by his fellow chiefs that the intruder was dangerous and must be driven out. He decided to go to Stanley's camp with two hundred armed followers, lull him with friendly words and then launch a surprise attack. Stanley's spies warned him what was afoot and, outnumbered about five to one, Stanley devised a plan to defuse the situation without bloodshed.

He ordered his askaris to hide in the bush surrounding the camp or to conceal themselves behind huts and tents, and when Ngalyema arrived, he found Stanley apparently unguarded, seated by his tent and deep in a book, while only a handful of his Zanzibaris lay around the camp, seemingly half asleep. Encouraged by this peaceful scene, Ngalyema advanced noisily up to the camp, drums beating and trumpets blowing. Then, as his soldiers stood menacingly close by, he approached Stanley, followed by his teen-aged son.

"Ngalyema was moody-browed, stiff and most unbrotherly in his responses to my welcome," Stanley recalled, "while I looked like one almost ready to leap into his arms with an irrepressible affection." After a few perfunctory pleasantries, the chief ordered Stanley to pack up and return whence he came, threatening war if he refused. Stanley, pretending to be taken aback, offered him lavish presents and insisted that all he wanted was a place near the river where "many white men would come to trade."

Ngalyema was not to be moved. "Enough!" he shouted. "We do not want any white men amongst us." As he turned to summon his soldiers, he noticed a large Chinese gong, normally used to rouse the camp at dawn, which Stanley had purposely placed by his tent. "What is this?" Ngalyema inquired. "It is a fetish," Stanley replied. "Let me hear it," demanded Ngalyema. "No, Ngalyema, the sound of the gong will bring trouble. I dare not—it is the war fetish."

The chief was insistent. Stamping his foot on the ground, he demanded: "I must hear it now. Beat it now." Feigning extreme reluctance, Stanley struck the gong, and at this prearranged signal his askaris appeared as if by magic, dropping down from trees, springing up from the bush, appearing from behind huts, brandishing their rifles and screaming like avenging demons.

Ngalyema's soldiers fled in blind panic, dropping their muskets as they ran. The chief himself was so terrified that he clung to Stanley, pleading for protection from the fetish warriors, while the chief's son in turn clung to his father's robes. "Keep fast hold of me," Stanley cried. "I will defend you, never fear!" Then, barking out an order, he made his askaris stop their caterwauling and fall into disciplined line.

Silence fell on the camp, and Ngalyema and his son emerged trembling from behind Stanley's protective cover. When Ngalyema had recovered his composure, he broke into a broad grin. "I was not afraid, was I?" he said. "See, all my people are run away. Ay me, such braves!" But when Stanley offered to sound the gong again, he blurted out: "No, no; don't touch it. Ay, verily, that must be a bad fetish."

There were weeks of haggling and bickering to come before Stanley got Ngalyema's signature to his treaty, but the successful ruse was a turning point in their relations, and once Ngalyema did sign, the less powerful local chiefs quickly fell into line. The eventual outcome was that the north bank of Stanley Pool remained French territory and the south became Belgian—a division which exists to this day, with the Republic of Zaire as successor to the Belgian Congo, and the People's Republic of the Congo as successor to the French Congo.

One more immediate consequence of Stanley's pact with Ngalyema was the formal establishment of the post on the Pool's southern shore, which became Léopoldville. Stanley used that name for the first time in writing in a letter to Strauch dated April 14, 1882, otherwise another testy diatribe about the performance of his officers.

With Leopoldville established, Stanley pushed on by steamboat, intending to place more posts all the way up to Stanley Falls, almost a thousand miles upstream. He built his next station at Mswata, another sixty miles up the river, and explored the Kwa, a tributary of the Congo, with the Danish officer Christophersen. At the head of the Kwa lay an undiscovered lake, which Stanley named Lake Leopold II.

While circumnavigating this lake, Stanley again fell victim to the fever which had almost carried him off the year before, and it soon became clear to Christophersen that he was too ill to carry on. Accordingly, the Dane brought Stanley back to Léopoldville, where he was carried ashore unconscious. From there he was taken downstream to Vivi, below the last cataract.

There Stanley handed over command, on Strauch's instructions, to a German naturalist and geologist named Peschuel-Loesche, who had been recruited by Leopold for a scientific mission. On July 15 Stanley sailed for Europe from Luanda.

WHEN Brazza returned, sick and exhausted, to France he at first found little more enthusiasm for the Congo in French ruling circles than Stanley had found in London four years earlier. The French were going through a phase of waning interest in colonial expansion, and were furthermore curiously complacent about Leopold's machinations. Belgium's diminutive size and lack of diplomatic and military muscle was one of the factors that persuaded them that their northern neighbor could not be a serious contender for imperial status. Also, they seem to have been taken in by Leopold's professions of altruism. Ferdinand de Lesseps, builder of the Suez Canal and president of the French committee of the AIA, for one, persuaded himself that Leopold's objectives were "not only scientific, but at the same time, one may venture to say, the most humanitarian of our century."

Guessing that Brazza would receive a cool reception in Paris, Leopold tried to co-opt him as he had Stanley. "We must explain to him that Belgium wants absolutely nothing," the king told Strauch, "that our committee is an international one." Accordingly, he invited Brazza to Brussels. The Frenchman came, but was not taken in by the king's wiles. As Leopold would recall, he declined to "take an interest in our enterprises."

Stanley arrived in Brussels himself not long afterward and, imagining that his task was done, went to Strauch to deliver a final report. As much mystified as anyone by Leopold's sleight of hand, he was under the impression that his five-year contract with the AIA, signed in 1878, had been superseded by his three-year contract with the CEHC the following year. Strauch insisted this was not so, apparently neglecting to state that the CEHC itself no longer existed.

Stanley pleaded that his doctors had warned him it would be suicidal for him to return to the Congo. Strauch coldly insisted that he must go back and fulfill his contract as soon as he was better. It was a stalemate until the next day, when Leopold applied a more persuasive kind of pressure: "Surely, Mr. Stanley, you cannot think of leaving me now, just when I most need you?" Leopold knew his man. With exemplary if misguided loyalty, Stanley gave in. "My powers of resistance failed me and in a weak moment I assented to part once more for the Congo, on or about November 1."

Before returning, Stanley launched a campaign aimed at discrediting Brazza's treaty with Makoko. This was not appreciated by Leopold, who, still anxious to keep his activities as low-profile as possible, wanted to avoid publicity. "What can be done to keep Stanley quiet?" he asked Strauch. His concern was justified, for the public feud which now broke out between Stanley and Brazza was to be a major factor in persuading the French parliament to change course and ratify the treaty.

Stanley was not popular in France. The French tended to sneer at his unpolished style, and were anyway going through one of their periodic fits of Anglophobia. Stanley insisted that he was an American "and therefore free of all political leanings and interested in Africa solely as an unhappy continent," but they were not convinced. Nor did they accept Stanley's assertions, in statements to the Paris press, that Brazza's treaty was legally and morally worthless since Makoko had been tricked into signing it and anyway had no paramount authority over the other chiefs in his area.

Brazza in turn discredited his rival by playing on his warlike reputation. Conveniently forgetting that he had himself fought several battles in legitimate self-defense, Brazza declared: "I never was in the habit of travelling around Africa as a warrior like Mr. Stanley, always accompanied by a legion of armed men, and I never needed to resort to barter because, traveling as a friend and not a conqueror, I everywhere found hospitable people."

This was great knockabout, helping to turn what might have remained an arcane dispute over a remote stretch of jungle into a popular cause, and raising Brazza to the status of a national hero. The affair came to a theatrical climax on the evening of October 20, when an ad hoc organization called the Stanley Club, largely composed of expatriate Americans, gave a dinner in Paris for their hero. Forewarned of this event, Brazza wrote a speech in English and spent days correcting its grammar and syntax, improving his accent, and practicing his delivery in front of a mirror. His plan was to gate-crash the dinner and, in proper naval fashion, blast his opponent out of the water.

Legend has it that on the day of the banquet the two men had a chance encounter in the street. Stanley supposedly told Brazza, "I'm going to have the pleasure of giving you a bit of a mauling this evening." Brazza merely bowed and went on his way smiling secretly.

At the dinner that evening Stanley repeated his argument that Makoko had been tricked into signing the treaty, which was anyway worthless, and stressed that he himself had gone to the Congo to serve an international committee, not a narrow national interest. In closing, he said with stunning self-righteousness that he could not join in a chorus of praise for Brazza, a man "who had brought an immoral diplomacy into a virgin continent."

At this point, Brazza himself entered the room and strode to the head table where the American ambassador, who was presiding, quickly recovered from his surprise and invited the interloper to sit on his right. Brazza accepted, shook hands with Stanley, and delivered his prepared speech. It was a tour de force. Instead of attacking Stanley he declared that he saw in him "not an antagonist, but simply a labourer in the same field, where our common interests . . . converge towards the same goal: the advance of civilisation in Africa."

"Gentlemen," he concluded, "I am a Frenchman and a naval officer, and I drink to the civilisation of Africa by the simultaneous efforts of all nations, each under its own flag." The French press was exultant, the public enraptured: the nimble Latin had triumphed over the ponderous Anglo-Saxon. Within six weeks the French parliament ratified the French Congo treaty.

# Chapter Nineteen

*AS PROMISED,* Stanley returned to the Congo in November. At Leopold's insistence, he did so clandestinely, as in 1879, for the French were anxious that he should not go back, and Leopold was keen not to offend his powerful neighbor. In Stanley's absence things had gone disastrously wrong. Peschuel-Loesche had proved utterly incapable of taking charge, and was even more at odds with his officers than Stanley had been. Three of them had sent a written complaint to Brussels, and the German had been sacked and sent back to Berlin by the time Stanley reached Vivi on December 20.

There he learned that, without his presence to keep them in line, the station commanders had fulfilled all his direst prophecies, warring needlessly with the natives, burning villages, letting their stations become overgrown and their steamboats fall into disuse. With the help of a number of new officers—many of them British and more up to Stanley's standards than their predecessors—he spent the first few months repairing the damage done in his absence.

While he supervised that task with his customary demonic energy, Stanley sent off three subexpeditions to secure the northern approaches to the Congo Basin by setting up stations and signing treaties along the Niari-Kouilou Valley. This effectively forestalled Brazza, who was mounting a new expedition on behalf of the French government. In time, this area immediately to the north of the Lower Congo and including a stretch of the Atlantic coast, would be a major bargaining chip, to be exchanged by Leopold for French acquiescence in his larger plans.

By now, with his new officers and a considerable number of Zanzibari reinforcements, Stanley's compact but formidable force resembled a nineteenth-century version of Pizzaro's small army of conquistadors. A French missionary, Father Augouard, estimated that Stanley had "about 100 white men, 600 blacks, eight steamers, a dozen Krupp guns, four machine-guns, 1,000 quick-firing rifles (14 rounds), over 2,000,000 cartridges, etc." at his disposal.

In August 1883, once he had got the Léopoldville station repaired, garrisoned and running efficiently, Stanley set off upriver with a flotilla of three steamboats and a whaler, bound for Stanley Falls and points in between. Leopold had been dissatisfied with the terms of the treaty Stanley had concluded with Ngalyema and others at the Pool and along the Lower Congo. "There must at least be added an article to the effect that they delegate to us their sovereign rights," Leopold had instructed Strauch. "The treaties must be as brief as possible and in a couple of articles they must give us everything. . . ."

They certainly did. Now the chiefs undertook "freely, of their own accord, for themselves and their successors for ever," to surrender to the Association their "sovereignty and all sovereign rights to their territories," and agreed "to unite and combine together" in a confederation. In return, the Association undertook to pay "one piece of cloth per month to each of the undersigned chiefs, besides presents of cloth in hand." The Association further undertook "to take . . . no occupied or cultivated lands, except by agreement, . . . to promote to its utmost the prosperity of the said country," and "to protect its inhabitants from all oppression or foreign intrusion."

After Stanley and his lieutenants had collected the signatures of more than three hundred chiefs and kings to this larcenous document, Leopold had the legal basis for his so-called Congo Free State— a misnomer if ever there was one—and Stanley felt inspired to say about the people he had duped: "An imposing family! And to think that I am under the obligation to love and defend the whole lot to the death."

By November, having set up and garrisoned two new stations along the Upper Congo, Stanley was approaching the first of the falls he had named after himself, where he proposed to set up his last river station. But in place of the bustling—if hostile—riverine life he had encountered here in 1877, a sinister silence lay over both banks of the mighty waterway. Mile after mile, he passed burned and abandoned villages, smashed canoes, ravaged fields. Slowly it dawned on Stanley what had happened: the Arab slavers, following belatedly in his footsteps, had overcome their fears and pushed downstream from Nyangwe.

At one point, Stanley's paddle-steamer, the forty-three-foot *En Avant*, passed a sizable native town lying in ruins. All the huts had been destroyed, the crops leveled, the palm and banana trees cut down, and on the river bank some two hundred survivors huddled in a state of total apathy. Through an interpreter, they said that the Arabs had attacked eight nights before, massacring most of the men and taking away the women and children.

As the *En Avant* continued upriver, passing one ruined settlement after another, Stanley felt "an impulse which was almost overpowering to avenge these devastations and massacres of sleeping people." But on reflection he decided that he could not "take the law into my own hands and mete out retribution." After all, he said, he "represented no constituted government, nor had I the shadow of authority to assume the role of censor, judge and executioner."

Eventually, Stanley reached the slavers' headquarters, a large camp by the river's edge where he went ashore to parley with the Arabs and investigate. He was greeted cordially enough by the slavers, and his Wangwana fell into animated Swahili conversation with their fellow Zanzibaris.

By questioning the slavers and consulting his maps, Stanley calculated that in eleven months they had ravaged an area of 35,000 square miles—bigger than Ireland. Adjoining the Arabs' quarters was a camp of huge sheds containing 2,300 newly enslaved natives awaiting shipment to the east coast. They were all women and children, close to starvation, "in a state of utter and supreme wretchedness," and, chained together in batches of twenty, wallowing in filth and excrement. Stanley departed the next day, "being in a hurry to leave such scenes," and pushed on to the first cataract, where he set up the station which eventually became the city of Stanleyville (now Kisangani).

Leaving a Scots engineer named Binnie in command, with plenty of provisions and a force of thirty-one askaris, Stanley began the return trip to Léopoldville on December 10. The time was approaching for his return to Europe at the end of his contract period, and he planned to leave once he had handed over to his successor. To fill that post, he had recommended Britain's General Charles Gordon—"Chinese" Gordon, as he was known for his exploits in the Far East—and with the agreement of the British War Office, Gordon had been to Brussels, where he was interviewed by the king.

Leopold told Gordon that he was principally concerned with suppressing the slave trade in the Congo, and the devout and idealistic Englishman took him at his word. Writing to Stanley following his audience with Leopold, Gordon was enthusiastic:

> I hope you will stay on and we will, God helping, kill the slave-traders in their haunts, for if we act together in the countries where they hunt, and make treaties with the chiefs, we can prevent their raids and truly stop the slave-trade. . . . No such means of cutting at root of slave-trade was ever presented as that which God has, I trust, opened out to us through the kind disinterestedness of His Majesty.

Stanley did not quite know what to make of this letter. "I gather from [Gordon] that he has some views hostile to the slave trade in the Soudan," Stanley said in a letter to Strauch. "A very laudable purpose, undoubtedly, but I am not told whether we are to abandon the Congo and be diverted from our work of settling, extending and consolidating along this river, to make raids upon Soudanese slave-traders in the Nile basin. In short, the whole affair is very mysterious to me."

His reference to the Sudan and the Nile basin is puzzling, or perhaps disingenuous. Nowhere in Gordon's letter is there any mention of this area, and his reference to "act[ing] together in the countries where [the slavers] hunt" would seem to apply more to the Congo than to the Sudan. In fact, Leopold was secretly planning to extend his control beyond the Congo basin into the Bahr el-Ghazal region of southwestern Sudan, a move which would subsequently put him at odds with the British. But it seems unlikely that he would have mentioned this intention to Gordon, whom he considered, for all his potential value to him, to be "most indiscreet."

In the event, Gordon never went to the Congo. The British government suddenly found it necessary for him to return to the Sudan—where he had until recently been governor—to deal with the revolt of the Mahdi and his fundamentalist followers. They were to murder him on the steps of his residence in Khartoum almost exactly a year later. Leopold hurriedly recruited another English soldier, Colonel Sir Francis de Winton, to take over as administrator general of his Congo interests, and on June 8, 1884, Stanley handed over to de Winton at Vivi and sailed for Europe.

His achievements during his five years in the Congo were prodigious. He had established twenty-two garrisoned stations along the Congo and its tributaries, put a fleet of steamboats onto the river, built roads and even a short stretch of railway, acquired sovereignty of the land from the natives, and in general set up a political and commercial network that would serve as the physical foundation for a future nation.

That done, Stanley's usefulness to Leopold now was largely as a totemic figure, to be dusted off and displayed from time to time for public-relations purposes. Stanley all too clearly lacked the cool temperament and sinuous skills for diplomacy, which was more than ever where Leopold now needed to concentrate his efforts. Anyway, Leopold had no intention of sending Stanley back to the Congo, where he would inevitably expect to share administrative responsibilities with de Winton. A division of authority, Leopold told Strauch, would "only increase the disorder and disunion from which our affairs are suffering." As well, the king had promised the French, for devious diplomatic reasons, that he would recall Stanley and, implicitly, not let him return.

Kirk, too, had contributed his shilling's-worth toward convincing Leopold that Stanley's presence in the Congo would be more of a liability than an asset. "Bold explorer as he undoubtedly is, no one trusts him here," Kirk had said in a letter to the king from London in the spring of 1883, "and unfortunately I know too much of him to be able to say a word in his favour." However, Kirk did concede that there was so much to be done in the Congo that if the AIC employed "a better class of administrator to manage stations," there might be "room enough for a rough pioneer like Stanley."

Kirk—since 1882, Sir John Kirk—was on leave from Zanzibar at the time and advising the Foreign Office on African policy issues related to Leopold's claims to the Congo. That he should simultaneously have been in confidential correspondence with the Belgian monarch seems, to say the least, a conflict of interest, especially at a time when Britain was trying to secure international recognition of Portuguese sovereignty over the mouth of the Congo.

Whitehall's intention was not so much to damage Leopold as to exclude the French, but if allowed to succeed, its policies would seriously, and perhaps fatally, have undermined Leopold's interests. Accordingly, the king moved vigorously to block, or at least blunt, the proposed Anglo-Portuguese agreement by playing on British dislike of Portugal's traditional protectionism and tolerance of slavery while brandishing his own credentials as a free-trader and philanthropist.

To further this campaign, he enlisted the aid of influential British business associates, such as the shipping magnate Sir William Mackinnon, who hoped to profit from the exploitation of the Congo. And he wrote to his cousin "Bertie," the Prince of Wales, complaining that the Liberal Prime Minister William Gladstone was planning to "rob" him for the benefit of Portugal.

In all this, Kirk played a most ambiguous role, keeping Leopold's chef de cabinet, Jules Devaux, up to date on the provisions of the Anglo-Portuguese treaty as they evolved. He told Devaux that the whole of the official correspondence relating to the matter had "fallen into my hands," and even sent him a full text of the treaty—marked "Strictly Private and Confidential"—as finally revised. "You will understand that I have not been idle," he told Devaux, "for each revise has been under my eye and little by little we are getting your ideas edged in."

Leopold fought the treaty on two fronts: in Britain, to stop its passage through Parliament, and abroad to prevent the concurrence of the other major powers. He lost the battle in Westminster, but was considerably more successful abroad, claiming his first victory in Washington, where he had sent his lackey Sanford to lobby Congress and the administration of President Chester A. Arthur. Although he had little time for Stanley personally, Sanford capitalized on the explorer's fame and presumed American nationality* to bolster his royal patron's case. He wined, dined and propagandized so effectively that although (or perhaps because) both the executive and the legislature were clearly confused by the whole issue—believing that the AIA and the AIC were interchangeable terms and that the CEHC was still in existence—he was soon able to report success.

A joint resolution of Congress called on President Arthur to recognize the AIC's blue-and-gold flag as "that of a friendly government," which he duly did on April 22, 1884, to the dismay of the Portuguese and the disgust of the British. "The United States government have committed an act of great folly," sniffed a Foreign Office mandarin.

Only twenty-four hours later, Leopold effected an even more stunning diplomatic coup—the acquiescence of France in his Congolese land-grab. Although the French had been the most dangerous opponents of his ambitions, Leopold had grasped that they were also, paradoxically, his best potential allies. With superb adroitness he made the French an offer they could not refuse: a secret treaty giving France a first option on his Congolese holdings if at any time he found he had to relinquish them.

The French, underestimating Leopold's tenacity and confident that he would indeed soon find the Congo far too big a mouthful to digest, took the bait. But in so doing, they had to recognize the legitimacy of the holdings they hoped to inherit. The gain was all Leopold's.

With France and America on his side, and the British fuming in the wings, Leopold now needed only Germany's backing to win the game. And in June 1884 Otto von Bismarck, the German Chancellor, in effect joined the team by flatly refusing to accept the Anglo-Portuguese treaty.

---

* In fact, Stanley became a naturalized American citizen on May 15, 1885.

It was not that Bismarck had been taken in by Leopold's protestations of altruism. He scribbled the word "Swindle!" alongside a pious note from Brussels about the king's desire to destroy the slave trade, and "Fantasies" alongside another note outlining Leopold's plans for a confederation of free states. But the Germans were in dispute with Britain over Fiji, Samoa and a minor southwest African territory called Angra Pequena, and Bismarck killed the Anglo-Portuguese treaty as a show of retaliatory diplomatic muscle. A few weeks later he gave formal recognition to the International Association.

But the maneuvering over the Congo—and sharp differences between France and Britain and Britain and Germany—had convinced Bismarck that "the scramble for Africa," as it came to be called, must be contained before it led to war between the great powers. In concert with the French government, he accordingly sponsored an international conference in Berlin, to ensure that Africa would be carved up in an orderly and peaceful fashion. And it was toward Berlin, where the delegates of fourteen interested nations gathered on November 15, 1884, that Leopold now directed his attentions.

His delegation went into the conference with the cards stacked in its favor. Since the Belgians were presumed to know more about the Congo than anyone else, one of Leopold's two principal delegates, Baron Auguste Lambermont, was named *rapporteur* to the conference. From this position of considerable influence, Lambermont—and by extension Leopold, who was in constant touch by telephone from Brussels—was in a position to steer the proceedings in whatever direction he wished.

In addition, Leopold's hired man Sanford had managed to get himself appointed one of Washington's two official delegates to the Berlin Conference. Since Sanford's fellow delegate, the U.S. ambassador to Berlin, was both malleable and incompetent, Sanford had little difficulty in ensuring consistent U.S. support for Leopold's positions. Stanley sat with the American delegation, too, as technical adviser, although like Sanford he was still on Leopold's payroll. Conflict of interest was clearly not the major concern then that it is nowadays.

By the time the Berlin Conference wound up on February 25, 1885, Leopold's personal dominion over 900,000 square miles of the Congo Basin had been formally recognized by all the nations represented. The great powers, assured of free trading rights in the Congo, considered it better for this African heartland to be in neutral hands than to remain a potential *casus belli* between them.

By royal decree of May 29 that year, Leopold declared himself King-Sovereign of the Congo Free State. Almost simultaneously, Stanley's massive two-volume account of how he had made possible the creation of that anomalous—and soon to become infamous—entity was published in London, with editions in seventeen other languages to follow.

Stanley had submitted the galley proofs to Leopold for his approval and had written a fulsome dedication to "the generous monarch who so nobly conceived, ably conducted, and munificently sustained the enterprise which has obtained the recognition of all the great powers of the world. . . ." Ever conscious of his own "base origins," Stanley was always naively willing to attribute to the nobly or wealthily born virtues which they did not possess and to which he felt he could only aspire.

The more perceptive recognized that, for all his faults, Stanley was a far better man than his patron. Recalling a London reception for Leopold, at which the Belgian monarch was accompanied by Stanley, the explorer's friend Henry Lucy noted: "As the two men strolled through the brilliant throng, it was pretty to see the ladies curtsying and the gentlemen bowing to the tall, mild-featured, tailor-made man whom the accident of family circumstance had made king, while they permitted themselves to stand erect as Stanley brushed by. Yet if there was a king of men in the room it certainly was not Leopold II."

# Chapter Twenty

*A* *PORTRAIT* photograph of Henry Stanley taken in 1885, when he was forty-four, reflects the qualities for which his age held him in awe. From under a high-peaked safari cap of his own design, its back flap framing a stern and truculent face, he looks out at a world that is his to conquer. This is the quintessential "Smasher of Rocks," grizzled, vigorous, indomitable, his gimlet gaze projecting an uncomplicated belief in his own powers to endure and overcome and in such current verities as white civilization's innate superiority and the virtues of hard work.

The "idleness" of the African is to Stanley as grave a vice as his "savage beliefs" and "naive superstitions," and wage labor one of the blessings that colonization will confer upon him. But Stanley does not discriminate; a willingness to work and a determination to succeed are the ultimate measure of any man, black or white. One cannot doubt that he means every word when he proclaims: "For thriftlessness the world has naught but contempt; for natural debility, only pity; for vice, condemnation; for failures, oblivion."

A portrait in oils by Robert Gibb, made in the same year, shows us something the photograph has missed. It is very much the same face, but the eyes seem wary, apprehensive, almost fearful; they reflect doubt as much as determination, deep hurt as much as steely resolve. This was the Stanley who shared the skin of the assertive, empire-building Bula Matari, a more sympathetic Stanley—insecure, lonely, at times despairing.

With the Berlin Conference behind him and his Congo book finished, he felt his life empty of purpose. Reneging on his six-year-old promise to appoint Stanley Director-General of the Congo Free State when it formally came into being, the Belgian king fobbed him off with the Order of Leopold and an extension of his $5,000-a-year contract as a consultant. With that and his book royalties Stanley had no money worries, but for a man of his temperament mere financial stability was of small account. For want of some grand project to engage his restless energies and bolster his self-regard, he was increasingly listless, depressed and irascible.

*Stanley in a "Bula Matari" pose. A Smasher of Rocks, but no breaker of hearts. (The Autobiography of H. M. Stanley, 1908)*

Above all, he was emotionally starved. He had few close friends and, increasingly, he felt the lack of a woman in his life. He had told an indifferent Leopold of his desire to find a wife but, as Stanley confessed to an acquaintance in America, he was dismally ill-equipped for the business of courting.

"I am absolutely uncomfortable when speaking to a woman," he wrote, "unless she is such a rare one that she will let me hear some common sense. . . .

It was during the Berlin Conference that Stanley met Marie von Bunsen when he was invited to her parents' home. She had imagined he would be "more vital, smarter, more a man of the world," and was disappointed to find him so ill at ease and such a poor conversationalist, except on the subject of Africa and its people. He struck her as being "of the tough Conquistadore [sic] type with the outward habit of a disgruntled farmer and the phraseology and vocabulary of an American journalist."

But clearly Stanley admired her—"He was greatly interested in you," an elderly American woman who was a mutual acquaintance told Marie some years later—and when they met again soon afterward at a U.S. embassy Thanksgiving Day reception and dinner, he contrived to escort her in to the dining room and sit next to her. But still he managed to appear "aloof, indifferent, stiff." She noted also that he still seemed embittered at the incredulity and disparagement he experienced on his return from finding Livingstone and "the exaggerated charges of cruelty launched against him after the Congo expedition." She "realized the element of tragedy and felt a good deal of sympathy for the man," but never imagined that he was taken with her, even when Sanford half jestingly asked her: "Why won't you be queen of Africa? You have only to say the word."

Several years later, Marie spotted Stanley at a crowded reception in London "standing in the background, flattened against the wall, embittered, like a whipped dog. I intended to go across to speak to him, but some acquaintances intercepted me and when I looked for him again he had left."

Soon after returning to London from the Berlin Conference, Stanley took a lease on an apartment in New Bond Street, moving in with a Congolese boy named Baruti and a recently hired valet-housekeeper named William Hoffmann. If Baruti was a successor to Kalulu as a kind of living trophy of Stanley's travels, Hoffmann—a seventeen-year-old Londoner of German extraction—may be seen as the latest in a line of impressionable youths, like Lewis Noe and Edwin Balch, who were taken up by Stanley.

Hoffmann was an apprentice bag-maker and met Stanley when delivering a purchase to a woman customer staying in the same private hotel. "One day, soon after our first meeting," Hoffmann would recall, "he came up to me and put his hands firmly on my shoulders. 'Would you like to leave the bag trade and look after me instead?' he asked. For a moment I was speechless with surprise. . . . [It] seemed too wonderful to be true. . . ."

Hoffmann had absolutely no previous experience of the kind of work Stanley was offering him. In his memoirs he theorized that Stanley hired him partly because of his fluency in German and French. Stanley's motivation was obviously deeper and more complex than the need for a live-in interpreter, however, and his hiring Hoffmann was the start of a curiously ambivalent master-servant relationship that was to endure, on and off, until Stanley's death.

One obvious inference is that the hiring of Hoffmann is another sign of Stanley's latent homosexuality. If so, it does not seem to have deterred him from his search for a wife. After his failure to impress Marie von Bunsen, Stanley tried to initiate a relationship with an anonymous Austrian woman who had written to him via his publisher. He sent her his photograph and asked for hers in return.

"With women, generally I am very shy," he confided, ". . . though I might be bold enough on paper." He said that in affairs of the heart he had once been "an enthusiastic soul"—a reference, presumably, to his courtship of Virginia, Katie and Alice—but that now "the motions and sentiments of my soul lie dormant." But the correspondence led nowhere.

Stanley confessed his handicap to Alexander Bruce, the husband of Agnes Livingstone. "My timidity is unconquerable," he wrote on the eve of a visit to Newstead Abbey, where he apparently thought of paying court to one or other of the by now grown-up daughters of his landed friends the Webbs.

To propose and be refused would be my death, which would not be a politic ending. Were I assisted by a good friend—firm, reliant, like yourself—to push me forward, I might venture. I am rich enough to keep half-a-dozen economically, but not rich enough to deck my bride with Kohinoors. . . .

In the event, when Stanley went to Newstead he soon realized that the young women with whom he had played when they were children had no eyes for a middle-aged man such as himself, especially when there were "young gentlemen" of their own age on hand.

Then, in the summer of 1885, he was introduced by Edwin Arnold to Dorothy Tennant, and for a while his amatory hopes seemed to prosper. Socially, "Dolly" Tennant was everything that Stanley was not—a member by birth of the British Establishment. She claimed descent from Oliver Cromwell, her grandfather had been an admiral, and her deceased father an author, landowner and Member of Parliament, while her mother, Gertrude, was one of the grandes dames of Victorian London, whose elegant home in Richmond Terrace, off Whitehall, was a virtual open house for the artistic, literary and political elite of the day.

There was a streak of well-fed bohemianism in the Tennant women. In her youth, as daughter of the British naval attaché in Paris, Dolly's mother had known—quite possibly in the Biblical sense—that *épateur* of the bourgeoisie, Gustave Flaubert. As a London hostess she was on terms of personal friendship with the pre-Raphaelite painters George Frederic Watts and Sir John Millais, for whom both her daughters, Dolly and Evelene, occasionally modeled. Dolly herself had studied art in Paris and at London's Slade School, and by the time she met Stanley she was established as a genre painter of coy Grecian nudes and perky London street urchins.

Edwin Arnold's son Julian would recall Dolly as being "tall and statuesque, handsome in face and figure," and moving "like some goddess of old story come down from the home of her rest." As for her painting,

> Her nymphs were delicately finished studies of nude maidens disporting themselves in the woods of ancient Greece. The canvas seldom extended a foot in height, but she mounted them in gilt frames so deeply recessed that the holder had a sense of distance. I asked her why she sank her dainty sprites in frames so deep, and ecstatically she answered, "I like to compel all eyes that gaze upon these pictured nymphs to climb golden steps before they may feel themselves worthy to worship at the Shrine of Grace."

Dolly's perceptions of the London street urchins who posed for her appear, according to Arnold, to have been of the same simpering quality:

> When in her walks she chanced to see some tiny, tousle-haired, bare-footed crossing-sweeper, wearing garments so ragged that they showed

much of their owner's body . . . she would offer him dinner and a tip if he would pose for her. The resulting experiences brought their surprises. When the door of her palatial home was opened by a flunkey, gorgeous in a cutaway coat, yellow vest, knee-breeches, pink stockings and powdered hair, one of her ragged and dirt-stained companions gazed awestruck at the apparition and remarked, "Why does your brother dress in that rummy way?" The same urchin, after giving appreciative attention to a substantial meal, looked up from his empty plate and exclaimed, "My eye, but yer mother can cook!"

It may be unfair to Dolly Tennant to judge her personality solely by way of Julian Arnold's syrupy recollections. She and Watts corresponded frequently on terms of intellectual and artistic equality and enjoyed an apparently lifelong platonic friendship. In other ways, too, she showed herself capable of steely resolve. Nevertheless, there is something oddly disembodied about her, even by Victorian standards, and one suspects that, like Stanley, she was deeply repressed sexually. She was thirty-four years old, and probably a virgin, when Stanley came on the scene. There is no record that she had ever been engaged or otherwise emotionally involved with a man, and her diary discloses that in the middle of her fourth decade she was still sharing a bedroom with her mother and addressing her nightly diary entries to her father, who had been dead for fifteen years.

Dolly's first meeting with Stanley seems to have been at a dinner party in her home on June 24, 1885, attended also by Gladstone and his cabinet colleague Joseph Chamberlain, who were then in the middle of a general-election campaign. Dolly's diary entry for the day of the party shows that she was in something of a twitter. "Oh God help me. Do help me. What am I to do?" she wrote. It is not clear whether her panic arose from the prospect of meeting Stanley, whose Congo book she was then reading, or because of the high-profile politicians who would also be present.

At dinner she sat between Stanley and Gladstone, whose exchanges were somewhat strained. Stanley shared the widespread view that Gladstone's lack of firmness and dispatch had contributed directly to the death of Gordon at Khartoum four months previously. Gladstone tended to see Stanley, as did many reformers and men of the cloth, as a ruthless buccaneer whose African adventures reflected little credit on the white man's civilization. While holding the ring between the two lions who flanked her, Dolly's sympathies clearly lay with Stanley, who must have been in better than usual form that night. Addressing her dead father later, she wrote: "I felt a friendship immediately. I felt I cared for him. I know he cared back for me. . . . Dearest, goodnight."

One might have thought that a woman of such refinement would find Stanley rather too rough a diamond, but it seems clear that she set her cap at him from the start. Although Dolly was not a portraitist, she invited him to sit for her. "I would let you be very comfortable," she assured him, "you shall smoke and feel just as though you were in your own tent." So Stanley began making regular visits to 2 Richmond Terrace, where Dolly committed him, session by session, to canvas and charmed him with her conversation.

His defenses fell rapidly, for it is evident that by mid-July he had confided to her the story of his unhappy courtship of Alice Pike. "Strange to say," he told his friend Alexander Bruce, "I had just told her the story of the Lady Alice when in came her mother and spoke about Gordon's never marrying, and says she, 'I am sure he must have been jilted by some girl in the past of whom no one has heard yet.' . . . So very apropos of what I had been saying! My young lady friend and I looked up and our eyes mutually served to say, 'What a coincidence.' "

Dolly had some observations of her own on that subject to relay to the ghost of her father:

> I wish Alice had died, because then, though separate, he could have thought of her with love, and he would not have mistrusted mankind. I felt so sorry for him, not because of this only, but there is a loneliness and disappointment about his life which he will not allow. . . .

Stanley sought Bruce's advice: "Do you think I am making any progress in this affair du coeur? I cannot see it. . . . If I have to propose to her—do you know, I rather think I will not have the courage. And then, there is a mother in this case, and I am rather afraid of her. I think it would be a boon to shy people like myself if there were no such people as mothers."

Between August and November, Dolly was vacationing with her mother, but Stanley kept in touch with her by letter. There was not yet any overt talk of love between them, and Stanley remained on the rack of anxiety and self-doubt. He even took the advice of an elderly female acquaintance to sleep with a piece of wedding cake under his pillow so that he would dream of his future bride. "But alas, I might as well have stuffed my pillow with hop flowers," he wrote. "Such a dreamless, uninteresting sleep I do not remember to have passed for months."

In January Dolly gave him a silver token for his watch chain, inscribed "Bula Matari tala."* Plainly, she had marriage in mind, for her diary entries at this time are full of references to the subject in general, and in one she said that despite her thirty-five years she felt young, energetic and "passionately loving."

In February, Stanley became ill with gastritis, a recurring ailment originating in the hardships of his African travels, and Dolly and her mother visited his sickbed in New Bond Street. "He wore a kind of brown silk vest with short sleeves, and his arm was bare," she wrote in her diary that night. "He grasped my hand eagerly with all his old vigour, looking so delighted to see me. He looked very brown and copper coloured, enhanced I suppose by the white pillow."

When he was sufficiently recovered, Stanley went on a convalescent tour to Nice, Rome, Naples and the Italian lakes. His doctor had put him on a rigorous milk diet, and at the outset he was still very weak physically. "I cannot even walk a mile without fatigue," he wrote to a friend. But he had the strength to write Dolly a series of stiff, rambling letters—occasionally as long as twelve pages—describing his travels and discussing the politics of the day; he was particularly incensed at news from London of Gladstone's plans to give Ireland home rule, and in a letter from Rome he denounced the Tennants' dinner guest as a "traitor," "arch-sophist" and "monomaniac."

He was a good deal less daring when writing of more personal matters. After another long diatribe against the prime minister's Irish policies, some words about the climate, and observations on the beauty of a certain Italian princess, he signed off from Naples with a passage of excruciating awkwardness:

> Bearing you and yours in mind most faithfully, I seem to have had your company most days, though when I looked upon Pompeii's ancient streets I felt your absence most keenly, because this was a time when interchange of sentiments regarding the awful calamity would have seemed to have increased one's pleasure and interest in the scene. . . . Most faithfully yours, Henry M. Stanley.

Back in London by June, Stanley was again a frequent visitor to Richmond Terrace, and in the following month he, Dolly and her mother were among fifty guests of the shipping magnate Mackinnon on a cruise of the Scottish Isles. At the end of the cruise, the Tennants

---

* *Tala*—Swahili for "remember."

stayed on in Scotland as the house guests of landed friends while Stanley returned to London.

In his New Bond Street flat he wrestled with his self-doubts and insecurities for a fortnight before screwing up the courage to write a letter of proposal to "my dear Miss Dorothy" which, after another two days of indecision, he sent to Scotland by special messenger. In it, the swaggering, cigar-chomping, assertive little Yankee, conqueror of the Congo and smasher of rocks, reveals a timidity that would have shamed a suburban bank clerk.

> In one of my carefully-treasured notes received from you I read, "How long it takes people to explore one another." Eager and interested as I have always been with regard to you, I have been unable to explore with any satisfaction to myself your feelings toward me, and driven by misery and doubt, I have resolved to lay bare my own feelings and ascertain from you, if your goodness will extend so far, whether you can reciprocate them. You have dropped phrases in my hearing which have induced me to think that possibly I did not love in vain; if I have misconstrued them the punishment is mine . . . knowing how woefully ignorant I am of women's ways, I restrained myself, lest by giving expression to the ardour that possessed me, I should unknowingly give offence to one I have learned to esteem, admire and love with all my heart and soul. . . . Thus I went to you and came away, visit after visit, always perplexed and doubting, never certain of anything, but that you were the noblest and brightest of your sex and that I loved you. . . . You are in need of nothing. I cannot advantage you in anything, therein I am poor, helpless, trembling. I am rich only in love of you, filled with admiration for your royal beauty. . . . I have sat and brooded for hours over the possibilities and impossibilities, which confidence alternating with diffidence pictured. . . . For all the world I would not wound your feelings, nor offend any delicate susceptibilities. Nevertheless, bear without offence this declaration of mine, and tell me honestly and candidly to put an end to this exasperating doubt of mine.

Signing himself "Yours most devotedly, Henry M. Stanley," he implored her to let him know her answer as quickly as possible, saying that if she rejected him but did not wish to write she could merely send his letter back to him without comment.

In 1875 Dolly had been the model for a painting by Millais entitled "No!" In it, a beautiful young girl reads over a letter she has just penned, rejecting a proposal of marriage. Now, eleven years later, she enacted the same scene in earnest and turned Stanley down. Why and in what terms we do not know. The letter she wrote in reply to his fumbling proposal does not survive.

Stanley's leaden courtship style can hardly have been the reason, for clearly Dolly had been leading him on and turning her own thoughts to marriage. Similarly she had shown no sign of being deterred by the allegations of brutality which still attached to his name. His humble origins and social inadequacies might have had something to do with it, but those handicaps could hardly have been news to Miss Tennant. Most probably she was frigid and suffered a last-minute failure of nerve. Also, her mother's opposition to the match might have been a deciding factor. There is a hothouse quality to the closeness of the mother-daughter relationship, and one can

*Dorothy Tennant. "That woman entrapped me with her gush," stormed Stanley. (The Autobiography of H. M. Stanley, 1908)*

imagine the formidable Gertrude, fearing to be left alone in her declining years,* persuading Dolly to turn her suitor away.

Stanley's despair and anger—at Dolly for having led him on, at himself for having once more lowered his defenses—pervade a letter he wrote to Mackinnon:

> I have been living ever since my book left my hands last year in a fool's paradise. That woman entrapped me with her gush, and her fulsome adulations, her knicknacks inscribed with 'Remember Me,' her sweet scented notes written with a certain literary touch which seemed to me to be a cunning compliment to myself. . . .

His bitterness embraced Leopold, too. Like Dolly, the king had "kept me on the stretch of expectation always." Leopold's officials had fobbed him off with "We do not know exactly when we shall need you, but we shall let you know, my dear Mr. Stanley, in ample time to prepare." And so, he told Mackinnon, "I lived, constantly hoping, hoping here and hoping there—and after all both have come to nothing. I look back therefore with regret that nearly sixteen months of my life have been wasted with these artful people."

---

* In fact, she lived to be ninety-nine, surviving Stanley by fourteen years and yielding only eight years to her daughter.

# PART FIVE

# INTO THE HEART
# OF DARKNESS

[T]he wilderness had found him out early, and
had taken on him a terrible vengeance. . . .[I]t
had whispered to him things about himself
which he did not know, things of which he had
no conception till he took counsel with this great
solitude. . . .

*JOSEPH CONRAD*

# Chapter Twenty-one

STANLEY'S fruitless sixteen-month pursuit of Dorothy Tennant had at least taken his mind off the aimlessness of an existence in which he seemed now to have no mission. It had at last become clear that Leopold had no further use for him in the Congo, and Stanley had nothing in prospect but a lecture tour in America. But just as his sense of being both unloved and unwanted took him to the depths, a situation arose which put Stanley back in the public eye and right at the center of events in Africa.

In that autumn of 1886, British national pride was still smarting over the murder of Gordon at Khartoum by the followers of the Ayatollah Khomeini of the day, the Mahdi Mohammed Ahmed. The electorate had already punished the laggardly Gladstone for failing to rescue Gordon, and now the plight of a man whom the press characterized as a second Gordon seized the public's attention.

This was Emin Bey, governor of the Sudan's beleaguered Equatoria Province, a man whose exotic origins, murky past and bizarre religious preference would under normal circumstances have made him an unlikely focus for British concern. Little was known of Emin personally but that he was a German-born doctor of medicine and convert to Islam who, while serving the Egyptian government, had become one of Gordon's lieutenants in the Sudan.

After a long silence, word had now reached Britain that Emin and four thousand loyal Sudanese troops were standing fast against the further advances of the Mahdi's fanatical warriors, who had already overrun the neighboring Bahr el-Ghazal province and dragged its British governor, Lupton Bey, off to Khartoum in chains. A letter from Emin, addressed to Charles Allen, secretary of the Anti-Slavery Society, and published in *The Times,* aroused great public emotion:

> Ever since the month of May, 1883, we have been cut off from all communication with the world. Forgotten and abandoned by the Government, we have been compelled to make a virtue of necessity. Since the occupation of the Bar-Ghazal we have been vigorously attacked, and I do

not know how to describe to you the admirable devotion of my black
troops throughout a long war, which for them at least has no advantage.

In a later letter, to the Uganda missionary Alexander Mackay,
Emin said: "I am ready to stay and hold these countries as long as I
can until help comes, and I beseech you to do what you can to hasten
the arrival of such assistance." German he might be, or Turk or
whatever, and a Mohammedan at that, but the fellow was clearly a
white man through and through, and his plight a direct challenge to
the pride of Britain, whose Egyptian satrap had been turfed out of the
Sudan in such humiliating circumstances.

*Emin Pasha. German? Jew? Turk?*
*Whatever he was, this "second*
*Gordon" had to be rescued.* ("Emin
Pasha in Central Africa" [ed. Georg
Schweinfurth], London, 1888)

But at Number Ten Downing Street, now occupied by the Tory Lord Salisbury, the appeal fell on deaf ears. Salisbury considered Emin to be Germany's problem if anybody's, and had anyway been advised by his general staff that a military expedition to save him was out of the question. Nevertheless, public emotions had been aroused, and the antislavery and missionary lobbies were keeping the issue alive in the columns of the press. Then, even more powerful interests took up the cause.

These were commercial interests: Stanley's old friend Mackinnon and some of his business cronies conceived the idea of sponsoring a private expedition to relieve Emin, and in the process establish a profitable long-term British trading presence, hitherto confined to Zanzibar, on the mainland of equatorial East Africa. The expedition might also make an operating profit, since Emin was rumored to be in possession of vast quantities of ivory.

In Mackinnon's view only one man was qualified to lead such an expedition, and in October of 1886 he broached the idea to Stanley, who responded with the expected enthusiasm. They had a preliminary discussion of ways and means, and Mackinnon asked Stanley to draft a plan of campaign to show to potential subscribers. Stanley was due to leave for his American lecture tour in mid-November, but he assured Mackinnon that an escape clause in his contract would allow him to cancel and return to London if necessary.

Stanley began his tour in Boston, where Mark Twain, in fine chauvinistic form, introduced him to the audience as "an untainted American citizen who has been caressed and complimented by half the crowned heads of Europe." But a mere fortnight later Stanley was heading back to Europe, having received a cable from Mackinnon: YOUR PLAN AND OFFER ACCEPTED. AUTHORITIES APPROVE. FUNDS PROVIDED. BUSINESS URGENT. COME PROMPTLY. REPLY. Stanley immediately canceled the tour, to the dismay of his agent, and forfeiting earnings which he estimated at $40,000 (£8,000) sailed from New York within forty-eight hours, reaching London on Christmas Eve. That same evening he and Mackinnon were in conference.

In his draft plan of campaign Stanley had suggested four possible routes by which to reach Emin in Equatoria. Three of them were via the east coast and across or skirting Lake Victoria, involving a round-trip march of about three thousand miles from Bagamoyo, and taking an estimated eighteen to twenty months; the fourth involved traveling up the Congo River by steamboat and then marching east from the confluence of the Congo and the Aruwimi. Stanley favored the Congo route, claiming that it would be quicker and surer. But

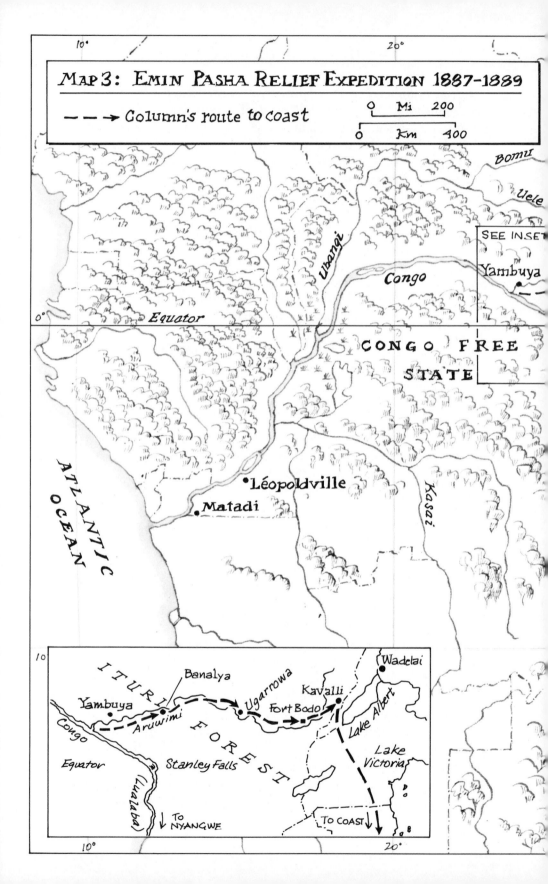

Map 3: Emin Pasha Relief Expedition 1887–1889

– – → Column's route to coast

0    Mi    200

0    Km    400

Bomu

Uele

Ubangi

Congo

SEE INSET

Yambuya

Equator

CONGO FREE STATE

ATLANTIC OCEAN

•Léopoldville

•Matadi

Kasai

Wadelai

ITURI

Banalya

Yambuya

Kavalli

Ugarrowa

Fort Bodo

Aruwimi

FOREST

Congo

Lake Albert

Lake Victoria

Equator

Stanley Falls

(Lualaba)

↓ TO NYANGWE

TO COAST ↓

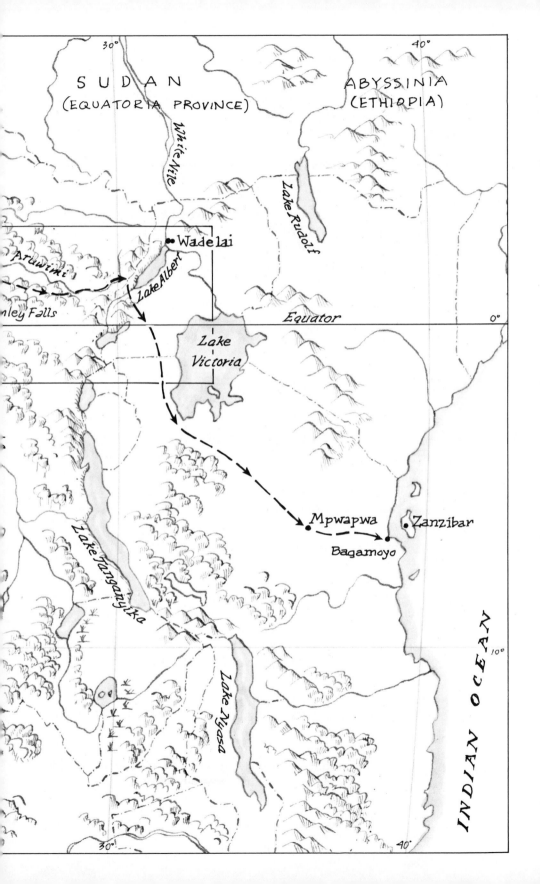

since the relief committee's ulterior objective in relieving Emin was to lay the groundwork for a trading empire in what is now Kenya and Uganda, Mackinnon and his associates preferred one or other of the east-coast routes.

Initially, Stanley bowed to their views, but there was another player in the game whose wishes could not be overlooked. This was King Leopold, to whom Stanley was still bound by contract. Apparently unknown to Mackinnon, Stanley obeyed Leopold's summons and took the boat train to Brussels on December 29 for an audience at the palace the following day. He arrived still resentful at Leopold's failure to make him Director-General of the Congo Free State, as promised.

The king explained that away by blaming it on "*haute politique, you know, to which we must all bend.*" Stanley took this to refer to continued pressure from the French, "who did not desire my presence in the Congo," and allowed himself to be won over by Leopold's calculated charm. As he recalled later: "The king was wonderfully benevolent, almost paternally so, and my hot anger at the 'tricks' I had conceived he had been playing me cooled."

Having put Stanley into a receptive frame of mind, Leopold made known his wishes. No matter what the relief committee might presently intend—and Leopold would be having a word with Mackinnon on the subject—he was to take his expedition to Equatoria via the Congo. For Leopold, as for Mackinnon, the relief of Emin was a secondary motive: now that the Egyptian Khedive no longer had the will or the means to hold on to Equatoria, it was up for grabs, and Leopold had long wanted to add that province, and perhaps Bahr el-Ghazal too, to his Congo Free State. By taking the Congo route Stanley would open up an overland trail between the Stanley Falls district and the Nile watershed, and Leopold's instructions were that having relieved and resupplied Emin he should sign him up to stay on, with his troops, as Leopold's viceroy.

The plan was a typically Leopoldian audacity, and there was a further example to come: the king had a secret offer of high employment to make to Stanley's old acquaintance, the notorious ivory- and slave-trader Tippu-Tib. In Zanzibar, where he would go to collect captains, askaris and porters for the relief expedition, Stanley should convey the king's offer to Tippu and use all his powers of persuasion to get him to accept. Sworn to secrecy about Leopold's intentions, Stanley returned to London that night. It is not clear when, if ever, he told Mackinnon of this meeting with Leopold, but it is striking that he made no mention of it in his subsequent account of the expedition, *In Darkest Africa.*

By now, the relief fund had closed with subscriptions totaling £21,500 (over $105,000). The major subscriber, contributing almost half the total, was the Egyptian government. Mackinnon himself put up only £2,000.

Stanley lost no time in ordering equipment and weapons for the expedition. These included 560 Winchester and Remington rifles and a quarter of a million rounds of ammunition, most of it intended for Emin's troops. Hiram Maxim, inventor of the Maxim Automatic Gun, donated one of his "wonderful weapons," with a firing rate of 600 rounds per minute. Other donations came from the drug company Burroughs and Wellcome ("nine beautiful chests," noted Stanley, "replete with every medicament necessary to combat the endemic diseases peculiar to Africa") and from Fortnum and Mason, the high-society provision merchants in Piccadilly ("40 carrier loads of choicest provisions. Every article was superb.").

Orders were cabled to agents in Zanzibar to hire 600 porters and purchase vast amounts of barter goods including 27,000 yards of various cloths, a ton and a half of beads and a ton of brass, copper and steel wire. Stanley then proceeded to select his staff officers from the hundreds who had volunteered.

The successful applicants included Major Edmund Barttelot of the Seventh Fusiliers and Lieutenant William Grant Stairs, a Canadian officer of the Royal Engineers, both of whom obtained unpaid leave from the army for the duration of the expedition; Captain Robert Nelson, lately of Methuen's Horse, who had fought in the Zulu Wars; Lieutenant John Rose Troup, who had been a police supervisor in the Congo and spoke fluent Swahili; William Bonny, a former sergeant in the army medical service; and two civilians—a big-game hunter and avid amateur naturalist named James Sligo Jameson, and a young sprig of the Anglo-Irish gentry named Arthur Mounteney Jephson—both of whom donated £1,000 to the fund before being accepted. Jephson's contribution came from his aunt, the wealthy Countess de Noailles. In addition, army surgeon Thomas Heazle Parke was signed on in Cairo, on the way to Zanzibar, as the expedition's medical officer.

While Stanley was immersed in these arrangements, Mackinnon received "a pleasant short letter from [Leopold] showing how anxious he is that the Congo route should be taken, and how unwilling to allow a break in the continuity of [Stanley's] connection with the

Congo State." With this gentle reminder that Stanley was his hired hand, Leopold urged Mackinnon "to banish any divergent sentiments and get all parties to agree to the Congo route."

This plainly vexed Mackinnon, who pointed out "the difficulties in the way of canceling existing arrangements" and "the great additional charge involved" in shipping Stanley's six hundred Zanzibaris all the way to the Congo. But Leopold held the whip hand, and Stanley made the decision easier by drawing up a list of the supposed advantages of going via the Congo.

These included "certainty of reaching Emin," since the riverboats would take the expedition "to a point 320 geographical miles" from its destination (a blatant miscalculation: the real distance was more than twice that far). Other perceived advantages were "allaying suspicion of Germans [who had territorial ambitions in East Africa] that underlying our acts were political motives," and "greater immunity from the desertion of the Zanzibaris who were fickle in the neighbourhood of Arab settlements." Stanley sweetened the pill for Mackinnon by pointing out that while taking the Congo route out, he could return via the east coast, signing commercial and territorial treaties with the native chiefs en route on behalf of Mackinnon's proposed Imperial British East Africa Company.

Leopold also eased the committee's dilemma by promising to place the Congo Free State's entire fleet of river steamboats at the disposal of the expedition, "inasmuch as will allow the working arrangements of its own administration. . . ." Under the circumstances, Mackinnon and his associates had no alternative but to concede, and the route change was agreed.

In a flurry of activity before sailing for Suez on January 21, Stanley was made a freeman of the City of London, went by cross-Channel ferry and train to Brussels for a last audience with Leopold, and came back to England for a meeting with the Prince of Wales, whom he found "very attentive."

Stopping over in Cairo, Stanley had a meeting with the Khedive and his prime minister, Nubar Pasha. They expressed doubts about the wisdom of the Congo route, as did the two noted German explorers, Georg August Schweinfurth and Wilhelm Junker. Also in Cairo, Stanley learned more about the mysterious Emin.

He was born Eduard Schnitzer, the son of well-to-do Jewish parents, in Prussian Silesia in March 1840. He had studied in Breslau and Berlin and practiced medicine in Albania, then part of the Ottoman empire, where he adopted the name Emin Effendi Hakim. Later, he went to Egypt as a medical officer until, working his way up through the ranks of the administration, he became a provincial governor under Gordon, with the rank of Bey. He followed the customs and outward forms of Islam, although there was some doubt whether he had formally converted to that religion.

Emin was formidably intellectual, a brilliant chess player and creditable pianist, reputedly the master of more than twenty languages and a dedicated naturalist, besides being an effective administrator. But much about him remained a mystery, including even his physical appearance. Junker told Stanley that he was tall, thin and extremely short-sighted. The last two attributes were accurate, the first was not; taking Junker's word for it, Stanley had a uniform made for Emin in Cairo, the trousers of which turned out to be six inches too long.

Other details of Emin's background remained shrouded in obscurity. In fact, that past was faintly scandalous, for Emin was an odd mixture of the scholarly and the picaresque. While in Albania he had joined the service of an Ottoman Pasha named Ismail Hakki, and while a member of his staff had carried on an affair with the Pasha's Transylvanian wife—a very dangerous pastime indeed. When the Pasha died rather suddenly, Emin had taken his widow home to Germany, claiming her as his own wife. There, it seems, he tired of her after a few months and, abandoning her with four children and six Circassian slave girls, absconded to Egypt. Since then, he had taken an Ethiopian wife, recently deceased, who had borne him a daughter.

Before Stanley left Cairo, he was given a firman by the Khedive, promoting Emin from Bey to Pasha and giving him and his officers and men the choice of returning to Egypt with Stanley and receiving all the back pay due to them, or of remaining in Equatoria on their own responsibility and without further claim on the Egyptian government.

On February 22, Stanley arrived in Zanzibar with his European officers, a detachment of sixty-one Sudanese soldiers and thirteen Somalis, his personal servant, Hoffmann, and Baruti, his Congolese ward. Zanzibar had changed considerably since he had last seen it. There was a telegraph office, a tall clock tower, a new sultan's palace, street lamps, horse-drawn carriages, steamrollers, and—a sign of Germany's rising influence in the region—six of the Kaiser's warships in the harbor. Many of Stanley's old traveling companions were on hand to greet him, and the valiant Uledi was among those who signed up for yet another expedition with Bula Matari.

Stanley lost no time in carrying out what he called "several little commissions." First was an audience with the Sultan Barghash, now

in failing health and within months of his death. Acting on Mackinnon's behalf, Stanley persuaded Barghash "how absolutely necessary
it was that he should promptly enter into an agreement with the
English"—that is to say with Mackinnon's nascent Imperial British
East Africa Company—to cede sovereignty over his nominal possessions on the mainland. Most uncharacteristically, but for reasons
which are not difficult to guess, Stanley felt constrained when writing
his account of the expedition to pass over this interesting exercise in
diplomacy in a mere paragraph. "It would take too long to describe
the details," he wrote.

Next, there was his business with Tippu-Tib, now enjoying a rest
on his native island from the violent affairs of the ivory- and slave-
trading empire he had established between the western shore of Lake
Tanganyika and the Upper Congo. Leopold, hav'ng paraded the need
to destroy the slave trade as justification for his claim to the Congo
Basin, now offered this notorious slaver, through Stanley, the governorship of the Congo Free State's Stanley Falls district.

This bizarre proposal was authentically Leopoldian. His fiefdom
and Tippu-Tib's were contiguous, and the Arabs and their
Manyuema auxiliaries, pushing ever deeper into the Upper Congo
from their old base at Nyangwe, had recently driven Leopold's garrison out of the Stanley Falls station. Intent on stopping these inroads, but lacking the capability to do so by force of arms, the king
had decided to try the tactic of co-option. Accordingly, he now proposed that Tippu-Tib should become his proconsul, with a regular
monthly salary and a free hand to exploit the Stanley Falls district's
plentiful resources of rubber, gum copal and ivory, provided only
that he abstained from slaving on Free State territory.

The proposal had obvious appeal to Tippu-Tib, now—like many
a gangster in prosperous middle age—yearning for a measure of
respectability and recognition. The injunction against slaving on Free
State territory, which in any case he never intended to honor, carried
the implication that it was all right to do so elsewhere. After an
exchange of telegrams with Brussels to iron out some details, Tippu-
Tib accepted Leopold's offer and prepared to sail with Stanley for the
Congo straightaway.

He also accepted a proposition Stanley made to him separately on
behalf of the relief expedition, to provide porters to carry ammunition to Emin and bring out the ivory—some $300,000 (£60,000)
worth, according to Junker—that he had supposedly stockpiled. After a good deal of haggling, Tippu-Tib agreed to provide six hundred

carriers at $30 (£6) per head to make the round trip from Stanley Falls to Equatoria and back, carrying boxes of ammunition one way and ivory the other.

Before sailing from Zanzibar, Stanley sent Emin a letter by native courier to say that he was on his way with "abundance of ammunition for your reeds, official letters from the Egyptian Government, a heavy mail from your numerous friends and admirers," and suggesting a rendezvous on the southern shore of Lake Albert. He conceded that the reasons for taking the Congo route were "principally political," but said he also felt it was more secure than the alternatives.

Stanley and his party, augmented by Tippu-Tib and a personal retinue of ninety-six, including thirty-five wives and concubines, sailed from Zanzibar for the Congo aboard the *Madura,* one of Mackinnon's British-India Line ships, on February 25, 1887. Their route took them to Matadi at the mouth of the Congo via Capetown, whose bustle and prosperity enormously impressed Tippu-Tib. Until then, he told Stanley, he had thought all white men to be fools, but now "I begin to think you must be very clever."


*IN BRITAIN* and throughout the English-speaking world the Emin Pasha Relief Expedition seemed a glorious and noble adventure, an undertaking to stir manly hearts and provoke womanly vapors. The motives of entrepreneurial greed and personal glorification that lurked behind the facade of high Victorian idealism were widely unrecognized. On the surface the venture was not only lofty-minded and altruistic, but extremely well founded.

After all, it was the biggest and most lavishly equipped African expedition ever mounted—that Maxim gun! those delicacies from Fortnum and Mason!—enjoying the blessings of the British government and the active support of the King of the Belgians. Lived there, indeed, a man with soul so dead he did not long to be with Stanley and his dauntless band on the Congo?

The reality was very different.

Even before the *Madura* reached the mouth of the Congo, the cracks began to appear. Stanley took a violent and almost instant dislike to his second-in-command, Barttelot, who was exactly the kind of privileged, drawling young swell he had learned to loathe. The dislike was mutual. In a shipboard letter to his sister, Barttelot described Stanley as "an extraordinary man. . . . I do not think he treats the fellows fairly. He has told us next to nothing about the business, and is very close on money matters." Writing to his father, Barttelot's forebodings sounded even more ominous: "I fancy some of us will regret the day we were born."

Well before that, the blacks had provided a disquieting foretaste of their likely behavior on the march. Only two hours out from Zanzibar, a "shindy" broke out between the Sudanese and the Zanzibaris over living space and, as Stanley said, "for a short time it appeared as though we should have to return to Zanzibar with many dead and wounded. . . . They were all professed Moslems, but no one thought of their religion as they seized upon firewood and pieces of planking to batter and bruise each other." Stanley and his white officers restored order only with great difficulty.

Shortly after the *Madura* dropped anchor at Matadi on March 18, Stanley learned to his shock that the fleet of five government-owned riverboats whose free use he had been promised by Leopold had been allowed to fall into a state of nearly total disrepair. This news put him into a vile mood; as he admitted, his "thoughts were not of the pleasantest" as he led his column in a twenty-eight-day march to Léopoldville, along the uphill road to the Congo plateau that he had built seven years before.

His young British officers soon realized that they had signed up to serve under an outrageously ill-tempered commander. On his good days Stanley was brusque and aloof, quick to criticize in the harshest terms when things went wrong and reluctant to praise even the most outstanding efforts. On his bad days, his rages were terrifying.

"He is a most excitable man, with a violent temper when roused," noted Stairs, ". . . he says and does a great many foolish things when he is in this state, for which afterwards he must be sorry. . . . [H]e holds such a tremendous leverage over us that for a single slip any of us might be put down as incompetent and dismissed at once."

Stanley was particularly hard on Barttelot, who told a friend that during a row over the conduct of the surly Sudanese troops "Stanley said it was in his power to ruin me in the Service." Having a splendid service record and excellent connections at the highest levels of the army, Barttelot dismissed that as "an empty threat, for it would take a good deal more than he could say to do that."

Jameson was astonished when Stanley, suffering from dysentery, blamed his condition "entirely" on Jameson, who was in charge of the cooking and ration arrangements on the march. "I have only you to thank for it," stormed Stanley. "I have had nothing but tea for two days, whilst you have had meat for your breakfast yesterday. . . ."

Meanwhile, the Sudanese, Somalis and Zanzibaris were behaving

*Edmund Barttelot. "I fancy," he*
*foresaw, "that some of us will regret*
*the day we were born." (The Life of*
*E. M. Barttelot, London, 1890)*

as an undisciplined rabble. Desertion, pilfering and insubordination were commonplace, and lazy porters frequently abandoned their loads, making it necessary for the officers to belabor them with sticks, fists and boots. "The work we are doing," said Jameson, "is not fit for any white man, but ought to be given to slave drivers." Noted Stairs: "Nothing that I have ever seen so demoralizes a man as driving negro carriers. . . . I should think in time a man would become a perfect brute if he did nothing else but this."

Inevitably, sickness soon began to exact its toll as fever and dysentery ravaged the expedition, while a chaotic supply situation, ensuring that the men received poor and insufficient rations, only added to the column's health and morale problems.

For all these tensions and troubles, Stanley's column must have presented a stirring sight in the early days of the march. The young adventurer Herbert Ward, who had spent three years working in the Congo and was now on his way home, encountered the expedition as he was heading for the coast, and was dazzled. First he saw a strapping Sudanese soldier come into sight over the brow of a hill, bearing—of all things—the standard of Gordon Bennett's New York Yacht Club.

> Behind him, astride of a fine henna-stained mule, whose silver-plated strappings shone in the morning sun, was Mr. Henry M. Stanley, attired in his famous African costume.* Following immediately in his rear were his personal servants, Somalis with their curious braided waistcoats and white robes. Then came the Zanzibaris . . . and a little further on the women of Tippoo-Tib's harem, their faces partly concealed and their bodies draped in gaudily-covered [sic] cloths. . . . A short distance further on, an abrupt turn of the narrow footpath brought into view the dignified form of the renowned Tippoo-Tib, as he strolled along majestically in his flowing Arab robes of dazzling whiteness, and carrying over his left shoulder a richly-decorated sabre. . . .

A brave show, indeed; the enraptured Ward begged Stanley to be allowed to join the expedition and was accepted. But by the time the column reached Leopoldville eleven men had died, twenty had deserted and twenty-six were too ill to go any farther. As well, the expedition had lost thirty-eight rifles and half its total of essential implements such as axes, bill-hooks, and shovels. Its food supplies were practically exhausted, and to his consternation Stanley found

---

*A Norfolk jacket and knickerbockers and a high-topped peaked cap with a sun flap protecting the back of the neck.

that the district around Léopoldville was in a condition of near-famine. This state of affairs reflected the priorities of those who had taken over the running of the Congo since Stanley's day. As Stairs observed: "Acres of bananas and manioc could have been planted, but, no, everything is ivory from morning to night. . . . They will never make anything of a State." In a later note, Stairs recorded the unanimous opinion of his fellow officers that the Congo Free State was "a huge, unwieldy mistake worked purely in the interests of the King of the Belgians. . . ."

The acute food shortage provided even more reason to get the column moving upriver as quickly as possible, and Stanley set about the task of acquiring the necessary means of transport in his usual steamroller fashion. He virtually commandeered the Baptist missionary vessel, *Peace*. Before leaving England he had asked Robert Arthington, the philanthropist who had given the steamer to the Baptists, for permission to use it. Arthington had refused, urging Stanley to "repent and believe the Gospel—with real sense, and live hereafter in happiness, light, and joy. . . ."

To make sure that no word of this refusal by Arthington reached the missionaries, Stanley checked through their incoming mail and abstracted any suspicious-looking letters. Then he turned the full force of his personality onto the head of the mission, Holman Bentley, who eventually handed over the craft. If he had not done so, said Bentley later, Stanley "would have taken her by force."

In similar style, Stanley seized an unfinished boat belonging to an ivory-trading company owned by Sanford, using the open hull as a barge. Through the governor of Stanley Pool he pressured another reluctant missionary into chartering his steamer, the *Henry Reid*, to the expedition for the not inconsiderable sum of $500 (£100) a month, and he bullied lesser Free State officials into carrying out urgent repairs to the dilapidated government boats.

This chaotic transport situation meant leaving many of his loads behind at Stanley Pool, to be sent for later, and Stanley was in a grim mood as he embarked his column for the nine-hundred-mile voyage upstream to the Aruwimi and Yambuya, where the march to Lake Albert was to begin. Before they left, Stanley issued orders to his officers regarding discipline:

> For trivial offences, a slight corporal punishment only can be inflicted, and this as seldom as possible. . . . Avoid irritating the men by being too exacting or showing unnecessary fussiness. . . . Be greatly forbearing—let the rule be, three pardons for one punishment. . . . Remember that the

labour of the men is severe, their burdens are heavy, the climate hot, the marches fatiguing, and the rations poor and often scanty. Under such conditions, human nature is extremely susceptible, therefore punishments should be judicious, not vexatious. . . . Serious offences, affecting the Expedition generally, will be dealt with by me.

This display of serene justice and calm forbearance astonished and irritated the officers in about equal measure. Apart from their own experience of Stanley's lack of such qualities, they noted that he was not at all slow to mete out severe corporal punishment when he lost his temper. Jameson recorded that when a box of ammunition went missing from his company, Stanley gave "all my chiefs . . . fifty cuts each with a stick, whilst they were held down on the ground."

There was certainly no justice or forbearance in Stanley's behavior when some of his Zanzibari headmen complained to him that Jephson and Stairs had confiscated food which they suspected the Wangwana had looted from an African village. The headmen claimed that, having paid for the food, the men had been unjustly treated, and Stanley chose to believe them rather than his officers. According to Jephson, this "occasioned a scene in which Stanley, to put it mildly, lost his temper and said things which have cast a gloom over everything." Jephson does not elaborate, and it is left to Jameson to fill in the details:

> The most disgraceful row I have ever heard of happened between Mr. Stanley and Jephson and Stairs. . . . He attacked them in a frantic state, stamping up and down the deck of the Peace. He called Jephson all sorts of names, "a G-d d-n son of a sea-cook." "You d-d ass, you're tired of me, of the Expedition, and of my men. Go into the bush, get. I've done with you. And you, too, Lieutenant Stairs, you and I will part today; you're tired of me, sir, I can see. Get; away into the bush." Then he turned around to the men (about 150) sitting down and spoke Swahili to the effect that the men were to obey us no more, and that if Lieutenant Stairs or Jephson issued any orders to them, or dared to lift a hand, they were to tie them up to trees. He had already told Stairs that he had only to lift his hand for the men to throw him into the sea. He lastly offered to fight Jephson. "If you want to fight, G-d d-n you, I'll give you a bellyful. If I were only where you are [Jephson was standing on the shore while Stanley paced the deck of the Peace] I'd go for you. It's lucky for you I'm where I am.". . . I had no idea until today what an extremely dangerous man Stanley was.

In his journal that night Stairs wrote: "I have stood more swearing at, heard more degrading things, and swallowed more intemperate language from another man today than I have ever before."

It is hard to find excuses for Stanley's behavior. By his own account, Stairs and Jephson were two of his most effective officers. But, as we have seen, Stanley's harsh early life and crippling lack of self-esteem had made him paranoid, while the accumulated physical legacy of his years in Africa—the malarial attacks, the acute gastritis, the blinding headaches—had soured a temperament that at its best was never sunny. And he was serving three masters—Leopold, Mackinnon and his own insatiable need for recognition—who drove him to succeed at all costs.

In this rancorous atmosphere, morale among the young officers and indiscipline among the men reached new lows as the flotilla of steamboats and barges made its way upriver. The brooding oppressiveness of the Congo itself added to a general sense of foreboding.

"It is peculiar," noted Jephson, "what a feeling of hatred the river inspires one with. One hates it as if it were a living thing—it is so treacherous and crafty, so overpowering and relentless in its force and overwhelming strength. . . . The Congo river god is an evil one, I am persuaded."

At Yambuya on the Aruwimi River, which enters the Congo about 120 miles below Stanley Falls, Stanley rid himself of Barttelot by putting him in command of the rearguard. Before leaving with the advance guard, Stanley attempted to placate his aggrieved second-in-command:

> Now, Major, my dear fellow, don't be silly. I know you feel sore because you are not to go with us in the advance. You think you will lose some kudos. Not a bit of it. Ever since King David, those who remain with the stuff, and those who go to war, receive the same honours. Besides, I don't like the word "kudos." The kudos impulse is like the pop of a ginger beer bottle, good for a V.C. or an Albert medal, but it effervesces in a month of Africa. It is a damp squib, Major. Think rather of Tennyson's lines: "Not once or twice in our fair island story/ Has the path of duty been the way to glory." There, shake hands on this, Major. For us the word is "Right Onward"; for you "Patience and Forbearance." I want my tea. I am dry with talking.

From a man whose career had been one long search for kudos it was an astounding display of hypocrisy and one that, far from mollifying, can only have increased Barttelot's loathing for Stanley.

Barttelot's task now was to wait for the steamers to bring up the rest of the ammunition, supplies and barter goods from Léopoldville while Stanley hurried ahead with 380 of the fittest men, due east through the vast Ituri Forest, for his momentous rendezvous with

Emin Pasha. According to Stanley's written instructions, when the loads were all received at Yambuya and Tippu-Tib's contracted six hundred porters had turned up, Barttelot and the rear column were to follow his trail through the forest and meet up with him at Lake Albert.

But this "very desirable" reunion, as Stanley called it, never came about. The rearguard would remain bogged down for fourteen months at Yambuya where, plagued by sickness and hunger, afflicted by a growing sense of futility and despair, surrounded by menacing slave-traders, and cheated and taunted by Tippu-Tib, they would steadily go to pieces in both body and spirit.

# Chapter Twenty-two

*THE* great Ituri rain forest stretches beyond the northernmost loop of the Congo in a 180-degree arc, covering an area of well over 200,000 square miles, or greater than France. Stanley had no idea what kind of conditions he would encounter en route for Lake Albert—"whether there are any roads, or what kind of natives, cannibals, incorrigible savages, dwarfs, gorillas."

On June 28, 1887, he set out into this vast unknown with Jephson, Stairs, Nelson, Parke, his servant Hoffmann, and the strongest and fittest of his African porters and askaris. He had optimistically estimated that he would reach Lake Albert in three months. In the event the journey took twice as long, and in conditions far worse than anything Stanley had imagined.

The forest was a frightful place—dark, dank and treacherous, a realm rarely penetrated by sunlight or enlightened by a glimpse of the sky, an all-enveloping, utterly hostile environment peopled by cannibals and pygmies made murderous by superstition and fear of strangers, teeming with poisonous snakes and swarms of relentless insects which seemed to harry the expedition every step of the way. "Of all the scenes of desolation for any human being to be left alone in!" wrote Parke. "I could not have fancied it before I came here."

Even the unflinching Smasher of Rocks was affected by the evil atmosphere of this "region of horrors," with its "dark, relentless woods" and the "ceaseless boom of the cataracts" as his column headed east, following the Aruwimi River. When they diverged from the meandering line of the river to take a more direct path through the forest, Stanley found that the sepulchral silence which replaced the roar of the rapids was no less oppressive.

For much of the way, the advance guard followed a foot-wide trail, marked out by the passage of native feet but frequently overgrown and blocked by creepers, through which an advance party of fifty had to hack their way with machetes and bill-hooks. Often the way was barred by gigantic fallen trees, or pits dug by the shadowy forest-dwellers to trap animals, and a completely fresh path had to be cut through the surrounding undergrowth. And always, when approaching a forest village, there was the danger of impaling a foot on one of the rows of poisoned skewers, concealed by leaves, set by the pygmies and other forest-dwellers who lurked invisibly a few feet away with bows drawn.

The hostility of the natives was not without good cause; Arab slavers had been that way, and any stranger was an object of fear and suspicion. But as Stanley's column advanced, taking whatever food they could find if barter was impossible, seizing women and children as guides and hostages, sometimes burning deserted villages, they created hostility on their own account.

The noise generated by such a large column on the move scared off game for miles around, and meat was rarely to be had. They subsisted mainly on the rice which they carried and manioc, or cassava, which they plucked from native plantations in the forest clearings. But manioc enfeebles while it sustains: the tuber contains a debilitating if rarely fatal poison and must be painstakingly prepared before it is entirely safe to eat. In their hunger-driven haste, Stanley's men would often fail to take the necessary precautions.

Frequently they would travel for days without passing any areas of cultivation, and then even such tainted nourishment as manioc was not available. In their worst periods they were forced to subsist for days on end on a kind of wild bean, berries, fungus, slugs, grubs, and ants.

While it was expedient to follow the path of the river, part of the expedition went by water in the *Advance*, their sectioned steel boat, rowing hard and occasionally poling against the current, with the sick aboard. At the outset, these included Stairs, who was prostrate for many days with fever. As they proceeded they managed to commandeer a growing number of native canoes, enabling Stanley to relieve the enfeebled land party of many man-loads.

Despite the hazards and hardships of the trail—and the tendency of the men to develop evil-smelling, gangrenous ulcers that quickly penetrated to the bone—the first three weeks passed without the loss of a man to death or desertion. Then two Zanzibaris vanished. At first it was thought that they had been captured by hostiles. Only later was it discovered that they had deserted, and soon others began to follow their example in twos and threes. So much for Stanley's belief that on the Congo route the porters would be less likely to run off.

On the thirty-sixth day out from Yambuya, the first death occurred when a porter succumbed to prolonged fever. In rapid succession five more men were lost by drowning and native attack and with them seventeen precious rifles. Then, during a skirmish on August 13, Stairs was hit just below the heart by a poisoned arrow. "The sensation was at first that of a knife being stuck into me," wrote Stairs, "and shortly afterwards my side stiffened and acute shooting pains set in. . . . Of [illegible] the evening, under morphia and opium, I remember nothing."

Surgeon Parke saved Stairs's life by sucking out the poison, but had to leave the arrowhead lodged in his ribs. Two Zanzibaris who were similarly wounded in the same skirmish were not so fortunate. They died in agony five days later. Stairs noted apprehensively: "Seeing those poor chaps die in convulsions quite close to me makes one feel a dread of the same thing happening to oneself."

Two days after the attack in which Stairs was wounded, Jephson led a land party of three hundred out into the forest with instructions to rendezvous upstream with the river-borne party, now consisting of the *Advance* and fourteen canoes. Jephson's column got lost, and an increasingly anxious Stanley sent three search parties out in different directions to look for them. Stanley himself remained in camp with the river party, now reduced to himself and Parke with twenty-nine sick and eight wounded, one of them Stairs.

Six days passed before Jephson and his party turned up, having lost three men during their wanderings. Jephson was suitably contrite and, clearly expecting a more than usually violent tongue-lashing, wrote Stanley a note saying: "I can understand how great your anxiety must have been, and deeply regret having caused it." But to his surprise, Stanley was "very quiet and nice about my having led the expedition astray."*

This seems to have been a deeply chastened Stanley. Instead of stoking up his fury, the anxiety of the past few days had cast him into deep gloom. "I am conscious of the insidious advance of despair towards me," he wrote in a diary note, "the last few days have begun to fill me with a doubt of success. . . ."

Another indication that Stanley's ruthless drive was faltering came a few days later when, after a number of Zanzibaris had deserted, taking supplies and rifles with them, he allowed himself to be dissuaded from hanging a man who was caught in the act. "The chiefs

*Stairs's recollection was different. Stanley gave Jephson "the slating he deserved," Stairs noted in his journal (August 20, 1887), but he was still suffering from his wound and possibly under the influence of pain-killing drugs, so perhaps we should take Jephson's word for it.

would not hear of it and he was only put in chains," wrote Jephson. "If I were Stanley I should hang the man whether the chiefs wished it or not. He will never stop desertions till he does."

Three weeks later, while continuing their eastward march, the column encountered a party of Arab slavers' Manyuema mercenaries, returning to their station from a foray to the south. At the invitation of their leader, Ugarrowa, Stanley's party followed them to their station and encamped nearby.

Stanley was greatly impressed by Ugarrowa's forest headquarters— "a large settlement, jealously fenced around with tall palisades," and by his "commodious, lofty and comfortable" private apartments. The slaver chief showed Stanley "all his treasures, including a splendid store of ivory," allowed his people to sell food to Stanley's caravan, and agreed, for $5 per man per month, to look after fifty-six sick and wounded—excluding Stairs, whom Stanley took with him— until Barttelot or someone else authorized by Stanley should come to pick them up.

The night after Stanley moved on from Ugarrowa's, as he was in camp a few hours' travel upriver, one of the slavers' canoes brought three Zanzibari deserters who had absconded with their rifles and ammunition. The next morning Stanley mustered all hands to debate the deserters' punishment, and this time the chiefs agreed that the sentence should be death. Stanley ruled that one of the three should be hanged immediately, one the next day, and the third the day after that. The condemned men drew straws, the unlucky one was strung up from a tree without further ceremony, and "before the last struggles were over the Expedition had filed out of the camp. . . ."

At dawn the next day, Stanley sent for the head chief, Rashid bin Omar, to discuss the pending execution of the second man. Stanley, according to his own account, was reluctant to go through with the hanging, hoping that the death of the first of the trio would be warning enough to the rest. Rashid agreed and fell in with Stanley's suggestion that they should make as if to carry out the second hanging but that at the last moment Rashid and the other chiefs should beg Stanley to show mercy.

They went through this charade, and Stanley describes how, having removed the noose from the deserter's neck, he launched into one of his colorful orations:

> "Enough, children! take your man, his life is yours. But see to it. There is only one law in future for him who robs us of a rifle, and that is death by the cord. . . ." Caps and turbans were tossed into the air. Rifles were

lifted, and every right arm was up as they exclaimed "Until the white cap [Stanley] is buried none shall leave him! Death to him who leaves Bula Matari! Show the way to the Nyanza! Lead on now—we will follow!". . . . Even the officers smiled their approval. Never was there such a number of warmed hearts in the forest of the Congo as on that day.

The episode reads like one of Stanley's familiar set-pieces, but is confirmed in its essentials by Jephson and Stairs. This was Stanley's leadership at its most effective: by sparing a life he earned far more obedience and loyalty than he could have gained by taking it.

As the expedition pushed deeper into the forest, frightening away the game by the noise of their advance and finding everywhere that the depredations of the slavers had ruined native agriculture, the shortage of food became desperate—and Stanley's men ever more ruthless in the methods they used to obtain it. Stairs describes an unprovoked attack on a peaceful and unsuspecting native village situated on an island some seventy-five yards out in the Aruwimi. What makes his account so disturbing is the utter lack of remorse with which this otherwise decent young Canadian describes the scene before he and his men opened fire.

> It was most interesting, lying in the bush watching the natives quietly at their day's work. Some women were pounding the bark of trees preparatory to making the coarse native cloth used all along this part of the river. Others were making banana flour by pounding up dried bananas. Men we could see building huts and engaged in other work, boys and girls running about, singing, crying, others playing on a small instrument common all over Africa, a series of wooden strips played over a bridge and twanged with the thumb and forefinger. All was as it is every day, till our discharge of bullets, when the usual uproar and screaming of women took place. . . .
>
> I opened the game by shooting one chap through the chest. He fell like a stone. . . . Immediately a volley was poured into the village. At first the natives ran, but rallying they peppered us well with their iron tipped arrows, but without effect. For some minutes we took pot shots at the heads as they appeared above the grass and huts and managed to drop a few more and then gradually they made off one by one till all was quiet.

Stairs sent swimmers to the island to ransack it, but "the only things they found were some spears, dried bananas and smoked elephant meat."

By October 5, hunger had reduced fifty-three of Stanley's men, including Nelson, to a state where they were too weak to march any farther. Stanley accordingly set up a camp for the invalids—Starvation Camp, as it was called by its inmates—before pushing ahead with the remainder of the expedition for the camp of a slaver named Kilonga-Longa, supposedly three days' march away. There, he hoped to obtain food to send back to Nelson and his companions.

Jephson had deep misgivings about this course. "It was a terrible position for Nelson to be left in," he wrote. "He had food for only two days and will have to exist on what he can pick up in the shape of fungus and roots, or if there are any fish in the river, he may be able to get a few. . . ."

By this time the usually equable Jephson was sufficiently affected by starvation to allow his pent-up resentments against Stanley to pour out onto the pages of his diary. He accused him of "practically abandoning" Nelson and marching off "without hardly taking the trouble to say goodbye" to him. Jephson also complained that Stanley had not been sharing equitably what little food there was, hogging the occasional chicken and portion of goat for himself. Stairs would make similar allegations later on. For the moment, though, all that any of them had to eat were bush beans that grew wild in the forest—"about the lowest form of food I have ever tasted," said Stairs, "and with very little sustaining power."

Weak and skeletal though they were, the approach of the expedition still struck the most terrible fear into the forest tribes, who fled at their approach. One day, when Jephson and his boatmen were fighting their way upstream against the rapids, they came across "the most extraordinary sight":

> [S]ome 50 natives, men, women and children, were in the rapid clinging to rocks and boughs of trees—they evidently thought the boat would come up the other side of the island . . . and were ducking and dodging behind the rocks with just heads above the water, trying to hide. Their terror was great as we approached. Women abandoned their children and made for the shore. It was piteous to see small children and babies swept past us in the rapid. . . .

Two days later Stanley shot the last of the expedition's donkeys, who seemed near death anyway, and distributed the meat "as carefully as though it were the finest venison." A free fight broke out for possession of the skin, bones and hooves. "A pack of hyenas could not have made a more thorough disposal," wrote Stanley. ". . . our men had become merely carnivorous bipeds, inclined to be as ferocious as any beast of prey."

In these desperate days, Jephson retained sufficient generosity of spirit to recognize that Stanley bore a greater burden than the other officers. His "anxiety has been frightful," wrote Jephson in the diary which, despite his privations, he kept up daily in a small, meticulous hand, "for the success of the expedition has been and is indeed hanging in the balance. . . . He has been very despondent and low and at times talks about it all in a very hopeless manner." Stairs tried to cheer his chief up: "I told him I did not think it was as bad as all that and asked him the distance to the Lake. He said 'To the Lake? None of us will ever see the Lake or anything else. Don't talk about the Lake.' "

Finally, eleven days after leaving Starvation Camp, they reached Kilonga-Longa's, at a place called Ipoto. There, the Manyuema gave them three goats and enough corn to allow each man six ears, promising also to send food back to Starvation Camp the following day. But soon relations began to deteriorate. Kilonga-Longa's cutthroats had clearly been expecting to obtain fine cloth and beads from Stanley's stores, but these had largely been lost and stolen. To pay for their food, Stanley's Zanzibaris were forced to trade their clothes and other personal property—and eventually even their rifles and ammunition.

"Despite entreaties for corn," wrote Stanley, "we could obtain no more than two ears per man per day. I promised to pay triple price for everything, on the arrival of the rear column, but with these people a present possession is better than a prospective one."

For this situation, both Jephson and Stairs held Stanley to blame. "It is perfectly scandalous the way he is treating the men," said Jephson, "—all sorts of promises of food when we reached the Arabs were held out to them to urge them forward when we were in the wilderness and now they have only had from him 4 heads of corn for two days." Stairs also used the term "scandalous," alleging that Stanley was feeding on "fowls, goat, porridge, beans, corn and bananas, while whatever we eat we pay for out of our now miserable supply of necessary clothing."

Meanwhile the treacherous Manyuema were stalling on their promise to provide porters to carry food back to Nelson. It was not until October 26, nine days after their arrival at Ipoto, that a seventy-strong party of Manyuema and Zanzibaris, commanded by Jephson, finally set out for Starvation Camp. En route they passed the skeletons of men who had died on the terrible inward march. When they finally reached Starvation Camp only Nelson and five of the fifty-two men left with him remained—the others having died, deserted, or gone foraging—and two of those were dying. Nelson himself was "worn and haggard-looking, with deep lines about his eyes and mouth," reported Jephson. "We clasped hands and then, poor fellow! he turned away and sobbed. . . ."

Jephson returned to Ipoto with Nelson to find that Stanley had pushed on to the east with Stairs and 146 men, leaving Parke behind with 29 men who were too sick to travel. He also left behind the steel boat, the Maxim gun, 47 rifles and a large amount of ammunition.

Whether he did his best for these men before leaving them is an open question. In his account of the expedition Stanley said that the night before he left Ipoto he entered into blood brotherhood with the chief of the Manyuema camp, to ensure proper treatment for his men. He also claimed to have entered into a written agreement to pay for their food with cloth to be provided by Barttelot when he turned up with the rear guard and the rest of the expedition's supplies and goods.

To ensure the goodwill of the Manyuema, Stanley said, he additionally gave their chief "a five-guinea rug, silk handkerchiefs, a couple of yards of crimson broadcloth, and a few other costly trifles," together with "a gold watch and chain value 49 pounds in London." But when Jephson arrived he found Parke "strong in his expressions of disgust at the way Stanley had left him without any proper arrangements being made."

"Stanley himself, so Parke tells me, took quantities of food and great numbers of chickens," wrote Jephson. "He did not even take the trouble to say good bye to Parke when he went, which to put it mildly was ungracious. It is really quite wonderful how little Stanley seems to care about the welfare of his officers. . . ."

Before setting out to catch up with Stanley, Jephson was himself reduced to selling "anything I could" to buy food for the journey, including 300 Remington cartridges for which the Manyuema gave him 350 ears of corn. "Probably Stanley will be very angry with what I have done," he noted. It took ten terrible days' march to catch up with Stanley's column, during which time Jephson discovered that flying ants, roasted until crisp, were "very good to eat."

But at Ibwirri, where he found Stanley encamped, there was food in plenty. The settlement lay just outside the slavers' zone of operations, and the natives, left in peace to tend their crops and look after their livestock, had "such abundance," as Stanley said, "that we might safely have rested six months without fear of starving." His men were gaining weight at the rate of one pound a day, "their eyes had become lustrous, and their skins glossy like oiled bronze."

Meanwhile, Stairs—his hunger sated—had found a new cause for complaint against Stanley. "Books . . . would now be worth their weight in gold," he wrote. "Stanley is so mean that he never offers the loan of any of his and does not like being asked for them. In the same manner, he is so devilish mean that he sticks to all the candles, never giving me one. . . ."

A week after Jephson rejoined Stanley, the column set off from this land of plenty, and four days later, climbing to a village on a hillside five hundred feet above a clearing, the expedition got its first exhilarating view of the open plain that lay beyond the forest. Jephson wrote:

> It is a glorious sight after being accustomed to the jungle for 6 months to see a splendid grassy plain dotted about with clumps of trees like a park; it looked almost as if it might be a distant view of Kent. . . . It was lovely just to sit and look at the open country—the men . . . are immensely delighted . . . and executed a sort of war dance which lasted nearly an hour. . . .

It took another four days' march to reach the grassland and, as Stanley reported, "we felt as if we had thrown all age and a score of years away as we stepped with invigorated limbs upon the soft sward of young grass. . . . [A]nd finally, unable to suppress our emotions, the whole caravan broke into a run."

Being in open country did much for Stanley's relations with his officers. Now, Stairs noted, he and Jephson got on much better with their commander. "He has taken our advice on many occasions and there is none of the old talk of 'conspiracy' and plotting that he used to rave about. . . ."

But the expedition's trials were by no means over. The natives of the plain were every bit as hostile as those of the forest, and the column, now numbering some 175 men, was harried constantly as it headed east across the grassland. Jephson found the warriors of the plains far more formidable than "the bush niggers we have been accustomed to hitherto." They had "long strong spears and large bows and stand up and shoot their long reed unpoisoned arrows like men and have some courage about them."

For all their courage, the natives kept their distance out of respect for the lethal reach of the expedition's "fire tubes." But after six days of harassment, Stanley, encamped in a strong position atop a hill, decided not to move any farther "until either the natives made friends with us or we gave them a good licking." He tried to negotiate peace, using as interpreter a Zanzibari who had a smattering of the local Zamboni language. But the natives seemed determined to drive the strangers out, and Stanley decided there was "no alternative but to inflict an exemplary lesson on them." Jephson described the action:

> Stanley had the people mustered and sent me to occupy a small village below the camp with 40 men, whilest [sic] Stairs was in readiness with another party to sally out if the natives should attack from the other side. They sent a man down into the valley to reconnoitre and he was instantly chased by 5 of our men and shot. The natives then began to descend from the hills with tremendous shouting and Stanley gave the order to burn all the villages round. Simultaneously Stairs and I sallied out. He with his party went along the North side of the valley whilest I swept around the south, burning everything, huts, granaries etc. as we went. . . .

The next day, when the natives again "began to get rather noisy," Stanley sent Jephson and Stairs out "to give them another lesson" and they burned "about two dozen villages . . . and captured a lot of chickens and goats." After this the Zamboni chief sued for peace, blaming the trouble on his hotheaded young warriors.

On December 13, they at last came in sight of Lake Albert, 2,500 feet below. "Cheer after cheer burst from the men," wrote Jephson, ". . . and several of them rushed madly up and down shouting out 'Nyanza, Nyanza, cheer for Bula Matari.' . . . Stanley had struck the exact place, Kavalli, he had been trying for. . . ."

But their joy was short-lived. Marching down to the lake shore, the expedition experienced what Stairs called "our worst piece of fighting since we landed in Africa. Every inch down this desperately steep hill the natives pushed us. Not till we had reached the plain below and crossed a largish river late in the evening did they give us any peace. . . ."

And when they got to Kavalli, where Stanley had hoped to rendezvous with Emin, their inquiries about the governor met a blank response. "Many, many years ago a white man came from the north in a smoke-boat, but he went away," they were told. Even worse, as he scrutinized the lake shore terrain and the surrounding hills Stanley realized that, unlike Victoria and Tanganyika, Lake Albert had no trees within twenty miles of the water suitable for making a large canoe. It was only four days by boat to Emin's headquarters at Wadelai, but having left the steel boat behind at Ipoto, they must either trek to Wadelai, an estimated twenty-five days' march through probably hostile territory, or else camp by the lake and wait for Emin to come to them.

There was a third alternative in what Stanley testily referred to as "the inexplicable absence of Emin or any news of him," and this was the one that Stanley favored. They would march back into the forest, make a fortified camp at some spot like Ibwirri where there was plenty of food, collect the invalids, ammunition and the abandoned *Advance* from Ugarrowa's camp and Ipoto and, leaving the sick and halt in camp, return once more to the lake, this time with the steel boat.

The decision makes sense only in the context of a situation which by now had become thoroughly muddled and hopelessly compromised. In its exhausted and impoverished condition the expedition looked less like a relief column than a pathetic group of refugees. If they could not at least hand over to Emin a reasonable quantity of ammunition, they might as well have stayed home. This may have been Stanley's principal motive in accepting the prospect of returning to the embrace of that frightful forest.

He argued that if they marched to Wadelai they might have to expend as many as twenty-five cases of ammunition fighting their way through, leaving virtually none for Emin. On the other hand, Stanley calculated, if they waited by the lake shore they would have a critical food problem. There was no cultivation on the acrid lake terrace, the natives living on fish and whatever grain they could get by barter from the natives of the plateau. Therefore he saw no alternative to returning to fetch the boat and more ammunition.

Jephson was amazed by this argument; he had found the lake shore to be teeming with game, on the wing and the hoof, and "all so tame and . . . little hunted by the natives [that] it would be easy to supply the whole expedition with meat."

> I said let us try anything, rather than turn back when we were on the eve of success. However, Stanley was against it, though Stairs was on my side, so we must make up our minds to the return journey. . . . Stanley has of course immense experience and marvellous powers of resource and I was rather astonished that with his resource he could not hit upon a feasible plan.

On December 17, after Stanley had sought to mollify Stairs and Jephson by sharing "a couple of bottles of fizz" with them, they began the long, hard climb back up to the plateau. They halted for an hour, "with feelings of utter dejection," at the spot from which they had first seen the lake. "How bitter it was," wrote Jephson, "to be sitting there knowing that we were returning and that all our work and labour had been in vain. . . . We marched along feeling as if we were going to an execution or a funeral."

On December 29 the forest closed in around them once more. Nine days later they were back at Ibwirri. There they set about building a stockade and planting corn, beans and tobacco. Stanley named their new stronghold Fort Bodo—Peaceful Fort. On January 18, Stanley sent Stairs with ninety-eight men and rifles to collect Nelson, Parke and every living man with them from Ipoto, plus the *Advance* and as many loads as they could manage. Twenty-five days later Stairs returned, having accomplished his mission, as Stanley said, "without a single flaw."

Parke looked "wonderfully well," Stanley noted, but Nelson was "prematurely old, with pinched and drawn features" and "the bent back and feeble legs [of] an octogenarian." Eleven of the men left at Kilonga-Longa's camp had died of starvation, having been ill-treated and given little or no food by the Manyuema. Life there, Parke reported, had been "almost intolerable."

In his official account of the expedition, Stanley would later observe that what Nelson and Parke endured at Kilonga-Longa's "required greater strength of mind and a moral courage greater than was needed by us during our stormy advance across the grass-land." But Jephson noted in his diary at the time that "Stanley tries to make as little as possible of what Nelson and Parke suffered and talks about their expecting to find themselves in an hotel."

After a four-day rest, the tireless Stairs was sent off on another mission—this time to Ugarrowa's camp, 183 miles away, to collect the invalids left there in September and to escort couriers who, from Ugarrowa's, would continue westward with maps and instructions for Barttelot and the rear column, by now presumably following Stanley's trail. Stanley said he would wait at Fort Bodo until March 25 before setting off back to the lake, moving at a pace that should enable Stairs to catch up with him and "participate in the honour of being present at the relief of Emin Pasha."

The day after Stairs left, "very much incensed" that Stanley had given him such a difficult deadline to meet, Stanley fell seriously ill with acute gastritis and a badly abscessed arm. Parke administered morphia and kept him on it for twenty-three days. At one point the arm was on the mend when, as Jephson noted, Stanley caused it to flare up again by hitting his servant Hoffmann on the head with a stick in "one of his ungovernable fits of rage—which by the way are of very frequent occurrence." Despite his savage moods, Parke and Jephson attended Stanley faithfully during his sickness, taking turns to sit up all night with him as, hardly sleeping, he lay in bed talking. Jephson paints a revealing picture of him at this time:

A few nights ago, by way of amusing himself he gave me a sketch of my character as he had observed it. He began by saying that my enthusiasm led me to exaggeration (perhaps that's true) and that I was full of cracks and prejudices, and in fact made me out to be a perfect fiend, to all of which I listened with a smile. But the thing he laid the most stress upon was my 'overweening pride—pride of birth and pride of self.' To the latter accusation I remarked that I did not see where my pride came in, for I had had many jobs to do since I had accompanied the Expedition, such jobs as are usually given to the very lowest and I had done them all without a word and without even thinking them derogatory. He said that perhaps I had, but that in doing them I had showed pride in every movement and turn of my body, though he admitted I had done them properly and well—and so on until he had contrived to paint a very nasty character. He said that at the age of eighteen had I been sent out for three years into a very tough life, say, three years before the mast in a coasting vessel, I should have borne the impress of it all my life and it would have improved my character to a very great extent. He said I had seen only the soft side of life. There he made a very great mistake, but I did not contradict him but smilingly asked if he had any other unpleasant traits to add to my character, upon which he said No, but added from what he had seen he had very great hopes of me and thought that I should return from this expedition greatly improved, which I thought was just as impertinent as his tirade against my character. He then gave me a sketch of his own character. He told me he had been just as impetuous and rash as I am when he was my age, but that time etc., had taught him to curb himself, and a whole lot more rubbish. He made himself out to be a St. John for gentleness, a Solomon for wisdom, a Job for patience and a model of truth. Whereas I do not suppose a more impatient, a more ungentle, a more untruthful man than Stanley could exist. He is most violent in his words and actions. The slightest little thing is sufficient to work him into a frenzy of rage. His sense of what is honourable is of the haziest description and he is certainly a most untruthful character—"Oh wad some power the giftie gie us."

On April 2 Stanley, Jephson and Parke with a party of 126 men left Fort Bodo for the lake, leaving the still-feeble Nelson in charge of the fort and hoping Stairs and his party would overtake them en route. Burdened as they were by the boat, the journey was slow and painful. But when they at last broke through into the grasslands, they found the natives less hostile than before. And soon they heard their first news of Emin. "About two moons after you passed us—when you came from the Nyanza—a white man called 'Malleju' or the Bearded One, reached Katzona's in a big canoe, all of iron," they were told.

This news produced mixed feelings in Stanley. "Had Emin, who expected us on December 15th, but taken the trouble to have sent his steamers a nine-hours' steaming distance from his station of Mswa, we should have met with his people December 14th. . . ." he grumbled.

All along the route the expedition was besieged by unarmed deputations from the various villages, wishing to make blood brotherhood. "They told us quite readily how many men we had killed," noted Jephson. "I forget the numbers, but it was sufficiently large to make them very anxious for our friendship."

At the village of Kavalli, a letter dated March 25—just over three weeks previously—was awaiting Stanley from Emin: "Be pleased, if this reaches you, to rest where you are, and to inform me by letter, or one of your people, of your wishes. . . . At the arrival of your letter, or man, I shall at once start for Nyamsassi, and from there we could concert our further designs." Stanley records that his men "became mad with enthusiasm," but does not describe his own feelings on at last making contact with the man he had gone to such enormous trouble, and suffered such tremendous hardship, to reach.

He penned a lengthy reply to Emin and sent Jephson and Parke on ahead with the *Advance*, a hand-picked boat crew of fifteen and fifty other men. Jephson's instructions were to proceed to Emin's station at Mswa, two days by boat up the western shore of the lake, deliver the letter, and return with Emin to where Stanley would be waiting for him. Seemingly unaware of the irony of the request, Stanley asked Emin to bring with him in his steamer "rations sufficient to subsist us while we await your removal, say about 12,000 or 15,000 lbs of grain."

The affluence of the supposedly desperate Emin Pasha, as compared with the relief column's bedraggled and impoverished state, was not lost upon Jephson when, on April 23, he arrived at Mswa.

> "[W]e looked as if we were in want of relief far more than they. I felt awfully dirty in my old worn out suit of Tweed beside the smart Nubian officer and even beside the servants, who were all dressed in suits of fresh white cotton cloth. . . . They brought me an enormous omellette and some delicious bread for my midday meal. I was very tired and . . . slept for 4 hours. I found that while I was asleep they had brought me a large round iron sponge bath full of water, a round piece of Soap, which Emin's people make here, and an Egyptian loofah. I had not ordered the

bath, so they must have thought I looked dirty. How delightful the bath was. . . ."

Emin himself was on an inspection tour farther up the lake and was due back the following day. In the event, he did not show up until the twenty-sixth. Jephson found him smaller than expected, "very foreign looking," and speaking English "very well, but with a strong foreign accent."

The next day, camped by the lake at Badzwa, Stanley saw a dark puff of smoke on the horizon, and two hours later Emin's eighty-five-foot steamer, *The Khedive*, dropped anchor nearby. Soon afterward, "amid great rejoicing, and after repeated salutes from rifles," Emin walked into camp, accompanied by Jephson and his second-in-command, the Italian Captain Gaetano Casati, and some of his Egyptian officers.

This time there were to be no memorable—or risible—words of greeting. As Stanley recorded it: "I shook hands with all and asked which was Emin Pasha? Then one rather small, slight figure, wearing glasses, arrested my attention by saying in excellent English, 'I owe you a thousand thanks, Mr. Stanley; I really do not know how to express my thanks to you.'" Stanley's recorded reply was: "Ah, you are Emin Pasha. Do not mention thanks, but come in and sit down. It is so dark out here we cannot see one another."

Inside his tent, by the light of a wax candle, Stanley beheld "a small, spare figure in a well-kept fez and a clean suit of snowy cotton drilling, well-ironed and of perfect fit. A dark grizzled beard bordered a face of a Magyar cast, though a pair of spectacles lent it somewhat an Italian or Spanish appearance." It was a face on which "there was not a trace . . . of ill-health or anxiety; it rather indicated good condition of body and peace of mind."

# Chapter Twenty-three

SEVENTEEN years before, spiteful critics had wondered aloud whether Stanley had saved Livingstone or vice versa; this time the question would have been apposite. By the time Stanley arrived on the scene, Emin Pasha, despite his earlier pleas for help, was not at all sure he needed to be relieved or wanted to be rescued.

True, he was under constant pressure from Kabba Rega, the warlike king of neighboring Bunyoro; true, the northernmost of his two battalions was of doubtful loyalty; and certainly his supplies of ammunition needed replenishing. But the main military threat seemed to have receded. Having beaten off an invasion attempt by the Mahdi's troops, Emin and his force of fifty Egyptian officers and fifteen hundred Sudanese soldiers—plus wives, concubines, servants, children and other hangers-on, making a total of some ten thousand—felt relatively secure and reasonably comfortable.

As Jephson had seen, they had plenty of food and were manufacturing many of their own necessities, such as cotton cloth, wax candles, soap, shoes and clothing. Emin himself seemed to have adapted particularly well to his circumstances, effective in his role as administrator and utterly absorbed in his self-appointed task of collecting and classifying specimens of Equatoria's abundant plant and insect life for the British Museum.

Thus, by April 1887, although aware that Stanley was on the way, Emin had made up his mind that he would "in no case abandon my people," should they prefer to stay put with their wives and families. "We have passed dark and troublous days together and I should consider it shameful to desert my post at this particular time," he said in a diary entry. In subsequent letters to the missionary Robert Felkin he reiterated his intention not to leave, although he would be glad to send home some of his fractious officers.

What Emin really needed from the outside at this point was a sense that the world was aware of his situation and concerned about his fate, and it was that need which Stanley and his bedraggled column fulfilled. So when Jephson told Emin of the public sympathy in Britain for his presumed plight, and of the hardships the expedition had endured in reaching him, he appeared to be genuinely moved. "The tears started in his eyes," noted Jephson, "and for a moment he looked away, and then he took my hand and said . . . 'If I lived for a hundred years I could not thank the English people enough for their disinterested kindness in sending me help when I have been abandoned by my own government for so many years.' "

By the time his tears had dried, though, the thirty-one cases of ammunition and the packet of letters which were all that Stanley was able to hand over must have seemed to Emin a distinctly meager result for all the effort and agony involved. And although his first two-hour exchange of views with Stanley was enlivened by the five half-pint bottles of champagne that Stanley had brought with him, it was not long before the two men began to grate on each other. Except for their mutual interest in Africa, Emin the courtly man of thought and Stanley the rough-hewn man of action had little in common.

It was Emin's evasiveness that particularly irritated Stanley. He had half expected the Pasha to be packed and ready to leave for the east coast immediately. But on April 30, he noted impatiently that although he had found Emin "most amiable and accomplished," he had been unable to gain the least idea of his intentions.

> [T]he Pasha's manner is ominous. When I propose a return to the sea to him, he has the habit of tapping his knee and smiling in a kind of 'We shall see' manner. It is evident he finds it difficult to renounce his position in a country where he has performed viceregal functions.

To spur Emin into making up his mind to leave, Stanley went over the options open to him. He reminded him that the Khedive had made it brutally clear that Egypt had no further interest in Equatoria and that if Emin stayed it would be at his own risk and responsibility. He pointed out that while the situation might seem stable enough now, it was fundamentally precarious, "surrounded as this lake is by powerful kings and warlike people on all sides, by such a vast forest on the west, and by the fanatical followers of the Mahdi on the north."

Emin countered that to move out with a total of perhaps ten thousand people would require a prodigious number of porters to carry the women and children. Stanley was dismissive. "The women must walk," he replied, and "for such children as cannot walk, they will be carried on donkeys, of which you say you have many. . . . Our women on my second expedition crossed Africa; your women, after a little while, will do just as well."

Resuming the dialogue the following day, Emin said that although he had no doubt the Egyptian officers would wish to leave, he was not at all sure about the men. Stanley urged him to muster his troops, read out the Khedive's letter and let them make their own choice. For his part, Casati declared: "If the Governor Emin goes, I go; if he stays, I stay." Increasingly impatient, Stanley said to Emin: "May I suggest then, Pasha, if you elect to remain here that you make your will?"

If for no other reason than his own glorification, Stanley's preference was to bring Emin back alive, but there remained the offers of employment from Leopold and Mackinnon if he insisted on staying. Should Emin sign up with Leopold—undertaking to keep law and order in Equatoria, maintain communications between the Upper Nile and the Congo, and provide "a reasonable revenue" for the Congo Free State's coffers—he could remain governor at a salary of $7,500 (£1,500) a year. If he would rather work for the British, Stanley would help him set up a secure base at the northeast corner of Lake Victoria, where, enjoying direct if uncertain communications with the coast and Zanzibar, he would be the East Africa Company's viceroy.

Despite his inclination to stay put, Emin wasted little time in refusing Leopold's offer. The route between Equatoria and the Congo was far too difficult and dangerous to maintain, he argued. But he viewed the East Africa Company's proposal more favorably and thought that his men might agree, especially as it was a comparatively short march to Lake Victoria.

As the dialogue continued, Stanley grew increasingly impatient at Emin's indecision. He was not in the least mollified by the arrival of gifts for himself and his officers from Emin's stations in the north. Indeed, the clothing, fresh fruit, honey, tobacco—and even a jar of pickles—which Emin pressed upon him only added fuel to Stanley's slow-burning resentment.

"These gifts," he grumbled, ". . . reveal that he was not in the extreme distress we had imagined, and that there was no necessity for the advance to have pressed forward so hurriedly. We left all our comforts and reserves of clothing behind at Yambuya. . . . I fear I shall have to travel far to go to the rescue of Major Barttelot and the rear column. God only knows where he is."

With Stanley the thought was the deed. He resolved to start back to find Barttelot, leaving Emin to go and consult the rest of his garrison. By the time he returned with the rear column to Lake

Albert, he hoped, Emin and his people would at last be ready to leave with him. At Emin's request he left Jephson behind as living proof that there was indeed a relief expedition on hand to escort them out of Equatoria and to read the troops a message that Stanley had composed at Emin's request: "I have come expressly at the command of Khedive Tewfik to lead you out of here and show you the way home. . . ."

On May 22, Stanley started back toward the forest. A detachment of Emin's Sudanese troops stood to attention and saluted as the column moved out, while "the Pasha fervently thanked us and bade us goodbye." Stanley's column included 130 Madi porters, provided by Emin. Most of them deserted the first day, and when Stanley sent back a messenger with this news Emin immediately sent his steamer north with instructions to bring back replacements.

A second message from Stanley that day told Emin of a significant geographical discovery he had made after only five miles' march—the sight, at some seventy miles' distance, of a vast snow-capped mountain. Taking a compass bearing on it before it disappeared from sight in the heat haze, Stanley concluded correctly that it must be a peak of the fabled Ruwenzori, or Mountains of the Moon. With this sighting, the last piece of the age-old riddle of the Nile's sources fell into place, for the Mountains of the Moon, never before located, had up to then existed only in legend dating back to the days of Ptolemy.

Strictly speaking, the discovery was not Stanley's at all, but Parke's and Jephson's. On April 20, while hurrying ahead to the lake with the *Advance,* they had seen the snow peak and had later reported it separately to Stanley. According to Parke, who was the first to tell him, Stanley seemed "a good deal interested." But when Jephson mentioned the matter after bringing Emin to Stanley's lake-side camp he "laughed at me and pooh poohed the idea."

Emin, unaware of Parke's and Jephson's part in the matter, gave full credit to Stanley for the sighting. "Allow me to be the first to congratulate you on your most splendid discovery," he wrote. "It is wonderful to think how, wherever you go, you distance your predecessors by your discoveries." Jephson confided his resentment to his diary: "He [Stanley] says nothing about Parke and I having seen it more than a month ago and having told him about it, but he makes it out to be his discovery."

With this latest feather in his explorer's cap, Stanley marched on toward the forest and Fort Bodo where, for a change, he found that all was well.

Lieutenant Stairs was first to show himself and hail us, and close after him Captain Nelson, both in excellent condition, but of rather pasty complexion. Their men then came trooping up, exuberant joy sparkling in their eyes and glowing in their faces, for these children of Nature know not the art of concealing their moods or disguising their emotions.

It had taken Stairs ten weeks to return to Fort Bodo from his mission to Ipoto, far too late for him to hope to catch up with Stanley at the lake. And so he had stayed put, missing the doubtful glory of being present at the link-up with Emin, but consoling himself by grousing about Stanley's having "taken almost all the quinine," and complaining that "with all his experience [he] cannot build a house worth anything."

After resting two days at the fort, Stanley mustered his men to select those who would accompany him onward in search of the rear column. On June 16 he set off at the head of a column consisting of 113 Zanzibaris, 95 Madi porters, 4 of Emin Pasha's soldiers, and his servant Hoffmann. He had decided to leave his white officers behind, although Parke and 14 Zanzibaris were to accompany him as far as Ipoto, to collect the dozen loads that had been left there and take them back to Bodo.

Stanley calculated that he would be back in about six months. But he had no illusions about the hardships that lay ahead. "Evil hangs over this forest as a pall over the dead," he wrote. "It is like a region accursed for crimes; whoever enters within its circle becomes subject to Divine wrath."

EVIL HAD indeed befallen Barttelot, Jameson and the rest of the rear column. By the time all the supplies and equipment had been brought up from Léopoldville, Barttelot had found that there were four times as many man-loads as porters. And as he waited in vain for Tippu-Tib to provide the carriers he had promised, even those he had began to perish, one by one. "It is horrible to watch these men slowly dying before your face, and not be able to do anything for them," wrote Jameson. "The moment a man falls really ill with dysentery, or any other affection [sic] of the stomach, he slowly wastes away, becoming a living skeleton, sometimes lingering for weeks before he finally goes out."

Within ten weeks of Stanley's departure, there were fifteen graves in the camp cemetery. After another three weeks, there were twenty-one. Three months later, there were forty-one graves, and after another four weeks, fifty. Barttelot wrote to Mackinnon: "I am afraid you will think I have been strangely dilatory at Yambuya but, believe me, I have done all in my power for the Expedition. I cannot arrest the death rate nor force Tippu, as I am entirely in his hands, and he knows it."

To his brother-in-law, Major Henry Sclater, Barttelot complained: "Stanley should never have left without his whole force, nor without Tippu-Tib's men. Of course, if he returns all the blame will be mine. . . ." Barttelot's letter was heavy with forebodings of his death and fears for his reputation. If he should live he could defend himself, but "if dead, please let Mackinnon read this letter." And to his father he wrote: "It is a disgusting life—nothing to read, no news, nothing to do. . . . It is no good my writing a long letter to you, for I cannot, simply. There is nothing to tell."

Stanley had taken the strongest porters and the best-disciplined askaris with him. "Seventy-six of the very worst were left," complained Jameson, "and only one chief called Munichandi, a man who is utterly worthless, as the men do not care one rush for what he says. Had Mr. Stanley tried, he could not have left a worse man as chief over the class of men left behind."

Barttelot imposed harsh discipline to keep these unpromising troops up to the mark. Day after day, camp routine began with the flogging of sentries who had been caught sleeping on watch. "It is sickening," wrote Jameson, ". . . but there is no help for it." When out foraging, Jameson and the others had little compunction about kidnapping women and children from villages in the area to force the natives to sell them food:

> Presently down came a woman with a load of manioc. . . . We let her come quite close, then made a dash and caught her. We tied her up and waited, when along came another woman with a baby. We caught her too, but she screamed fearfully, and I thought she would bring a perfect hornets' nest about us; but the noise of the rapids drowned her voice. . . . Major Barttelot was delighted when I returned with the captives. He sent [a boy] to his village to tell the chief that he would only give up the women for goats and fowls. . . .

In mitigation of such behavior, it should be stressed that the rearguard were in desperate straits for food. As Jameson recorded at one point: "We finished our last plantain to-day, and have only two more fowls left, a kid and a goat; I see no chance of getting any more, for the natives do not trade, or offer to, in the least. As a last resource we must catch some more of their women."

Jameson was the expedition's naturalist, and his months of en-forced idleness at Yambuya gave him the opportunity to collect many specimens of birds and insects, which acquisitions he noted enthusi-astically in this diary. But his scientific curiosity had a peculiarly cold-blooded dimension and he clearly had a tendency to view the natives as mere specimens. One day after a force of Tippu-Tib's Manyuema attacked a village on the other side of the Aruwimi, their Arab commander presented him with the severed head of a native. Jameson packed the head in a box full of salt to preserve the flesh and subsequently had it sent to London, to be dressed and mounted by Messrs. Rowland Ward, the taxidermists of Piccadilly. Bonny, the medical orderly, would report seeing it some time later in a glass case in Jameson's house. On another occasion Jameson recorded in his diary that "I had determined to begin collecting today in the natural history line, and succeeded in a much larger way than I intended, by collecting two native women, one baby and a boy."

For the first six weeks after Stanley's departure Barttelot and Jame-son were the only white men at Yambuya, Ward and Bonny being occupied downriver at Bolobo and Troup even farther downriver at Stanley Pool, waiting to bring up the loads that had been left behind by reason of the ramshackle condition of Leopold's Congo River fleet.

Two men thrown together under such circumstances are likely to become either fast friends or bitter enemies. Barttelot and Jameson were fortunate enough to find each other agreeable company. "I shall be proud to introduce Jameson to you," Barttelot wrote to his father. "I have seldom met a man like him—sweet-tempered as a woman, courageous, honest and a friend of all." For his part, Jameson said of Barttelot that "he is a real honest gentleman, and I cannot say more."

Ward, Troup and Bonny linked up with them when the steamer *Stanley* reached Yambuya on August 14, bringing the total strength of the rear guard to 251 men. Of the three new arrivals, Bonny was socially beyond the pale, being a mere ranker. As for Ward and Troup, although gentlemen they never warmed to Barttelot, a man of rigid mind and, like Stanley, given to violent outbursts of temper.

Ward, a quintessential civilian with an easygoing nature, was quite open about the fact that "somehow or another from the very start Barttelot and I failed to 'hit it off.' We viewed things in different lights: he through the strict, stern, rigid spectacles of discipline and with the autocratic manner of a British officer; while I, who had roughed it the world over, had the influence upon me which came of much adventure, and that cosmopolitanism which results from being vis-à-vis to every phase of life."

Both Ward and Troup also noted that, even by the standards of the day, Barttelot was deeply and violently prejudiced. "[H]e had an intense hatred of anything in the shape of a black man," wrote Troup, "for he made no disguise of this, but frequently mentioned the fact. His hatred was so marked that I was seized with great misgivings. . . ."

Barttelot's contempt for Blacks contributed greatly to the low state of morale among the rearguard. He imposed increasingly savage punishments for wrongdoing, culminating in a sentence of 300 lashes on a mission-educated Zanzibari named John Henry, whom he found guilty of desertion and theft. The flogging was administered in commutation of a death sentence, but John Henry died of his injuries anyway, whereupon Barttelot merely commented that "he must have been shot or hung sooner or later, for he was a monstrous bad character."

While despising the Blacks, Barttelot had little more time for the Arabs. His relations with Tippu-Tib, on whose goodwill he was ultimately so dependent, were never cordial, and he was frequently at odds with the other Arabs, whose marauding in the vicinity of Yambuya made him daily more nervous for the safety of his own camp and stores. As he said himself, in a letter to his father, "to deal with [the Arabs] you require an urbane disposition, a rare facility for lying, an impassible face, a suave and gentle manner and a limitless purse. None of these I possess, though they think I possess the latter, because they are told of the vast amount of stores I have, and think they must be mine; and because I don't give according to their ideas they hate me."

Still, even had Barttelot been a consummate diplomat, it is unlikely that he could have held Tippu-Tib to his agreement. In the manner of the East, the Arab leader was full of reassurances that the promised service was about to be performed but, for devious reasons of his own, never intended to perform it.

First, he undertook to deliver the six hundred porters to Yambuya by early July. When they had not arrived by late August Barttelot sent Jameson and Ward to Stanley Falls, a six-day trek, to buttonhole him. They found Tippu-Tib "bland, courteous and accommodating in every way." He told them he had sent five hundred men some weeks previously but said that they had been unable to find the expedition's camp. He assured his visitors he would immediately dispatch as many men as he could round up, and the two Englishmen returned, accompanied by Selim bin Mohammed, Tippu-Tib's nephew, who had been appointed headman of an Arab camp set up near Yambuya to pillage the surrounding countryside.

On their return, Ward went down with a fever and took to his tent. After five weeks, during which he hovered between life and death, he recovered to find that no porters had arrived and that "matters appeared to be precisely as they were when I had been taken ill."

At this point, Barttelot went to Stanley Falls in person, accompanied by Troup. Tippu-Tib assured him that the porters would be found, but that they might have to come from Kasongo, a major Arab outpost one month's journey upriver. The fact was that most of Tippu-Tib's manpower was away marauding for ivory and slaves. Barttelot had to take his bland assurances at face value and return empty-handed.

All this time there had been no news of Stanley, apart from wild and frequently conflicting rumors spread by the occasional deserter. Three letters he had written to Barttelot remained undelivered at Ugarrowa's camp, and Barttelot was beginning to wonder whether Stanley might already have relieved Emin and pushed on with him to the east coast.

In mid-February, Barttelot set out on yet another mission to Tippu-Tib at Stanley Falls, taking Jameson and a Syrian interpreter named Assad Farran with him and leaving Troup in command at Yambuya. When they got to the falls they discovered that Tippu-Tib was at Kasongo.

At this point Barttelot's behavior begins to seem decidedly irrational. Notwithstanding that he had not yet received the six hundred porters originally promised, he decided to ask Tippu-Tib to provide four hundred "fighting men" in addition, arguing that if Stanley was "in a fix" somewhere it would be useless going to his rescue with a force no bigger than the one Stanley himself had started out with. Barttelot accordingly sent Jameson and Farran on to Kasongo with this new request for Tippu-Tib while he himself—sick of a fever—turned back to Yambuya.

After he got back, "shattered and weak," on March 25 he made another seemingly irrational decision. Drafting a long telegram to the Relief Committee in London, he ordered Ward to proceed downriver with it to the coast, more than eleven hundred miles away, and thence by ship to a telegraph terminal at either Luanda or São Tomé.

Barttelot's telegram informed the committee that he had so far heard no news of Stanley, that Tippu-Tib had yet to provide the promised porters, and that he, Barttelot, had asked him for an additional four hundred fighting men. It added that when he got the porters and askaris he intended to start out after Stanley, leaving behind one officer at Stanley Falls with all the stores not absolutely needed on the march. The message asked for the committee's "advice and opinion" on this course of action and said that Ward would await their reply at the coast. Barttelot calculated that, returning to Yambuya by steamboat, Ward should be back with the committee's reply by about the first of July. But if Tippu-Tib's porters turned up before then, the message said, the rearguard would set off without waiting for him.

This alone made sending Ward to the coast quite pointless. It would take him at least two months to get there—if he got there at all, for the trip by canoe for a lone white man would be extremely hazardous. But, having sent him, Barttelot was now talking of leaving Yambuya before Ward came back with the committee's reply.

One may reasonably wonder whether Barttelot was losing his mind. He certainly seems to have fallen victim to some form of paranoia. He had already confided to his diary that he suspected Stanley might want to poison him, and three delphic diary entries between the time of his return from Stanley Falls and the date of Ward's departure for the coast provided further hints of paranoia. On March 25, Barttelot noted darkly that the "opportunity was taken to play me false," while he was down with fever. The following day, he recorded that "they have been playing the mischief while I have been away." And the day after that, he was "much upset at what I find. . . ." Exactly what he thought "they" had been doing in his absence, we are not told.

Both Ward and Troup commented on his agitated state of mind. "Poor Barttelot is almost beside himself with his fever, weakness, and the preparation of letters for me," noted Ward, while Troup observed that his commanding officer was "very excited," "distressed in mind," and "disturbed." Further evidence of Barttelot's mental condition came when Ward, on his way to the coast with Barttelot's telegram, was overtaken by a canoe bearing an extraordinary letter from his superior officer:

WARD, I am sending this to warn you to be very careful in the manner you behave below—I mean as regards pecuniary matters. I shall require at your hands a receipted bill for everything you spend, and should you be unable to purchase the champagne and the watch, you will not draw that 20 pounds. The slightest attempt at any nonsense I shall be down upon you for. I have given you a position of trust, so see that you do not abuse it. You will send me a receipt of this letter.

Ward rightly considered the letter to be a "gross insult" and determined to demand satisfaction on his return. Meanwhile, in camp at Yambuya, Barttelot was hearing "more disclosures" about his fellow officers, presumably from Bonny. Again, we have no idea what kind of disclosures were made, if any. Barttelot's diaries and letters were edited by his elder brother, who leaves us with ellipses, presumably to protect the reputations of his brother's fellow officers, who he may well have suspected were being wrongfully accused.

Another obsession of Barttelot's was that the Arabs and their Manyuema henchmen, who were camped nearby under Selim bin Mohammed, were planning to attack Yambuya with the aim of seizing the expedition's stores and ammunition. Relations were already strained, and Barttelot's diary entries contain such phrases as "Salem [sic] means mischief," "things look black," and "perhaps my days are numbered."

Barttelot decided that yet another trip to Stanley Falls was called for—this time to ask Tippu-Tib's lieutenant, "Bwana Nzige," to curb Selim. The Arab chief heard him out courteously and promised that Selim would be moved to another post. The following day Barttelot headed back toward Yambuya. En route he met Troup, who had been away on a foraging trip. Troup was concerned to find Barttelot "looking terribly ill and very disturbed."

Back at camp, Barttelot said, Bonny again "told me tales of Troup and Ward." Barttelot seems to have assumed that Bonny's motive for tale-bearing was resentment at being treated as a social inferior: "His continual cry is that he is every bit as good as we are, and must be treated the same." When Selim visited Yambuya to say that he was leaving, Barttelot remained suspicious. "This may be a blind," he noted. "I have sent men out to watch him."

Meanwhile, Jameson was at Kasongo, where Tippu-Tib, bland and courtly as ever, assured him that "he would give us all the men we wanted, and be ready to start on the 10th of the next moon." As for the extra fighting men, he would provide them too, "if not 400, then 300." Jameson tried to get him to sign a contract which Barttelot had drawn up, but Tippu-Tib demurred, saying that he would "settle everything with Stanley."

I strove to impress on him the necessity of speed and the value of a contract to himself, when he reiterated what he had said and seemed annoyed at my pressing the point. . . . I decided to accept his promise and leave him alone for the day, deferring any other questions till tomorrow, as he was evidently not in good humour. . . .

The following day, Jameson found Tippu-Tib in a better mood and during the course of a conversation got some idea of the Zanzibari's imperial ambitions, which he found "enormous, far greater than most people think . . . he evidently means to have the whole country up to Lake Albert Nyanza, and God knows how much of the Congo." Jameson was entirely bemused by his host and, seduced by his princely manner, he seems to have been willing to believe his soothing promises. At the same time, though, Jameson was aware that "we are entirely in the hands of Tippu-Tib and dare not have a row with him."

Finally it seemed that Tippu-Tib was about to fulfill his contract. The Arabs began assembling a fleet of canoes and loading porters, shackled together like slaves, onto them for the journey downriver to Stanley Falls and thence, ostensibly, to Yambuya. Tippu-Tib was himself to return to his governorate, and Jameson would travel with him as far as Stanley Falls. On May 5, more than three weeks after Jameson's arrival at Kasongo, they set off downriver.

It was a particularly uncomfortable trip for Jameson, hunched up "like a trussed chicken" all day in a canoe and tormented all night by clouds of mosquitoes. After a week's journey he found himself spending the night at a riverine village called Riba-Riba, where the local chief staged an entertainment for the Arab dignitaries. Drummers, their heads weirdly daubed with thick white clay, beat out intricate rhythms while men and women danced, "going through the most extraordinary contortions," and "sang a wild chant."

This was the prelude to a nightmarish incident. Tippu-Tib, leaning close to Jameson to be heard above the din, told him that the dancers were members of the Wacusu tribe and "terrible cannibals." He told how, some years before when he was marauding in the vicinity, he sent one night for water to drink and wash his hands from a nearby well. He could not understand why the water was so greasy and tasted so bad, and the following morning he went to investigate the well.

There he saw "a most horrible sight—the surface of the water was covered by a thick layer of yellow fat, which ran down over the sides." On enquiry, he discovered that the Wacusu, who had killed a number of enemy tribesmen in a battle the day before, had washed the butchered carcasses of their foes in the well before cooking and eating them.

According to his own account, Jameson scoffed at this story and told Tippu-Tib that it sounded far-fetched. At this, Tippu-Tib turned to an Arab named Ali, who sat on his other side, and murmured something. Ali addressed Jameson: "Give me a bit of cloth and see." Jameson described what happened next:

> I sent my boy for six handkerchiefs, thinking it was all a joke, and that they were not in earnest, but presently a man appeared, leading a young girl of about ten years old by the hand, and I then witnessed the most horribly sickening sight I am ever likely to see in my life. He plunged a knife quickly into her breast twice, and she fell on her face, turning over on her side. Three men then ran forward, and began to cut up the body of the girl; finally her head was cut off, and not a particle remained, each man taking his piece away down to the river to wash it. The most extraordinary thing was that the girl never uttered a sound, nor struggled, until she fell. . . . I never would have been such a beast as to witness this, but I could not bring myself to believe that it was anything save a ruse to get money out of me, until the last moment.

Jameson added that when he returned to his hut he "tried to make some small sketches of the scene while still fresh in my memory, not that it is ever likely to fade from it. No one here seemed to be in the least astonished by it."

Yet for all his professed horror over the incident, Jameson seems to have had no rancor toward its instigator. After only a paragraph break, his diary entry continued: "In the afternoon I had a long talk with Tippu-Tib. I explained to him that Mr. Stanley had left orders to communicate with the Committee when possible. . . ." And so forth; as reported by Jameson, the "long talk" was entirely to do with matters concerning the expedition. Not a word was said about the murder and dismemberment of the native girl.

Eleven days later, Jameson and Tippu-Tib reached Stanley Falls, where Barttelot was waiting for them. Some days of haggling followed, in which Tippu-Tib refused to provide the 400 fighting men Barttelot demanded but was finally pinned down to delivering not 600 but 430 Manyuema porters. Even with that reduced number there was a proviso: these were not slaves, but free men, said Tippu-Tib, and they would not carry a sixty-pound load each. The maximum was forty pounds per man, take it or leave it.

This was a crippling restriction. It meant that almost half the

*James Jameson, the gentleman-naturalist, looked on as a native girl was butchered and eaten. (The Story of the Rear Column, London, 1890)*

expedition's baggage would have to be left behind. But unless he was willing to remain at Yambuya indefinitely, Barttelot had no alternative but to agree. He did so with understandable bad grace.

Back at Yambuya, he put Jameson in charge of the dispiriting task of opening up the essential loads, reducing them to exactly forty pounds each (Tippu-Tib was insistent that they must not weigh an ounce more) and then sealing them up again. Barttelot had the surplus matériel loaded on the steamer *Stanley,* to be taken downstream to the Bangala River station and stored there. He also sent Troup and the interpreter Farran, both of them too sick to march, downstream on the *Stanley* and gave its captain a letter of instructions for Ward, who was then on his way back from his pointless mission to the coast, aboard the *En Avant.* In both tone and content, those instructions seem to confirm the impression that Barttelot was losing his mind:

> SIR—On arrival at Bangala you will report yourself to the chief of the station, and take over the stores from him belonging to the Expedition. You will remain at Bangala till you receive orders from the Committee concerning yourself and the loads.... On no account will you leave Bangala while you remain in the service of the Expedition.... Should you bring a telegram of recall for me, you will make arrangements with the chief of Bangala to forward it to the Falls, where a messenger awaits it. You will not, however, send any other message after me, nor will you on any account leave Bangala station unless you receive orders to that effect from the committee—EDMUND M. BARTTELOT.

Barttelot's dislike and paranoid suspicion of Ward had surely got the better of him. Having sent the man on a hazardous round trip of over three thousand miles with a message to London, he did not even want to know the answer, unless it were an order of recall. Furthermore, he effectively barred Ward from any further active part in the relief of Emin. Not surprisingly, Ward considered this "the unkindest act which had been done to me since I had been with the Expedition and on the impulse of the moment I felt inclined to throw everything up and return home."

But even in the face of such provocation Ward remained loyal to his commitments. Instead of transferring to the *Stanley* and traveling downstream to the coast and home, as he might well have done, he carried on to Bangala and his chore of looking after the surplus stores. As for the now-unwanted reply he brought back from the obviously bemused committee in London, it simply advised Barttelot to carry out the instructions Stanley had given before leaving Yambuya, adding: IF YOU CANNOT MARCH IN ACCORDANCE WITH THESE ORDERS, THEN STAY WHERE YOU ARE, AWAITING HIS ARRIVAL OR UNTIL YOU RECEIVE FRESH INSTRUCTIONS FROM STANLEY. The committee's only new instruction was not to engage any fighting men: Mackinnon and his partners were anxious to avoid the impression that the expedition had any warlike intent.

On June 11, Barttelot, Jameson, Bonny and the 141 black survivors of the original rear column left Yambuya with Tippu-Tib's Manyuema porters, heading—in Barttelot's words—"for abomination, desolation, and vexation, but I hope in the end success."

His misgivings were well founded. The Manyuema were an absolute rabble. They refused to acknowledge Barttelot's command, answering only to Tippu-Tib's man, an Arab named Muni Somai, who in the event had little or no control over them. They did as they pleased, halting when they felt like it, rifling their loads, getting drunk on palm wine, and loosing off ammunition at random. Soon an outbreak of smallpox began decimating their ranks, and at that point, the Zanzibaris—even the most trusted of them—started to desert.

This was altogether too much for Barttelot. He paraded the Zanzibaris, relieved them of their rifles and ammunition, and announced that he was going to Stanley Falls to obtain slave chains from Tippu-Tib. By this time the column had become hopelessly split, part of it, under Jameson, trailing some days behind. Accordingly, Barttelot left Bonny in command of the front section, telling him to concentrate the entire column at a village named Banalia and wait for him there.

Once at Stanley Falls, Barttelot asked Tippu-Tib to provide not only the slave chains, but sixty men to act as guards over the unruly porters. Tippu-Tib sold him four sets of chains and gave him a letter to Abdullah Kichamira, the Arab headman at Banalia, ostensibly authorizing him to provide the sixty guards.

Before leaving Stanley Falls to return to his column with his gyves and fetters, Barttelot dashed off a letter to his father. "Our march altogether up to the present has not been a success," he wrote with masterly understatement, "but I think I have now so arranged matters that I shall have no more stoppage." He was soon to be disillusioned once more. When he reached Banalia on July 17, drained by fever and plagued by his burgeoning paranoia, the headman flatly refused to provide the guards he wanted. Barttelot also found to his fury that the entire column had not consolidated at Banalia as instructed, and that Jameson's section was five days in the rear.

Barttelot was by now in a hair-trigger mood, made all the worse by the mutinous mood of the Manyuema, who were drinking, drumming, chanting and firing their rifles into the air as they celebrated a tribal festival. Barttelot, hardly the man to appreciate African folkways at the best of times, sent orders to Abdullah Kichamira and Muni Somai to keep their people quiet. His instructions were ignored.

The next day Barttelot tried again to pressure Kichamira into providing the sixty guards he wanted. Again the headman refused. Barttelot's first impulse was to march back to Stanley Falls to report the chief's insolence to Tippu-Tib, but Bonny dissuaded him. As night fell, the shooting, chanting and drumming resumed. While Barttelot and Bonny sat together a bullet was fired into their hut, passing over their heads and lodging in the roof. Barttelot, according to his own account, found the culprit and "punished him severely."

Before dawn the next morning the insistent sound of a woman chanting and beating a drum aroused Barttelot from an uneasy sleep. He sent a servant with another demand for silence. A few minutes later Barttelot and Bonny heard loud, angry voices in dispute, then two shots. Sending some of his Sudanese askaris on ahead with orders to arrest whoever was shooting, Barttelot dressed, seized a loaded revolver and left the hut, vowing—as Bonny stated in an official report to Stanley—that he would "shoot the first man I catch firing."

Pushing his way past the askaris and shouldering aside some Manyuema men, Barttelot marched up to the woman who was still chanting and drumming. He ordered her to stop. She ignored him. A shot rang out and Barttelot fell dead with a bullet through the heart. It had been fired by the woman's husband, a Manyuema headman named Sanga, through a loophole in the wall of a nearby house.

There was immediate pandemonium. Bonny, hearing screaming and wild shooting, "thought a general massacre had commenced." In the uproar and confusion the expedition's stores were looted and porter loads "scattered all over the place, some in the forest, in the rice field and in the village huts hidden away within and without, in fact everywhere. Some of the bead sacks and ammunition boxes had already been ripped or broken open, and the whole of their contents, or in part, gone."

With the aid of a few loyal Zanzibaris, Bonny did what he could to recover the looted stores, reassemble the abandoned loads, and bring the situation under control. He sent messages to Jameson and Tippu-Tib, telling what had occurred, then brought "the terrible day to a close" by sewing up Barttelot's body in a blanket and burying it.

Jameson received Bonny's message two days later and wrote a eulogy for his friend into his diary—"He was a straightforward, honest English gentleman; his only fault being a little too quick-tempered. . . . God knows what I shall do without him"—before hurrying ahead of the porters to each Banalia as quickly as possible.

There he completed Bonny's work of recovering as much of the expedition's stores as could be found and got together Barttelot's personal effects for shipping back to England before setting out for Stanley Falls, where, he was told, Barttelot's killer had gone. Reaching the falls a week later, Jameson demanded the punishment of Sanga and, intending to continue the rear guard's march in Stanley's footsteps, offered Tippu-Tib £500 out of his own pocket for the services of Rashid, one of his trusted nephews, to command the Manyuema porters.

Meanwhile, Sanga was tried by a court consisting of Tippu-Tib and four Belgian officers. He was found guilty of murder and summarily executed by firing squad. In his diary that night, Jameson recorded that as Sanga lay dying "the look he gave us was the most horrible I think I ever saw on a man's face."

When Jameson was unable to induce Rashid to take command of the Manyuema, Tippu-Tib himself offered to lead the rear guard to Lake Albert. But he said that instead of following Stanley's trail, he would go via Nyangwe and Ujiji, and he demanded a fee of £20,000, to be payable even if hostile native action should force the column to turn back. Jameson could not agree to such a proposition and, aware that Ward was now at Bangala, decided to make his way there by canoe to learn the committee's response to Barttelot's message and collect loads to replace those lost at Banalia.

A day after leaving Stanley Falls, Jameson caught a cold, which rapidly developed into a fever. On August 12, he wrote a diary entry describing a weirdly hallucinatory scene as he traveled downstream:

> Shot out of an open reach—fine clear night—into a dark narrow channel, not more than forty yards wide. All at once it became lit up with dozens of fires on both sides, throwing a bright light back into the forest and across the water. We glided on without a sound from us but the zip-zip of the paddles, drums beating, horns blowing, shouts and cries on every side. . . . Down this lane of fire and noise we went for nearly half a mile, when suddenly it opened out into a grand open reach of the river. . . . We shot away to our right, and soon left all the tumult behind.

Jameson reached Bangala on the sixteenth. Told of his arrival, Ward, who had learned of Barttelot's death only the day before, "rushed to the beach, and there saw a deathlike figure lying back in the men's arms, insensible. I jumped into the canoe, and, great Heavens! it was poor Jameson."

The following evening, Ward was at Jameson's bedside when drums begun to beat, signaling the end of the day's work at the station. At the sound, Jameson awoke from a coma, clutched Ward's hands, and murmured: "Ward! Ward! they're coming; listen. Yes! they're coming—now let's stand together." Those were his last words. An hour and a half later, as Ward tried to give him a spoonful of brandy, "he drew a long breath and his pulse stopped."

# Chapter Twenty-four

*THE* very day that Jameson died, Stanley reached Banalia, having covered the 460 miles from Fort Bodo in two months. He was aghast at the tale of woe that Bonny, the rear column's only surviving white man, told him, and what he saw within the "charnel yard" that was the rear guard's camp. "Pen cannot picture nor tongue relate the full horrors witnessed within that dreadful pest-hold," he wrote. "There were six dead bodies lying unburied and the smitten living with their festers lounged in front of us by the dozen . . . a deadly stench of disease hung in the air, and the most repellent sights moved and surged before my dazed eyes."

In a bravura display of the extraordinary energy and organizing ability of which he was capable when things were at their worst, Stanley rapidly restored the situation. Having got the living to bury the dead and the well to tend the sick, he moved the entire expedition six miles upriver to a healthier location. Next, he dispensed with the services of all but 61 of the unruly Manyuema carriers. With these, plus the Zanzibaris and Madis, he had brought with him, Stanley now had 283 porters for the 275 loads that were to be carried on the return journey to Lake Albert.

Before starting back on August 30, Stanley sent a letter to Bangala to tell Jameson, of whose death he was unaware, what he thought of the condition in which he had found the rear column. The passage of two weeks had done nothing to calm his outrage:

> I cannot make out why the Major, you, Troup, and Ward have been so *demented*—demented is the word. You understand English; an English letter of instruction was given you. You said it was intelligible—yet for some reason or another you have not followed one paragraph. You paid £1,000 to go on this Expedition; you have voluntarily thrown your money away by leaving the Expedition. Ward is not a whit better; he has acted all through, as I hear, more like an idiot than a sane being. . . .

Characteristically, Stanley had failed to consider that the initial and fatal error which led to the downfall and disintegration of the rear column might have been his own. It would certainly have been wiser to have waited for all the stores to be brought upriver, to have ensured that he had sufficient porters, and then to have marched to Emin's relief in one unified column instead of rushing ahead with an advance guard, leaving the rear column under the command of a man in whom, by his own account, he had little confidence. Under cruelly difficult circumstances Barttelot and Jameson had cracked, but it had been Stanley who helped create those circumstances.

Particularly unfair was his savage criticism of Ward, who had loyally and with great dispatch carried out the lawful, if irrational and malicious, orders of his superior officer. In other ways too, the tone of Stanley's letter to the dead Jameson was mean-minded. "You have left me naked," he complained, alluding to Barttelot's decision to include most of his personal belongings in the loads that were sent back to Bangala. "I have no clothes, no medicine; I will say nothing of my soap and candles, photograph apparatus and chemicals, two silver watches, a cap, and a score of other trifles." For Barttelot's death he did not even make a show of regret.

The march back to Fort Bodo was as terrible as it had been the first time. By the time the column got there on December 20, it had lost 106 lives out of 465 through starvation, sickness and native attacks. But after only two days' rest, Stanley mustered his force—now totaling 410 souls, including Stairs, Parke and the sick men who had been left under their care—and headed east yet again to the grasslands of Equatoria.

Stanley had been incensed to find that no word had reached Fort Bodo from Emin or Jephson. He was unaware that Emin's Egyptian and Sudanese officers and men had mutinied and for a while held both their commander and Jephson captive, or that, to make the situation in Equatoria even more chaotic, the Mahdists had launched a new attack and taken control of half the province. He might have realized that only *force majeure* could have kept an officer as loyal and energetic as Jephson from carrying out his duty to maintain contact. But as he marched for the third time to the lake, Stanley allowed his unjust anger to mount. He was little mollified even when, on approaching Kavalli, he received letters of explanation from Jephson and Emin, who by this time had escaped from captivity and were waiting at Tunguru at the head of the lake.

To Jephson, he sent a stinging reproach for his supposed dereliction of duty in failing to carry out an instruction to take porters to Fort Bodo and bring the goods stored there to a station to be set up on Lake Albert. "Eight months have elapsed and not one single promise has been performed," Stanley fulminated. And to Emin he sent a brusque demand that he make up his mind quickly whether or not he wanted to be evacuated: "If at the end of twenty days no news has been heard from you or Mr. Jephson I cannot hold myself responsible for what may happen."

In his letter to Jephson, Stanley described the fate of the rear column—not omitting to complain again at the loss of his personal effects and to comment harshly on the performance of the officers he had left in charge—and asked: "Are the Pasha, Casati and yourself to share the same fate? If you are still the victims of indecision, then a long good night to you all, but while I retain my senses I must save my expedition. You may be saved also if you are wise."

On receipt of Stanley's letter, Jephson commented mildly enough that it "greatly wants in common sense and I think the way he speaks about the officers of the rearguard is not very pleasant." But he loyally obeyed Stanley's order to proceed immediately to Kavalli and there, on February 6, Stanley "received me in his usual calm way, tempered however by a smile. I think he was glad to see me."

Over dinner, Jephson told Stanley that, after nine months, Emin had still not made up his mind whether or not he wished to leave Equatoria. But a week later, when Stanley and Jephson were again at dinner, native messengers brought news that Emin was in camp on the lake shore, en route for Kavalli, having sailed from Tunguru with a number of his people. Delighted at this unexpected turn of events, and assuming that it meant Emin had at last made up his mind to leave, Stanley leaned across the table and said: "Shake hands on it old fellow, we'll be successful after all." Jephson did so "most heartily" and told Stanley that "if anyone deserved success he did."

The following day, Jephson led a party out to meet Emin and escort him to Kavalli. Jephson was so pleased to see Emin that he "felt almost inclined to hug the dear old pasha." But within a day his feelings had turned to exasperation, for Emin and his officers insisted on bringing huge amounts of unnecessary baggage with them, including massive grindstones, beer jars and iron bedsteads.

"At that rate," wrote Jephson, "20,000 carriers would not be sufficient to take these people to the coast and we have only about 250. . . . One felt so indignant and helpless when one saw one of our hard worked, patient, faithful Zanzibaris toiling in the sun up the mountain side staggering under the weight of a load belonging to some of these worthless people. . . ."

Stanley was no less indignant: "The Pasha, 200 loads! Casati . . . eighty loads! Vita, the apothecary, forty loads! Marco, the Greek, sixty loads! = 380 loads for four persons!" As for the hard-pressed Zanzibaris, they often came close to mutiny as they struggled up to the plateau with the Emin party's impedimenta.

When Emin finally turned up at Kavalli, looking "like a Professor of Jurisprudence . . . despite his fez and white clothes," Stanley was further exasperated to find that he and his accompanying officers were by no means ready to leave for the coast. Emin was still not certain that he wanted to go, while his senior Egyptian officer, one Selim Bey, asked for time to return to Wadelai, Emin's old headquarters on the Nile, to collect those of his comrades, plus their families, who might want to join them. It was a ten-day round trip by steamer from the nearest point on the lake, and Stanley grudgingly allowed "a reasonable time" for this mission to be carried out.

Stanley's officers joined him in fuming at the delay. Stairs found the "apathy, indifference . . . and absolute helplessness" of Emin and his people "quite beyond understanding." Yet, for all that, Stairs could not remain indifferent to Emin's charm. He was "such a funny looking little man with his crooked nose and spectacles, peering over some insect, that one always feels inclined to laugh at him. But he is a good old soul, so kind and generous and so sympathetic."

When a month had passed and Selim Bey had not returned, Stanley's patience gave out. It was long past time for him to bear his living trophy, Emin Pasha, back to civilization and write "finis" to another epic adventure. Accordingly, he gave Emin an ultimatum: he would break camp and start the march to the coast on April 10, either with or without him and his followers. Emin was plainly uneasy about abandoning Selim Bey and the others at Wadelai, but accepted the deadline.

With only five days to go, Stanley learned by messenger from Wadelai that Emin's people there were still at odds among themselves and that none were ready to leave. At the same time his camp spies reported that Emin's men at Kavalli were planning to mutiny and seize the relief expedition's arms to prevent their leaving on the tenth. When Stanley stormed into Emin's tent to tell him about this alleged plot, the pasha was incredulous. "I do not think that anyone would be so wicked," he said.

Stanley impatiently shrugged off Emin's objection and offered him a choice. Either Stanley would force the issue, staging a showdown with Emin's people by telling them to prepare for immediate depar-

ture and threatening force against any show of resistance, or else
Emin must agree to slip away secretly with "a trustworthy escort," to
be followed within a few days by Stanley, leaving the mutinous
Sudanese and Egyptians behind. When Emin replied that he saw no
need for either alternative, assuring him that he and his people were
ready to depart on the tenth as promised, Stanley lost his temper. He
had long since become contemptuous of Emin's shortcomings as a
disciplinarian and his constant willingness, in face of much evidence
to the contrary, to believe only the best of his followers.

Now Stanley "stamped his foot upon the ground and said in a
convulsed voice: '. . .! I leave you to God, and the blood which will
now flow must fall upon your own head!' " He rushed out of the
tent, blowing his alarm whistle to muster his men, leaving Emin
"pale with rage and indignation." Emin told Casati: "I have been
covered with insults. Stanley has passed every limit of courtesy. . . ."
Meanwhile, the Zanzibaris were herding Emin's men at gunpoint
into the camp square, where Stanley began to harangue them.

"If you have the courage, point your guns at my breast," he cried.
"I am here alone and unarmed." In fact, he had a Winchester rifle in
one hand, a revolver at his belt and 100 armed Zanzibaris at his
back. None of Emin's malcontents took up the challenge, and Stanley
continued his harangue: "My orders alone are to be obeyed here, and
whoever resists I will kill him. . . ."

He commanded all who were willing to leave with him for the
coast to move to one side and, as Casati reported, "in a moment
everyone moved, and all was changed; the terrible conspirators were
quiet as lambs." Was there ever, in fact, a conspiracy? The evidence
for it was slender, and it seems more likely that Stanley staged the
whole scene to pre-empt any further vacillation by Emin.

Duly, at dawn on the tenth, the caravan moved out, burning the
camp behind them. The relief expedition numbered 360 and Emin
Pasha's people 600, including 380 women and children. There was
no question who had the upper hand; 294 of Stanley's men had guns,
while Emin's people mustered only 40 among them. Counting local
native carriers, the total caravan numbered more than 1,500 souls
and, Jephson estimated, stretched for three miles.

Only three days out, Stanley was stricken with an attack of gastritis so painful that Parke prescribed morphine injections. Then
Parke and Jephson went down with fever, and as a result of these
afflictions, the march was held up for four weeks. During the en-
forced stop, relations between Stanley's men and "these miserable,

yellow-bellied Egyptians," as Stairs called them, grew ever worse. As for Stanley and Emin, they "hate each other now, to an extent almost incredible," said Stairs.

By May 7, although too weak to walk, Stanley decided to resume the march. Before breaking camp he ordered Stairs to bury twenty-five cases of the ammunition the relief expedition had, at such cost and suffering, brought all the way from Zanzibar to give to Emin. There was no further need for it, and now the heavy cases were simply an impediment. The following day the column set out again, with Stanley borne in a hammock.

Resuming the march did not improve his relations with Emin. "Though polite, [Emin] yet smarted under resentment for the explosion of April 5th," wrote Stanley. But there were more fundamental reasons for discord:

> Our natures were diametrically opposed. . . . He was learned and industrious and a gentleman, and I could admire and appreciate his merits. But the conditions of our existence prohibited a too prolonged indulgence in these pleasures. . . . I knew he was an ardent collector of birds and reptiles and insects, but I did not know that it was a mania with him. He would slay every bird in Africa; he would collect ugly reptiles, and every hideous insect; he would gather every skull until we should become a travelling museum and cemetery, if only carriers could be obtained. . . .

Jephson had more serious cause for complaint. He was shocked by the way Emin allowed his officers and men to treat the plateau natives who had been rounded up and pressed into service as carriers. "The constant brutal ill treatment of the slaves by the Pasha's people, is getting beyond anything," he wrote, "and is enough to bring the judgement of destruction and utter annihilation on the expedition."

After the relief expedition's return to England, Stanley's many critics would be all too quick to cast him, as they had in the past, in the role of the brutal freebooter, and Emin as the gentle scholar, bullied by Stanley—for his own glorification—into leaving his beloved Equatoria and abandoning his men at Wadelai. But Jephson, no uncritical admirer of Stanley's, saw things in a very different light. Of the treatment of prisoners he wrote:

> When we were by ourselves . . . such few natives as the Zanzibaris caught were kindly treated and looked after and soon became content to follow the caravan without any restraint being put upon them. . . . But now that Emin Pasha, who has been represented as one of the champions of Anti Slavery . . . has come into our camp, scenes of the most disgrace-

ful cruelty . . . are of daily occurrence. . . . [A] strong indignation arises in one when one thinks how the sympathies of Europe have been tricked and played with and how we have been duped into giving our best energies towards helping and rescuing a man and his people utterly unworthy of our help or even of our sympathy.

In addition to his vacillation, weakness and toleration of brutal behavior by his officers and men, Emin was guilty, in Jephson's view, of pettiness and spite. He was "in his way as dangerous a man as Stanley and tries to put one in very nasty positions; only he does it in a meaner and more ungenerous way than Stanley does, and that is saying a good deal."

Shouting matches between Stanley and Emin became increasingly frequent. On one occasion, after Emin refused to order a company of his men to take their turn on rearguard duty, both were seen to be in a towering rage, and Emin was heard to shout: "I think you had better leave me here, I wish you had never come to help me." To which Stanley replied:" "You are a most thankless and ungrateful man."

From that time on, Emin avoided Stanley as much as possible and focused his attentions, apart from his scientific studies, on his little daughter, Ferida, the child of his deceased Abyssinian wife. She was carried in a hammock by two bearers, and for much of the march Emin rode immediately behind them on his donkey.

While Emin played the loving and protective father, the cruelties perpetrated by his men against the native carriers continued unchecked. On July 22, Jephson noted in his diary that two women slaves had been beaten to death that day and that the Pasha's "Turks" were such sadists that even the Manyuema would not sell a slave to them. "The Pasha should do something to stop it," wrote Jephson, "but he is more incapable and impotent than ever, nor do I think he greatly cares. . . ."

The caravan's march, south by southeast, was enlivened by tantalizing views of the snow-capped Ruwenzoris, the recording of whose height (17,000 feet) and location was the principal scientific achievement of the relief expedition. Stanley set up his photographic apparatus to capture "the snowy breasts of Ruwenzori uplifted," as—with uncharacteristically direct erotic imagery—he called the range. But the distance was too great for good results.

In camp on July 21 or 23—depending on whether Jephson's or Stanley's diary entry was the most accurate—the expedition received a visit from the Prince Royal of Ankole, through whose father's domains the party was traveling. After undergoing the necessary rites of blood brotherhood with this "sweet-faced, gentle looking boy of about thirteen or fourteen," Stanley put on a display of the expedition's firepower.

First, he had a group of his riflemen discharge five rounds each, "to the boy's great admiration." Then Stairs showed off the Maxim's paces, raising clouds of dust as he peppered a hillside some four hundred yards distant. This display "simply sent [the prince] into ecstasies," recorded Stanley, "and to prevent him crying his soul out in rapture, he laid his hand firmly over his mouth."

To some who witnessed this scene, the prince's gesture looked like evidence of terror rather than rapture. Whatever it was, he must have carried back to his father the warning that it would be most imprudent to interfere with Stanley's caravan. That was surely Stanley's intention. He was nevertheless restrained in his use of the Maxim; in the almost three years that the expedition lasted, it was fired in anger only once. This occurred some two months after the display for the Ankole prince, when marauding Wasukuma tribesmen massed to attack Stanley's camp. The Maxim spewed out 150 rounds at a range of 300 yards, but according to both Stanley and Jephson only one man was killed.

When he came to write his account of the expedition, Stanley wisely made little of the incident. Belatedly, he had learned the value of discretion over sensationalism. And Jephson, though frequently critical of his chief, found no cause to fault his way of dealing with hostile tribesmen. "Stanley is ever ready to make friends and do it thoroughly," he noted, "or if needs be to fight and do it thoroughly. That's what I like, there are no half measures, no little petty compromises. . . ."

By mid-August, although the column had sustained grievous losses through desertion and death, morale among the Zanzibaris was high, for now they had entered territory—part of present-day Tanzania— where the natives spoke a little Swahili. On August 21, they came across a further sign of their growing proximity to civilization: an abandoned French mission station. And a week later, they marched into a mission station that was very much a going concern: that of the intrepid Reverend Alexander Mackay, of England's Church Missionary Society, who had been chased out of Uganda by Mutesa's grandson, the psychopathic King Mwanga.

Stanley and his people rested three weeks at Mackay's, where they first learned of Jameson's death and where Stairs received word that his father had died almost two and a half years before. At Mackay's the column acquired a number of pack mules and riding asses, replenished their food stocks, and took on loads of beads, cloth and brass wire that had been stockpiled there for them. There was also a large stock of European provisions, sent up from Zanzibar, and a number of English and American newspapers, many of them containing items about the expedition. "Dozens of reports, letters and leading articles," as Jephson observed, "all vieing with each other in the utter falseness and improbability of their conjectures."

The column set out on the last lap to the coast "in high spirits," following the well-traveled Arab traders' route southeast toward Bagamoyo, and but for their brush with the Wasukuma, the march was uneventful. They were now entering territory which had lately come under German tutelage, a fact first brought home to them when the porters of a caravan going in the opposite direction greeted them with cries of "*guten Morgen.*"

By the end of October they were at Mpwapwa, where the Germans had just set up a garrison, commanded by a Lieutenant Rochus Schmidt. Two weeks further on they were met by Captain Freiherr von Gravenreuth—who enjoyed the soubriquet "Lion of the Coast" for his vigorous suppression of the Arabs who had dared to challenge German rule. Gravenreuth was at the head of a hundred troops and accompanied by two American reporters, Thomas Stevens and Edward Vizetelly.

Vizetelly was from Stanley's old paper, the New York *Herald,* and brought with him "quite a number of well-selected articles for personal comfort and some provisions," as a gift from Gordon Bennett. But it was Stevens, from the New York *World,* who seems to have hit it off best with Stanley. Stevens was impressed by his apparently good physical condition and brisk morale, finding him "good yet for another two or three more such expeditions" and "adept in dry humour." Stanley opened up to him in a way he seldom did with casual acquaintances, confessing his failures with the opposite sex. By Stevens' account, Stanley said:

> [N]obody can say I'm not good looking; and in many other respects I compare favourably with men who have been markedly successful with the ladies; but I have always fallen short of success. . . . The young women will never take me seriously. When I talk seriously, they won't believe I am sincere. They expect nonsense; moonshine is not in my line, and so in the end I have to take refuge with their mothers and grandmothers.

Stevens came to the conclusion that Stanley suffered from an excess of old-fashioned chivalry, regarding a woman, if young and beautiful, as "a sort of wingless angel—a superior being who was made for rough man to admire at a respectful distance, but not to be approached too closely without sacrilege."

By December 3 the column was close enough to the coast to hear the sound of the evening cannon rolling across the calm waters from Zanzibar. The following morning, at the Kingani River ferry, they were met by the German military governor, Major Hermann von Wissmann, who escorted Stanley and Emin into Bagamoyo in triumph, leaving the column to follow on under the command of Stairs. The streets were decorated with palm fronds in Stanley's and Emin's honor, the locals turned out to cheer them, and in the square in front of Wissmann's headquarters a battery of artillery were drawn up to fire a salute.

"[O]n our left," wrote Stanley," close at hand, was the softly undulating Indian Sea, one great expanse of purified blue. 'There, Pasha,' I said. 'We are at home!' 'Yes thank God,' he replied. At the same time, the battery thundered the salute in his honour, and announced to the war-ships at anchor that Emin, the Governor of Equatoria, had arrived at Bagomoyo."

Emin's fervent "Thank God" may have been as much an expression of gratitude for his pending separation from Stanley as a hallelujah for his deliverance from danger. In the past few weeks the mutual dislike of rescuer and rescued had been intensified by sentiments of a nationalistic nature. Impressed by the signs of his native land's new-found imperial muscle, and flattered by the attentions bestowed on him by his countrymen, the deracinated Emin was beginning to feel like a German again, and Stanley, for all his Yankee accent and mannerisms and his Belgian connections, to seem in his eyes very much a creature of the rival British imperium.

"On the whole, and in spite of all English opposition, German influence appears to be slowly but surely taking deeper root," wrote Emin with evident satisfaction, "and I only hope an advance column will be sent out as soon as possible towards Lake Victoria and that eventually Uganda will be occupied before it is too late.

"It is curious to observe," he added, "how little Stanley can rid himself of his English prejudices. He is fond of acting the cosmopolitan; and therefore, in speaking to us, approves of the extension of German domination, but in unguarded moments, when we are alone, he reproaches me with my German proclivities."

Emin found a similar attitude among Stanley's officers. They were "superlatively English and look down upon us Germans from a sublime altitude," he noted, adding: "And then people talk about German narrow-mindedness and particularism!"

At Bagamoyo, following their triumphal entry, Emin and Stanley were entertained to "a sumptuous lunch" by Wissmann and his officers, and the champagne flowed freely. Worried about its effects after so long without exposure to the grape, Stanley was careful to dilute his champagne with mineral water. But "the Pasha was never gayer than on this afternoon, when surrounded by his friends and countrymen he replied to their thousand eager questions. . . ." In fact, Emin seems to have been childishly delighted to discover what a celebrity he had become; there was even a telegram of welcome and congratulations from the Kaiser!

At four that afternoon, the 530-odd other survivors of the fifteen-hundred-mile march from Equatoria filed into Bagamoyo, "making a brave show" under the command of Stairs. With commendable German efficiency the fit were swiftly and smoothly assigned to huts already built for them near the beach, while the sick were tended to in an improvised field hospital.

By 7:30 that evening all was ready for the lavish banquet Wissmann had prepared for Emin, Stanley and their officers, to which he had invited the local consular corps, German military and naval officers, various missionaries, and representatives of British and German trading companies. The band of the German cruiser *Schwalbe* was on hand "to give éclat to what was a very superb affair for Bagamoyo." Again the champagne flowed copiously, again Stanley was careful to dilute his well, and again "the Pasha was supremely gay and happy."

After toasts had been proposed and replied to, Emin was seen moving from one end of the table to the other, conversing animatedly with hosts and fellow guests. Nobody noticed when he walked out onto the balcony for some fresh air, or when—no doubt owing to the combined effects of poor eyesight and good champagne—he blundered over the balcony rail and fell fifteen feet to the ground. If he cried out as he fell, the sound was drowned by the noisy celebrations of the Zanzibaris, who were also feasting and drinking, and some time passed before anyone took note of his absence from Wissmann's banquet.

It was one of the Zanzibari revelers who spotted Emin's crumpled, unconscious form, and Lieutenant Rochus Schmidt who first went to his assistance, dousing him with cold water in an attempt to rouse him. When that expedient failed, Emin was hustled to hospital, while word of what had happened was sent up to Wissmann and his guests.

Emin lay unconscious all night. Parke examined him when he came to and concluded that, although serious, his injuries were not life-threatening; he was badly bruised and in pain, but his skull had not been fractured. But two German naval surgeons came to a different conclusion; Emin, they said, had indeed fractured his skull, near the base, and only one in five of such cases ever recovered. Whatever the truth, Emin could clearly not be moved for the time being, and so when Stanley made his triumphal return to Zanzibar a day later aboard a British warship, it was without his living trophy.

Before leaving, Stanley visited Emin, whom he found "in great trouble and pain." His bedside manner left something to be desired.

> "Well, Pasha," I said, "I hope you don't mean to admit the possibility that you are to die here, do you?" "Oh! no. I am not as bad as that," and he shook his head. "By what I have seen, Pasha, I am entirely of the same opinion. A person with a fractured head could not move his head after that manner. Goodbye. Dr. Parke will remain with you until dismissed by you, and I hope to hear good news from him daily." We shook hands and I withdrew.

The Germans soon made it clear that the British doctor's presence was unwelcome and, himself sick, Parke soon left for Zanzibar and a stay in hospital. Now that they had Emin to themselves, his compatriots began working on him to join the service of German East Africa instead of returning to Cairo. Meanwhile, receiving no word of Emin's progress, Stanley sent his steward Sali to Bagamoyo to get a firsthand report on his condition. Sali came back claiming that the Germans had warned him never to visit Bagamoyo again.

In a final effort to get Emin to Zanzibar, and thence to Cairo, Stanley sent Jephson to see him. It was futile; Emin refused to leave, even though he obviously retained a soft spot for Jephson. "You I shall never forget," he said as they parted company, "for you have been my companion and friend through those months of our imprisonment together, those months which were the worst of my life."

He sent no message back to Stanley, who was basking in the accolades descending on him from around the world by telegraph as he rested in Zanzibar. Indeed, Stanley never heard again from the man he had gone to such lengths to rescue, and eventually Emin did join the German colonial service in East Africa. The following April, still weak and by now half blind, he led an expedition to Uganda, hoping to add that territory to Germany's possessions.

But before he got there, Britain and Germany signed a treaty designating their respective spheres of influence, under which Uganda was allotted to the British. Emin blundered on, ever deeper into the interior, his health and spirit broken, but still avidly collecting, preserving and classifying birds, insects and plants. In October 1892, at a Manyuema village some eighty miles from Stanley Falls, he was murdered by Arab slavers.

# Chapter Twenty-five

$A$N ARMCHAIR philosopher seeking a metaphor for the absurdities and contradictions of the human condition could surely find it in the story of the Emin Pasha Relief Expedition. From conception to conclusion it juxtaposes squalor with idealism, duplicity with selflessness, nobility with brutality, high courage with low farce. How apposite that Emin should bring the whole preposterous adventure to an end by falling drunkenly over a balcony rail! But the subplot of the rear column, and the complete moral collapse of Barttelot and Jameson, adds a further element—one of sheer horror.

Victorian society, cocooned in self-righteousness, turned away in disbelief when controversy over the fate of the rear column lifted the lid on a box full of horrors too ghastly to contemplate, attributing to Barttelot and Jameson crimes of which no English gentleman could possibly be guilty. A hundred years on, we are less incredulous; the killing fields of Flanders, the gas chambers of Auschwitz, the execution sheds of the workers' paradise and the interrogation cells of John Vorster Square, among countless other twentieth-century abominations, leave us in little doubt of civilized man's unlimited capacity for individual and collective frightfulness.

Perhaps the uproar throughout the autumn and winter of 1890 about the behavior of two officers of Stanley's rear column was the beginning of the end of innocence. That long-forgotten controversy pre-echoed the greater uproar to come over the systematic atrocities committed in the name of Leopold's Congo Free State, which were themselves just a sampling of what the future had in store.

The controversy was set off when Stanley, on his return from Africa, pinned the blame for the failure of the rear column on "the irresolution of its officers, neglect of their promises, and indifference to their written orders." In angry rebuttal, Barttelot's brother and Jameson's widow rushed separately into print. Introducing a collection of his brother's journal entries and letters home, Walter Barttelot sought to show that, in truth, the officers of the rear column were the innocent parties and Stanley the guilty one. Barttelot portrayed the entire expedition as a fraud, in which Emin's plight was used as a pretext for furthering Leopold's imperial ambitions, Mackinnon's commercial interests and Stanley's insatiable hunger for acclaim. He accused Stanley of recklessness and irresponsibility in plunging ahead with his advance party and leaving Barttelot in command of a couple of hundred diseased and disgruntled cripples "without proper food, deserted for fourteen months, without carriers, and in the power of Tippu Tib."

The near-simultaneous publication of Jameson's letters and diaries painted a similar picture. Troup also weighed in, with a book in which he derided Stanley's claim to Christian principles ("He showed no outward sign of religious fervour . . . we heard no prayers") and philanthropic intent ("He has no more philanthropy than my boot"), and claimed that the entire expedition was a fiasco ("Emin . . . had to relieve Stanley [and] was taken almost by force to the coast"). Even by the hero of the hour, such allegations could not easily be brushed aside; Stanley attempted to do so by revealing information about Jameson and Barttelot that he had hitherto kept to himself.

In an interview with the New York *Herald,* shortly before sailing to America for a lecture tour, Stanley refused to retract or modify a word of his censure of Barttelot and claimed that, out of deference to the family, he had told "only part of the truth." The attacks by Barttelot's brother, he warned, "may rouse me to declare to the world that which I know." He added with heavy emphasis that "Barttelot was killed—killed, I say, not murdered."

When the *Telegraph* buttonholed him in Liverpool as he was about to board ship, Stanley stoked the fires higher by saying that things had occurred among the rearguard officers that were "too horrible to describe in all their barbarity—things which were they fully described would make an Englishmen's blood boil and his cheeks flush with shame."

Such statements plunged Stanley headfirst into the caldron. Accusing him of "mud-throwing and running away," the *St. James Gazette* commented: "To fling out vague, but terribly serious charges against a dead man, accompanied only by a general hint that the author may perhaps make them good at some future period, is a rather dastardly proceeding. . . . [T]hat is not the conduct of a 'hero' or even a gentleman."

Either of his own volition or at Stanley's instigation, Bonny now entered the lists with a lengthy signed statement in *The Times.* In this, he detailed the matters which Stanley claimed to have omitted from his official account of the expedition out of consideration for the Barttelot and Jameson families.

By his own account, Jameson had become aware about two weeks before his death that "the most foul reports" about his buying a girl to be eaten by cannibals at Riba-Riba had reached the outside world. They had been carried by the interpreter Assad Farran, who had been present at the time, and sworn to by him in an affidavit before Belgian officers at a downstream Congo River station while Farran was on his way home. The Syrian was later to recant his affidavit for reasons which, though obscure, are not hard to guess: the pressures for a cover-up from the influential relief committee would have been enormous.

Farran's story was that Jameson had bought the slave girl from the Arabs for twelve lengths of cloth, fully aware that she was to be slaughtered to satisfy his "scientific" curiosity about cannibalism. Farran alleged that while the girl was killed, dismembered and eaten, "we were watching them all the time, and Mr. Jameson was drawing every act that was going on."

Jameson's version, which in self-defense he immediately sent to Mackinnon and the relief committee, asserted that he had never expected that the girl would be killed and that he had made the sketches after the event. "The girl never looked for help," he insisted, "for she seemed to know it was her fate, and never stirred hand, foot or head. . . ."

Now, Bonny alleged that Jameson himself had confessed to him the truth of Farran's version, showing him the sketches he had made and describing the scene in detail. Bonny told *The Times:*

> I cannot now describe each of the six sketches, but they begin with the picture of the girl being brought down tied by one hand to the native, who holds in his right hand the fatal knife. He is then represented thrusting the knife into the girl, while the blood is seen spurting out. Then there is the scene of the carving up of the girl, limb by limb, and of the natives scrambling for the pieces and running away to cook them, and the final sketch represents the feast.

These sketches, said Bonny, were now—or had been until recently—in the possession of Mrs. Jameson, as was the pickled human head which Jameson had sent back to London earlier. Stanley himself added to this Grand Guignol the information that "the story, as Mr. Bonny told it to me, was not only current in the camp but it was current all along the Congo, from Stanley Pool to Nyangwe.

"If Mr. Jameson had not shown the sketches and had not appeared to take pride in the fact that he was the only living European who had ever seen this atrocious act of cannibalism," Stanley continued, "Assad Farran's story . . . would never have been deemed sufficient evidence to cause me to believe that any white man could be capable of such an act."

In the case of Barttelot, Bonny's indictment suggests not so much the complete moral collapse of Jameson as a descent into homicidal insanity, exacerbated by racial revulsion. There is ample evidence from other sources that Barttelot nursed an obsessive hatred of Blacks. To this Bonny added the information that he was "in the habit of standing before the natives showing his teeth and trying to frighten them by grinning at them like a fiend." He also used to go about the camp wielding a steel-tipped cypress staff, prodding and hitting the Blacks at random.

Bonny gave a horrific account of the fatal flogging, at Barttelot's command, of John Henry, the mission-educated Zanzibari whose crime had been to steal Barttelot's revolver and trade it for food.

> Four big Sudanese in our party, not one of them under 6ft. in height, were selected to deliver the punishment. Each man was to deliver 75 lashes. John Henry never uttered a sound after the first 30 lashes, as he became insensible to the pain. This scene was the most horrible I ever saw. Mortification set in, the man's flesh fell off in pieces to the ground, and his body swelled to twice its ordinary size. Within 24 hours, John Henry died.

Bonny went on to give a nightmarish description of the forty-eight hours leading up to Barttelot's death at Banalia. It seems that he arrived from Stanley Falls in a vile mood, which became positively murderous when the headman, Abdullah Kichamira, refused his demands for extra men. Barttelot grew so abusive that neither Kichamira nor any of his people would give him living quarters, and Barttelot was forced to share Bonny's hut.

In a sudden fit of rage the next day, Bonny said, Barttelot kicked his servant boy Soudi so savagely that he eventually died of the injury.* He also attacked a Manyuema woman, sinking his teeth into her cheek. This occurred in full view of the village and camp, and a crowd of enraged Blacks might have beaten Barttelot to death in retaliation if Bonny had not driven them off.

---

*Soudi—a "wise little boy of about thirteen," Stanley called him—died almost three months later, though whether from the injury Barttelot had inflicted it is impossible to say. According to Stanley, the cause of death was a gangrenous ulcer on his leg, presumably where Barttelot had kicked him, which left four inches of bone exposed.

And that evening, after the bullet was fired into their hut, Barttelot seized the man he believed responsible, stabbed him "quite 30 times" with his steel-tipped staff, before "beating the man's brains out before the eyes of all in the village." This started another near-riot in which, Bonny says, he again only just managed to save Barttelot from the wrath of the Manyuema "by knocking him down myself . . . for then they thought I meant punishing him."

"During all that night of the 18th," Bonny continued, "as on the previous night, the firing of guns was going on all over the village, as an expression of the hatred in which Major Barttelot was held, and the only wonder is that we were not both killed."

This was the background against which, as Bonny told it, Barttelot rushed out of his hut the following morning, revolver in hand, threw himself at the woman drummer, and was shot dead by her husband. It was this version of events that led Stanley to insist that Barttelot was "killed, not murdered," and that no court in England would have convicted Sanga, because he shot to defend his wife, whom Barttelot was frenziedly kicking and beating.

That Jameson had, indeed, witnessed the butchering of the slave girl at Riba-Riba and that Barttelot was given to murderous rages against the Blacks under his command was beyond dispute. But the uneasy consensus among the elite of the English-speaking world, was that the worst allegations against the two officers must be false. Farran—whom Jameson's diary had repeatedly described as dirty, lazy, useless and dishonest—was wished away as a typically malicious Levantine liar, while Bonny was merely a noncommissioned malcontent, motivated by resentment that the other officers had refused to accept him as a social equal.

But what about Stanley's role in giving currency to these allegations? Well, there were those who were ready to say that he always had been a cad, willing to say or do anything to vindicate himself. Altogether the whole business was just too distasteful, so the best thing was to draw a veil over it and let the uproar die down. Which is what happened. Stanley was conveniently out of the country, lecturing in America where the controversy was far less acute, and somehow it became possible in the public mind to acquit Barttelot and Jameson without censuring the popular hero of the hour.

One person who could not put the matter out of his mind was a Polish-born British sea captain named Joseph Conrad, who had personal knowledge of the Congo and had sensed for himself its power to corrupt the white intruder. He had been in command of a Congo riverboat while the rear-column controversy was at its height, taking the vessel all the way upstream, past the confluence of the Aruwimi, to Stanley Falls. Many Conrad scholars believe that the story of Stanley's rear column was the direct inspiration for *Heart of Darkness*, his haunting meditation on civilized man's capacity for evil. Some have speculated that Conrad's depraved and doomed inner station manager, Kurtz, was based on Barttelot.

But Jameson seems a more likely model. Unlike Barttelot, but like Kurtz, Jameson was a cultivated, even idealistic man until "the wilderness found him out." Like Kurtz, Jameson "had been present at certain midnight dances ending with unspeakable rites." It is not difficult to imagine Jameson's dying words being not those which Ward reported, but those which Conrad put into the mouth of Kurtz: *"The horror! The horror!"*

*THE CONTROVERSY* over the rear column largely obscured a small but singular omission from Stanley's account of the relief expedition, an omission that, like the rear-column story itself, hinted at behavior too vile for public disclosure. In all the thousand pages of *In Darkest Africa*, Stanley did not once mention—either by name or even indirectly—his personal servant, William Hoffmann, although Hoffmann was at his side from start to finish.

Hoffmann is almost equally ignored in all the other officers' letters, diaries and reconstructed accounts of the expedition. Jephson, for example, refers to him just once, and then only as Stanley's "German servant." Stairs mentions him a few times, but only disparagingly—he had been "flogged . . . for stealing [Stanley's] porridge"; he was "really about as low a character as one can possibly imagine." Others treat Hoffmann as if he did not exist at all. Even when every allowance is made for Victorian class attitudes, the plebeian Hoffmann's invisibility is striking. What did he do to condemn himself to such unpersonhood? All we have to go on, apart from the eloquence of the omission itself, is the six-page record of court-martial proceedings against Hoffmann that was found long afterward among Stanley's private papers.

The record discloses that during the expedition Stanley four times dismissed Hoffman but took him back each time. It may have been difficult for him to do otherwise; Hoffmann could hardly have been abandoned on the march, Stanley was frequently ill and in need of personal attention, and Hoffmann more than anyone knew what his needs were. In short, the malefactor was indispensable, whatever his offense.

The first dismissal seems to have occurred when Stanley was ill with gastritis at Fort Bodo in February 1888, and—as Jephson recorded in his diary—hit Hoffmann across the head with a stick, injuring his own right arm in the process. According to the court-martial document, the reason for this dismissal was that Hoffmann was a liar and "filthy in his person."

This could hardly mean that he failed to wash often enough, or to clean his fingernails. In context, it looks like a euphemism for an act that could not be committed to the record. Some have theorized that Hoffmann was driven by starvation to indulge in cannibalism, but that can hardly have been the case in this instance, for there was plenty of food at Fort Bodo. More plausibly, the phrase cloaks some act of gross sexual indecency.

However that may be, the court-martial charges against Hoffmann—brought in the final stages of the march to the coast—relate only to theft, mainly alleging that he asked junior officers for various articles, ostensibly on Stanley's behalf, and kept them for himself. Stanley himself took no part in the proceedings.*

As he and his entourage were sailing from Zanzibar bound for Suez and home, Stanley got rid of Hoffmann by pressuring him to sign a year's contract to work for Sir Francis de Winton, by now administrator of the Imperial British East Africa Company, in Mombasa. But that was not the end of their relationship; in 1892 Stanley used his influence to get Hoffmann a posting as a junior officer with the Congo Free State administration; in 1897 he took Hoffmann with him as companion-servant on a trip to South Africa. And when he drew up his will he included a special bequest of £300 to Hoffmann, "as an expression of esteem and admiration for his continued services in Africa."

---

*Hoffmann was, presumably, found guilty. An inconclusive document relating to his court-martial is in the Stanley Family Archives.

# PART SIX

# THE LION IN WINTER

I vowed in my heart that he should never return
to the country that had taken so much of his
splendid vitality.

*DOROTHY STANLEY*

# Chapter Twenty-six

*A HERO'S* welcome awaited Stanley in Europe at the conclusion of the Emin Pasha Relief Expedition, but he was in no hurry to partake of it. Having once again left the dangers and hardship of the wilderness behind him, he began to fear the snares and hazards of civilization—the speeches, the banquets, the cheering crowds, the backbiting and the inevitable criticism. Accordingly, he lingered in Zanzibar until the end of December and, after arriving in Cairo in mid-January of 1890, rented a secluded villa where he sat down to write his account of the expedition.

At first he experienced an uncharacteristic case of writer's block. "I could not, immediately, dash off two consecutive sentences that were readable," he recalled. "A thousand scenes floated promiscuously through my head, but, when one came to my pen-point, it was a farrago of nonsense. . . ."

Eventually, by starting in the middle of his narrative, he got going and, in a prodigious burst of energy, writing steadily from 6:00 A.M. to midnight every day, he turned out 300,000 words in fifty days. Coincident with those labors, he also managed to dictate answers to 400 letters and 100 telegrams.

As Stanley wrote, the surviving officers of the expedition cooled their heels at Shepheard's Hotel in Cairo; it had been agreed that they would return as a group with Stanley at their head. Before going into seclusion at his villa, he had posed with them in a photographer's studio. They make an absurdly incongruous picture, arranged among the potted palms in their newly purchased natty gents' suitings, peering morosely over their almost identical walrus moustaches, looking altogether more like a suburban bank manager and his staff than the heroes of a desperate adventure.

And there is a sad and significant omission. The ex-workhouse boy Stanley did not see fit to invite the ex-ranker Bonny to join the gentlemen survivors—Jephson, Stairs, Nelson and Parke—for the commemorative photograph. By the same token, when they sailed from Alexandria on April 7, bound for the Italian port of Brindisi, Bonny traveled second class while the others went first.

From Brindisi, Stanley made a triumphant progress through Italy and France to Brussels, where Leopold had arranged a spectacular reception and drove in an open carriage with his famous employee through cheering crowds to the palace. Stanley was very much in favor with the king once more, and Leopold, in one of his manically expansive moods, offered him £100,000 to recruit an army of Congolese warriors, march them north along the Nile to Khartoum and annex the Sudan to the Congo Free State. Not surprisingly, Stanley declined the offer and headed for London bearing less onerous tokens of the king's regard—the Grand Cross of the Order of Leopold and the Grand Cross of the Congo.

In Britain, Stanley's reception was ecstatic. He was feted every-

*Stanley and his officers, back in Cairo:*
*like suburban bankers on a staff outing.*
*(The Autobiography of H. M. Stanley, 1908)*

where he went, and it seemed that everyone, from the Queen down, wanted to hear of his exploits from his own lips. The Queen also wanted him to accept a knighthood and was quite put out when he politely but cryptically declined the honor. The reason, which he preferred not to disclose, was that he had taken out U.S. citizenship in 1885—not so much from any excess of feeling for America as to protect his book royalties from unscrupulous publishers who, in the era before international copyright agreements, could pirate the works of foreign authors with impunity.

Despite his refusal of the knighthood, Victoria had him to dinner at Windsor Castle and afterward wrote more kindly of him than before. This time, Stanley was "the wonderful traveller and explorer."

Like the Sovereign, the Royal Geographical Society went out of its way to honor him and staged a mammoth reception at the Albert Hall. Ten thousand of the elite—members of royalty and the peerage, distinguished industrialists, churchmen, politicians, scientists, authors, and journalists—applauded as Stanley received a special gold medal from the president of the RGS, the resoundingly named Sir Mountstuart Grant-Duff. It was, said Stanley, "by far the grandest assembly I ever saw."

He was no less of an idol to the lower orders, and advertising and mercantile interests were quick to cash in on his name. Tin mugs bearing Stanley's likeness sold briskly, he was invited to endorse a well-known brand of cigar, and the United Kingdom Tea Company issued an advertisement showing Stanley and Emin enjoying steaming mugs of its brew in a jungle setting. "Well, Emin old fellow," says Stanley, "this cup makes us forget all our troubles." To which Emin replies, with an impressive grasp of the British officer idiom: "So it does, old boy."

The music hall comedians perpetrated some truly terrible jokes, along the lines of "I say, I say, I say, why did it take Stanley so long to find Emin Pasha?" "I don't know, why did it take him so long to find Emin Pasha?" "Because there's no M in Pasha." On a minimally more elevated plane, a song entitled "The Victor's Return" had the refrain "On, Stanley, on! were the words of yore/ On, Stanley, on! let them ring once more." The weekly *Spectator* condemned this kind of thing as "offensive to good taste," but indulged in some hyperbole of its own by likening Stanley's epic march to that of Xenophon and the Ten Thousand.

Meanwhile, Stanley's publisher Marston was rushing *In Darkest Africa* to press. The first edition went on sale in mid-June and in a matter of weeks had sold 150,000 copies and was being translated into five languages.


AMONG the torrent of mail Stanley found waiting for his attention on his return was one letter in a painfully familiar hand. Dorothy Tennant, who had spurned his offer of marriage almost four years previously, was offering to renew the relationship. "Dear Mr. Stanley," she wrote, "I shall be so deeply glad to see you again, not because you have done great things, but because you have come back safe, because I feared I might never see you again."

Still smarting from the pain of rejection, Stanley did not reply. When they met by chance at a reception a few days later, Dorothy grasped his hand and asked him to visit her at Richmond Terrace the next day. He said stiffly that he might come, but failed to turn up. She wrote to him again, saying that she "only wanted to say goodbye to you, so do not mind coming. I also want to give you back something you gave me." The following day she wrote yet again, bidding him a lengthy "farewell forever," which ended: "Well, dear Mr. Stanley, goodbye. . . . I shall, I promise you, avoid going where we might meet, and if ever you think of me, don't let it be as a poor craven spirit, but as a woman who, though she deserves to suffer, has done so bravely, on the whole."

She signed herself "Your sincere friend, Dorothy Tennant." This time Stanley replied. His tone was angry and reproachful. She had treated him in a way he would not have treated "the most degraded pygmy." Her refusal had been like "a barbed arrow that entered deeper and deeper into my heart." But by the very fact of answering he had sold the pass. And she, far from avoiding places where they might meet, turned up at a reception for him that very evening. There, as London society ebbed and swirled about them, she whispered to him that she would be his wife if he would have her.

Stanley's defenses were crumbling fast. That night he wrote to say that they should try to forget the past and remain good friends. But he admitted that "from a settled indifference, your words have created in me a profound sympathy." Dorothy now took pen in hand to deliver the coup de grace. She had prayed night and day for three years that he would forgive her for rejecting him, she said. She prayed now that he would accept her offer to be his bride:

> Oh, Bula Matari, listen to me. If I made you suffer, I have expiated the wrong done. Remember the difference between us. You were a man, you

knew more of life, you had loved before. I was a girl, unacquainted with love. . . . When your letter came, I was unprepared, and I felt afraid. . . .

*A girl unacquainted with love.* Preposterous-sounding, but perhaps the truth, and no doubt the underlying reason for her initial rejection of Stanley's proposal. At thirty-five Dorothy Tennant had been a frightened virgin; at thirty-nine, she was perhaps even more frightened, but now by the prospect of perpetual spinsterhood. And perhaps she also realized that Stanley would have as little interest as she in what Victorians called the "physical side" of marriage—that he had no lust to slake and, like her, needed rather the emotional fulfillment and companionship of connubial life. In this, at least, they were a perfectly matched couple, and within a week Dolly, as he now called her, was on the telephone to *The Times* dictating an engagement announcement. A few days after that, the date and venue for the wedding were set—July 12, in Westminster Abbey.

During their brief engagement, Gladstone, the eighty-year-old Liberal Party leader and former and future prime minister, dropped into the Tennants' house for a cup of tea and a chat. Stanley had "looked forward to the meeting, believing—deluded fool that I was!—that a great politician cares to be instructed about anything but the art of catching votes." He was accordingly disappointed by the Great Man's response to his suggestions on East African policy.

First, Gladstone initiated a hair-splitting argument over the difference between a port and a harbor, then he took Stanley to task for having named two peaks in the Ruwenzoris after Gordon Bennett and Mackinnon. Herodotus had spoken of them twenty-six centuries before as Crophi and Mophi, said Gladstone, and it was "intolerable that classic names like those should be displaced by modern names." Stanley replied, correctly enough, that Herodotus wrote only from hearsay and had located the Crophi and Mophi of legend over a thousand miles to the north of mounts Gordon Bennett and Mackinnon.

But Gladstone would have none of that—and none of Stanley's plea for him to support a scheme to construct a railway from the coast at Mombasa to Uganda. Stanley had represented the purpose of such a railway as a means of suppressing the slave trade, but the wily old Whig no doubt concluded that Stanley's real purpose was to advance his friend Mackinnon's commercial interests.

The news of Stanley's engagement created a sensation. Good wishes poured in from all sides, as did gifts, including a locket set with thirty-eight diamonds for the bride from Queen Victoria and a gold bracelet from King Leopold. Not everyone was enthusiastic, though. When the journalist and bon viveur Frank Harris heard that Dolly—"who was a very charming girl"—was to marry the lion of the season, he observed that "it seemed to me true; she was about to marry the king of the beasts, for Stanley was to me always a force without a conscience."

But Harris was in a minority. The Abbey was packed with the rich and famous for the wedding—dukes, duchesses, statesmen, politicians, generals, and a group of distinguished fellow explorers. The groomsmen were the surviving officers of the Emin Pasha Relief Expedition, this time including Bonny. The best man was the Belgian Count d'Aarche, acting on behalf of King Leopold.

The groom himself was in considerably less than good form. Two days before the wedding he had been laid low by a savage attack of the gastritis that had almost cost him his life in the Ituri Forest. Parke tended him around the clock as he lay in agony in his bed in New Bond Street, and not until the last moment was Stanley strong enough to struggle up and make his way to the Abbey, leaning heavily on a stick and aided by Parke. During the service he sat, pale and suffering, in an armchair but rose painfully to his feet to make his way down the aisle with Dolly, who laid her bouquet on Livingstone's tomb as they passed it.

As they were leaving the Abbey, Stanley was seized with stomach cramps so severe that Sir John Millais had to take his place and escort Dolly to her waiting carriage. The hoi polloi on the street outside mistook Millais for the bridegroom and pressed forward, cheering lustily. "I'm not Stanley," cried Millais. "I wish I were. Lucky dog; lucky dog!" But his disclaimer went unheard over the hubbub.

After Stanley had been helped into the carriage and it began to move away, the crowd got quite out of hand. In a diary note to her long-dead father that night, Dolly wrote: "The police struggled in vain to keep back the fighting, shouting, maddened people. I felt so faint and dreaded seeing some horror, some terrible accident. I closed my eyes, and only opened them when I felt the carriage go rather quicker. A reinforcement of mounted policemen had come to the rescue."

The reception was held at Richmond Terrace, only a few hundred yards from the Abbey, where the newlyweds were to make their home with the formidable Gertrude. Stanley was too ill to take part. He lay on a sofa in a darkened room while Dolly mingled with their guests in the garden. When the bride and groom left by train for their honeymoon in the New Forest, they were necessarily accompanied by the devoted Parke.

Despite his sickness, Stanley, like Dolly, found time to write a note in his journal before turning in that night:

> . . . I was too weak to experience anything save a calm delight at the fact that I was married, and that now I shall have a chance to rest. . . . [I]t is all so very unreal. During my long bachelorhood, I have often wished that I had but one tiny child to love; but now, unexpectedly as it seems to me, I possess a wife; my own wife. . . .

Under Parke's ministrations, Stanley recovered rapidly, and in four weeks he and Dolly left for a lengthy tour of the Continent. In Switzerland the Stanleys met the vacationing Sir Richard and Lady Burton. No longer the swaggering "Ruffian Dick" of old, Burton seemed to Stanley to be "much broken in health." Stanley urged him to write his memoirs, but Burton demurred, saying he would have to tell the truth about too many people. "Be charitable to them and write only of their best qualities," said Stanley, to which Burton replied with a flash of his old fire: "I don't care a fig for charity; if I write at all, I must write truthfully, all I know."

In his journal that night, Stanley wrote: "What a grand man! One of the real great ones of England he might have been, if he had not been cursed with cynicism. . . . If he had a broad mind, he would curb these tendencies and thus allow men to see more clearly his grander qualities."

In Italy, the newlyweds met Casati, who, despite his earlier ill-feelings toward Stanley, had written a very fair assessment of him in his about-to-be-published memoirs: "Reserved, laconic and not very sociable, he does not awake sympathy; but on closer acquaintance he is found to be very agreeable, from the frankness of his manner, his brilliant conversation, and his gentlemanly courtesy."

The Stanleys returned to London via Ostend, where Stanley presented his bride to Leopold and spent four days as the king's guest before returning to London. It was just as Stanley was about to leave for a lecture tour in America at the end of October, that the controversy over the rear column broke with the force of a tropical storm.

Aside from the allegations and counterallegations as between Stanley and his officers, the controversy called into question the rationale and justification for the exploration and colonization of Africa. The deeply disillusioned Troup had a novel contribution to make:

You ask me what England had better do with Africa. I say that she had better let it alone. . . . There is, I have no doubt, money to be made in Africa, but no white man can live in the central portion of the continent to colonise it. The natives had rather die than work. Nature has provided them with all they want, and they are contented and happy until the European gives them civilisation with the alternative to make money for him and receive beads, or not work and receive lashes. The black is far happier in his comfortable grass hut than are the thousands of dwellers in the slums of the great cities of civilised Europe, and I believe he represents as high a standard of morality. He will not bear civilisation but will be exterminated first, as the red man in America and his brother black in Australia has been.

An editorial in the *Spectator* also subjected the aims and ethics of African exploration to critical analysis:

The work itself operates as a law of selection, and the explorers who succeed are almost invariably men of reckless courage, of indurated hearts, and of true domineering temper, the temper which will slay rather than suffer its will to be unfruitful. And finally . . . they are frequently men [who believe] that the Negro desires severity, and [have] the idea that severity does not hurt him as it hurts other human beings. . . . Some of them regard the race with kindly contempt, some with malignant contempt, but with almost all contempt is the substratum of their thoughts.

At the other end of the spectrum, a satirical weekly called *Funny Folks* broke into rhyme:

> And when the heat of Afric's sun
> Grew quite too enervating,
> Some bloodshed with the Maxim gun
> Was most exhilarating!
> He found the sport a sweet relief,
> And nothing if not "manly"—
> The ever-joking, mirth-provoking, brandy-soaking,
>    robber chief,
> The coming Viscount Stanley.

The controversy over the rear column caused rather less stir on the other side of the Atlantic, where this time Stanley's lecture tour was a critical and commercial success. He brought an entourage that included his wife, his mother-in-law, Jephson, and several servants. Major James B. Pond, his lecture agent, provided a luxurious Pullman car, named *The Henry M. Stanley,* to transport them from city to city. It featured a kitchen, a bathroom, three bedrooms, a drawing room equipped with a grand piano, and an observation platform. The itinerary spanned the continent, from coast to coast and from Canada to Texas. The gross receipts for Stanley's first lecture in New York City amounted to $18,000, and his personal earnings for the whole tour reached $60,000.

Although the American press did not subject Stanley to the kind of heavyweight criticism he had to suffer in Britain, he was an irresistible target for the satirists. " 'How I Found the Consommé' would be a very appropriate subject for Explorer Stanley to tackle," said the Washington *Post.* "Somebody ought to organise a relief expedition to find H. M. Stanley," joked the New York *World.* And the Chicago *Daily News,* observing the limpet-like qualities of Gertrude Tennant, had merciless fun at Stanley's expense in an article headlined "How Stanley Won His Mother-in-Law."

The sketch imagined an exchange between Stanley and Gertrude in which Mrs. Tennant refuses to consent to the marriage unless he promises to take her into his household as well. Reluctantly, Stanley accepts the condition, and Gertrude cries: "She is yours, and so am I!"

After six months, the Stanleys were back in London for the start of a British lecture tour. Stanley began to find the lecture round exhausting. "Rest! Ah, my dear! we both need it—I more than you," he wrote from one provincial town to Dolly, who had remained with Gertrude at Richmond Terrace, "existence is mere prolonged endurance." When his tour took him to North Wales he was treated as a native son. Eight special trains were laid on to bring in country folk who wanted to hear him speak at Caernarvon, some forty miles from his birthplace.

"[A]s I moved through the crowd," wrote Stanley, "I felt hands touch my coat, then, getting bolder, they rubbed me on the back, stroked my hair, and, finally, thumped me hard, until I felt that the honours were getting so weighty I should die if they continued long. Verily, there were but few thumps between me and death!"

Stanley had been invited to preside at the next Eisteddfod—the annual festival of Welsh song and poetry that is central to the cultural identity of the people of the Principality—but he was not at all sure that he wanted to accept this signal honor, for he was no Welsh nationalist.

"My travels in the various continents have ill-prepared me for sympathising with such a cause," he wrote to Dolly. "If I were to

*The Stanleys on tour in the U.S.: public acclaim, a private train, but no time for old friends in New Orleans. (Library of Congress)*

speak truly my mind I should recommend Welshmen to turn their attention to a closer study of the English language, literature, and characteristics, for it is only by that training that they can hope to compete with their English brothers for glory, honour and prosperity."

For all that, Stanley was not above playing to the Welsh gallery. As he waited for his train to pull out of the station at Caernarvon on the morning after his lecture, he made a display of reading a copy of the local Welsh-language newspaper, to the great delight of the crowd which had gathered on the platform to see him off.

It seems clear that marriage to Dolly had at last brought Stanley the emotional fulfillment he had sought all his life. From one stop he wrote to tell her of his "great relief" at being able to reveal himself to another person—"not to be chilled and have to shrink back."

> Between mother and child, *you* know the confidence and trust that exist; *I* never knew it; and now, by extreme favour of Providence, the last few years of my life shall be given to know this thoroughly. Towards you I begin trustfully to exhibit my thoughts and feelings. . . .

But Stanley remained a lightning conductor for the malice of others. He had been married less than a year when rumors began to circulate that he was treating his wife as harshly as his enemies said he used to treat his Africans, and that the marriage was breaking up. James Gordon Bennett, still nursing his old grudge against the employee who had upstaged and then outflanked him, sent Aubrey Stanhope, one of his star reporters, to Switzerland—where the Stanleys were vacationing after his British lecture tour—to confront Stanley with these rumors. Stanhope hated the assignment, not least because he was aware that Stanley was "a particularly irascible man, whose health . . . rendered him exceedingly irritable."

To make matters worse, Stanley was nursing a broken ankle, having slipped and fallen badly during a country walk across a muddy meadow—a strange mishap for a man who had crossed and recrossed Africa without so much as a sprain. Despite his discomfort, Stanley welcomed his old colleague warmly, and they talked for three days before Stanley asked if there was any particular reason for his visit. Perhaps there was some matter connected with Africa that Stanhope wanted to discuss? No, replied Stanhope, it was something quite different—and then, taking a deep breath, he blurted out: "Do you beat your wife?"

There was a shocked silence. Then, as his anger mounted, Stanley's right hand doubled into a fist. "Now kill me," Stanhope said to himself. But Stanley held back his wrath and, recalling his own days as a general-assignment reporter, muttered: "God! I used to do that myself."

Grimly, Stanley scribbled a signed denial of the rumors and then asked Dolly, who had not been present during the interview, to do likewise. "I am very much astonished and disgusted," she wrote, "with the reports in a New York newspaper that my married life is unhappy and that I am separated from my dear husband."

On their return to Britain a few days later, Stanley was able to derive one small benefit from having broken his ankle: it gave him the perfect excuse to avoid opening the Eisteddfod without giving offense.

In October 1891, the Stanleys were on the move again—this time to Australia and New Zealand on another lecture tour. Dolly's mother came, too. En route to the Antipodes, the Stanleys were invited to Ostend by Leopold, who told the explorer that he had "a big task on hand for you when you are ready." But Dolly had other ideas for her husband's future, and they very definitely did not include his going back to the Congo, or any other part of Africa.

On their return to London in the summer of 1892 she persuaded him to renounce his American nationality and become a naturalized citizen of his native land, so that he could stand for election to Parliament. As an MP, Dolly hoped, Stanley would find the occupational fulfillment he might otherwise seek in the Dark Continent.

# Chapter Twenty-seven

STANLEY hated electioneering, and when he got there he quickly came
to hate the House of Commons. The fearless lion of African exploration was a timorous rabbit in the political jungle.

While Americans say that a candidate *runs* for office, the British
say that he *stands,* and in Stanley's case that was certainly the more
appropriate verb. In the general election of 1892, he offered himself,
only ten days before the poll—and with extreme diffidence and ill-
disguised lack of fervor—to the electors of North Lambeth, just
across the Thames from Westminster. Carrying the colors of the
Liberal-Unionists,* he was "howled down by an organised rabble"
at his first meeting, an experience which so unnerved him that when
he was defeated by the Radical incumbent he hoped it was the end of
his political career.

But Dolly would have none of that. Despite his reluctant candi-
dacy, Stanley had been beaten by only 130 votes, and she was determined that he should try again at the next election. He agreed to
do so, but only for her sake and after warning her that "you must not
expect any enthusiasm, any of that perseverant energy which I have
shewn elsewhere." He went on to complain that

> this political work involves lying, back-biting, morally damaging your
> opponent in the eyes of the voters, giving and receiving wordy abuse. . . .
> I cannot find the courage either to open my lips against my opponent, or
> to put myself in a position to receive from him and his mindless myrmi-
> dons that filthy abuse they are only too eager to give. . . . You remember
> that meeting in Lambeth. Well! I have been through some stiff scenes in
> my life, but I never fell so low in my own estimation as I fell that day. . . .

Stanley further advised Dolly that he would never ask any man for
his vote, never address an open-air meeting, never canvas door-to-

---

*The right wing of the Liberal Party, whose members had hived off in protest against
Gladstone's policy of Home Rule for Ireland. Even if he had not been opposed to Home Rule,
it is hard to imagine Stanley accepting the leadership of the man who had told him off about
Mophi and Crophi.

door—never, in short, kiss babies or shake hands with complete strangers on street corners. She accepted his terms and nursed his constituency for him until the next election in the summer of 1895. Stanley found the campaign as distasteful as before, and the Liberal and Radical newspapers at times virulently abusive. On the eve of polling day one leading Liberal journal, reviving all the old charges against him, declared that Stanley's course through Africa had been "like that of a red hot poker drawn across a blanket" and that he nightly slept "on a pillow steeped in blood."

Dolly wore herself out on her husband's behalf, and when the polls closed on election day she retired to an attic room of the Liberal-Unionist Club in Lambeth to rest while the votes were counted. A red signal in the night sky around midnight would mean victory for Stanley; a blue light, victory for his Radical opponent.

"Suddenly," Dolly wrote later, "the sky flushed pink over the roofs; to the west, a rosy fog seemed gently to rise, and creep over the sky; and, soon, a distant, tumultuous roar came rolling like an incoming tide, and I went down to meet my Stanley!"

He was carried in, "looking very white and stern," on the shoulders of his cheering supporters. As he passed Dolly she caught his hand, which was so cold it seemed to freeze her own. Called on to make a victory speech, Stanley stood on the table where his supporters had set him down and said: "Gentlemen, I thank you, and now goodnight!" In the carriage that took them home to Richmond Terrace, he remained silent, except to say: "I think we both need rest; and now for a pipe."

After taking his seat in the Commons on August 12, 1895, Stanley recorded his impressions of his first week as an MP. He was far from overwhelmed by his venerable surroundings in the Mother of Parliaments ("any of the State houses in America would offer superior accommodation") and by the lackluster oratory of his fellow members ("we listened to the most dreary twaddle it has ever been my lot to hear"). He found late-night sittings especially wearing:

> I was so tired when I came home that I felt as if I had undergone a long march. The close air of the House is most deleterious to health, for the atmosphere of the small chamber after the confinement of about three hundred and fifty members for 11 hours, must needs be vitiated. We are herded in the lobbies like so many sheep in a fold; and among my wonders has been that so many eminent men would consent voluntarily to such a servitude, in which I cannot help seeing a great deal of degradation.

The golden age of African exploration was now passed, and although there was still enough magic attached to his name to ensure his election, Stanley was made to feel somewhat passé in the House. A different style of speaking was required from that of the lecture hall. "I have not got the art!" he admitted. "First, I have not the patience; and then again, I disdain the use of the art, on principle. I want to say what I have to say, right out, and be done with it, which does not tend to elegance." Even when African affairs were being debated, he often failed even to catch the Speaker's eye and had to listen to members with little or no real knowledge of the subject hold forth. "The House," he grumbled, "takes no interest in any one's personal qualifications."

When his term as an MP ended in July 1900, Stanley said farewell to the Commons with relief. Nothing could persuade him to stand again.

Between his two election campaigns he had started writing his frequently mendacious autobiography, but the work went fitfully, and he was never to complete it. The man who in 1891 had turned out 300,000 words in seven weeks now found it impossible to squeeze out more than a few paragraphs at a time. He was never to get beyond his discharge from the Union army at the age of twenty, the rest of his life story being sketched in after his death by Dolly from his notes, letters and journals.

And his health was wretched. He was constantly subject to savage attacks of gastritis, complicated by bouts of malaria, and when the old sickness struck it did so with agonizing force. Dolly wrote:

> During Stanley's malaria attacks, the shivering preceding the hot stage was so violent that the bed he lay on would shake, and the glasses on the table vibrate and ring. I might . . . find him in bed, covered with blankets, quilts, even great-coats; with chattering teeth and hurried speech, he would bid me get hot water bottles to pack around him. Then, when the cold fit had passed, and the heat had reached its maximum, he would speak to me reassuringly, and tell me not to fear, that all would be well; that it was only "Africa in me.". . . I vowed in my heart that he should never return to the country which had taken so much of his splendid vitality.

On a visit to Spain in 1896 he was suddenly attacked by gastritis while they were on a train from Toledo to Madrid. So severe were the pains that by the time they reached Madrid he was barely conscious. Dolly spoke no Spanish and knew nobody in the capital. She got

Stanley to a hotel where a doctor was called to attend him. But day by day he grew weaker. In desperation Dolly decided to get him back to England and only did so "with the greatest difficulty." Back in London it took him three months to recover.

The attacks kept recurring. Often he would call out to Dolly in the middle of the night, and she knew by the sound of his voice that the agony was upon him. "I think Stanley feared nothing in the world as he feared those first ominous stabs of pain," wrote Dolly, "but when the spasms were steadily recurrent, and no doctor could give him any relief, Stanley accepted the pain and weakness, silently and stoically."

It was too late for Stanley and Dolly to have a child of their own, and so they decided in 1896 to adopt a baby boy from Stanley's home district in North Wales. They named him Denzil Morton and had him baptized with water from Lake Albert which Stanley had kept sealed in a bottle since his return from the Emin Pasha expedition. Stanley thought the child "a model of infantile beauty [who] promises to be remarkable for his intelligence," and although he was little more than a year old bought him picture books and toys more suitable to a child of four.

When Stanley was ill, Dolly recalled, he liked to have the child placed on the bed beside him. Once when Denzil was there, Stanley looked up at Dolly and said: "Ah! it is worth while now to get well." His joy in the child seems genuine, and touching, revealing an unexpectedly tender side of his prickly personality. While in Brighton just before Christmas of 1896, Stanley wrote home:

> Warmest greetings to darling little Denzil, our own cherub! Possibly, I think too much of him. If I were not busy with work and other things, I should undoubtedly dwell too much on him . . . look where I may, his beautiful features, lightened up with a sunny smile, come before my eyes all the time! I see him in your arms, and I marvel greatly at my great happiness in possessing you two!

And ten months later, while sailing to South Africa, Stanley wrote to Dolly that there were "several wee things in arms on board, and I shake hands with them all in turns, every morning, as my 'devoir' to our Denzil." He was deeply affected when one of the babies on board died of meningitis and was buried at sea.

By the autumn of 1898, Stanley had decided that they must have a country home, and he plunged into house-hunting with something of his old vigor. He collected the lists of estate agents throughout the Home Counties surrounding London and inspected fifty-seven prop-

*The lion in winter: a seat in the Commons, a country house, and a wife and child to love. (The Autobiography of H. M. Stanley, 1908)*

erties before finding one he liked. It was a rambling (and quite hideous) mock Tudor manor named Furze Hill, in Pirbright, Surrey, about thirty miles from the capital.

Stanley had it electrified and renovated extensively before they moved in during September of the following year, doing much of the work himself. "Everything Stanley planned and executed was to last," Dolly recalled, "to be strong and permanent. He replaced the window frames by stone; the fences were of the strongest and best description; even the ends of the gate and fence-posts, he had dipped in pitch, and not merely in tar, that the portion in the ground might resist decay. It was his pride and joy that all should be well done. . . ."

Furze Hill had extensive grounds containing a small wood, which Dolly named the Aruwimi Forest. A stream which ran through it was named the Congo and a pond "Stanley Pool." Stanley, she said, was "amused at my fancy." Time, ill-health and the pleasures of family life had turned the Smasher of Rocks into a thoroughly domesticated animal. And along with domesticity came a title. In her Birthday Honors List of 1899, Queen Victoria conferred the Grand Cross of the Bath on Stanley—not the highest degree of knighthood available, to be sure, but one which nevertheless confirmed that he had at last been formally accepted into English society.

The recognition had come, as the *Pall Mall Gazette* said, "long after the intrepid African explorer had ceased to expect titular honours," but not before controversy connected with his work in Africa had completely died down. For the previous three years, word had been seeping out of the Congo alleging hideous ill-treatment of the natives by agents of King Leopold's administration and of the companies to whom Leopold had sold concessions for the exploitation of the territory's resources.

An American missionary named Murphy made startling allegations of the use of forced labor in the Congo to obtain rubber, for which there was by now a booming world market. As Murphy told it, and as later investigation confirmed, the administrator of each district set a weekly quota for the amount of rubber that had to be brought into his headquarters by the natives.

> It is collected by force; the soldiers drive the people into the bush. If they will not go they are shot down, and their left hands cut off and taken as trophies to the Commissaire. . . . [T]he hands of men, women and children are placed in rows before the Commissaire who counts them to see that the soldiers have not wasted cartridges.

A Swedish missionary named Sjoblom added grisly detail. To preserve the severed hands until they could be shown to a Commissaire, the Free State's soldiers would smoke them in small kilns, he alleged. "I have many times seen this done." An Englishman named Parminter, one of the few non-Belgians still allowed to work in the Upper Congo, told of seeing a detachment of soldiers return from the pursuit of recalcitrant rubber-gatherers with strings of severed ears. When a sergeant showed these trophies to the Commissaire, he was congratulated for his zeal. Parminter also alleged that an unnamed Belgian lieutenant had given two native women 200 lashes each and then ordered his men to cut their breasts off and leave them to die.

The diary of a former British officer of the Free State named Edward Glave—who died in 1897 while trying to repeat Stanley's voyage down the Congo—told of natives who failed to collect enough rubber being flogged with the *chicotte,* a whip made of raw hippopotamus hide that was "trimmed like a corkscrew, with edges like knife blades, and hard as wood." Everywhere he went in the Congo, Glave reported, he heard the story of "rubber and murder, slavery in its worst form."

Leopold professed shock and horror at such stories and, insisting that they must be isolated incidents and in no way represented official policy, had regulations drawn up which ostensibly forbade the ill-treatment of the Blacks. He also set up a tame Commission for the Protection of the Natives.

Leopold's sympathizers, among them Stanley, pointed out that in administering a vast and savage region such as the Congo, occasional lapses were inevitable. But Stanley was outraged at the suggestion that such behavior was widespread and routine. Indeed, he wrote to *The Times* denouncing Parminter's "foul fictions" in terms so strong that the editor declined to publish his letter for fear of a libel suit. Stanley thought the letter was "exceedingly moderate," but toned it down sufficiently to permit publication.

All the same, Stanley had misgivings about the situation in the Free State, for on the day his rebuttal appeared in *The Times* he wrote to Leopold urging that "something should be done to prevent this continual supply of Congo sensations." A few more incidents of the kind would provoke "a fearful uproar" in Britain, he warned, and jeopardize prospects for a renewal of Leopold's mandate when it came up for great-power review in 1905.

In another display of his private reservations about the true state of affairs in the Congo, Stanley noted in his journal that he had declined recent offers to return to work there "because to go back would be to see mistakes consummated, and to be tortured daily by seeing the effects of an erring and ignorant policy."

> I would be tempted to re-consitutute a great part of the governmental machine, and this would be to disturb a moral malaria injurious to the reorganiser. We have become used to call vast, deep layers of filth "Augean Stables"; what shall we call the years of stupid government, mischievous encroachments on the executive, years of unnecessary unqualified officers, years of cumbersome administration, years of neglect at every station, years of confusion and waste in every office?

Stanley obviously felt passionate on the subject, but about exactly what aspect of it? Phrases like "moral malaria" and "deep layers of filth" suggest an anger more profound than seems likely to be inspired simply by mismanagement and incompetence, however gross. Yet even in a private diary note Stanley could not admit to himself the likely existence of hideous and systematic cruelties in the state which had been largely his creation.

Indeed, in the introduction to a book on the Congo by a former Free State officer, published in 1898, Stanley went out of his way to lavish praise on Leopold for "his matchless sacrifices on behalf of the inhabitants of the region." Leopold had earned "the gratitude of the civilised world," he wrote, and added: "Who can doubt that God chose the King for His instrument to redeem this vast slave park?"

The most charitable explanation for this excessive loyalty to Leopold is that Stanley had managed to convince himself—as even the missionary societies had done up to this point—that the Congo atrocities were not systematic and that Leopold would put things to rights now that some isolated cases had been exposed. In fact, what had been revealed to date was merely the tip of the iceberg, as detailed reports in later years by the British consular officer Roger Casement and the crusading journalist Edmund Morel would convincingly demonstrate.

These left no doubt that, in response to royal demands for evergreater revenues, district administrators and the agents of the Congo's concession companies had a free hand to use whatever means they chose to make their territories profitable. Apart from the widespread practice of cutting off hands—and sometimes feet as well—Leopold's soldiers and the company askaris also kidnapped women and held them hostage to make their menfolk collect rubber, ivory, palm oil or whatever other natural product was in demand.

The British Foreign Office became concerned, not just for humanitarian reasons, but because it was plain that Leopold was violating his undertaking to permit free trade in the Congo by giving monopolies to the concession companies, many of which existed only on paper and were actually under his control. The Foreign Office instructed Casement to investigate the situation, and he was horrified at what he found. Whole areas he had once known as heavily populated were now virtually deserted. "Infamous! Infamous shameful system," he wrote in his diary, ". . . terrible oppression of these poor people."

When his official report was published in February 1904, it created a sensation. Leopold fought a dogged rearguard battle to discredit Casement's findings, but was eventually forced by international pressure to pass control of his misnamed Free State to the Belgian government, which henceforth administered the Congo in a more humane if still deeply authoritarian fashion.

Leopold's forced-labor policy had, by reliable estimate, caused the deaths of some three million Congolese, while boosting the revenues of his slave state tenfold. And although Stanley was not responsible for that policy, its hideous consequences would inevitably leave a stain on his achievements in the Congo. But by the time Casement's report came out, Stanley was past caring. In April 1903 he had suffered a stroke which left him paralyzed down one side of his body.

"Months passed," Dolly recorded; "spring, summer, autumn, Stanley lay there, steadfast, calm, uncomplaining; never by word or sigh did he express grief or regret. He submitted grandly, and never seemed to me greater, or more courageous, than throughout that last year of utter helplessness and deprivation. Stanley, the very embodiment of proud independence, was as weak and helpless as a little child!"

In fact, his condition improved for a while, so that he could sit in the garden in an invalid chair, and even—with a display of his old indomitable will—walk a few steps and speak a few words. He returned to Richmond Terrace for the winter, and the following Easter went back to Furze Hill.

But on April 17, 1904, exactly a year after his stroke, he was smitten again, this time by pleurisy. Ten days later, at his own request, he was taken by ambulance back to town. "Where will they put me when I am—gone?" he asked Dolly. "In Westminster Abbey," she replied. "Yes," said Stanley, "they will put me beside Livingstone."

By May 5 it was clear that he was dying, and for days he slipped in and out of consciousness. On the night of May 9 his mind was wandering. "I have done—all—my work—I have—circumnavigated," he murmured. Later, according to Dolly, he cried out: "Oh! I want to be free!—I want to go—into the woods—to be free!"

As the nearby Big Ben struck four next morning, he awoke and asked Dolly: "What's that?" She told him, and he said: "Four o'clock? How strange! So that is Time! Strange!" As six o'clock struck, his breathing stopped.

On May 17, Stanley's coffin was carried into Westminster Abbey for the funeral service. But he was not to be buried there. The Dean of Westminster, the Reverend Joseph Armitage Robinson, who by tradition had the absolute right to decide in such matters, had ruled against it. The final rejection.

Instead, Stanley was cremated and his ashes buried in the village churchyard at Pirbright. Dolly had a huge block of granite brought from Dartmoor as his headstone and had it engraved with a cross and the legend: "Henry Morton Stanley, Bula Matari, 1841–1904, Africa."

IT WAS Stanley's posthumous misfortune that his name should have been so inextricably linked with the Congo. That was almost certainly the reason why Robinson refused him burial in the Abbey, and why to this day he enjoys less repute than he deserves. But for his imperishable "I presume," he might be all but forgotten.

Posterity has been kinder to Leopold II. That rapacious and conscienceless monarch is still highly regarded in Belgium, if nowhere else. After all, his Free State loot paid for the beautification of Brussels and the construction of some edifying museums and art galleries.

If, in decline, Stanley was willing to gloss over the atrocities perpetrated by Leopold's agents, one may plead mitigating circumstances: his wretchedly poor health; his sense of obligation to a patron who had made it possible for him to achieve great things; his understandable reluctance to believe that an undertaking he had pioneered could have had such a shameful outcome. Like selective memory, selective belief is a common enough human failing.

This does not relieve Stanley of the accusation of moral equivocation, but one may doubt that he would have tolerated, let alone perpetrated, the kind of horrors that occurred under his successors in the Congo. For all his well-attested ruthlessness, there is a ring of credibility to his claim that Africa had taught him "real, heartfelt sympathy for the natives with whom one has to deal."

Africans should be regarded not as "mere brutes," he said, but as "children, who require, indeed, different methods of rule from English or American citizens, but who must be ruled in precisely the same spirit, with the same absence of caprice and anger, the same essential respect to our fellow-men."

There, it may be said, speaks the authentically patronizing voice of white Victorian racism. But Stanley's was at least a benign racism, lacking the venomous contempt expressed by such contemporaries as Burton and Baker, and ameliorated by a genuine interest in the native people and stirrings of conscience in his dealings with them. And it must be said that whatever miseries and injustices white penetration brought to Equatorial Africa, it did at least drive out the Arab slave-traders, whose depredations would surely have depopulated the center of the continent in a generation or two.

In any case, the issue of race may be an historical red herring. Victorian colonialism was more about the conquest of nature—an irresistible challenge to a society besotted with its scientific and technological prowess—than about the immemorial subjugation of "backward" races by more "advanced" societies. In Africa, western man found nature in its most primal and challenging form, and the "savages" who attacked the explorer as he carved his way through forest, swamp and bush were just one more natural hazard.

It needs to be said, too, that Stanley's observations on how to rule the African differ very little from the rationale advanced nowadays by Black African despots in defense of the one-party systems that keep them in office.

Nowhere is that more the case than in the Congo, now the Republic of Zaire, which President Mobutu Sese Seko rules as an absolute dictator and plunders with a panache that Leopold himself might have admired. True, the hands and feet of recalcitrants are no longer chopped off wholesale, but since seizing power in 1965, the once-penniless Mobutu has, according to U.S. State Department estimates, accumulated a private fortune of over $5 billion.

For comparison, it may be noted that the per-capita income of his people, at $150 a year, is the eighth-lowest in the world and in real terms only 10 per cent of what it was in 1960, when Zaire became independent. Under the fatherly rule of one of the world's wealthiest men, more than one-third of all Zairean children die of disease and malnutrition before reaching the age of five.

Mobutu has shown only a little more regard for the human rights of his people than he has for their material well-being. In welding over two hundred disparate tribes into something like a nation, he has put in place a highly repressive system of state security, in which torture, arbitrary arrest and prolonged detention without trial are systematic. In a country where hardly anything else works and the impressive communications infrastructure left behind by the Belgians has been allowed to fall into almost total disrepair, the intelligence services function with awesome efficiency.

None of which should be construed as an argument in favor of colonialism, least of all the blatantly piratical brand practiced by Leopold. It is surely axiomatic that the white subjugation and exploitation of Black Africa, in which Stanley played such a pioneer role, was reprehensible. But colonialism was a product of its age, a phenomenon as historically inevitable in the mid-to-late nineteenth century as was its passing a hundred years later. The materialistic, inquiring, acquisitive, self-admiring Europe of the Victorian era could no sooner have left the map of Africa blank and its "empty" spaces unoccupied than the tide could cease or the sun stand still.

And in Stanley the age found, par excellence, the man. At his worst, he was a bully, a braggart, a hypocrite and a liar; at his best he was steadfast, brave, enduring, resourceful, and an inspired leader. It was those qualities that Lieutenant Stairs acknowledged when, amid the horrors of Starvation Camp, he inspired the "poor skeletons" who had survived to resume their march through the forest by telling them of Bula Matari's exploits at Lake Albert:

> It was this, that carried the whole body of Zanzibaris onwards when nothing but despair stared us in the face. It was this that has enabled Stanley to push through everything and get through where others might have stuck. He carried on his men by his example and presence, his feelings were theirs. These natives he understood to a nicety. Never perhaps will any of us five Europeans ever see a man who could make men "spring" to a thing like Stanley could.

And while, in his relations with his junior officers, much of Stanley's behavior seems dismayingly mean-spirited, allowance should be made for the corrosive effects of crushing responsibility, constant sickness and ever-present danger. Nor could Stanley's uncongenial disposition have been unusual among explorers of his day. As Stairs noted: "White men in this strange country seem to have a universal suspicion of each other. . . . To put it plainly, every white man . . . thinks everyone else either a rogue or a good-for-nothing."

And should Stanley be condemned for the fact that a savagely deprived childhood rendered him something of an emotional cripple? The obvious depth of his feelings for Livingstone and Dolly, and his unabashed love for his adopted son, surely give the lie to those who depict him as totally unable to forge meaningful human relationships. As for his apparent sexual ambivalence, well, Stanley was certainly not the only eminent Victorian to display homosexual tendencies—in his case almost certainly repressed—tendencies which, in any case, are no longer viewed with such deep disdain.

Stanley had learned early on not to expect happiness. "I was not sent into the world to be happy," he declared toward the end of his life, "nor to search for happiness. I was sent for a special work." He was wrong on that score, though he little realized it. Happiness—or something approximating that condition: release from the demons that had pursued him since childhood—was precisely what he had been seeking in Africa. For surely his epic journeyings were not so much a search for an old man lost in the wilderness, for rivers and mountains, lakes and deserts, as an escape from a society in which he felt acutely uncomfortable and a quest for self-esteem.

How paradoxical that not Africa, but Dolly and domesticity, should ultimately have brought him a measure of the balm he so desperately needed.

# Epilogue

Wᴏʀᴅ reached Dorothy Stanley a month or so after her husband's death that a certain Mrs. Katie Bradshaw of Pendleton, Manchester— the former Katie Gough-Roberts, of Denbigh—was in possession of letters from Stanley dating back to the period of their engagement. Dolly became concerned. She planned to edit and complete Stanley's unfinished autobiography, and was determined that it should reflect only credit and honor on her late husband. She wanted no unauthorized material to appear in print, but it seemed that Mrs. Bradshaw was being approached by publishers to sell the letters and photographs that she had kept all these years.

Dolly took legal advice and, finding that in law the documents were rightly Mrs. Bradshaw's property, she asked Stanley's friend, the pharmaceuticals magnate Henry Wellcome, to act for her in getting the lady to disgorge those treasures, either gratis or for payment. Wellcome went about the task with a heavy hand. It would be "a dishonourable act and a grave breach of faith," he told Katie, for her to sell to a publisher "letters and memoranda which were written under the most sacred pledge of fidelity that can be made between man and woman."

Wellcome's hectoring can hardly have helped, especially as a Welsh nationalist journalist calling himself Morien the Bard was pressuring Mrs. Bradshaw from the opposite direction. He wanted the letters, and in particular the autobiography, to be published in order to establish Stanley as a Welsh, not an English, national hero.

Letters went to and fro for more than three years, and Wellcome's agents called on Mrs. Roberts several times before she finally parted with the documents for £150 at the end of November 1907. Dolly wrote an ecstatic letter of thanks to Wellcome ("It is such *triumph*— and would have been such a relief to Stanley") and put the documents into the fire.

By this time, Dolly had also become concerned about William Hoffmann, who had written to say that he had it in mind to write his memoirs of his years in Stanley's service. At first she was reluctant to give her approval on the grounds, as she told Wellcome, that "he

writes badly and might unwittingly do ill-service" to Stanley's reputation. But after Hoffmann wrote again in August 1905, to say that
the Barttelot family had invited him to pay them a visit ("they are still
after the details of the fate of their relative") she became thoroughly
alarmed.

"I have such misgivings about this Hoffmann," Dolly wrote, . . .
"What can the Barttelots want to get at him for? Only for some
mischief? And I mistrust Hoffmann through and through; they only
have to intoxicate him and bribe him, and there is no knowing what
he may say. . . . [H]e is a weak, untruthful man. . . ."

In fact, Hoffmann would pepper Wellcome with begging letters for
the next quarter of a century. A tentative whiff of blackmail adheres
to some of these, as though Hoffmann had some secret to reveal
about his master that could be bought off.

"I mite have been better off," he wrote on one occasion, "had I
been wicked and earnt money, as some people wanted me to give
some details of my late master, which will never be as I promised him
it will go to my grave with me as Stanley was my dear beloved master
and what I know is in my heart."

But when Hoffmann's unctuous, self-serving and heavily ghosted
memoirs were published in 1938, they provided no revelations and
no new insights. Hoffmann characterized Stanley as "a kind, cheerful
companion, so interested in my welfare, and so interested in the wild
life of the forest," and himself as the ever-loyal servant and friend,
one of the few people Stanley felt he could trust and confide in, a
welcome visitor to his master's home right up to the time of his
death.

In the early 1900's, Lewis Noe, too, emerged from the past with
vague hints of damaging information concerning Stanley. He wrote
to Dolly to say that he had a number of letters and photographs,
which "of course I would be unable to spare . . . for less than *one
hundred dollars.*" This seems a pitifully small sum for one intent on
blackmail, and perhaps that was not Noe's intent. But the tone of the
letter was troubling; he mentioned, *inter alia,* "a peculiar experience" during his trip with Stanley to Asia Minor, "the details of
which journey would interest you, providing you wished to hear the
*good and bad.*"

Dolly certainly did not want to hear the bad. Again, she turned to
Wellcome, who sent an employee of the Burroughs Wellcome New
York office to see Noe, long since married and still living on Long
Island. Noe was bought off more quickly—and more cheaply—than
Mrs. Bradshaw, and in return for his original price of $100, turned

over the letters and photographs in a few days. They shared the same fate as those retrieved from Katie Bradshaw.

Henceforward, apart from Hoffmann's ineffectual begging letters down the years to Wellcome, the ghosts of Stanley's past were no longer heard from. To her credit, Alice Pike Barney had the good taste not to trumpet the memories and fantasies she cherished of her *grand amour* as a girl. She saved these for the novelettish memoirs which she dictated to her amanuensis in the late 1920s, but which were mercifully never published.

The officers who returned from the Emin Pasha expedition with Stanley all died young—Stairs of sickness in the Congo in 1892, after leading an expedition to Katanga; Nelson in the same year in Kenya, while in the employ of the British Imperial East Africa Company; Parke of a heart attack in Scotland, in 1893; Bonny of consumption and generalized debility caused by drink, drugs and poverty in an army hospital in 1899; and Jephson, after years of failing health, in Ireland in 1908.

As for Dolly, despite her fierce loyalty to Stanley's memory, she remarried within less than three years of his death. It was a curious alliance. At forty, Henry Curtis, a Harley Street physician, was sixteen years her junior, and Dolly never called herself "Mrs. Curtis," insisting on being known as "Lady Stanley." After her death in 1926 her ashes joined those of her Bula Matari in the churchyard at Pirbright.

# A Note on Sources

*EVEN* the greatest of men may—to borrow the recent phrase of a Whitehall mandarin—prove to be "economical with the truth" about themselves. But as we have seen, Stanley went further than mere economy. He was a liar and a fantasist on a scale to rival his unquestionably heroic achievements as an explorer, and it is only in the last two decades that the dense smoke screen he created has begun to dissipate.

For that, much credit must go to the British journalist and Africanist, Richard Hall. His researches for his biography *Stanley: An Adventurer Explored* (Collins, London, 1974; Houghton Mifflin, Boston, 1975) were a model of hard-nosed and painstaking investigative technique, which the present author acknowledges with admiration and cites with gratitude.

Building on the solid foundation established by Hall, I believe I have been able to shed even more light on Stanley's elusive and not entirely sympathetic personality. New documentary sources include the hitherto unpublished expedition journals of William Grant Stairs and memoirs of Alice Pike Barney.

A word should be said here about the disposal of Stanley's private papers. Up to 1974, Hall was the only biographer—excluding Frank Hird, the gullible (or biddable) author of the 1935 authorized biography—to be give access to the Stanley Family Archives, which at that time were unclassified and unindexed. Eight years after Hall's book was published, this collection was sold by Stanley's adoptive grandson, Richard, and was swallowed up in what one can only describe as an academic black hole.

Put up for auction by Christie's in New York in November 1982, the Stanley archives were purchased for 30 million Belgian francs by the Société Générale de Banque of Brussels on behalf of the Musée Royal de l'Afrique Centrale. The successful joint bidders were Herman Libaers, ex-Grand Marshal of the Royal Belgian Court, and Professor Marcel Luwel, curator of the museum and author of a 1959 biography of Stanley. The authorities in Brussels considered their acquisition so important that they sent a Belgian Air Force plane to fly the document collection back to Belgium. Since then, access to the papers has been consistently denied to outsiders, including the present author, on the grounds that they have still not been classified or indexed.

Fortunately for interested parties less privileged than Professor Luwel, most of the collection was copied before the British government allowed it to be exported, and those microfilms and photocopies are accessible to researches at the British Library in London (Ref. RP 2435, Boxes 1 8, Batches 1 5). However, the diaries of Dorothy Tennant Stanley and important personal letters from Stanley to her, and vice versa, were not among the documents copied, and I am grateful to Hall for permission to quote from these.

I must also record my appreciation for permission to quote from *Stanley's Despatches to the New York Herald* (Boston University Press, 1970), editor Norman R. Bennett; *The Diary of A. J. Mounteney Jephson* (Cambridge University Press/ The Hakluyt Society, 1969), editor Dorothy Middleton; *The Unpublished Letters of H. M. Stanley* (Chambers, London, 1957), editor Albert Maurice; *The Exploration Diaries of H. M. Stanley* (Kimber, London, 1961) editors Richard Stanley and Alan Neame; and the following: Neil Ascherson, *The King Incorporated* (Allen and Unwin, London, 1963); Barbara Emerson, *Leopold II of the Belgians* (St. Martin's, New York, 1979); Brian Inglis, *Roger Casement* (Hodder and Stoughton, London, 1973); Tim Jeal, *Livingstone* (Heinemann, London, 1973); Dana L. Thomas, *The Media Moguls* (Putnam, New York, 1981); Richard West, *Brazza of the Congo* (Cape, London, 1972)

And then there are those local historians whose articles and monographs so often contain information that adds depth and detail which might otherwise go unnoticed. Professional biographers invariably owe a debt to such little-recognized researchers, and in this respect I would like to acknowledge my debt to Ivor and Lucy Jones, Bob Owen, and W. Wynne-Woodhouse of North Wales, Mary Willis Shuey and John S. Kendall of the American South, and Douglas L. Wheeler, historian of the American West.

# A Note on Sources

*EVEN* the greatest of men may—to borrow the recent phrase of a Whitehall mandarin—prove to be "economical with the truth" about themselves. But as we have seen, Stanley went further than mere economy. He was a liar and a fantasist on a scale to rival his unquestionably heroic achievements as an explorer, and it is only in the last two decades that the dense smoke screen he created has begun to dissipate.

For that, much credit must go to the British journalist and Africanist, Richard Hall. His researches for his biography *Stanley: An Adventurer Explored* (Collins, London, 1974; Houghton Mifflin, Boston, 1975) were a model of hard-nosed and painstaking investigative technique, which the present author acknowledges with admiration and cites with gratitude.

Building on the solid foundation established by Hall, I believe I have been able to shed even more light on Stanley's elusive and not entirely sympathetic personality. New documentary sources include the hitherto unpublished expedition journals of William Grant Stairs and memoirs of Alice Pike Barney.

A word should be said here about the disposal of Stanley's private papers. Up to 1974, Hall was the only biographer—excluding Frank Hird, the gullible (or biddable) author of the 1935 authorized biography—to be give access to the Stanley Family Archives, which at that time were unclassified and unindexed. Eight years after Hall's book was published, this collection was sold by Stanley's adoptive grandson, Richard, and was swallowed up in what one can only describe as an academic black hole.

Put up for auction by Christie's in New York in November 1982, the Stanley archives were purchased for 30 million Belgian francs by the Société Générale de Banque of Brussels on behalf of the Musée Royal de l'Afrique Centrale. The successful joint bidders were Herman Libaers, ex-Grand Marshal of the Royal Belgian Court, and Professor Marcel Luwel, curator of the museum and author of a 1959 biography of Stanley. The authorities in Brussels considered their acquisition so important that they sent a Belgian Air Force plane to fly the document collection back to Belgium. Since then, access to the papers has been consistently denied to outsiders, including the present author, on the grounds that they have still not been classified or indexed.

Fortunately for interested parties less privileged than Professor Luwel, most of the collection was copied before the British government allowed it to be exported, and those microfilms and photocopies are accessible to researches at the British Library in London (Ref. RP 2435, Boxes 1 8, Batches 1 5). However, the diaries of Dorothy Tennant Stanley and important personal letters from Stanley to her, and vice versa, were not among the documents copied, and I am grateful to Hall for permission to quote from these.

I must also record my appreciation for permission to quote from *Stanley's Despatches to the New York Herald* (Boston University Press, 1970), editor Norman R. Bennett; *The Diary of A. J. Mounteney Jephson* (Cambridge University Press/ The Hakluyt Society, 1969), editor Dorothy Middleton; *The Unpublished Letters of H. M. Stanley* (Chambers, London, 1957), editor Albert Maurice; *The Exploration Diaries of H. M. Stanley* (Kimber, London, 1961) editors Richard Stanley and Alan Neame; and the following: Neil Ascherson, *The King Incorporated* (Allen and Unwin, London, 1963); Barbara Emerson, *Leopold II of the Belgians* (St. Martin's, New York, 1979); Brian Inglis, *Roger Casement* (Hodder and Stoughton, London, 1973); Tim Jeal, *Livingstone* (Heinemann, London, 1973); Dana L. Thomas, *The Media Moguls* (Putnam, New York, 1981); Richard West, *Brazza of the Congo* (Cape, London, 1972)

And then there are those local historians whose articles and monographs so often contain information that adds depth and detail which might otherwise go unnoticed. Professional biographers invariably owe a debt to such little-recognized researchers, and in this respect I would like to acknowledge my debt to Ivor and Lucy Jones, Bob Owen, and W. Wynne-Woodhouse of North Wales, Mary Willis Shuey and John S. Kendall of the American South, and Douglas L. Wheeler, historian of the American West.

# Chapter Notes

PAGE

## CHAPTER 1

3 "The best evidence," Stanley AUT, preface.

"Those to whom," *ibid.*, p. xv.

"I make enemies," Stanley to Harry Johnston, Feb. 15, 1885, SFA.

4 "He hardly looked at me," Bunsen, *The World I Used to Know,* p. 149.

"Oh, I want to be free," AUT, p. 515.

5 "One of the first things," AUT, p. 6.

"A stout old gentleman," *ibid.*, p. 7.

6 "The way seemed interminable," *ibid.*, p. 10.

"It took me some time," *ibid.*, p. 12.

7 "The king of the school," *ibid.*, p. 22.

8 "Learnt the tricks of the trade," quoted in Wynne-Woodhouse, *Hel Achau* 15.

"Indecent liberties," *ibid.*

"Very broken English," Report of the Commission on Education in Wales, 1849, PRO.

"A respectable mechanic," *Western Mail,* March 11, 1889.

9 "My superior in strength," AUT, p. 31.

"Whenever he received," *Western Mail,* March 11, 1889.

"Particularly fond of geography," *ibid.*

10 "Francis came up to me," AUT, p. 29.

" 'Never again' I shouted," *ibid.*, p. 33.

11 "I have forgotten a million things," *ibid.*, p. 40.

12 "At meal-times," *ibid.*, p. 48.

"He did not stoop," *ibid.*, p. 50.

13 "His heart was altogether," *ibid.*, p. 59.

"The finances of the family," *ibid.*, p. 63.

"How would you like to sail?" *ibid.*, p. 67.

15 "But there rose up," *ibid.*, p. 68.

"Now then, come out of that," *ibid.*, p. 69.

"Just as Francis," *ibid.*, p. 73.

## Notes

Regarding AUT, to Stanley's own reticences, evasions and misrepresentations must be added those of his widow, Dorothy, who edited the unfinished manuscript and completed it with excerpts from his notebooks before allowing it out for publication. Like Sir Richard Burton's widow, who burned her husband's erotic writings on his death, Dorothy Stanley rigorously suppressed important but "discreditable" clues to her husband's personality. In this and subsequent chapters, therefore, AUT, like many autobiographies, is not an invariably reliable source. Hall's researches first cleared up many of the mysteries and uncertainties concerning the circumstances of Stanley's birth, down to its exact date. The work "H. M. Stanley and Wales," written by Lucy M. and Ivor Wynne-Jones and published locally to mark the centenary of Stanley's discovery of Livingstone, contains much valuable material on Stanley's origins and childhood. Most of the comments on sexual depravity at St. Asaph's which are quoted by Wynne-Woodhouse were deleted from the published *Report of the Commission on Education in Wales*, 1849. The accounts of the "respectable mechanic" and "Mrs. Jones" were contained in a lengthy letter, signed "T.L.L.W., St. Asaph," to the editor of the *Western Mail*, a Welsh national newspaper published in Cardiff. The St. Asaph Workhouse records may be examined at the Hawarden Record Office.

## CHAPTER 2

17 "The tumultuous sensation," AUT, p. 81.

18 "Presently there bounced in," *ibid.*, p. 84.

19 "He was so modest," *ibid.*, p. 107.

"She was never seen," *ibid.*, p. 111.

20 "They had a swing," *ibid.*

21 "Within a few weeks," *ibid.*, p. 94.

22 "A fragile little lady," *ibid.*, p. 99.

23 "Near midnight," *ibid.*, p. 112.

24 "In my earliest dreams," *ibid.*, p. 119.

"With such a man," *ibid.*, p. 127.

25 "At some place below," *ibid.*

"Month after month of absolute silence," *ibid.*, p. 161.

27 "He was very kind," Kendall, *Louisiana Historical Quarterly*, p. 819.

"Suddenly, of heart disease," New Orleans *Daily Picayune*, Nov. 3, 1878.

28 "A soft heart but a hard head," Shuey, *Southwest Review*, p. 201.

29 "A lady of undoubted veracity," New Orleans *Daily States*, April 16, 1891.

### Notes

The local historians, John S. Kendall, of New Orleans (*Louisiana Historical Quarterly*, July 1937), and Mary Willis Shuey, of Dallas (*Southwest Review*, July 1940), must be given credit for establishing, independently of each other, the identity and background of Stanley's shadowy "adoptive father" in their papers, entitled respectively "Old New Orleans Homes and Some of the People Who Lived in Them," and "Stanley in New Orleans." Kendall and Shuey both exposed the falsehood of Henry Hope Stanley's supposed death in 1861. However, in a later paper, "Young Stanley: Arkansas Episode" (*Southwest Review*, July 1942), Shuey revealed that, unlike Kendall, she had been taken in by the story of Mrs. Stanley's death in 1859. Research carried out on the present author's behalf in New Orleans has brought to light further detail, such as the clinching evidence provided by estate records of Mrs. Stanley's death in 1878, and documents showing that her husband purchased their house on the corner of Annunciation Square, at 904 Orange Street, from William M. Goodrich, an Episcopalian minister, in 1858. Although it is clear that the explorer-to-be never lived in it, that house was subsequently designated "the boyhood home of Sir Henry Morton Stanley" by the Orleans Parish Landmarks Commission. Henry Hope Stanley's other house, Stanley Hall, at Arcola, was destroyed by fire in 1929. Interestingly, Henry Hope Stanley spent the Civil War years in England, having gone back at the outbreak of a conflict in which, as a British citizen, he appears to have felt he had no stake. He returned to New Orleans at the end of the war to resume his business and, according to Kendall, "fortune was as friendly to him now as she had been before."

Clippings from all three New Orleans daily newspapers—the *Daily States,* the *Times-Democrat* and the *Picayune*—in March and April 1891, reveal local resentment that on returning to the scenes of his youth Stanley avoided old friends and acquaintances. A contributor to the *Picayune* reeled off the names of men still living in the city who had supposedly been friends of Stanley's and challenged them: "What say you . . . can you meet and in a body give greeting to the companion of your youth upon his return to his old home?" However, no such meeting took place. The "lady of undoubted veracity" interviewed in the *Daily States* was obviously resentful at Stanley's refusal to see her when she called on him at the St. Charles Hotel. But even allowing for her resentment, and taking into account her insistence on remaining anonymous, it is hard to imagine that she could have invented Stanley's mendacious account, given to her in New York, of how he had acquired his new name. If she had wanted to discredit him she could surely have dreamed up something far more damning. "I know no reason why he should refuse to see me," she said. "I wanted nothing and had nothing to say against him, but perhaps he was ashamed of old acquaintances of thirty years ago. . . . When he left New Orleans he did so suddenly that no one knew when or where he had gone, and no one knew of any reason why he had left."

## CHAPTER 3

30 "Afflicted young and old," AUT, p. 155.

"Several of the richer men," *ibid.,* p. 154.

31 "The poor American settler," *ibid.,* p. 156.

"His father owned," *ibid.,* p. 163.

"had a secret scorn," *ibid.,* p. 213.

32 "I hastily hid it," *ibid.,* p. 165.

34 "How the cannon bellowed," *ibid.,* p. 192.

"I cannot forget," *ibid.,* p. 195.

35 "Now, Mr. Stanley," *ibid.,* p. 199.

"Within a week," *ibid.,* p. 209.

36 "My condition at this time," *ibid.,* p. 214.

37 "With what pride," *ibid.,* p. 219.

"Wrecked off Barcelona," *ibid.,* p. 220.

38 "Boarding with Judge X," *ibid.,* p. 220.

"He was full of aspirations," SDNYH, p. 406.

39 "Infested with Indians," *ibid.,* p. 431.

49 "He told me of diamonds," *ibid.,* p. 408.

"Scourged me with a whip," *ibid.,* p. 410.

41 "The first night," *ibid.,* p. 413.

"Mr. Cook and myself," Journal, Sept. 18, 1866, SFA.

"If ever the condition of men," SDNYH, p. 435.

### Notes

Much detail confirming Stanley's account of his time in Cypress Bend and the circumstances of his enlistment in the Dixie Greys is to be found in Shuey's "Young Stanley: Arkansas Episode." In dealing, in AUT, with the ill-fated expedition to Turkey, Stanley's widow refers to Noe only once, and then not by name: he is merely "the American lad whom they had brought with them as an attendant," and there is no reference to the controversy in which Noe was a leading figure after Stanley's discovery of Livingstone. Details about that controversy and other valuable information relating to this period in Stanley's life are contained in appendices to SDNYH. It was Hall's researches that nailed Stanley's lie about the supposed shipwreck of the *Jehu*.

### CHAPTER 4

43   "John Rowlands, formerly of this parish," Cadwalader Rowlands, *H. M. Stanley*, pp. 70–71.

"Gratefully, and, . . . gracefully," *ibid.*, p. 72.

"Make a man of you," *Western Mail*, March 11, 1889.

45   "Having made up my mind," SDNYH, p. 424.

"The American Traveller," *ibid.*, pp. 420–21.

46   "Four deadheads and four who paid," W. A. Kelsoe, St. Louis Reference Record, quoted in Hall, *Stanley*, p. 151.

"Not without benefit," MET, vol. 1, p. vi.

47   "The Indian War has at last," Wheeler, "H. M. Stanley's Letters," *Bulletin of the Missouri Historical Society*, April 1961, p. 272.

"If the present," *ibid.*

48   "Coarse black hair," MET, vol. 1, p. 42.

"Extermination is a long word," *ibid.*, p. 134.

"A thoroughly sensible" outfit, *The Westerners' Brand Book*, quoted in Hall, *Stanley*, p. 152.

49   "These women are expensive," MET, vol. 1, p. 166.

"He stands six feet one," *ibid.*, p. 6.

"If we have been mistaken," Wheeler, "Stanley's Letters," p. 277.

50   "Wronged children of the soil," *ibid.*, p. 280.

Satanta "beside himself with joy," *Kansas Historical Quarterly*, Autumn 1967, p. 258.

51   "I love the land," MET, vol. 1, p. 248.

"Were these people," *Kansas Historical Quarterly*, p. 278.

52   "A kind of apprenticeship," MET, vol. 1, p. xii.

"I have had occasion," Rowlands, *H. M. Stanley*, pp. 155–56.

### Notes

Stanley's visit to Denbigh and St. Asaph's—not mentioned in his autobiography and expunged from his diaries—was reported in the Denbigh *Free Press* and authenticated by Cadwalader Rowlands, whose book contains a reproduction of Stanley's entry in the Denbigh Castle visitors' book. Stanley's promotional flyer for his abortive lecture series was shown by Noe to his New York *Sun* interviewer. He had apparently been sent it by Stanley, who remained in correspondence with him until January 1869. Stanley's later doctoring of his dispatches to the *Democrat*, for publication in MET, is revealed by a comparison of that work with the compilations by Wheeler and an unnamed compiler/editor for the Kansas Historical Society. Details of Stanley's employment by the *Democrat* are in Jim A. Hart, *History of the St. Louis Globe-Democrat*. Details of Hancock's mission are in Oliver Knight, *Following the Indian Wars*.

## CHAPTER 5

53  "Practiced a rigid economy," AUT, p. 223.

The Herald "compelled support," Seitz, *The James Gordon Bennetts,* foreword.

54  "The sons of bitches," Thomas, *Media Moguls,* p. 18.

"I wish I could offer you," AUT, p. 228.

56  "Feelings of no great love," C and M, p. 298.

57  "I say, old boy," *ibid.,* p. 268.

"Oh, Anglo-Indian officers," *ibid.,* p. 356.

"One young lordling," *ibid.,* p. 338.

58  "Indian patties, brain cutlets," *ibid.,* pp. 351–52.

"After being in the saddle," *ibid.,* p. 410.

59  "There are men at the top," *ibid.*

60  "Even in the act," *ibid.,* p. 416.

"The last sounds," *ibid.,* p. 425.

62  "Waving a bloody rag," Lucy, *Sixty Years in the Wilderness,* vol. 2, p. 175.

"Onward adown the pass," C and M, p. 499.

63  "I urged Sayed," *ibid.,* p. 502.

64  "I must keep a sharp lookout," Journal, June 28, 1868, SFA.

### Notes

Seitz provides invaluable information about Stanley's employer. Thomas relates how Bennett scandalized New York society by urinating in the fireplace. C and M contains a reworking of Stanley's dispatches to the *Herald* from Abyssinia; the published originals are on microfilm at the New York Public Library. For the best overall view of the Abyssinian campaign, see Alan Moorehead's *The Blue Nile.* Sir Henry Lucy, a British journalist who knew Stanley well in later life, was told of the "bloody rag" incident by a colleague.

## CHAPTER 6

65  "What a curious custom," AUT, p. 237.

66  "For six days," *ibid.,* p. 238.

"The more tasks," *ibid.,* p. 240.

"Had I been a leper," *ibid.,* p. 239.

67  "Honest, original and wise," King, *Scribner's Monthly,* p. 106.

"The uncouth young man," SDNYH, p. 438.

68  "The atmosphere stifled him," King, *Scribner's Monthly,* p. 112.

"The bill for our excursions," Balch, *Geographical Review,* p. 279.

"To my dear young friend," *ibid.,* p. 279.

"A wife! My wife!" AUT, p. 231.

69  "Her name was Virginia," *ibid.,* p. 233.

"Whatever misgivings," *ibid.,* p. 235.

70  "We exchanged regards," *ibid.,* p. 236.

"Dear Sir, I want a favour," Stanley to Hekekyan Bey, Sept. 14, 1868, British Library, Additional Manuscripts.

71  "When a well-to-do solicitor," Journal, March 3, 1869, SFA.

"This admiration begot," Jones and Jones, *Stanley and Wales,* pp. 21–23.

72 "Mother is in raptures," Journal, March 9, 1869, SFA.

73 "Personal instances of ferocity," AUT, p. 242.

"The slightest inattention," *ibid.*, p. 243.

74 "Down came my pictures," HIFL, p. xv.

75 "Describe whatever is interesting," *ibid.*, p. xviii.

77 The "distinct impression," Seitz, *op. cit.*, p. 303.

78 "The free and easy habit," New Orleans *Times-Democrat*, July 21, 1890.

### Notes

Re Stanley's middle name, it is interesting that, as early as 1865, Stanley suggested to Noe that he use the name "Morton" in signing on for the Eighth New York Mounted Volunteers after the two had deserted from the navy. Documents pertaining to Stanley's engagement to Katie Gough-Roberts are in Royal Geographical Society archives in London. His letters to her were destroyed after his death in 1904 by his widow, who acquired them from Katie. But Katie had made a copy of the autobiographical letter, quoted above, which surfaced in Jones and Jones.

### CHAPTER 7

81 "The sky is one of cerulean tint," Journal, Jan. 6, 1871, SFA.

"The Baghdad . . . of East Africa," HIFL, p. 5.

82 "Learn the necessity," *ibid.*, p. 9.

83 "I was too far," SDNYH, p. 4.

"Totally ignorant of the interior," HIFL, p. 21.

85 "A capital navigator," *ibid.*, p. 27.

86 "I heard anecdotes," *ibid.*, p. 14.

"A very difficult man," *ibid.*, p. 15.

88 "The dull and lazy dhows," *ibid.*, p. 41.

"Half a dozen times," SDNYH, p. 11.

89 "Had I not gone," Kirk to Foreign Office, Feb. 18, 1871, PRO.

"Does it not appear," SDNYH, pp. 34–35.

### Notes

As well as describing the tensions between Webb and Kirk, Bennett, in "Stanley and the American Consuls at Zanzibar" (*Essex Institute Historical Collections*, 100, 1964) and "American in Zanzibar: 1865–1916" (*Tanganyika Notes and Records*, March 1963) gives much valuable detail about life in Zanzibar during the 1860s and 70s.

### CHAPTER 8

94 "He knows how to come round," Kirk, *Zambezi Journal*, March 14–17, 1859.

95 "The strangest disease," *Last Journals of Livingstone* vol. 1, p. 93.

"It is the old, old way," quoted in Moorehead, *The White Nile*, p. 100.

97 "We left Bagomoyo," SDNYH, p. 14.

"First the white man," *ibid.*, p. 17.

98 "As we do geese and turkeys," HIFL, p. 147.

"I would advise you," *ibid.*, p. 161.

"There is one of us," *ibid.*, p. 292.

98 "Its powerful verses," AUT, p. 253.

99 "The villages are very pretty," *Last Journals,* vol. 2, p. 104.

"The men here deny," *ibid.,* p. 117.

100 "A comfortable place," HIFL, p. 262.

101 "Wherever he is," SDNYH, p. 23.

"I am distressed," *Last Journals,* vol. 2, p. 132.

102 "Before I had got," *ibid.,* p. 133.

103 "On the first day," SDNYH, p. 24.

104 "After this event," *ibid.,* p. 26.

105 "The people all ran away," *Last Journals,* vol. 2, p. 145.

"A large spear," *ibid.,* p. 146.

"From each hole," *ibid.,* p. 147.

106 L. "felt as if dying," *ibid.,* p. 153.

106–7 "Now, Mr. Shaw," HIFL, p. 315.

107 "A miserable, ten-dollar affair," *ibid.,* p. 321.

108 "A sickly yellow hue," SDNYH, p. 65.

"Came on in a sidelong way," HIFL, p. 344.

109 "See, it is broad enough," SDNYH, p. 76.

"Shereef was evidently a moral idiot," *Last Journals,* vol. 2, p. 155.

110 "Hurrah! This is Livingstone," HIFL, p. 385.

"So that I might have," SDNYH, p. 88.

111 "What would I not have given," HIFL, p. 411.

113 "It was the dignity," SDNYH, p. 51.

"I looked upon Livingstone," *ibid.,* p. 93.

114 "Up to this moment," AUT, p. 264.

"You didn't really say it," Grierson, *Donald Francis Tovey,* p. 2.

## Notes

SDNYH provides an invaluable service to students of African exploration in general and the personality of Henry Stanley in particular. The footnotes and appendices are especially useful. HIFL necessarily gives a far fuller and more detailed account of Stanley's first expedition than his hurriedly composed newspaper reports, but like his autobiography needs to be read with a certain amount of caution. As reproduced in HIFL, his supposed diary entries do not seem always to be spontaneous, and some have almost certainly been revised if only to enhance the narrative. Others play down or omit altogether his descriptions of the violent punishments he frequently inflicted on his men. In this regard, his dispatches to the *Herald* had already given rise to some disapproving comment. Still, we need not doubt the passages which draw attention to Stanley's unquestionable qualities of courage, resolve and decisiveness. As to Stanley's professed piety, it may be significant that his account of being drawn back to God and the Bible by the vastness of Africa was written long after the event and appears only in AUT.

## CHAPTER 9

115 "Too much engrossed," HIFL, vol. 2, p. 413.

"There we sat," LT, Aug. 17, 1872.

"The man's heart," SDNYH, p. 94.

116 "You have brought me new life," *ibid.*, p. 96.

"He is not an angel," HIFL, vol. 2, p. 430.

"His religion," *ibid.*, p. 434.

117 "I am very happy," Ward, *A Voice from the Congo*, p. 172.

118 "A son to a father," Livingstone to Rev. W. Thompson, Nov. 1872, LMS archives.

"Benevolently paternal," Journal, Nov. 16, 1871, SFA.

"Since I became the recipient," HIFL, vol. 2, p. 497.

119 "Beautiful, bewitching," *ibid.*, p. 584.

"No sun shone," *ibid.*, p. 586.

120 "Two of us gone," *ibid.*, p. 598.

121 "There was not a doubt of it," Journal, Feb. 14, 1872, SFA.

"Oh, France! Oh, Frenchmen!" HIFL, vol. 2, p. 606.

122 "He looks but forty-five," SDNYH, p. 123.

"The regret I feel," AUT, p. 279.

"Had you not better," Journal, March 13, 1872, SFA.

S. "took long looks," HIFL, vol. 2, p. 625.

123 "MARCH! Why do you stop," *ibid.*, p. 627.

## CHAPTER 10

124 "A few bottles of champagne," HIFL, vol. 2, p. 649.

"While I was travelling," *ibid.*, p. 650.

125 "We never doubted," LT, Nov. 12, 1872.

"Splendid success!," HIFL, vol. 2, p. 653.

"The wind out of our sails," *ibid.*, p. 654.

"His hair was quite grey," NYH, Sept. 2, 1872.

126 "I am not going to expose," HIFL, vol. 2, p. 675.

"Why did they not mention," *ibid.*, p. 661.

"The truth is," *ibid.*, p. 661.

"I do not grudge," *ibid.*, p. 678.

127 YOU ARE NOW AS FAMOUS, Journal, July 10, 1872, SFA.

"There is one point," RGS *Proceedings* 1871–72.

128 "I must endeavour," Journal, July 31, 1872, SFA.

"What a welcome!" *ibid.*, Aug. 1, 1872.

129 "First they would sneer," letter of Aug. 25, 1872, in Quentin Keynes Collection, London.

"Our best thanks," Rawlinson to Stanley, LT, Aug. 8, 1872.

131 "A person like myself," Journal, Aug 18, 1872, SFA.

"You caused the world to believe," HIFL, vol. 2, p. 683.

Victoria's "high appreciation," LT, Aug. 31, 1872.

132 "I almost laughed," AUT, p. 290.

"A determined, ugly little man," Weintraub, *Victoria*, p. 513.

"Let it be understood," LT, Nov. 12, 1872.

133 S. "basely slandered," SDNYH, p. 427.

134 "Proud to call my friend," *ibid.*, p. 434.

"Stanley's "profound astonishment," *ibid.*, p. 447.

135 A "curiously sore" subject, Lucy, *Sixty Years*, p. 182.

"A perfect porcupine," Augusta Fraser, *Livingstone and Newstead*, p. 202.

"He was always at his best," *ibid.*, p. 198.

136 "I have never seen eyes," *ibid.*, p. 194.

"Under all his roughness," *ibid.*, p. 196.

137 "There sprang into his bosom," Seitz, *op. cit.*, p. 299.

"Who was Stanley?" *ibid.*, p. 300.

"Bennett let Stanley know," *ibid.*, pp. 299–300.

138 "Intolerably dull," NYH, Dec. 4, 1872.

"When Bennett sent for me," Seitz, *op. cit.*, p. 299.

"Stanley's played out," New York *Sun*, Dec. 7, 1872.

"The discoverer of Livingstone," New York *Sunday Mercury*, Dec. 8, 1872.

"Next to himself," New Orleans *Times-Democrat*, July 21, 1890.

"His egotism was attractive," *ibid.*

139 S. could "see things as they are," Burton, "Supplementary Papers to the Mwata Cazembe," Huntington Library, San Marino, California.

"All the actions of my life," AUT, p. 489.

"It was owing to repeated attacks," *ibid.*, p. 526.

### Notes

Stanley's acerbic comments about Rawlinson, the "gentleman geographers" of the RGS, Dawson, and the British press, which appeared in the first edition of HIFL, were deleted from later editions. So were his criticisms of Kirk—indeed, in some later editions Kirk's name does not even appear in the index. Stanley's "biography letter" to Katie Gough-Roberts, and other letters from him to her, were purchased from Mrs. Bradshaw by Stanley's widow and destroyed. But a copy of the biography letter survived and was reproduced in Jones and Jones. The recollections of Stanley's anonymous colleague were published in the *Times-Democrat* at the time of Stanley's lecture visit to New Orleans. Burton's comments on HIFL are in the Huntington Library's comprehensive collection of Burton documents, acquired in 1986 from London's Royal Anthropological Institute.

### CHAPTER 11

141 "When a man returns," AUT, p. 535.

143 A "stately little gentleman," C and M, p. 22.

"Self assured and cool," Harris, *My Life and Loves*, p. 227.

144 "Swayed by fears," C and M, p. 181.

"The firing," *ibid.*, p. 199.

"The utmost danger," Harris, *op. cit.*, p. 228.

"As cool and self-possessed," Wolseley, *Story of a Soldier's Life*, vol. 2, p. 342.

145 "Not by any means," C and M, p. 165.

"Many little things," *ibid.*, p. 167.

"The streets were numerous," *ibid.*, p. 230.

"Foul smells so suffocating," *ibid.*, p. 231.

146   "Dear Livingstone!" AUT, p. 295.

"I have a spur," *ibid.*, p. 297.

147   "Each man has his own way," *ibid.*, p. 295.

"I was stricken dumb," Stanley to Agnes Livingstone, March 18, 1874, NLS.

### Notes

Stanley, with an ever-keen eye for a best seller, gathered together his dispatches from West Africa and resurrected those from his coverage of the Abyssinian campaign to make the two-part volume *Coomassie and Magdala: the Story of Two British Campaigns in Africa.* In the preface he noted that "the story of Magdala was written five years ago. The reader will perceive it to be in a fresher style than the story of Coomassie. . . . The story of Coomassie is dull compared to that of Magdala; but it is more heroic. . . ."

### CHAPTER 12

151   "Could you, and would you," TDC, vol. 1, p. 2.

"Springing from his chair," Arnold, *Giants in Dressing Gowns*, p. 74.

152   "Good looking, stout," Journal, May 13, 1874, SFA.

153   "I fear that . . . I shall fall in Love," *ibid.*, May 17.

"She has sworn," *ibid.*, June 13.

154   "Two years is such a long time," *ibid.*, July 11.

"We solemnly pledge ourselves," document dated July 12, 1874, SFA.

"She raised her lips," Journal, July 17, 1874, SFA.

"She repeated her vows," *ibid.*, July 18.

156   "Her lovely white arms," ABM.

"This young girl," *ibid.*

"Alice's lips parted," *ibid.*

"Why had she been so stupid?" *ibid.*

### Notes

The typescript of Alice Pike Barney's memoirs was bequeathed to the National Museum of American Art in Washington by her amanuensis, William Huntington, who died in 1986, aged seventy-nine. The manuscript (ABM) was found there in 1988 by the present author. Huntington was a nineteen-year-old student when he went to work for Mrs. Barney, at the time a prominent Washington socialite and amateur painter of considerable private fortune. On her death in 1931, she left her home and its contents (Studio House, Sheridan Circle, Washington, D.C.) with an endowment for its upkeep to the National Museum of American Art, a branch of the Smithsonian Institution. But her manuscript remained in the possession of Huntington with instructions that it should remain unpublished as long as her two daughters lived, presumably because of its unflattering portrayal of her husband. Her younger daughter, Laura Dreyfus-Barney, lived on in Paris until the age of ninety-four, a flamboyantly colorful lesbian who was the subject of a 1976 biography (Jean Chalon, *Portrait of a Seductress: The World of Natalie Barney*). Alice's biographer, Jean Kling, told the present author that Mrs. Barney dictated her memoirs to Huntington, often waking him in the middle of the night when inspiration seized her. Huntington was one of a string of young men, mostly homosexuals, whom Mrs. Barney employed as secretary/amanuenses. In 1911—by then long since divorced from Barney—she married one of these. He deserted her five years later to run away with another man. As Alice grew older she became obsessed with the idea that she should have married Stanley, and she kept a photograph of him at her bedside. Jilting Stanley was "the biggest mistake of my life," she told her last secretary. The inscribed copy of HIFL which

Stanley gave her before leaving for his trans-Africa expedition is now in the Rare Books Department of the Library of Congress.

## CHAPTER 13

158 "This is rather an unkind," Journal, July 8, 1874, SFA.

159 "Over 1200 letters," TDC, vol. 1, p. 6.

160 "Capable of great love," *ibid.*, p. 47.

161 Stanley's "paramount idea," SDNYH, p. 154.

"In this manner," TDC, vol. 1, p. 84.

"The ranks become broken," *ibid.*, p. 84.

162 "A sharp throb of regret," SDNYH, p. 188.

"Unprecedentedly successful," *ibid.*, p. 188.

"The heat was intense," ED, p. 31.

"Added to the torments," *ibid.*, p. 31.

"Both nature and man," SDNYH, p. 193.

"Out of the ordinary," *ibid.*, p. 193.

163 "A more cheerless Christmas," ED, p. 35.

"Your kind woman's heart," Stanley to Pike, Dec. 25, 1874, SFA.

"I do love dancing," Pike to Stanley, *ibid.*, Dec. 2, 1874.

"Clapped in chains and flogged," ED, p. 37.

164 "It sickens me," TDC, vol. 1, p. 108.

"How inexpressibly satisfied," *ibid.*, p. 111.

"Their manly beauty," SDNYH, p. 196.

165 "More auspicious lands," *ibid.*, p. 197.

"His tongue thickly coated," TDC, vol. 1, p. 114.

"A shriek of sorrow," *ibid.*, p. 116.

166 "Ye are women," *ibid.*, p. 126.

"In a mood to pray," *ibid.*, p. 127.

167 "Long before noon," SDNYH, p. 202.

"I am happy to say," *ibid.*, p. 202.

"No sooner," ED, p. 53.

"Many a stout fellow," *ibid.*, p. 53.

"Such rapid thinning," *ibid.*, p. 54.

168 "Fifty-one were for hanging," *ibid.*, p. 55.

"We conveyed the body," TDC, vol. 1, p. 135.

"A sudden hurrahing," *ibid.*, p. 142.

169 "Sing, O friends," *ibid.*, p. 142.

## Notes

Stanley's exploration diaries, which are one of the sources drawn upon for this and succeeding chapters dealing with his second expedition, remained undiscovered until 1960, when his grandson Richard Stanley found them in a box file at the explorer's last home, Furzehill, Pirbright, Surrey. These important documents—in a meticulously neat hand and perfectly preserved, despite the frequently appalling conditions in which they were written—were edited with the assistance of Alan Neame and published in 1961. As Neame says in his introduction, the diaries convey "a tireless persistence more than any other personal quality." And, written as they were for Stanley's own reference rather than for publication, they may be taken as truthful. Still, the diary entries are generally too brief and cryptic to provide sufficient information and color for a full description of Stanley's epic coast-to-coast journey. Hence the frequent references to TDC and SDNYH, which put flesh on the day-to-day skeleton. There are some discrepancies between ED on the one hand and TDC and SDNYH on the other. None of these involve major falsification, but where there are interesting divergences these will be pointed out.

## CHAPTER 14

170 "As I look," SDNYH, p. 206.

"The very hour," Stanley to Pike, March 4, 1875, SFA.

"For she realized," ABM.

"She did not read them," *ibid.*

171 "People with . . . tails," TDC, vol. 1, p. 153.

"Where are the brave fellows?" AUT, p. 306.

"Wild beyond description," TDC, vol. 1, p. 157.

174 "The man fell dead," SDNYH, p. 217.

"Fired over their heads," TDC, vol. 1, p. 180.

"Amid a concourse," SDNYH, p. 219.

175 "Issuing out," *ibid.*, p. 219.

"Tall and slender," *ibid.*, p. 219.

"A murderous despot," Kaggwa, *Kings of Buganda*, p. 162.

"I have seen in Mutesa," ED, p. 70.

"The outward sweep," Speke, *Journal of Discovery*, p. 286.

176 "A look of glee," *ibid.*, p. 290.

"Nearly every day," *ibid.*, p. 337.

"The capital was nicknamed," Kaggwa, *op. cit.*, p. 162.

"He allowed the Arabs," *ibid.*, p. 158.

"False and contemptible," ED, p. 71.

"By one conversation," SDNYH, p. 226.

177 "Here, gentlemen," *ibid.*, p. 227.

178 "Each one of us," de Bellefonds' Journal, April 13, 1875, SFA.

"Extremely well informed," SDNYH, p. 223.

179 "No sooner," *ibid.*, p. 244.

"With one desperate effort," *ibid.*, p. 246.

This "extraordinary result," *ibid.*, p. 247.

"Four shots killed," *ibid.*, p. 247.

180 "Resigned ourselves," *ibid.*, p. 248.

"A rare young man," *ibid.*, p. 229.

181 "The hated island," ED, p. 193.

"After approaching," SDNYH, p. 259.

181 "Work of punishment," *ibid.*, p. 260.

"But I refused," *ibid.*, p. 260.

182 "This outrage," *Saturday Review*, Aug. 23, 1876.

He "still shoots negroes," quoted in Coupland, *Exploitation of East Africa*, p. 327.

"And there in the presence," *ibid.*, p. 327.

"Howling dervishes," NYH, Nov. 7, 1876.

"Humane but impractical," *ibid.*, Sept. 17, 1877.

183 "Remembering the bitter injuries," SDNYH, p. 257.

"Several killed and wounded," TDC, vol. 1, p. 292.

"As God is my judge," Stanley to King, May 19, 1875, SDNYH p. 458.

Notes

Stanley's descriptions of his two battles at Bumbireh are here drawn mainly from SDNYH rather than ED and TDC. This is because the dispatches are fuller and more detailed than the briefer accounts in ED, and lack the self-exculpatory afterthoughts of TDC. The dispatches agree in most essentials with the diary entries, but where they are at variance this is made clear in the text.

CHAPTER 15

185 "The sound of sonorous drums," ED, p. 96.

"Received with joy," *ibid.*, p. 99.

"They fight desperately," *ibid.*, p. 98.

"Mutesa is like a child," *ibid.*, p. 103.

186 "The great war drum," *ibid.*, p. 109.

"No, no, you are liars," *ibid.*, p. 110.

187 "Remaining here . . . is certain death," *ibid.*, p. 112.

A "great folly," SDNYH, p. 269.

Mirambo "so different," ED, p. 118.

"I daily fed," Stanley to Pike, June 2, 1876, SFA.

188 "The question of the Lualaba," Stanley to Edward Levy, Aug. 13, 1876, SDNYH, p. 465.

189 "Not received one encouraging word," Stanley to Pike, Aug. 14, 1876, SFA.

S's faith "utterly destroyed," TDC, vol. 2, p. 64.

190 "Unless the traveller," *ibid.*, p. 66.

"The surviving children," ED, p. 123.

"The slave trade elsewhere," SDNYH, p. 318.

191 "Invite their friends," *ibid.*, p. 321.

192 "The redoubted . . . Tippu-Tib," ED, p. 132.

"He was . . . straight and quick," TDC, vol. 2, p. 95.

193 "Slaves cost nothing," ED, p. 134.

194 "If I merely struck," SDNYH, p. 332.

"Was it right?" *ibid.*, p. 348.

"I can die," Stanley to King, Nov. 1, 1876, SFA.

195 "A fearful time of it," ED, p. 134.

Path was "so slippery," TDC, vol. 2, p. 133.

Tippu-Tib "seemed bent," ED, p. 137.

"I never was in . . . such a place," TDC, vol. 2. pp. 139–40.

196 "This great river," ibid., p. 190.

### Notes

Stanley's account of tossing a coin with Pocock to decide whether they should head north or turn south may have been a piece of journalistic invention. The incident is not mentioned in his diary, although it appears in SDNYH and, in a greatly embellished form, in TDC, and became part of the Stanley legend. In TDC the coin is tossed six times, not three, and when it consistently comes down tails they draw straws, always with the same result until Stanley says: "It is of no use, Frank. We will face our destiny, despite the rupee and the straws."

### CHAPTER 16

197 "One of them threw a spear," ED, p. 139.

"Everybody in a panic," TDC, vol. 2, pp. 157–58.

198 "Sons of Zanzibar," ibid., p. 198.

"One protracted torture," ED, p. 146.

"A region of fable," SDNYH, p. 360.

199 "Gentle and quiet behaviour," ED, p. 147.

"Terribly trying day," ibid., p. 152.

200 "A Fall 50 yards in width," ibid., p. 152.

"The cheers we gave," TDC, vol. 2, p. 234.

201 "A sight that sends the blood tingling," ibid., p. 270.

202 "Our blood is up," ibid., p. 272.

"Proved the people," ibid., p. 273.

"The human and 'soko' skulls," ibid., p. 274.

"A foolhardy feat," ED, p. 159.

"Twenty-six fights," ibid., p. 160.

203 "With great loss," ibid., p. 163.

"We glide down," ibid., p. 163.

"Suddenly I heard," ibid., p. 164.

"The fight of fights," ibid., p. 164.

204 "Without any cause," ibid., p. 169.

"Horrible and slow," ibid., p. 173.

205 "My heart aches," ibid., p. 177.

"Borne on the crests," ibid., p. 180.

206 "Gunpowder was abundant," TDC, vol. 2, p. 358.

"On suddenly arriving," ibid., p. 360.

207 "His many inestimable qualities," ED, p. 192.

"Benumbing their faculties," TDC, vol. 2, p. 405.

208 "That white medicine paper," ED, p. 193.

208 "A sheet of paper," *ibid.*, p. 193.

"They would prefer," *ibid.*, p. 193.

"The [Zanzibaris] try me," *ibid.*, p. 194.

"Crossed over," *ibid.*, p. 195.

209 "They have no money," *ibid.*, p. 197.

"Attacked and destroyed," *ibid.*, p. 199.

"After embracing me," *ibid.*, p. 201.

210 "A miserable little village," *ibid.*, p. 202.

"Dear Sir," TDC, vol. 2, pp. 447–48.

"Sundry small things," ED, p. 203.

211 "Ye Gods! Just think," SDNYH, p. 340.

"Not to exact too much," SDNYH, p. 342.

"A state of torpid brooding," TDC.

"I feel his loss," Stanley to Henry Pocock, Sept. 2, 1877, SDNYH, p. 355.

213 "Very lonely and depressed," Marston, *After Work*, p. 226.

"Dear Morton," Barney to Stanley, Nov. 17, 1877, SFA.

214 "She had made it possible," ABM.

## Notes

A comparison of ED with TDC shows that Stanley's later descriptions of events, while far more detailed, generally correspond faithfully enough with his diary entries. Where TDC departs from ED, Stanley is usually embellishing for dramatic effect rather than falsifying. For example, in his TDC version of the "medicine paper" incident involving the Mowa, Stanley says that he burned a volume of Shakespeare similar in size and color to his notebook, instead of a mere sheet of paper on which he had scribbled. Also, he dates this incident before Pocock's death, although it is clear from ED that it occurred afterward. In TDC Stanley occasionally cites what purport to be verbatim entries from his diary. In most cases, the original entries have, in fact, been added to and embellished—though, again, not falsified. Similarly, while TDC does not exaggerate the number of battles fought on Stanley's way downriver, it may well exaggerate the odds encountered. Had the expedition been as heavily outnumbered as often as TDC suggests, its casualties would surely have been greater. Still, W. Holman Bentley, a Baptist missionary who interrogated members of Stanley's expedition some years later, found that their recollections of the journey tallied with Stanley's. He also defended Stanley against the usual allegations of having been needlessly aggressive.

## CHAPTER 17

217 *Il faut à la Belgique*, quoted in Ascherson, *The King Incorporated*, p. 47.

"Something doing in Africa," Emerson, *Leopold II*, p. 72.

"Leopold is subtle," Daye, *Leopold II*, p. 30.

"Artful and deceitful," Emerson, *op. cit.*, p. 35.

219 "In no way motivated," *ibid.*, p. 77.

"A fine chance," Leopold to Solvyns, Nov. 17, 1877, APR.

"The great traveller," *ibid.*

220 "So sick and weary," TCFFS, vol. 1, p. 21

221 "I had hoped," Hird, *H. M. Stanley*, p. 171.

"All that Mr. Farler has stated," Kirk to Lord Derby, May 1, 1878, PRO.

223 "Anyone who knows," Bentley, *Pioneering on the Congo,* vol. 1, p. 64.

"More and more unfit," TCFFS, vol. 1, p. 23.

"A purely exploratory mission," Leopold to Solvyns, Nov. 17, 1877, Emerson, *op. cit.,* p. 85.

224 "Various persons of more or less note," TCFFS, vol. 1, p. 26.

"It has been pretty evident," Hird, *op. cit.,* p. 177.

"Care must be taken," Leopold to Strauch, Jan. 8, 1884, UL, pp. 20–21.

"Belgium doesn't need a colony," Daye, *op. cit.,* p. 203.

225 "It is clearly understood," Strauch to Stanley, date uncertain, UL, pp. 22–23.

226 "It would be madness," Stanley to Strauch, July 8, 1879, TCFFS, vol. 1, p. 54.

### Notes

In 1953 the Belgian historian Albert Maurice went to London to authenticate and purchase from a dealer a packet of recently discovered letters from Stanley to Colonel Strauch and others concerned with his expedition to the Congo on behalf of King Leopold. The letters—four hundred faded sheets, some of them written in an obviously fevered hand—were undoubtedly authentic. They shed interesting new light not only on the personality of Stanley but also on the mission he undertook for Leopold's shady Comité d'Études du Haut Congo, and are now in the possession of the Museé Royal de l'Afrique Centrale. Much of the history of the so-called Congo Free State and its founding remains murky thanks to Leopold's wholesale destruction of documents when, as a consequence of the international hue and cry over conditions there, he was forced to cede control of the colony to the Belgian government in 1908. As Leopold's hatchet man Strauch said: "The voices which, in default of the destroyed archives, might speak in their stead have systematically been condemned to silence for considerations of a higher order." But not all of the incriminating documents were burned. They and Stanley's unpublished letters tell us enough to confirm that Stanley was—it seems unwittingly—a key player in what turned out to be perhaps the greatest criminal enterprise of the colonial era.

### CHAPTER 18

227 "The interest of the enterprise," Strauch to Stanley, Dec. 30, 1879, UL, p. 32.

"I am not a party," Stanley to Strauch, Feb. 6, 1880, *ibid.,* p. 34.

228 "The gentleman is tall," TCFFS, vol. 1, p. 232.

"It will take you six months," *ibid.,* p. 234.

229 "Mr. Stanley has taken," UL, p. 44.

"Pressed down by a crate," Stanley to Strauch, June 12, 1881, *ibid.,* p. 47.

"Again and again, I strove," TCFFS, vol. 1, p. 275.

"Always something new," Stanley to Strauch, June 12, 1881, UL, p. 52.

230 "Accepted the reproaches," AUT, p. 348.

"Repulsive if inflicted," Stanley to Strauch, June 12, 1881, UL, p. 49.

"Be kind to your blacks," Stanley to Popelin, May 16, 1879, TCFFS, vol. 1, p. 46.

"In sheer despair," Stanley to Strauch, April 7, 1882, UL, p. 118.

231 "Good at business," Stanley to Strauch, March 25, 1882, *ibid.,* p. 109.

"Stupid to the highest degree," *ibid.,* p. 159.

"It is indispensable," Leopold to Stanley, Dec. 31, 1881, *ibid.,* p. 137.

"It is but fair," *ibid.,* p. 138.

"The mere rumour," Stanley to Leopold, April 14, 1882, *ibid.,* p. 136.

232 "You know the white brother," UL, p. 156.

"Covetous and grasping," TCFFS, vol. 1, p. 305.

"Ngalyema . . . has desired me," Stanley to Strauch, Jan. 6, 1882, UL, p. 98.

233 "Ngalyema was moody-browed," TCFFS, vol. 1, p. 335.

235 "Not only scientific," UL, p. 149.

"Take an interest in our enterprises," Leopold to Strauch, Sept. 10, 1882, *ibid.*

"Surely, Mr. Stanley," Hird, *H. M. Stanley*, p. 186.

236 "What can be done . . .?" UL, p. 151.

"Free of all political leanings," *ibid.*, p. 155.

"I never was in the habit," West, *Brazza of the Congo*, p. 121.

"I'm going to have the pleasure," *ibid.*, p. 122.

237 "An immoral diplomacy," UL, p. 155.

"Not an antagonist," *ibid.*

CHAPTER 19

238 "About 100 white men," UL, p. 160.

239 "There must at least," Leopold to Strauch, Oct. 16, 1882, *ibid.*, p. 161.

"Freely, of their own accord," TCFFS, vol. 2, p. 196.

"An imposing family!" UL, p. 164.

240 "An impulse that was almost overpowering," TCFFS, vol. 2, p. 143.

"Utter and supreme wretchedness," *ibid.*, p. 147.

"I hope you will stay on," Gordon to Stanley, Jan. 1, 1884, *ibid.*, pp. 226–27 n.

241 "I gather from [Gordon]," Stanley to Strauch, April 23, 1884, TCFFS, vol. 2, pp. 226–27.

242 "Only increase the disorder," Leopold to Strauch, April 23, 1884, UL, p. 166.

"Bold explorer as he is," Kirk to Leopold, March 21, 1883, APR.

"You will understand," Kirk to Devaux, May 1, 1883, *ibid.*

244 "Swindle . . . Fantasies," quoted in Ascherson, *op. cit.*, p. 132.

245 "As the two men strolled," Lucy, *op. cit.*, pp. 232–33.

CHAPTER 20

246 "For thriftlessness," TCFFS, p. xiv.

248 "I am absolutely uncomfortable," Stanley to Edward King, Aug. 1, 1884, SFA.

"More vital, smarter," Bunsen, *op. cit.*, p. 149.

"Standing in the background," *ibid.*, p. 152.

249 "One day soon after," Hoffmann, *With Stanley*, p. 1.

"With women, generally," Stanley to "The Unknown Madame or Mademoiselle," April 11, 1885, NLW.

"My timidity is unconquerable," Stanley to Bruce, undated, NLS.

250 "Tall and statuesque," Arnold, *Giants in Dressing Gowns*, p. 79.

251 "Oh God help me," entry cited in Hall, *op. cit.*, p. 280.

"I felt a friendship," *ibid.*, p. 280.

252 "I would let you be," *ibid.*

252 "Strange to say," Stanley to Bruce, July 18, 1885, NLS.

　　"I wish Alice," Hall, *op. cit.*, p. 281.

　　"Do you think," Stanley to Bruce, July 18, 1885, NLS.

　　"But alas," Stanley to Baroness von Donop, Nov. 19, 1885, WP.

253 "He wore a kind of . . . vest" Hall, *op. cit.*, p. 282.

　　"Bearing you and yours," *ibid.*, p. 283.

254 "In one of my," *ibid.*, p. 283.

256 "I have been living," Stanley to Mackinnon, Sept. 23, 1886, MP.

### Notes

Gertrude Tennant's real or imagined affair with Flaubert began after they met in Trouville and, according to a memoir she wrote after the novelist's death, she "loved him passionately, adoringly." They wrote to each other over the decades, and Flaubert sent her a signed copy of his masterpiece, *Madame Bovary*. Dorothy Tennant's work was exhibited at the Royal Academy in 1886 ("An Arab Dance"), 1887 ("In Trouble" and "A Socialist"), 1889 ("A Load of Care"), 1893 ("Henry Morton Stanley"), 1896 ("The Bather"), 1900 ("The Forsaken Nymph") and 1903 ("Leap Frog").

### CHAPTER 21

259 "Ever since the month of May, 1883," Emin to Allen, Dec. 31, 1885, IDA, vol. 1, p. 26.

260 "I am ready to stay," Emin to Mackay, July 6, 1886, *ibid.*, p. 28.

261 YOUR PLAN AND OFFER ACCEPTED, Mackinnon to Stanley, Dec. 11, 1886, *ibid.*, p. 34.

264 "Haute politique, you know," Hird, *op. cit.*, p. 222.

　　"The King was wonderfully benevolent," *ibid.*, p. 223.

265 "Nine beautiful chests," IDA, vol. 1, p. 38.

　　"A pleasant short letter," Mackinnon to Stanley, Jan. 4, 1887, IDA, vol. 1, p. 44.

266 "Difficulties in the way," Mackinnon to Stanley, Jan 7, 1887, *ibid.*, p. 44.

269 "Abundance of ammunition," Stanley to Emin, Feb. 23, 1887, *ibid.*, p. 63.

　　Stanley "an extraordinary man," Barttelot to Edith Sclater, March 14, 1887, Barttelot, W., *The Life of E. M. Barttelot*, p. 68.

270 "I fancy some of us," Barttelot to Sir Walter Barttelot, March 17, 1887, *ibid.*, p. 71.

　　"For a short time it appeared," IDA, vol. 1, p. 72.

　　"He is a most excitable man," SJ, April 15, 1887.

　　"Stanley said it was in his power," Barttelot, *op. cit.*, diary entry, April 8, 1887, p. 82.

　　"I have only you to thank," Jameson, *Story of the Rear Column*, diary entry March 31, 1887, p. 16.

272 "The work we are doing," *ibid.*, March 29, 1887, p. 14.

　　"Nothing that I have ever seen," SJ, April 13, 1887.

　　"Behind him, astride," Ward, *With Stanley's Rear Guard,* p. 12.

273 "Acres of bananas," SJ, April 23, 1887.

　　"A huge, unwieldy mistake," *ibid.*, May 31, 1887.

　　"Repent and believe," Arthington to Stanley, Jan. 15, 1887, IDA, vol. 1, p. 47.

　　"For trivial offences," *ibid.*, p. 97.

274 "All my chiefs fifty cuts," Jameson, *op. cit.*, diary entry April 18, 1887, p. 25.

"Occasioned a scene," Jephson, *Diary,* May 27, 1887, p. 99.

"The most disgraceful row," Jameson, *Story of the Rear Column,* diary entry May 20, 1887, p. 47.

"I have stood more swearing," SJ, May 27, 1887.

275 "Now, Major, my dear fellow," IDA, vol. 1, p. 128.

### Notes

For the first time, Stanley was accompanied on an expedition by a group of well-educated and articulate fellow whites, all of whom, except Bonny, kept diaries, and it is instructive to compare Stanley's account with theirs. But the journals and letters of Jameson and Barttelot, who did not survive the expedition, were edited by close relatives before being published in a controversy that arose after Stanley published his own version of events. Jameson's widow and Barttelot's brother might have tampered with certain passages in pursuit of their declared intention to vindicate the dead men's reputations. The versions published by Troup, Ward and Parke might also be considered self-serving in certain respects, but nothing of the kind can be imputed to either Jephson or Stairs, who made no attempt to publish. Jephson's diaries remained undiscovered until 1955 and were edited by an objective historian of high repute before being published. Stairs's journals languished unnoticed altogether until the present author unearthed them in 1989. While neither account bears directly on the controversy involving Barttelot and Jameson, both journals have the reassuring stamp of uncalculated spontaneity. For the sake of clarity, the present author has taken the liberty of correcting Jephson's and Stairs's occasionally erratic punctuation.

### CHAPTER 22

277 "Whether there are any roads," IDA, vol. 1, p. 124.

"Of all the scenes," Parke, *My Personal Experiences,* p. 115.

This "region of horrors," IDA, vol. 1, p. 138.

279 "The sensation was at first," SJ, Aug. 13, 1887.

"Seeing these poor chaps die," *ibid.*, Aug. 18, 1887.

"I can understand," IDA, vol. 1, p. 191.

"Very quiet and nice," Jephson, *Diary,* Aug. 20, 1887, p. 140.

"I am conscious," IDA, vol. 1, p. 191.

"The chiefs would not hear of it," Jephson, *Diary,* Sept. 4, 1887, p. 145.

280 "A large settlement," IDA, vol. 1, p. 207.

"Before the last struggles," *ibid.*, p. 213.

"Enough, children!" *ibid.*, p. 215.

281 "It was most interesting," SJ, Sept. 28, 1887.

282 "It was a terrible position," Jephson, *Diary,* Oct. 6, 1887, p. 159.

"About the lowest," SJ, Oct. 10, 1887.

"Some 50 natives," Jephson, *Diary,* Oct. 13, 1887, p. 164.

"A pack of hyenas," IDA, vol. 1, p. 231.

283 Stanley's "anxiety has been frightful," Jephson, *Diary,* Oct. 16, 1887, p. 166–67.

"I told him I did not think," SJ, Oct. 16, 1887.

"Despite entreaties," IDA, vol. 1, p. 243.

283 "It is perfectly scandalous," Jephson, *Diary*, Oct. 19, 1887, p. 169.
"Fowls, goats, porridge, beans," SJ, Oct. 19, 1887.

284 "Worn and haggard-looking," IDA, vol. 1, p. 248.
"A five-guinea rug," *ibid.*, p. 253.
"Strong in his expressions," Jephson, *Diary*, Nov. 2, 1887, p. 181.
"Probably Stanley will be angry," *ibid.*, Nov. 3, 1887, p. 183.
"Such abundance," IDA, vol. 1, p. 271.

285 "Books . . . would now be worth," SJ, Nov. 14, 1887.
"It is a glorious sight," Jephson, *Diary*, Nov. 30, 1887, p. 197.
"We felt as if," IDA, vol. 1, p. 292.
"He has taken our advice," SJ, Dec. 12, 1887.
"Until either," Jephson, *Diary*, Dec. 9, 1887, p. 201.

286 "No alternative," IDA, vol. 1, p. 315.
"Stanley had the people," Jephson, *Diary*, Dec. 10, 1887, p. 203.
"Began to get rather noisy," *ibid.*, Dec. 11, 1887, p. 204.
"Cheer after cheer," *ibid.*, Dec. 13, 1887, p. 206.
"Our worst piece of fighting," SJ, Dec. 13, 1887.
"Many, many years ago," IDA, vol. 1, p. 332.

287 "The inexplicable absence," *ibid.*, p. 335.
"All so tame," Jephson, *Diary*, Dec. 15, 1887, p. 213.
"With feelings of utter dejection," *ibid.*, Dec. 17, 1887, p. 215.

288 "Without a single flaw," IDA, vol. 1, p. 362.
"Required greater strength," *ibid.*, p. 360.
"Stanley tries to make," Jephson, *Diary*, Feb. 8, 1888, p. 225.
"Participate in the honour," IDA, vol. 1, p. 363.
"Very much incensed," SJ, Feb. 16, 1888.
"One of his ungovernable fits," Jephson, *Diary*, Feb. 26, 1888, p. 228.

289 "A few nights ago," *ibid.*, Feb. 26, 1888, p. 228.

290 "Had Emin . . . taken the trouble," IDA, vol. 1, p. 379.
"They told us quite readily," Jephson, *Diary*, April 15, 1888, p. 237.
"Be pleased," IDA, vol. 1, p. 390.
"Rations sufficient to subsist," *ibid.*, p. 391.
"We looked as if," Jephson, *Diary*, April 23, 1888, p. 246.

291 "Very foreign looking," *ibid.*, April 27, 1888, p. 249.
"I shook hands with all," IDA, vol. 1, p. 396.
"A small, spare figure," *ibid.*, p. 396.

## CHAPTER 23

292 "In no case abandon my people," Schweitzer, *Emin Pasha*, vol. 1, p. 263.

293 "The tears started," Jephson, *Diary*, April 27, 1888, p. 250.
"The Pasha's manner," IDA, vol. 1, p. 401.
"The women must walk," *ibid.*, p. 403.

294 "If the Governor Emin goes," *ibid.*, p. 406.

"These gifts . . . reveal," *ibid.*, p. 422.

295 "I have come expressly," *ibid.*, p. 427.

"A good deal interested," Parke, *op. cit.*, p. 220.

Stanley "laughed at me," Jephson, *Diary*, May 26, 1888, p. 256.

"Allow me to be," IDA, vol. 1, p. 432.

296 "Lieutenant Stairs was first," *ibid.*, p. 454.

"Taken almost all the quinine," SJ, April 28, 1888.

"Evil hangs over," IDA, vol. 1, p. 465.

"It is horrible to watch," Jameson, *op. cit.*, diary entry July 29, 1887, p. 95.

297 "I am afraid you will think," Barttelot to Mackinnon, March 27, 1888, Barttelot, *op. cit.*, p. 219.

"Stanley should never have left," Barttelot to Sclater, March 28, 1888, *ibid.*, p. 221.

"It is a disgusting life," Barttelot to Sir Walter Barttelot, March 18, 1888, *ibid.*, p. 209.

"Seventy-six of the very worst," Jameson, *op. cit.*, diary entry June 7, 1887, p. 77.

"Presently, down came a woman," *ibid.*, July 10, 1887, p. 84.

"We finished our last plantain," *ibid.*, July 21, 1887, p. 92.

298 "I had determined to begin," *ibid.*, July 10, 1887, p. 83.

"I shall be proud," Barttelot to Sir Walter Barttelot, June 1, 1888, Barttelot, *op. cit.*, p. 297.

"Somehow or another," Ward, *op. cit.*, p. 33.

299 "He had an intense hatred," Troup, *With Stanley's Rear Column*, p. 145.

"He must have been shot," Barttelot, *op. cit.*, April 26, 1888, p. 231.

"To deal with [the Arabs]," Barttelot to Sir Walter Barttelot, June 1, 1888, *ibid.*, pp. 298–99.

"Bland, courteous, and accommodating," Ward, *op. cit.*, p. 45.

301 "Opportunity was taken," Barttelot, *op. cit.*, March 25, 1888, p. 212.

"Poor Barttelot," Ward, *op. cit.*, p. 92.

"WARD, I am sending," *ibid.*, p. 96.

302 "More disclosures," Barttelot, *op. cit.*, March 30, 1888, p. 221.

"Looking terribly ill," Troup, *op. cit.*, p. 245.

"His continual cry," Barttelot to Sclater, (no date), Barttelot, *op. cit.*, p. 291.

"He would give us all the men," Jameson, *op. cit.*, diary entry April 12, 1888, p. 254.

303 "Enormous, far greater," *ibid.*, April 15, 1888, p. 258.

304 "I sent my boy," *ibid.*, May 11, 1888, p. 291.

306 "SIR—On arrival," Ward, *op. cit.*, p. 115.

"The unkindest act," *ibid.*, p. 116.

307 IF YOU CANNOT MARCH, IDA, vol. 1, p. 515.

"For abomination, desolation and vexation," Barttelot to Mrs. E. Sandham, June 7, 1888, *op. cit.*, p. 295.

"Our march altogether," Barttelot to Sir Walter Barttelot, July 5, 1888, *ibid.*, p. 341.

308 "Punished him severely," *ibid.*, p. 350.

"Shoot the first man," IDA, vol. 1, p. 518.

308 "Thought a general massacre," *ibid.*, p. 519.

309 "A straightforward, honest English gentleman," Jameson, *op. cit.*, letter, July 21, 1888, p. 338.

"The look he gave us," *ibid.*, Aug. 7, 1888, p. 362.

"Shot out of an open reach," *ibid.*, Aug. 12, 1888, p. 368.

310 "Rushed to the beach," Ward, *op. cit.*, p. 118.

## CHAPTER 24

311 "Pen cannot picture," IDA, vol. 1, p. 521.

"I cannot make out," Stanley to Jameson, Aug. 30, 1888, Jameson, *op. cit.*, pp. 365–66.

313 "Eight months have elapsed," Stanley to Jephson, Jan. 17, 1889, IDA, vol. 2, p. 124.

"If at the end of twenty days," Stanley to Emin, *ibid.*

"Received me in his usual calm way," Jephson, *Diary*, Feb. 6, 1889, p. 332.

"Shake hands on it," *ibid.*, Feb. 13, 1889, p. 333.

"At that rate," *ibid.*, Feb. 15, 1889, p. 334.

314 "The Pasha, 200 loads!" IDA, vol. 2, p. 147.

"Apathy, indifference," SJ, March 3, 1889.

"Such a funny-looking," SJ, March 17, 1889.

"I do not think," Casati, *Ten Years in Equatoria*, vol. 2, p. 249.

315 Stanley "stamped his foot," *ibid.*, p. 249.

"If you have the courage," *ibid.*, p. 250.

"In a moment everyone moved," *ibid.*, p. 250.

315–16 "These miserable, yellow-bellied," SJ, May 4, 1889.

316 "Our natures were diametrically opposed," IDA, vol. 2, p. 267.

"The constant brutal ill treatment," Jephson, *Diary*, April 26, 1889, p. 346.

"When we were by ourselves," *ibid.*, April 26, 1889, p. 346.

317 "In his way as dangerous," *ibid.*, May 5, 1889, pp. 350–51.

"I think you had better leave me," *ibid.*, June 13, 1889, p. 362.

"The Pasha should do something," *ibid.*, July 22, 1889, p. 383.

"The snowy breasts," IDA, vol. 2, p. 333.

318 "Sweet-faced, gentle looking," *ibid.*, p. 378.

"Stanley is ever ready," Jephson, *Diary*, June 13, 1889, p. 360.

319 "Dozens of reports," *ibid.*, Aug. 28, 1889, p. 398.

"Quite a number of well-selected articles," IDA, vol. 2, p. 450.

"Good yet for . . . two or three more," Stevens, *Scouting for Stanley*, p. 260.

"Nobody can say," *ibid.*, p. 263.

320 "On our left, close at hand," IDA, vol. 2, 453–54.

"On the whole," Schweitzer, *Emin Pasha*, p. 328.

321 "The Pasha was never gayer," IDA, vol. 2, p. 457.

"To give eclat," *ibid.*, p. 458.

322 " 'Well, Pasha,' I said," *ibid.*, p. 465.

" 'You I shall never forget," Jephson, *Emin Pasha*, p. 477.

## CHAPTER 25

324  "The irresolution of its officers," Stanley to Mackinnon, Aug. 5, 1889, *The Standard*, Aug. 25, 1889.

325  "Without proper food," Barttelot, *op. cit.*, pp. 3–4.

"He showed no outward sign," *The Globe*, Oct. 24, 1890.

"Only part of the truth," NYH, Oct. 26, 1890.

"Too horrible to describe," DT, Oct. 27, 1890.

"Mud-throwing," *St. James Gazette*, Oct. 28, 1890.

326  "The most foul reports," Jameson to Ethel Jameson, Aug. 3, 1888, Jameson, *op. cit.*, p. 356.

"We were watching them," Emin Pasha Relief Expedition official report, MP.

"The girl never looked for help," *ibid.*

"I cannot now describe," LT, Nov. 10, 1890.

"The story, as Mr. Bonny told it," *ibid.*

327  "In the habit of standing before the natives," *ibid.*

"Four big Sudanese," *ibid.*

328  "Killed, not murdered," NYH, Oct. 26, 1890.

329  "Flogged . . . for stealing," SJ, Oct. 17, 1887.

"Really about as low," SJ, Feb. 9, 1889.

## CHAPTER 26

333  "I could not, immediately," AUT, p. 411.

335  "By far the grandest," *ibid.*, p. 419.

"Offensive to good taste," *Spectator*, May 3, 1890.

336  "I shall be so deeply glad," Tennant to Stanley, April 26, 1890, Hall, *Stanley*, p. 336.

"I only want to say goodbye," T to S, May 5, 1890, *ibid.*, p. 336.

"Well, dear Mr. Stanley," T to S, May 6, 1890, *ibid.*, p. 336.

"Oh, Bula Matari," T to S, May 9, 1890, *ibid.*, p. 337.

337  "Looked forward to the meeting," AUT, p. 419.

338  "A very charming girl," Harris, *op. cit.*, p. 742.

"I'm not Stanley," Millais, *Life and Letters*, vol. 2, p. 69.

339  "I was too weak," AUT, p. 423.

"Be charitable," *ibid.*, p. 423.

340  "You ask me what," Boston *Herald*, Oct. 1, 1890.

"The work itself," *Spectator*, Nov. 15, 1890.

341  "Rest! Ah, my dear," Stanley to Dolly, undated, AUT, p. 429.

"As I moved through the crowd," Stanley to Dolly, June 16, 1891, *ibid.*, p. 431.

"My travels," Stanley to Dolly, undated, *ibid.*, p. 430.

343  "Not to be chilled," Stanley to Dolly, June 20, 1891, *ibid.*, p. 432.

"A particularly irascible man," Stanhope, *On the Track of the Great*, p. 152.

344  "I am very much astonished," *ibid.*, p. 152.

## CHAPTER 27

345 "Howled down by an organised rabble," AUT, p. 439.

"You must not expect," *ibid.*, p. 443.

346 "A red hot poker," *ibid.*, p. 466.

"Suddenly, the sky flushed," *ibid.*, p. 466.

"I was so tired," *ibid.*, p. 476.

347 "I have not got the art!," *ibid.*, p. 480.

"During Stanley's malaria attacks," *ibid.*, p. 483.

348 "I think Stanley feared," *ibid.*, p. 484.

"A model of infantile beauty," Stanley to Leopold, Sept. 16, 1896, SFA.

"Warmest greetings," AUT, p. 485.

350 "Everything Stanley planned," *ibid.*, p. 507.

"It is collected by force," Inglis, *Casement*, p. 46.

351 "I have many times," *ibid.*, p. 46.

"Something should be done," Stanley to Leopold, Sept. 16, 1896, SFA.

"Because to go back," AUT, p. 536.

352 "His matchless sacrifices," Burrows, *Land of Pygmies*, p. ii.

353 "Infamous! Infamous," Inglis, *op. cit.*, p. 72.

"Months passed," AUT, p. 513.

"Where will they put me . . .?" *ibid.*, p. 514.

354 "Real, heartfelt sympathy," LT, Dec. 9, 1890.

356 "It was this, that carried," SJ, undated.

"White men in this strange," *ibid.*, Feb. 15, 1889.

357 "I was not sent into the world," AUT, p. xvii.


## EPILOGUE

359 "A dishonourable act," Wellcome to Bradshaw, Aug. 31, 1904, copy in RGS archives.

"It is such *triumph*," Lady Stanley to Wellcome, Dec. 2, 1904, *ibid.*

359–60 "He writes badly," Lady Stanley to Wellcome, Aug. 20, 1904, *ibid.*

360 "They are still after the details," Hoffmann to Lady Stanley, Aug. 14, 1905, *ibid.*

"I have such misgivings," Lady Stanley to Wellcome, Aug. 15, 1905, *ibid.*

"I mite have been better off," Hoffmann to Wellcome, Aug. 13, 1920, *ibid.*

"A kind, cheerful companion," Hoffmann, *With Stanley*, p. 73.

"Of course I would be unable," Noe to Lady Stanley, undated but apparently late Sept. 1907, RGS.

# Bibliography

## WORKS BY H. M. STANLEY:

HIFL *How I Found Livingstone*. 2 vols. London, 1872.
*My Kalulu*. London, 1873.
*C and M Coomassie and Magdala*. London, 1874.
TDC *Through the Dark Continent*. 2 vols. London, 1878.
TCFFS *The Congo and the Founding of Its Free State*. 2 vols. London, 1885.
IDA *In Darkest Africa*. 2 vols. London, 1890.
MET *My Early Travels and Adventures in America and Asia*. 2 vols. London, 1895.
AUT *The Autobiography of H. M. Stanley*. Ed. Dorothy Stanley. London, 1909.
ED *The Exploration Diaries of H. M. Stanley*. Ed. Richard Stanley and Alan Neame. London, 1961.
SDNYH Ed. Norman R. Bennett. Boston, 1970. *Stanley's Despatches to the New York Herald, 1871–72, 1874–77*.
UL *The Unpublished Letters of H. M. Stanley*. Ed. Albert Maurice. London and Edinburgh, 1957.

## BIOGRAPHICAL AND GENERAL

Anstruther, Ian. *I Presume: Stanley's Triumph and Disaster*. London, 1956.
Anstey, Roger. *Britain in the Congo in the 19th Century*. Oxford, 1962.
———. *King Leopold's Legacy*. Oxford, 1966.
Arnold, Julian. *Giants in Dressing Gowns*. Chicago, 1942.
Ascherson, Neal. *The King Incorporated: Leopold II in the Age of Trusts*. London, 1963.
Baker, Sir Samuel. *The Albert Nyanza*. 2 vols. London, 1866.
———. *Exploration of the Nile Tributaries of Abyssinia*. London, 1868.
———. *Ismailia*. 2 vols. London, 1874.
Barttelot, Edmund M. *The Life of Edmund Musgrave Barttelot*. Ed. Walter G. Musgrave. London, 1890.
Bentley, W. Holman. *Pioneering on the Congo*. 2 vols. London, 1900.
Brodie, Fawn. *The Devil Drives: A Life of Sir Richard Burton*. New York, 1967.
Bunsen, Marie von. *The World I Used to Know, 1860–1912*. London, 1930.
Burrows, Guy. *The Land of the Pygmies*. London, 1898.
Burton, Sir Richard. *The Lake Regions of Central Africa*. 2 vols. London, 1860.
Cairns, H. A. C. *Prelude to Imperialism: British Reactions to Central African Society, 1840–90*. London, 1965.
Cameron, Verney Lovett. *Across Africa*. 2 vols. London, 1877.
Casati, Gaetano. *Ten Years in Equatoria and the Return with Emin Pasha*. 2 vols. London, 1891.
Chaille-Long, Charles. *Central Africa*. London, 1876.
Conrad, Joseph. *Heart of Darkness*. London, 1902.
Coupland, Reginald. *The Exploitation of East Africa, 1856–90*. London, 1939.
———. *Livingstone's Last Journey*. London, 1945.
Daye, Pierre. *Leopold II*. Paris, 1934.

————. *Stanley*. Paris, 1936.

Emerson, Barbara. *Leopold II of the Belgians, King of Colonialism*. New York, 1979.

Farwell, Byron. *The Man Who Presumed*. London, 1957.

Fraser, Augusta. *Livingstone and Newstead*. London, 1913.

Glave, Edward J. *Six Years of Adventure in Congo-Land*. London, 1895.

Grierson, Mary. *Donald Francis Tovey*. Oxford, 1951.

Hall, Richard. *Stanley, an Adventurer Explored*. London, 1974.

Harris, Frank. *My Life and Loves*. New York, 1960.

Hird, Frank. *H. M. Stanley, the Authoritative Life*. London, 1935.

Hoffman, William. *With Stanley in Africa*. London, 1938.

Inglis, Brian. *Roger Casement*. London, 1973.

Jameson, James S. *The Story of the Rear Column of the Emin Pasha Relief Expedition*. Ed. Mrs. J. A. Jameson. London, 1890.

Jeal, Tim. *Livingstone*. London, 1973.

Jephson, A. J. M. *Emin Pasha and the Rebellion at the Equator*. London, 1890.

————. *The Diary of A. J. Mounteney Jephson*. Ed. Dorothy Middleton. Cambridge, 1969.

Jones, Roger. *The Rescue of Emin Pasha*. London, 1972.

Kaggwa, Sir Apolo. *The Kings of Buganda*. Trans. and ed. M. S. M. Kiwanuka. Nairobi, 1971.

Kirk, John. *The Zambesi Journal and Letters of Dr. John Kirk*. Ed. R. Foskett. 2 vols. London, 1965.

Knight, Oliver. *Following the Indian Wars: The story of newspaper correspondents among the Indian campaigns*. Oklahoma, 1960.

Livingstone, David. *Missionary Travels and Researches in South Africa*. London, 1857.

————. *The Last Journals of David Livingstone*. Ed. Horace Waller. London, 1874.

Livingstone, David and Charles. *Narrative of an Expedition to the Zambesi*. London, 1866.

Lucy, Sir Henry. *Sixty Years in the Wilderness*. Vol. 2. London, 1912.

Luwel, Marcel. *Stanley*. Brussels, 1959.

Marston, Edward. *After Work*. London, 1904.

Millais, J. G. *The Life and Letters of Sir John Everett Millais*. Vol. 2. London, 1899.

Moorehead, Alan. *The White Nile*. London, 1960.

————. *The Blue Nile*. London, 1962.

Nutting, Anthony. *Gordon: Martyr and Misfit*. London, 1966.

Parke, Thomas Heazle. *My Personal Experiences in Equatorial Africa*. London, 1891.

Pond, James B. *Eccentricities of Genius*. London, 1900.

Rowlands, Cadwalader. *Henry M. Stanley: the Story of his Life from Birth in 1841 to his Discovery of Livingstone. 1871*, London, 1872.

Schweitzer, G. *Emin Pasha, His Life and Work*. 2 vols. London, 1898.

Seitz, C. Don. *The James Gordon Bennetts, Father and Son*. Indianapolis, 1928.

Simpson, Donald. *Dark Companions*. London, 1975.

Slade, Ruth. *King Leopold's Congo*. Oxford, 1962.

Smith, Iain R. *The Emin Pasha Relief Expedition, 1886–90*. Oxford, 1972.

Speke, John Hanning. *Journal of the Discovery of the Source of the Nile*. London, 1863.

Stanhope, Aubrey. *On the Track of the Great*. New York, 1914.

Stevens, Thomas. *Scouting for Stanley in East Africa*. New York, 1890.

Strachey, Lytton. *Eminent Victorians*. London, 1918.

Symons, A. J. A. *Emin, Governor of Equatoria*. London, 1950.

Thomas, Dana L. *The Media Moguls*. New York, 1981.

Tippu Tib. *The Life of Hamed bin Muhammed el Murjebi*. Introduced by Alison Smith, trans. W. H. Whitely. Nairobi, 1959.

Troup, John Rose. *With Stanley's Rear Column*. London, 1890.

Wasserman, Jakob. *Bula Matari: Stanley, Conqueror of a Continent*. New York, 1933.

Ward, Herbert. *My Life with Stanley's Rear Guard*. London, 1891.

————. *A Voice from the Congo*. London, 1910.

Wauters, A. J. *Stanley's Emin Pasha Expedition*. London, 1890.

Weintraub, Stanley. *Victoria: An Intimate Biography.* New York, 1987.
West, Richard. *Brazza of the Congo.* London, 1972.
Wolseley, Lord. *The Story of a Soldier's Life.* 2 vols. London, 1904.


PROCEEDINGS, PAPERS, PERIODICALS AND PAMPHLETS

Anon. "A British Journalist Reports the Medicine Lodge Peace Councils." *Kansas Historical Quarterly* Autumn, 1967.
Balch, Edwin. "American Explorers of Africa." *The Geographical Review* 5 June 1918.
Bennett, Norman R. "Stanley and the American Consuls at Zanzibar." *Essex Institute Historical Collections* 100 (1964).
Burton, Richard. "Ocean Highways." *The Geographical Review* 1 (1873).
Casada, James A. "Henry M. Stanley: the Explorer as Journalist." *Southern Quarterly* XV, 4 (July 1977).
———. "The Emotional Underpinnings of the British Exploration of East Africa." *Proceedings of the South Carolina Historical Association,* 1973.
Keltie, J. Scott. *Geographical Journal* XLIX (1917).
Kendall, John S. *Louisiana Historical Quarterly* July 1937.
King, Edward. "An Expedition with Stanley." *Scribner's Monthly* 5 (1872).
Owen, Bob. "Stanley's Father, I Presume." *Hel Achau, Journal of the Clwyd Family History Society* 15 (Spring 1985).
Shuey, Mary Willis. "Stanley in New Orleans." *Southwest Review* xxv (1939–40).
———. "Young Stanley; Arkansas Episode." *Southwest Review* xxvii (1941–42).
Wheeler, Douglas L. *Bulletin of the Missouri Historical Society.* April 1961.
Wynne-Jones, Lucy M. and Ivor. "H. M. Stanley and Wales." St. Asaph, the H. M. Stanley Exhibition Committee, 1972.
Wynne-Woodhouse, W. "Elizabeth Parry of Denbigh, an Extraordinary Woman, and Henry M. Stanley, her son, an Extraordinary Man." *Hel Achau* 15 (Spring 1985).


ARCHIVES, INSTITUTIONS, LIBRARIES AND COLLECTIONS

APR   Archives du Palais Royal, Brussels.
SFA   British Library, London, for Stanley Family Archive.
LMS   London Missionary Society.
NLS   National Library of Scotland, Edinburgh.
NLW   National Library of Wales, Cardiff.
ABM   National Museum of American Art (Smithsonian Institution), Washington, D.C., for Alice Barney Manuscript.
SJ    Nova Scotia Public Archives, for Stairs Journals.
PRO   Public Records Office, London.
RCS   Royal Commonwealth Society, London.
RGS   Royal Geographical Society, London.
MP    School of Oriental and African Studies, London, for Mackinnon Papers.
WP    Wellcome Institute, London, for Henry S. Wellcome Papers.


NEWSPAPERS

Principally, *The Times* of London (LT), the New York *Herald* (NYH), and the *Daily Telegraph* (DT). Miscellaneous others.

# Index

*Note:* Numbers in italics denote illustrations.

# A NOTE ABOUT THE AUTHOR

*AFRICA* is one of five continents in which John Bierman has lived during a long career as a journalist, but the one to which he feels most drawn. He spent the years 1959–63 based in Nairobi, during which time he covered much of the ground over which—under far more difficult and dangerous circumstances—Stanley had passed long years before. Since leaving Africa, Bierman has worked mainly as a BBC news correspondent, in the Middle East, South and Central Asia, the Caribbean, Latin America, Eastern Europe, the United States, and Canada. He now lives in Toronto, where he writes on international affairs for *Maclean's* magazine.

# A Note on the Type

THE TEXT of this book was set in Sabon, a typeface designed by Jan Tschichold (1902–1974), the well-known German typographer. Because it was designed in Frankfurt, Sabon was named for the famous Frankfurt type founder Jacques Sabon, who died in 1580 while manager of the Egenolff foundry.

Based loosely on the original designs of Claude Garamond (c. 1480–1561), Sabon is unique in that it was explicitly designed for hot-metal composition on both the Monotype and Linotype machines as well as for film composition.

Composed by American–Stratford Graphic Services, Inc.

Brattleboro, Vermont

Printed and bound by Courier Companies, Inc.,

Westford, Massachusetts

Designed by Margaret Wagner